Entertainment Law

DELMAR CENGAGE Learning

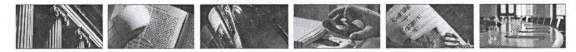

Options.

Over 300 products in every area of the law: textbooks, online courses, CD-ROMs, reference books, companion websites, and more – helping you succeed in the classroom and on the job.

Support.

We offer unparalleled, practical support: robust instructor and student supplements to ensure the best learning experience, custom publishing to meet your unique needs, and other benefits such as Delmar Cengage Learning's Student Achievement Award. And our sales representatives are always ready to provide you with dependable service.

Feedback.

As always, we want to hear from you! Your feedback is our best resource for improving the quality of our products. Contact your sales representative or write us at the address below if you have any comments about our materials or if you have a product proposal.

Accounting and Financials for the Law Office • Administrative Law • Alternative Dispute Resolution • Bankruptcy Business Organizations/Corporations • Careers and Employment • Civil Litigation and Procedure • CLA Exam Preparation • Computer Applications in the Law Office • Constitutional Law • Contract Law • Court Reporting Criminal Law and Procedure • Document Preparation • Elder Law • Employment Law • Environmental Law • Ethics Evidence Law • Family Law • Health Care Law • Immigration Law • Intellectual Property • Internships Interviewing and Investigation • Introduction to Law • Introduction to Paralegalism • Juvenile Law • Law Office Management • Law Office Procedures • Legal Nurse Consulting • Legal Research, Writing, and Analysis • Legal Terminology • Legal Transcription • Media and Entertainment Law • Medical Malpractice Law Product Liability • Real Estate Law • Reference Materials • Social Security • Sports Law • Torts and Personal Injury Law • Wills, Trusts, and Estate Administration • Workers' Compensation Law

---

DELMAR CENGAGE Learning
5 Maxwell Drive
Clifton Park, New York 12065-2919

For additional information, find us online at:
www.delmar.cengage.com

DELMAR
CENGAGE Learning™

Entertainment Law

by

Jeffrey A. Helewitz
Leah K. Edwards

DELMAR
CENGAGE Learning

Australia • Brazil • Japan • Korea • Mexico • Singapore • Spain • United Kingdom • United States

Entertainment Law
Jeffrey A. Helewitz, Leah K. Edwards

Vice President: Dawn Gerrain

Director of Editorial: Sherry Gomoll

Acquisitions Editor: Pamela Fuller

Editorial Assistant: Sarah Duncan

Director of Production: Wendy A. Troeger

Production Manager: Carolyn Miller

Production Editor: Betty L. Dickson

Director of Marketing: Donna J. Lewis

Channel Manager: Wendy Mapstone

Cover Design: Dutton and Sherman Design

For product information and technology assistance, contact us at
Cengage Learning Customer & Sales Support, 1-800-354-9706

For permission to use material from this text or product, submit all requests online at **cengage.com/permissions**
Further permissions questions can be emailed to
permissionrequest@cengage.com

Library of Congress Control Number: 2003046256

ISBN-13: 978-0-7668-3584-9

ISBN-10: 0-7668-3584-7

Delmar
Executive Woods
5 Maxwell Drive
Clifton Park, NY 12065
USA

Cengage Learning is a leading provider of customized learning solutions with office locations around the globe, including Singapore, the United Kingdom, Australia, Mexico, Brazil, and Japan. Locate your local office at: **international. cengage.com/region**

Cengage Learning products are represented in Canada by Nelson Education, Ltd.

For your course and learning solutions, visit **delmar.cengage.com**

Visit our corporate website at **cengage.com**

Printed in the United States of America
1 2 3 4 5   14 13 12 11 10

FD344

TABLE OF CONTENTS

Chapter 3   Legal Structures of the Entertainment Industry 53

Chapter 4   Television 121

Chapter 5   Film 145

PREFACE

Entertainment law has become an extremely important specialty in the legal profession; for this reason, a serious need exists for a basic text that can provide the legal practitioner with a concise, effective, informative, and up-to-date analysis of the legal principles involved in an entertainment law practice.

Entertainment Law is designed to combine the best of textbooks, reviews, and practical material in one comprehensive and straightforward text. The materials that have been selected for inclusion in this book have been chosen with an eye to providing material that highlights the general law and the most important exceptions in all major areas of the entertainment business. No other book currently on the market affords the scope of material covered in *Entertainment Law.*

Entertainment Law differs from other books in the field because it includes

- Detailed but concise discussions of every area of entertainment law, providing the reader with all of the general legal concepts in the field

- Cases selected for their discussions of basic entertainment law concepts

- Exercises specifically designed to generate classroom discussions

- Exhibits from different areas of the entertainment industry.

Organization of *Entertainment Law*

The text is divided into ten chapters covering the areas of entertainment law discussed in other texts. However, unlike the other books, *Entertainment Law* provides detailed and comprehensive prose discussions on each area of the law so that both the student and the practitioner can develop an overall understanding of the field. The text details the different industries and their own legal peculiarities, which is completely lacking in all of the other texts on the market. Each specific topic is highlighted by a judicial decision chosen for its discussion of the area of law under review. Each chapter concludes with Exercises that can be used to generate classroom discussions of the law by providing practical assignments for the reader. These ten questions are designed to test the student's knowledge of the basic concepts discussed and offer a direct "hands-on" approach to dealing with an entertainment law practice. The text is written in a manner that is comprehensible to law, paralegal, and undergraduate students and that is compatible with any method of instruction.

Each chapter is constructed in a similar format, beginning with an introduction outlining the basic principles that will be covered in the body of the chapter. The chapters are arranged to take the student from the most basic concepts through complex analyses and provide numerous examples of the principles discussed, taken from typical examples in the industry. In this fashion, the examples help the student to comprehend the entertainment industry from a practical point of view. Unlike most texts that merely provide lists of terms used in the chapters, *Entertainment Law* provides key terms and their definitions in the text margins. These marginal notes redefine the terms used throughout the text to reinforce the chapter terminology in the mind of the student. Each chapter concludes with a chapter summary that provides a concise recapitulation of the subject matter covered.

Supplemental Teaching and Learning Materials

- The **Instructor's Manual with a Test Bank** is available on line at http://www.paralegal.delmar.com in the Instructor's Lounge under Resource. Written by the authors of the text, the *Instructor's Manual* contains a sample course syllabus, chapter outlines, teaching suggestions, and a test bank with answers.

- **WESTLAW®**—Delmar's online computerized legal research system offers students "hands-on" experience with a system commonly used in law offices. Qualified adopters can receive ten free hours of WESTLAW®. WESTLAW® can be accessed with Macintosh and IBM PC compatibles. A modem is required.

- **Strategies and Tips for Paralegal Educators**, a pamphlet by Anita Tebbe of Johnson County Community College, provides teaching strategies specifically designed for paralegal educators. A copy of this pamphlet is available to each adopter. Quantities for distribution to adjunct instructors are available for purchase at a minimal price. A coupon in the pamphlet provides ordering information.

- **Survival Guide for Paralegal Students**, a pamphlet by Kathleen Mercer Reed and Bradene Moore, covers practical and basic information to help students make the most of their paralegal courses. Topics covered include choosing courses of study and notetaking skills.

- **Delmar's Paralegal Video Library** —Delmar is pleased to offer the following videos at no charge to qualified adopters:

  - *The Drama of the Law II: Paralegal Issues Video*
    ISBN: 0-314-07088-5
  - *The Making of a Case Video*
    ISBN: 0-314-07300-0

Please note the Internet resources are of a time-sensitive nature
and URL addresses may often change or be deleted.

Contact us at **westlegalstudies@delmar.com**

ACKNOWLEDGMENTS

The author and publisher would like to thank the following reviewers who provided valuable feedback and suggestions during the review and edit of this text:

Scott A. Hauert
Phoenix College

M. Ruth Harrison, J.D.
Yavapai College

Alex Yarbrough
Virginia College

Robert Diotalevi
Florida Gulf Coast University

Angela R. Ericson
Everest College

Chelsea Campbell
Lehman College

Mimi K. Flaherty
RETS Tech Center

Richard Martin
Washburn University

Patricia Greer
Berkeley College

Adam Epstein
University of Tennessee

Ramona P. DeSalvo
Southeastern Career College

Kathryn Myers
Saint Mary of the Woods College

Richard Lewis
Saddleback College

INTRODUCTION:
WHAT IS ENTERTAINMENT LAW?

Entertainment law is comprised of legal principles and business practices. Legal principles control business operations and create recognized areas of law. Business practices make the business operations financially lucrative. Traditionally, entertainment law has embraced six forms of media: movies, television, live theater, music, sports, and publishing. Entertainment law professionals analyze these areas of the industry from the perspective of several functional branches: production (the creation of entertainment material), distribution (to retailers), and retailing (to the entertainment consumer).

Entertainment law envelops four basic areas. The entertainment law professional must:

1. Evaluate and apply both common law and statutory law from a variety of legal disciplines to the complex concept of entertainment
2. Consider business, or corporate, implications
3. Decipher collective bargaining and employment law issues
4. Consider the economic evaluation of a given project and its impact.

CHAPTER

1

CONSTITUTIONAL CONSIDERATIONS

CHAPTER OVERVIEW

constitutional law
Law derived from the
United States Constitution
that is not otherwise set
out in a statute or a
legislatively created law.

freedom of speech
The right of a citizen to
say (or write) exactly what
he or she thinks without
fear of governmental
retribution.

This chapter discusses the constitutional considerations applicable to the field of entertainment law. The intent is to provide a *general overview* of constitutional protections afforded to both the individual artist and to the overall entertainment industry. **Constitutional law,** law derived from the United States Constitution, is a vast and complex area, and a definitive discussion of all of its aspects is beyond the scope of this text.

The United States Constitution grants the protection of **freedom of speech.** Freedom of speech can be defined as the right of an artist to say or write exactly what he or she thinks without fear of governmental retribution (with certain exceptions designed to protect the public safety and welfare). This constitutional protection of free speech, which appears in the First Amendment to the Constitution (see Exhibit 1-1), and the penumbra of free speech covering the concept of privacy form the basis of much litigation in the area of entertainment law. This principle, however, does not confer an absolute right to speak or publish without responsibility.

This chapter will focus on the following constitutional protections that directly relate to the entertainment industry:

- The right to privacy
- Obscenity
- The control of one's name and likeness
- Defamation.

THE RIGHT TO PRIVACY

The right to privacy is the right to be left alone. The concept of a right to privacy in one's own person has its roots in "The Right to Privacy," an article written in 1890 by Louis D. Brandeis, a former Supreme Court Justice, and Samuel D. Warren.

A person's right to privacy is necessary to protect thoughts and sentiments expressed in writing, painting, and the arts. Failure to protect these rights could result in the inability of artists to express their creativity and eventually profit from their art. The protection of the private individual's privacy is distinct from the protection of the privacy of a public figure. Public figures, such as movie stars, professional athletes, and recording artists, do not retain their privacy to the same extent as do private persons.

A person can suffer an invasion of privacy in any of four different ways:

1. Intrusion upon his or her seclusion or solitude or into his or her private affairs

— Example

A celebrity may have a claim that his privacy is invaded if the paparazzi are constantly snapping photographs. The more the paparazzi delve into the celebrity's private life, the more likely his or her right to privacy based on intrusion upon seclusion or solitude will be infringed upon.

2. Public disclosure of embarrassing private facts about the individual

— Example

Information relating to a basketball player's sexual escapades that resulted in a sexually transmitted disease could constitute a public disclosure of an embarrassing fact if such confidential information was obtained without authorization.

3. Publicity which places the individual in a false light in the public eye

—— *Example* ————————————————————

A rock star whose girlfriend was arrested for firing a gun in a popular club may have a claim of invasion of privacy if publicity falsely places the rock star as the one arrested or the connection between him and his girlfriend is detrimental to his image.

4. Appropriation, for one person's advantage, of another's name or likeness.

—— *Example* ————————————————————

If a company sells busts of a famous opera singer for profit, the singer whose profile was used as the model for the bust may claim that his right to privacy has been invaded unless he has authorized such use.

tort
Civil wrong.

right of publicity
A right of publicity involves the use of aspects of one's own personality for economic gain.

This right to secure one's privacy is protected by principles known as tort law. A **tort** is a civil wrong that is not protected under any other distinct area of law. The first three of the above-identified torts involve one's right to be free from unwarranted intrusions into one's personal solitude. The fourth category of privacy invasion involves a property right that courts and commentators commonly refer to as the **right of publicity**. A right of publicity involves the use of aspects of one's own personality for one's own economic gain.

The degree of intrusion upon an individual's privacy interest depends on two factors:

1. The intrusiveness of the method whereby that privacy interest is invaded
2. The strength of the individual's privacy interest.

Such determinations are especially complicated when ascertaining whether or not a celebrity's privacy interest has been infringed upon. This is primarily because the celebrity, by definition, has agreed to put him or herself in the public's eye, thus diminishing his or her privacy interest.

common law
Law evolving from judicial precedent rather than statute.

Generally, the right to privacy is not a common-law doctrine. **Common law** is defined as law evolving from judicial precedent rather than by statute. The following are general common-law principles that apply to an entertainment professional's right to privacy:

1. The right is generally applied to the person and not to the property.

—— *Example* ————————————————————

In a newspaper, there appeared a likeness of an artist placed by a likeness of an ill–dressed and sickly looking person. Above the likeness of the artist were the words "Do it now. The man who did." Above the likeness of the other person were the words "Do it while you can. The man who didn't." Below the two pictures were the words "These two pictures tell their own story." The photographs were used to advertise life insurance. The picture of the artist was taken from a negative and was made without his consent. Such publication of a picture of a person, without his consent, as a part of an advertisement used for the purpose of exploiting a business, may be considered a violation of the right to privacy of the person whose picture is reproduced. Thus, the artist may claim that his right to privacy has been invaded.

---

2. The right to privacy does not exist where the aggrieved has consented to the action.

— *Example*

In order to help his friend make some money, a professional golfer agrees to let his friend use his picture on T-shirts the friend wants to sell. Because the golfer agreed to this use, he cannot later claim that his friend invaded his privacy rights.

The law does not recognize a right of privacy in connection with that which is inherently a public matter, such as proposed congressional regulation of the film industry. However, the unprovoked publicizing of a person's private affairs and activities may be the basis for a cause of action for invasion of privacy. When an artist's life has ceased to be private, or to the extent it has ceased to be private, the right of privacy is revoked. In other words, a celebrity has a limited right to privacy because of his or her fame. The life of the celebrity is subject to legitimate life of the public snooping.

In addition to the willing public figure, those who have been thrust into the limelight may lose their right to privacy. This may include people who are merely associated, even unwittingly, with interesting events. An example would be groupies who follow rock stars around the country. Those seeking notoriety are considered to have waived their right to personal seclusion.

— *Example*

A man on a mission decides to hang glide his way onto the observation deck of the Statue of Liberty to promote his relatively unknown hang gliding performance-art theater. Unfortunately, he does not accomplish his goal, but ends up tangled on the flame of her torch. Embarrassed by his failed attempt, he alleges that the *Daily Press* violated his right of privacy when they took a picture of his failed attempt and published it in their paper. Because the hang glider sought notoriety, even though his attempt failed, his right to privacy is waived as a result of his voluntary thrust into the limelight.

Public figures and celebrities are not afforded the same right to privacy as are private individuals because:

A. They seek publicity and consent to it, and therefore cannot complain about the publicity.

B. Their lives and the details of them are already public and cannot be regarded as their own private business.

C. The press has certain protected rights guaranteed by the Constitution (freedom of speech) to inform people about legitimate matters of public interest.

3. If the information is considered news if it or is the result of a news event, there can be no claim of right to privacy (note the example of the hang glider).

The right to be left alone and to be protected from undesired publicity is not absolute, but must be balanced against the public interest to newsworthy information, as is consistent with the constitutional assurances of freedom of speech and of the press. The determining factors are the content and character of the news and not the right of the individual to be left alone. If the use of a person's name or picture is secondary to legitimate news value, his or her right of privacy has not been unlawfully invaded. In fact, the right to privacy may not prohibit publication of any matter that may be of public or general interest.

Therefore, if a television actor has a habitual drug habit and the media covers his court appearance, the character of the news (the habitual drug problem), will be balanced against the right of the individual to be left alone. Here, since the actor puts himself in the public's view every day, there will be a lower standard when it comes to determining whether the character of the news has legitimate value.

— Example

A woman returned to her apartment building only to discover an intruder and the body of a famous stage director. She fled the scene of the crime. A reporter published her name in his paper in an article he had written, stating that she was the one who found the body. The police requested that he not release her name since she could identify the murderer. The police thought that the release of her name might put her in danger. Under these circumstances the reporter and his newspaper are not entitled to absolute privilege simply because the murder was news. The interest of the state to protect witnesses and conduct criminal investigations and the interest of the woman are superior to the public's interest in the content of the news.

Example

A prostitute was tried and acquitted for murder. After her acquittal, she abandoned her life of crime and became entirely rehabilitated. Thereafter, some film producers made, photographed, produced, and released a film entitled *The Red Kimono*, based on her life story. The film was made without her knowledge or consent. This caused her friends to scorn and abandon her. The incidents portrayed in the film appeared in the records of her trial for murder, which is a public record and open to the perusal of all. However, the producers went further and used the true name of the woman in the formation of the plot. This publication by the producers of the unsavory incidents in the woman's past after she had reformed, coupled with the use of her true name, was not justified and is a direct invasion of her right to privacy.

4. The right can only be violated by means of a permanent publication to a third party.

permanent publication
Something fixed in a tangible format.

A **permanent publication** is defined as something fixed, or permanently established, that the general public has seen or heard about. It cannot be a mere statement said out loud to one's self.

—— *Example* ——

The host of a well-known talk show and her guest do not agree on the issue of gun control. During the show they avidly debate the issue. The guest and the host continue to debate the issue in the Green Room after the taping of the show is complete. In an effort to stay clear of the mayhem, the crew and staff leave the room and the host and her guest are left alone. Things get personal, and the host yells, "I am going to tell everyone about your secret affair with your secretary!" The guest wants to sue the host. The judge asks who heard the statement. When he finds out that no one heard the statement and there was no permanent publication of the statement, he dismisses the case.

5. Some jurisdictions also hold that the right to privacy is only invaded if such publication results in gain or profit.

—— *Example* ——

Anytown is a locality that recognizes that the right to privacy is violated when publication results in gain or profit. While walking down a street in Anytown, a local politician overhears a conversation about the use of his likeness on a flyer. The flyer is to promote a local band. On the flyer is a picture of the politician attending one of the band's previous concerts. If the politician can prove that the band sold tickets and made a profit from the sale of such tickets, then the politician will be able to recover from his suit in this jurisdiction.

Loss of the Right to Privacy

estoppel
The theory that one is barred from applying a principle of law in a given situation.

The right to privacy is not an absolute right, meaning that it does not automatically attach to a given activity, and may not apply to an individual in some situations. Consent, either express or implied, may waive the right. **Estoppel** is a theory that states that one is barred from applying a principle of law in certain circumstances. Estoppel applies when the aggrieved party is barred from the claim of invasion of privacy because the party has previously consented to the action. Again, if the person is a public figure he or she may not qualify for protection because of his or her implied consent to publicity by becoming a public figure. Someone who becomes involved, intentionally or unintentionally, in a matter of public interest may also waive his or her right to privacy.

Further, the right of privacy, like other individual rights, may be waived. This waiver may be effectuated by the person, by anyone authorized by the person, or by anyone the law empowers to act on the individual's behalf. This assumes the effect of such waiver will not bring before the public matters of a purely private nature which law or public policy demands shall be kept private. The right to privacy may also be lost by either a course of conduct that bars its assertion or by consent.

— *Example*

A famous movie actress agrees to the making of an all-access documentary of her life. If, when the documentary is released, she does not like the section about her non-marital child, she cannot claim her right to privacy was violated because she consented to the all-access making of the film.

express waiver
Voluntary and deliberate actions that relinquish a right.

implied waiver
A person's actions that cause another to believe that a right has been relinquished.

A waiver of the right to privacy may be either express or implied. An **express waiver** results from a person voluntarily and deliberately acting to relinquish a right. An **implied waiver** results from a person acting in such a manner that another person would reasonably believe that person meant to relinquish a right. The right may be waived completely or only in part; it may be waived for one purpose and still be asserted for another; and it may be waived as to one individual, class, or publication, and retained as to all others.

— *Example*

A novelist is asked for permission to use his or her life story for a magazine article. The novelist does nothing about the request. The magazine may reasonably believe that the novelist has implicitly waived a right to privacy by not objecting to this use.

The right to privacy directly affects the entertainment industry in one of two ways. First, the personal aspects of an artist's life may be afforded protections against being made public. Second, private details about a person may not be used as the basis of an artistic work without consent.

OBSCENITY

obscene
Material is obscene if to the average person applying contemporary standards to the dominant theme it ... appeals to prurient interests.

Material is **obscene** if the "average person, applying contemporary standards to the dominant theme of the material taken as a whole, appeals to prurient interests." In other words, if the material is so indecent that it would outrage the community's notions of decency, it is considered obscene. Liability may occur only if the act has gone beyond the limits of decency.

Historically, there has been great debate over what is considered obscene. Some of the most notorious instances center around book burning. Books such as *Lady Chatterley's Lover* were burned because a group of people determined the topic and material to be obscene and therefore felt it should be banned. Obscenity laws have also banned great classics such as the movie *Last Tango in Paris* and the novel *Ulysses*, to name a few. It is because of the obscenity law's power to dictate that something should not be made available to the public that it is such an important concept for the entertainment industry.

— *Example* —————————————————————

A magazine publishes nude photographs of an actress. If a particular community finds the pictures obscene, the magazine may be pulled from that market. Furthermore, if the pictures were published without the actress's permission, then she may have a claim of invasion of privacy.

CONTROL OF LIKENESS AND NAME

name
What one calls oneself.

likeness
An image or picture.

false attribution
Attributing a characteristic to a person in instances in which such characteristic does not apply.

In earlier days, the courts did not always recognize that the First Amendment granted protection to names and likenesses. A **name** is simply that, what one calls oneself. A **likeness** is an image or picture.

One has protection over one's name and/or likeness by being able to stop another from presenting that name or likeness in a false light. In this context, **false attribution**—attributing a characteristic to a person in instances in which such a characteristic does not apply—and the right of publicity—a variation on the right to privacy— provide recourse for the wrongful use of the person's name. Courts will generally prohibit the unauthorized commercial use of a person's name as an illicit expropriation of the proprietary interest in one's identity. However, the legal cause of action is limited to those acts that result in economic harm to the person whose name or likeness was affected by the usurper. This theory is based upon the idea that creators have a right to exploit their own identities for their own economic advantage. They are entitled to enjoin the use of their names, not only to prevent others from profiting from the economic benefits in their identity, but also to prevent false attribution to their names that could result in a diminution of the economic value of the name or likeness. An illustration of false attribution is akin to the previous example used for the right of publicity that places the individual in a false light.

A cause of action based on false light aims to protect an individual's honor and reputation. False attribution may damage a reputation and result in a claim of defamation. This may be an especially successful cause of action in cases in which an author's name is attributed to a work of a different genre or to a work of inferior quality.

Defamation as a cause of action can be used as a tool to enforce a creator's right of integrity. Breach of a work's integrity implies that the work has somehow been transformed into an inferior one. Publication or display of an inferior work may damage the creator's reputation or standing in either the community at large or in a particular artistic community, such as the motion picture industry.

— Example

A popular artist has recently completed a show at a chic gallery in Greenwich Village in New York. In a review of the show, a reporter makes reference to an awful painting that appeared in the show. If the artist did not paint the piece, he could have a claim because the article implies an inferior quality work.

Similarly, a tort action of invasion of privacy based on the false-light theory provides recourse for the creator's right to integrity. This cause of action does not require injury (or likelihood thereof) to the plaintiff's reputation; rather, it requires highly offensive or misleading accounts for which the plaintiff may recover emotional distress damages. A creator of a work may be able to show that the alteration of the work caused, in essence, a false attribution of the creator's name that led to emotional distress.

— Example

Assume that the painter from the previous example is not financially damaged, but as a result of this misleading account he can no longer paint. His emotional distress may be enough for recourse against the author of the article.

DEFAMATION

defamation
Tort involving false statements about a person that are communicated to another person, resulting in ridicule or contempt of the person they were said or written about.

slander
Verbal defamation.

libel
Written defamation.

defamation per se
Statements so defamatory so as to be determined defamatory on their face.

Defamation is a tort involving false statements about a person that are communicated to another person, the result of which is ridicule or contempt of the person about whom they were made.

Defamation is either verbal or written. Verbal defamation is called **slander**. Written defamation is referred to as **libel**. In order to show defamation the following elements must be proven:

1. A defamatory statement

   A statement is defamatory if it injures an individual's reputation and exposes him or her to public hatred, contempt, ridicule, or degradation. When the defamatory meaning is not apparent on its face, the plaintiff has the burden of pleading and proving such extrinsic facts.

   Some statements are so defamatory that they are considered **defamation per se**, meaning they are defamatory on their face, and the individual does not have to prove that the statements harmed his reputation.

— *Example*

At a press conference for the opening of a new musical, to get back at his costar, the comedic sidekick hints that the leading man is a Communist at a time when Communism is taboo. As a result, the show is panned and closes, and the leading man cannot find subsequent work. The statement may be considered defamation per se and he may be able to recover without proving the statement harmed his reputation.

Absent defamation per se, a plaintiff must establish proof of damage to reputation in order to recover any damages for mental anguish. Evidence of a person's poor reputation is generally an admissible defense that the defendant can use to reduce the amount of the award he or she may have to pay because the plaintiff's reputation was poor to begin with. In other words, a person may be "libel-proof" if his or her reputation has been previously and irreparably tarnished.

— *Example*

Suzy Pornstar is not likely to recover for defamation if she claims that a reporter falsely reported the number of sexual partners she had been with because her reputation would most likely preclude her from recovery—she may be considered libel-proof on this matter.

2. Published to third parties

Defamatory statements must be communicated to a third party. A party cannot defame someone by speaking to the alleged defamed person alone or by talking to oneself.

3. The speaker or writer knew or reasonably should have known the statement to be false.

— *Example*

If the reporter who wrote that the leading man from the previous example was a Communist could have easily found out that he was not one by looking at his voter's registration card, which he carries with him at all times, he would not have exercised reasonable care in writing the article.

The alleged defamer is liable if he or she knew or should have known by the exercise of reasonable care (see the negligence standard discussed on page 12) that the statement was false. Therefore, if the defendant could have reasonably ascertained that the statement was false—for example, by asking a friend or reading an article—the defendant will be held liable.

Defenses to Defamation

Truth

Truth is always a defense to a claim of defamation. No true statement can result in defamation. The requirement that the statement be false is essential.

— *Example* —

If the voter registration card for the leading man from the previous examples identifies him as a Communist, then the reporter may not be found to have committed libel because the statement is true.

Actual Malice

New York Times v. Sullivan, reprinted in part in the Judicial Decision at the end of this chapter, provided the actual malice standard for public officials. In that case, the aggrieved party was a public official who supervised the Montgomery Police Department. The *Times* printed an advertisement stating that the police had attempted to terrorize Martin Luther King, Jr., and his entourage. It was decided that public officials must prove "actual malice" against a defendant. The Supreme Court articulated the actual malice standard, saying that a statement made relating to a public official's conduct is not defamatory unless made "with knowledge that it was false" or with "reckless disregard for whether it was false or not."

Distinction for Private Figures   In a series of libel actions brought by private figures against media defendants, it has been held that the First Amendment does not require actual malice. Instead, each state is free to establish its own standard of **negligence**—failure to adhere to a defined standard of care—short of **strict liability**—being held responsible regardless of the degree of care exercised—to address defamation as it affects media defendants. A fuller discussion of this kind of tort law appears in chapter 9.

When a public figure brings an action based on defamation that concerns statements involving no issue of public interest, he or she can recover for injuries without a showing of actual malice. However, when a private figure files a defamation claim based on a statement relating only to matters of private concern, that person is not required to show even ordinary negligence in order to recover damages.

Public figures are defined as those persons who become well-known through no purposeful action of their own, including those who have become especially prominent in the affairs of society. They also include those who occupy positions of power and influence and those who have thrust themselves to the forefront of particular public controversies in order to influence the resolution of the issues

negligence
Failure to adhere to a defined standard of care.

strict liability
Being held responsible regardless of the degree of care exercised.

involved. In other words, most people in the entertainment industry may be considered public figures who must show malice or actual damage to prevail in a suit based on libel or slander.

Statements Made to the Government and Its Representatives Statements made to the government and its representatives in the course of petitioning the government for redress of grievances are absolutely protected from any and all defamation claims.

—— *Example* —————————————————

A television reporter for a daily newspaper, in response to the United States Senate's request, states that the Congressman she saw while reporting on an international peace treaty convention used government funds to bring his wife and his girlfriend with him. The Congressman claims that the statement is defamatory. The reporter is protected from defamation claims.

Qualified Privileges

A statement is protected by qualified privilege if made (absent the showing of actual malice) for a proper occasion, a proper motive, and based upon reasonable cause. An example of a proper occasion would be testifying on the witness stand at a trial or administrative proceeding.

—— *Example* —————————————————

The stagehand of a Broadway show slips on a piece of scenery and injures herself. The stage manager, in response to a worker's compensation claim, gives information that he believes is true—the stagehand was drunk. He will not be held liable for defamation.

Opinion Defense

The First Amendment protects statements of opinion because opinions are not capable of being proven true or false and because the injured cannot prove that the defamer reasonably interpreted the statement as actual fact.

A statement is an opinion when:

1. It addresses matters of public concern
2. It is expressed in a manner that can be proven neither true nor false
3. It cannot be *reasonably* interpreted as actual fact.

—— *Example* —————————————————

Arthur Author writes a novel about a popular politician. After researching his main character, Arthur believes him to be a womanizer. If in his portrayal he has a character express an opinion as to this unfavorable characteristic, Arthur could successfully defend himself on the ground that the statement was expressed as the opinion of the character.

Consent

consent
An implied or express permission.

While rare, **consent** is a defense to defamation. Consent is either implied or express permission to do something. When one consents to the release of information, he cannot allege injury as a result of the released statement.

Legal Obligation to Publish and Privileges Created by Statute

If a person is legally required to publish a statement, he or she cannot be held liable for defamation. Responses to court subpoenas, formal requests for information from government agencies, and so forth, fall into this category. Statements made pursuant to state or federal statute are protected by a qualified privilege, not an absolute one. See the example for qualified privileges on page 12.

CHAPTER REVIEW

Freedom of speech can be defined as the right of a citizen to say or write exactly what he or she thinks without fear of governmental retribution (with certain exceptions designed to protect the public safety and welfare). The right to privacy is the right to be left alone.

Waiver or loss of the right of privacy may be occasioned if the published material is obscene. Material is obscene if the "average person, applying contemporary standards to the dominant theme of the material taken as a whole, appeals to prurient interest." In other words, if the material is so indecent that it would outrage the community's notions of decency, it is considered obscene.

One specific right of privacy recognized by the court is the right to control one's name and likeness. Such a right protects people from subjection to false attribution.

The right of privacy is not an absolute right and may not apply to an individual in some situations. Consent, either express or implied, may waive the right. Estoppel, or the theory that one is barred from applying the principle, may also apply. If the person is a public figure they may not qualify for protection. Someone who becomes involved, intentionally or unintentionally, in a matter of public interest may waive his or her right to privacy.

Defamation is a tort involving false statements about a person that are communicated to another person, thus resulting in ridicule or contempt of the person they were said or written about.

Defamation is either verbal or written. Verbal defamation is called *slander*. Written defamation is referred to as *libel*. The application of standards applied to defamation is the same as those of the principles discussed above with respect to the right of privacy.

With respect to an entertainer, the responsibility of interacting with the public places him or her in a precarious position. Not only do people in the public eye need to be held liable for what they do, but *they* also need to be protected from the public.

JUDICIAL DECISION

The following case is the seminal decision concerning free speech involving a public official.

New York Times Co. v. Sullivan
376 US 254 (1964)

We are required in this case to determine for the first time the extent to which the constitutional protections for speech and press limit a State's power to award damages in a libel action brought by a public official against critics of his official conduct.

Respondent L. B. Sullivan is one of the three elected Commissioners of the City of Montgomery, Alabama. He testified that he was "Commissioner of Public Affairs and the duties are supervision of the Police Department, Fire Department, Department of Cemetery and Department of Scales." He brought this civil libel action against the four individual petitioners, who are Negroes and Alabama clergymen, and against petitioner the New York Times Company, a New York corporation which publishes the *New York Times*, a daily newspaper. A jury in the Circuit Court of Montgomery County awarded him damages of $500,000, the full amount claimed, against all the petitioners, and the Supreme Court of Alabama affirmed.

Respondent's complaint alleged that he had been libeled by statements in a full-page advertisement that was carried in the *New York Times* on March 29, 1960. Entitled "Heed Their Rising Voices," the advertisement began by stating that "As the whole world knows by now, thousands of Southern Negro students are engaged in widespread non-violent demonstrations in positive affirmation of the right to live in human dignity as guaranteed by the U.S. Constitution and the Bill of Rights." It went on to charge that "in their efforts to uphold these guarantees, they are

being met by an unprecedented wave of terror by those who would deny and negate that document which the whole world looks upon as setting the pattern for modern freedom. ..." Succeeding paragraphs purported to illustrate the "wave of terror" by describing certain alleged events. The text concluded with an appeal for funds for three purposes: support of the student movement, "the struggle for the right-to-vote," and the legal defense of Dr. Martin Luther King, Jr., leader of the movement, against a perjury indictment then pending in Montgomery.

The text appeared over the names of 64 persons, many widely known for their activities in public affairs, religion, trade unions, and the performing arts. Below these names, and under a line reading "We in the south who are struggling daily for dignity and freedom warmly endorse this appeal," appeared the names of the four individual petitioners and of 16 other persons, all but two of whom were identified as clergymen in various Southern cities. The advertisement was signed at the bottom of the page by the "Committee to Defend Martin Luther King and the Struggle for Freedom in the South," and the officers of the Committee were listed.

Of the 10 paragraphs of text in the advertisement, the third and a portion of the sixth were the basis of respondent's claim of libel. They read as follows:

Third paragraph:

In Montgomery, Alabama, after students sang `My Country, 'Tis of Thee' on the State Capitol steps, their leaders were expelled from school, and truckloads of police armed with shotguns and tear-gas ringed the Alabama State College Campus. When the entire student body protested to state authorities by refusing to re-register, their dining hall was padlocked in an attempt to starve them into submission.

Sixth paragraph:

Again and again the Southern violators have answered Dr. King's peaceful protests with intimidation and violence. They have bombed his home almost killing his wife and child. They have assaulted his person. They have arrested him seven times—for 'speeding,' 'loitering' and similar 'offenses.' And now they have charged him with 'perjury'—a felony under which they could imprison him for ten years. ..."

Although neither of these statements mentions respondent by name, he contended that the word "police" in the third paragraph referred to him as the Montgomery Commissioner who supervised the Police Department, so that he was being accused of "ringing" the campus with police. He further claimed that the paragraph would be read as imputing to the police, and hence to him, the padlocking of the dining hall in order to starve the students into submission. As to the sixth paragraph, he contended that since arrests are ordinarily made by the police, the statement "They have arrested [Dr. King] seven times" would be read as referring to him; he further contended that the "They" who did the arresting would be equated with the "They" who committed the other described acts and with the "Southern violators." Thus, he argued, the paragraph would be read as accusing the Montgomery police, and hence him, of answering Dr. King's protests with "intimidation and violence," bombing his home, assaulting his person, and charging him with perjury. Respondent and six other Montgomery residents testified that they read some or all of the statements as referring to him in his capacity as Commissioner.

It is uncontroverted that some of the statements contained in the paragraphs were not accurate descriptions of events which occurred in Montgomery. Although Negro students staged a demonstration on the State Capitol steps, they sang the National Anthem and not "My Country, 'Tis of Thee." Although nine students were expelled by the State Board of Education, this was not for leading the demonstration at the Capitol, but for demanding service at a lunch counter in the Montgomery County Courthouse on another day. Not the entire student body, but most of it, had protested the expulsion, not by refusing to register, but by boycotting classes on a single day; virtually all the students did register for the ensuing semester. The campus dining hall was not padlocked on any occasion, and the only students who may have been barred from eating there were the few who had neither signed a preregistration application nor requested temporary meal tickets.

Although the police were deployed near the campus in large numbers on three occasions, they did not at any time "ring" the campus, and they were not called to the campus in connection with the demonstration on the State Capitol steps, as the third paragraph implied. Dr. King had not been arrested seven times, but only four; and although he claimed to have been assaulted some years earlier in connection with his arrest for loitering outside a courtroom, one of the officers who made the arrest denied that there was such an assault.

On the premise that the charges in the sixth paragraph could be read as referring to him, respondent was allowed to prove that he had not participated in the events described. Although Dr. King's home had in fact been bombed twice when his wife and child were there, both of these occasions antedated respondent's tenure as Commissioner, and the police were not only not implicated in the bombings, but had made every effort to apprehend those who were. Three of Dr. King's four arrests took place before respondent became Commissioner. Although Dr. King had in fact been indicted (he was subsequently acquitted) on two counts of perjury, each of which carried a possible five-year sentence, respondent had nothing to do with procuring the indictment.

Respondent made no effort to prove that he suffered actual pecuniary loss as a result of the alleged libel. One of his witnesses, a former employer, testified that if he had believed the statements, he doubted whether he "would want to be associated with anybody who would be a party to such things that are stated in that ad," and that he would not re-employ respondent if he believed "that he allowed the Police Department to do the things that the paper say he did." But neither this witness nor any of the others testified that he had actually believed the statements in their supposed reference to respondent.

The cost of the advertisement was approximately $4800, and it was published by the *Times* upon an order from a New York advertising agency acting for the signatory Committee. The agency submitted the advertisement with a letter from A. Philip Randolph, Chairman of the Committee, certifying that the persons whose names appeared on the advertisement had given their permission. Mr. Randolph was known to the *Times'* Advertising Acceptability Department as a responsible person, and in accepting the letter as sufficient proof of authorization it followed its established practice. There was testimony that the copy of the advertisement which accompanied the letter listed only the 64 names appearing under the text, and that the statement, "We in the south ... warmly endorse this appeal," and the list of names thereunder, which included those of the individual petitioners, were subsequently added when the first proof of the advertisement was received. Each of the individual petitioners testified that he had not authorized the use of his name, and that he had been unaware of its use until receipt of respondent's demand for a retraction. The manager of the Advertising Acceptability Department testified that he had approved the advertisement for publication because he knew nothing to cause him to believe that anything in it was false, and because it bore the endorsement of "a number of people who are well known and whose reputation" he "had no reason to question." Neither he nor anyone else at the *Times* made an effort to confirm the accuracy of the advertisement, either by checking it against recent Times news stories relating to some of the described events or by any other means.

Alabama law denies a public officer recovery of punitive damages in a libel action brought on account of a publication concerning his official conduct unless he first makes a written demand for a public retraction and the defendant fails or refuses to comply. Respondent served such a demand upon each of the petitioners. None of the individual petitioners responded to the demand, primarily because each took the position that he had not authorized the use of his name on the advertisement and therefore had not published the statements that respondent alleged had libeled him. The *Times* did not publish a retraction in response to the demand, but wrote respondent a letter stating, among other things, that "we ... are somewhat puzzled as to how you think the statements in any way reflect on you," and "you might, if you desire, let us know in what respect you claim that the statements in the advertisement reflect on you." Respondent filed this suit a few days later without answering the letter. The *Times* did, however, subsequently publish a retraction of the advertisement upon the demand of Governor John Patterson of Alabama, who asserted that the publication charged him with "grave misconduct and ... improper actions and omissions as Governor of Alabama and Ex-Officio Chairman of the State Board of Education of Alabama." When asked to explain why there had been a retraction for the Governor but not for respondent, the Secretary of the *Times* testified: "We did that because we didn't want anything that was published by the *Times* to be a reflection on the State of Alabama and the Governor was, as far as we could see, the embodiment of the State of Alabama and the proper representative of the State and, furthermore, we had by that time learned more of the actual facts which the ad purported to recite and, finally, the ad did refer to the action of the State authorities and the Board of Education presumably of which the Governor is the ex-officio chairman ... ." On the other hand, he testified that he did not think that "any of the language in there referred to Mr. Sullivan."

The trial judge submitted the case to the jury under instructions that the statements in the advertisement were "libelous per se" and were not privileged, so that petitioners might be held liable if the jury found that they had published the advertisement and that the statements were made "of and concerning" respondent. The jury was instructed that, because the statements were libelous per se, "the law ... implies legal injury from the bare fact of publication itself," "falsity and malice are presumed," "general damages need not be alleged or proved but are presumed," and "punitive damages may be awarded by the jury even though the amount of actual damages is neither found nor shown." An award of punitive damages—as distinguished from "general" damages, which are compensatory in nature—apparently requires proof of actual malice under Alabama law, and the judge charged that "mere negligence or carelessness is not evidence of actual malice or malice in fact, and does not justify an award of exemplary or punitive damages." He refused to charge, however, that the jury must be "convinced" of malice, in the sense of "actual intent" to harm or "gross negligence and recklessness," to make such an award, and he also refused to require that a verdict for respondent differentiate between compensatory and punitive damages. The judge rejected petitioners' contention that his rulings abridged the freedoms of speech and of the press that are guaranteed by the First and Fourteenth Amendments.

In affirming the judgment, the Supreme Court of Alabama sustained the trial judge's rulings and instructions in all respects. It held that "where the words published tend to injure a person libeled by them in his reputation, profession, trade or business, or charge him with an indictable offense, or tend to bring the individual into public contempt," they are "libelous per se"; that "the matter complained of is, under the above doctrine, libelous per se, if it was published of and concerning the plaintiff"; and that it was actionable without "proof of pecuniary injury ..., such injury being implied." It approved the trial court's ruling that the jury could find the statements to have been made "of and concerning" respondent, stating: "We think it common knowledge that the average person knows that municipal agents, such as police and firemen, and others, are under the control and direction of the city governing body, and more particularly under the direction and control of a single commissioner. In measuring the performance or deficiencies of such groups, praise or criticism is usually attached to the official in complete control of the body." In sustaining the trial court's determination that the verdict was not excessive, the court said that malice could be inferred from the *Times'* "irresponsibility" in printing the advertisement while "the *Times* in its own files had articles already published which would have demonstrated the falsity of the allegations in the advertisement"; from the *Times'* failure to retract for respondent while retracting for the Governor, whereas the falsity of some of the allegations was then known to the *Times* and "the matter contained in the advertisement was equally false as to both parties"; and from the testimony of the *Times'* Secretary that, apart from the statement that the dining hall was padlocked, he thought the two paragraphs were "substantially correct." The court reaffirmed a statement in an earlier opinion that "There is no legal measure of damages in cases of this character." It rejected petitioners' constitutional contentions with the brief statements that "The First Amendment of the U.S. Constitution does not protect libelous publications" and "The Fourteenth Amendment is directed against State action and not private action."

Because of the importance of the constitutional issues involved, we granted the separate petitions for certiorari of the individual petitioners and of the *Times*. We reverse the judgment. We hold that the rule of law applied by the Alabama courts is constitutionally deficient for failure to provide the safeguards for freedom of speech and of the press that are required by the First and Fourteenth Amendments in a libel action brought by a public official against critics of his official conduct. We further hold that under the proper safeguards the evidence presented in this case is constitutionally insufficient to support the judgment for respondent.

I

We may dispose at the outset of two grounds asserted to insulate the judgment of the Alabama courts from constitutional scrutiny. The first is the proposition relied on by the State Supreme Court— that "The Fourteenth Amendment is directed against State action and not private action." That proposition has no application to this case. Although this is a civil lawsuit between private parties, the Alabama courts have applied a state rule of law which petitioners claim to impose invalid restrictions on their constitutional freedoms of speech and press. It matters not that that law has been applied in a civil action and that it is common law only, though supplemented by statute. The test is not the form in which state power has been applied but, whatever the form, whether such power has in fact been exercised.

The second contention is that the constitutional guarantees of freedom of speech and of the press are inapplicable here, at least so far as the *Times* is concerned, because the allegedly libelous statements were published as part of a paid, "commercial" advertisement. The argument relies on *Valentine v. Chrestensen* where the Court held that a city ordinance forbidding street distribution of commercial and business advertising matter did not abridge the First Amendment freedoms, even as applied to a handbill having a commercial message on one side but a protest against certain official action on the other. The reliance is wholly misplaced. The Court in *Chrestensen* reaffirmed the constitutional protection for "the freedom of communicating information and disseminating opinion"; its holding was based upon the factual conclusions that the handbill was "purely commercial advertising" and that the protest against official action had been added only to evade the ordinance.

The publication here was not a "commercial" advertisement in the sense in which the word was used in *Chrestensen*. It communicated information, expressed opinion, recited grievances, protested claimed abuses, and sought financial support on behalf of a movement whose existence and objectives are matters of the highest public interest and concern. That the *Times* was paid for publishing the advertisement is as immaterial in this connection as is the fact that newspapers and books are sold. Any other conclusion would discourage newspapers from carrying "editorial advertisements" of this type, and so might shut off an important outlet for the promulgation of information and ideas by persons who do not themselves have access to publishing facilities—who wish to exercise their freedom of speech even though they are not members of the press. The effect would be to shackle the First Amendment in its attempt to secure "the widest possible dissemination of information from diverse and antagonistic sources" *Associated Press v. United States*, 326 US 1, 20). To avoid placing such a handicap upon the freedoms of expression, we hold that if the allegedly libelous statements would otherwise be constitutionally protected from the present judgment, they do not forfeit that protection because they were published in the from of a paid advertisement.

II

Under Alabama law as applied in this case, a publication is "libelous per se" if the words "tend to injure a person ... in his reputation" or to "bring [him] into public contempt"; the trial court stated that the standard was met if the words are such as to "injure him in his public office, or impute misconduct to him in his office, or want of official integrity, or want of fidelity to a public trust ... ." The jury must find that the words were published "of and concerning" the plaintiff, but where the plaintiff is a public official his place in the governmental hierarchy is sufficient evidence to support a finding that his reputation has been affected by statements that reflect upon the agency of which he is in charge. Once "libel per se" has been established, the defendant has no defense as to stated facts unless he can persuade the jury that they were true in all their particulars. His privilege of "fair comment" for expressions of opinion depends on the truth of the facts upon which the comment is based. Unless he can discharge the burden of proving truth, general damages are presumed, and may be awarded without proof of pecuniary injury. A showing of actual malice is apparently a prerequisite to recovery of punitive damages, and the defendant may in any event forestall a punitive award by a retraction meeting the statutory requirements. Good motives and belief in truth do not negate an inference of malice, but are relevant only in mitigation of punitive damages if the jury chooses to accord them weight.

The question before us is whether this rule of liability, as applied to an action brought by a public official against critics of his official conduct, abridges the freedom of speech and of the press that is guaranteed by the first and Fourteenth Amendments.

Respondent relies heavily, as did the Alabama courts, on statements of this Court to the effect that the Constitution does not protect libelous publications. Those statements do not foreclose our inquiry here. None of the cases sustained the use of libel laws to impose sanctions upon expression critical of the official conduct of public officials. The dictum in *Pennekamp v. Florida*, 328 US 331, 348–349, that "when the statements amount to defamation, a judge has such remedy in damages for libel as do other public servants," implied no view as to what remedy might constitutionally be afforded to public officials. In *Beauharnais v. Illinois*, 343 US 250, the Court sustained an Illinois criminal libel statute as applied to a publication held to be both defamatory of a racial group and "liable to cause violence and disorder." But the Court was careful to note that it "retains and exercises authority to nullify action which encroaches on freedom of utterance under the guise of punishing libel"; for "public men, are, as it were, public property," and "discussion cannot be denied and the right, as well as the duty, of criticism must not be stifled" (*Id.*, at 263–264, and n.18). In the only previous case that did present the question of constitutional limitations upon the power to award damages for libel of a public official, the Court was equally divided and the question was not decided (*Schenectady Union Pub. Co. v. Sweeney*, 316 US 642 [376 US 254, 269]). In deciding the question now, we are compelled by neither precedent nor policy to give any more weight to the epithet "libel" than we have to other "mere labels" of state law. (*NAACP v. Button*, 371 US 415, 429). Like insurrection, contempt, advocacy of unlawful acts, breach of the peace, obscenity, solicitation of legal business, and the various other formulae for the repression of expression that have been challenged in this court, libel can claim no talismanic immunity from constitutional limitations. It must be measured by standards that satisfy the First Amendment.

The general proposition that freedom of expression upon public questions is secured by the First Amendment has long been settled by our decisions. The constitutional safeguard, we have said, "was fashioned to assure unfettered interchange of ideas for the bringing about of political and social changes desired by the people" (*Roth v. United States*, 354 US 476, 484). "The maintenance of the opportunity for free political discussion to the end that government may be responsive to the will of the people and that changes may be obtained by lawful means, an opportunity essential to the security of the Republic, is a fundamental principle of our constitutional system" (*Stromberg v. California*, 283 US 359, 369). "[I]t is a prized American privilege to speak one's mind, although not always with perfect good taste, on all public institutions," (*Bridges v. California*, 314 US 252, 270), and this opportunity is to be afforded for "vigorous advocacy" no less than "abstract discussion" (*NAACP v. Button*, 371 US 415, 429 [376 US 254, 270]). The First Amendment, said Judge Learned Hand, "presupposes that right conclusions are more likely to be gathered out of a multitude of tongues, than through any kind of authoritative selection. To many this is, and always will be, folly; but we have staked upon it our all" (*United States v. Associated Press*, 52 F. Supp. 362, 372 [D.C. S. D. N. Y. 1943]). Mr. Justice Brandeis, in his concurring opinion in *Whitney v. California*, 274 US 357, 375–376, gave the principle its classic formulation:

> Those who won our independence believed ... that public discussion is a political duty; and that this should be a fundamental principle of the American government. They recognized the risks to which all human institutions are subject. But they knew that order cannot be secured merely through fear of punishment for its infraction; that it is hazardous to discourage thought, hope and imagination; that fear breeds repression; that repression breeds hate; that hate menaces stable government; that the path of safety lies in the opportunity to discuss freely supposed grievances and proposed remedies; and that the fitting remedy for evil counsels is good ones. Believing in the power of reason as applied through public discussion, they eschewed silence coerced by law—the argument of force in its worst form. Recognizing the occasional tyrannies

of governing majorities, they amended the Constitution so that free speech and assembly should be guaranteed.

Thus we consider this case against the background of a profound national commitment to the principle that debate on public issues should be uninhibited, robust, and wide-open, and that it may well include vehement, caustic, and sometimes unpleasantly sharp attacks on government and public officials. See *Terminiello v. Chicago*, 337 US 1, 4; *De Jonge v. Oregon*, 299 US 353 [376 US 254, 271] 365. The present advertisement, as an expression of grievance and protest on one of the major public issues of our time, would seem clearly to qualify for the constitutional protection. The question is whether it forfeits that protection by the falsity of some of its factual statements and by its alleged defamation of respondent.

Authoritative interpretations of the First Amendment guarantees have consistently refused to recognize an exception for any test of truth—whether administered by judges, juries, or administrative officials—and especially one that puts the burden of proving truth on the speaker. (Cf. *Speiser v. Randall*, 357 US 513, 525–526). The constitutional protection does not turn upon "the truth, popularity, or social utility of the ideas and beliefs which are offered" (*NAACP v. Button*, 371 US 415, 445). As Madison said, "Some degree of abuse is inseparable from the proper use of every thing; and in no instance is this more true than in that of the press" (*Elliot's Debates on the Federal Constitution* (1876), p.571). In *Cantwell v. Connecticut*, 310 US 296, 310, the Court declared:

> In the realm of religious faith, and in that of political belief, sharp differences arise. In both fields the tenets of one man may seem the rankest error to his neighbor. To persuade others to his own point of view, the pleader, as we know, at times, resorts to exaggeration, to vilification of men who have been, or are, prominent in church or state, and even to false statement. But the people of this nation have ordained in the light of history, that, in spite of the probability of excesses and abuses, these liberties are, in the long view, essential to enlightened opinion and right conduct on the part of the citizens of a democracy.

That erroneous statement is inevitable in free debate, and that it must be protected if the freedoms of expression (376 US 254, 272) are to have the "breathing space" that they "need ... to survive,"

(*NAACP v. Button*, 371 US 415, 433), was also recognized by the Court of Appeals for the District of Columbia Circuit in *Sweeney v. Patterson*, 76 US App. DC 23, 24, 128 F2d 457, 458 (1942), cert. denied, 317 US 678. Judge Edgerton spoke for a unanimous court which affirmed the dismissal of a Congressman's libel suit based upon a newspaper article charging him with anti-Semitism in opposing a judicial appointment. He said:

> Cases which impose liability for erroneous reports of the political conduct of officials reflect the obsolete doctrine that the governed must not criticize their governors. ... The interest of the public here outweighs the interest of appellant or any other individual. The protection of the public requires not merely discussion, but information. Political conduct and views which some respectable people approve, and others condemn, are constantly imputed to Congressmen.
>
> Errors of fact, particularly in regard to a man's mental states and processes, are inevitable. ... Whatever is added to the field of libel is taken from the field of free debate.

Injury to official reputation affords no more warrant for repressing speech that would otherwise be free than does factual error. Where judicial officers are involved, this Court has held that concern for the dignity and (376 US 254, 273) reputation of the courts does not justify the punishment as criminal contempt of criticism of the judge or his decision (*Bridges v. California*, 314 US 252). This is true even though the utterance contains "half-truths" and "misinformation" (*Pennekamp v. Florida*, 328 US 331, 342, 343, n.5, 345). Such repression can be justified, if at all, only by a clear and present danger of the obstruction of justice (see also *Craig v. Harney*, 331 US 367; *Wood v. Georgia*, 370 US 375). If judges are to be treated as "men of fortitude, able to thrive in a hardy climate," (*Craig v. Harney*, supra, 331 US 376), surely the same must be true of other government officials, such as elected city commissioners. Criticism of their official conduct does not lose its constitutional protection merely because it is effective criticism and hence diminishes their official reputations.

If neither factual error nor defamatory content suffices to remove the constitutional shield from criticism of official conduct, the combination of the two elements is no less inadequate. This is the lesson to be drawn from the great controversy over the *Sedition Act of 1798*, 1 Stat. 596, which first crystallized a national awareness of the central meaning of the First Amendment (see *Levy, Legacy of Suppression* (1960), at 258 et seq.; *Smith, Freedom's Fetters* (1956), at 426, 431, and passim). That statute made it a crime, punishable by a $5,000 fine and five years in prison, "if any person shall write, print, utter or publish ... any false, scandalous and malicious (376 US 254, 274) writing or writings against the government of the United States, or either house of the Congress ..., or the President ..., with intent to defame ... or to bring them, or either of them, into contempt or disrepute; or to excite against them, or either or any of them, the hatred of the good people of the United States." The Act allowed the defendant the defense of truth, and provided that the jury were to be judges both of the law and the facts. Despite these qualifications, the Act was vigorously condemned as unconstitutional in an attack joined in by Jefferson and Madison. In the famous *Virginia Resolutions of 1798*, the General Assembly of Virginia resolved that it

> doth particularly protest against the palpable and alarming infractions of the Constitution, in the two late cases of the `Alien and Sedition Acts,' passed at the last session of Congress ... . [The Sedition Act] exercises ... a power not delegated by the Constitution, but, on the contrary, expressly and positively forbidden by one of the amendments thereto—a power which, more than any other, ought to produce universal alarm, because it is levelled against the right of freely examining public characters and measures, and of free communication among the people thereon, which has ever been justly deemed the only effectual guardian of every other right (4 *Elliot's Debates*, supra, pp.553–554).

Madison prepared the Report in support of the protest. His premise was that the Constitution created a form of government under which "The people, not the government, possess the absolute sovereignty." The structure of the government dispersed power in reflection of the people's distrust of concentrated power, and of power itself at all levels. This form of government was "altogether different" from the British form, under which the Crown was sovereign and the people were subjects. "Is (376 US 254, 275) it not natural and necessary, under such different circumstances," he asked, "that a different degree of freedom in the use of the press should be contemplated?" (*Id.*, pp.569–570). Earlier, in a debate in the House of

Representatives, Madison had said: "If we advert to the nature of Republican Government, we shall find that the censorial power is in the people over the Government, and not in the Government over the people" (4 *Annals of Congress*, p.934 (1794)). Of the exercise of that power by the press, his Report said: "In every state, probably, in the Union, the press has exerted a freedom in canvassing the merits and measures of public men, of every description, which has not been confined to the strict limits of the common law. On this footing the freedom of the press has stood; on this foundation it yet stands ..." (4 *Elliot's Debates*, supra, p.570). The right of free public discussion of the stewardship of public officials was thus, in Madison's view, a fundamental principle of the American form of government (376 US 254, 276).

Although the Sedition Act was never tested in this Court, the attack upon its validity has carried the day in the court of history. Fines levied in its prosecution were repaid by Act of Congress on the ground that it was constitutional (see, e.g., *Act of July 4*, 1840, c.45, 6 Stat. 802, accompanied by H.R. Rep. No. 86, 26th Cong., 1st Sess. (1840)). Calhoun, reporting to the Senate on February 4, 1836, assumed that its invalidity was a matter "which no one now doubts" (*Report with Senate Bill No. 122*, 24th Cong., 1st Sess., p.3). Jefferson, as President, pardoned those who had been convicted and sentenced under the Act and remitted their fines, stating: "I discharged every person under punishment or prosecution under the sedition law, because I considered, and now consider, that law to be a nullity, as absolute and as palpable as if Congress had ordered us to fall down and worship a golden image" (*Letter to Mrs. Adams*, July 22, 1804, 4 *Jefferson's Works* (Washington ed.), pp.555, 556). The invalidity of the Act has also been assumed by Justices of this Court. (See Holmes, J., dissenting and joined by Brandeis, J., in *Abrams v. United States*, 250 US 616, 630; Jackson, J., dissenting in *Beauharnais v. Illinois*, 343 US 250, 288–289; Douglas, *The Right of the People* (1958), p.47. See also Cooley, *Constitutional Limitations* (8th ed., Carrington, 1927), pp.899–900; Chafee, *Free Speech in the United States* (1942), pp.27–28. These views reflect a broad consensus that the Act, because of the restraint it imposed upon criticism of government and public officials, was inconsistent with the First Amendment.

There is no force in respondent's argument that the constitutional limitations implicit in the history of the Sedition Act apply only to Congress and not to the States. It is true that the First Amendment was originally addressed only to action by the Federal Government, and (376 US 254, 277) that Jefferson, for one, while denying the power of Congress "to control the freedom of the press," recognized such a power in the States (see the 1804 *Letter to Abigail Adams* quoted in *Dennis v. United States*, 341 US 494, 522, n.4 (concurring opinion)). But this distinction was eliminated with the adoption of the Fourteenth Amendment and the application to the States of the First Amendment's restrictions (see, e.g., *Gitlow v. New York*, 268 US 652, 666; *Schneider v. State*, 308 US 147, 160; *Bridges v. California*, 314 US 252, 268; *Edwards v. South Carolina*, 372 US 229, 235).

What a State may not constitutionally bring about by means of a criminal statute is likewise beyond the reach of its civil law of libel. The fear of damage awards under a rule such as that invoked by the Alabama courts here may be markedly more inhibiting than the fear of prosecution under a criminal statute (see *City of Chicago v. Tribune Co.*, 307 Ill. 595, 607, 139 NE 86, 90 (1923)). Alabama, for example, has a criminal libel law which subjects to prosecution "any person who speaks, writes, or prints of and concerning another any accusation falsely and maliciously importing the commission by such person of a felony, or any other indictable offense involving moral turpitude," and which allows as punishment upon conviction a fine not exceeding $500 and a prison sentence of six months (Alabama Code, Tit. 14, 350). Presumably a person charged with violation of this statute enjoys ordinary criminal-law safeguards such as the requirements of an indictment and of proof beyond a reasonable doubt. These safeguards are not available to the defendant in a civil action. The judgment awarded in this case—without the need for any proof of actual pecuniary loss—was one thousand times greater than the maximum fine provided by the Alabama criminal statute, and one hundred times greater than that provided by the Sedition Act (376 US 254, 278). And since there is no double-jeopardy limitation applicable to civil lawsuits, this is not the only judgment that may be awarded against petitioners for the same publication. Whether or not a newspaper can survive a succession of such judgments, the pall of fear and timidity imposed upon those who would give voice to public criticism is an atmosphere in which the First Amendment freedoms cannot survive. Plainly the Alabama law of civil libel is "a form of regulation that creates hazards to protected freedoms markedly greater than those that attend reliance upon the criminal law" (*Bantam Books, Inc., v. Sullivan*, 372 US 58, 70).

The state rule of law is not saved by its allowance of the defense of truth. A defense for erroneous statements honestly made is no less essential here than was the requirement of proof of guilty knowledge which, in *Smith v. California*, 361 US 147, we held indispensable to a valid conviction of a bookseller for possessing obscene writings for sale. We said:

> For if the bookseller is criminally liable without knowledge of the contents, ... he will tend to restrict the books he sells to those he has inspected; and thus the State will have imposed a restriction upon the distribution of constitutionally protected as well as obscene literature. ... And the bookseller's burden would become the public's burden, for by restricting him the public's access to reading matter would be restricted. ... [H]is timidity in the face of his absolute criminal liability, thus would tend to restrict the public's access to forms of the printed word which the State could not constitutionally (376 US 254, 279) suppress directly.
>
> The bookseller's self-censorship, compelled by the State, would be a censorship affecting the whole public, hardly less virulent for being privately administered. Through it, the distribution of all books, both obscene and not obscene, would be impeded." (361 US 147, 153–154.)

A rule compelling the critic of official conduct to guarantee the truth of all his factual assertions—and to do so on pain of libel judgments virtually unlimited in amount—leads to a comparable "self-censorship." Allowance of the defense of truth, with the burden of proving it on the defendant, does not mean that only false speech will be deterred. Even courts accepting this defense as an adequate safeguard have recognized the difficulties of adducing legal proofs that the alleged libel was true in all its factual particulars (see, e.g., *Post Publishing Co. v. Hallam*, 59 F. 530, 540 (C.A. 6th Cir. 1893); see also Noel, *Defamation of Public Officers and Candidates* 49 Col. L.Rev. 875, 892 (1949)). Under such a rule, would-be critics of

official conduct may be deterred from voicing their criticism, even though it is believed to be true and even though it is in fact true, because of doubt whether it can be proved in court or fear of the expense of having to do so. They tend to make only statements which "steer far wider of the unlawful zone" (*Speiser v. Randall*, supra, 357 US, at 526). The rule thus dampens the vigor and limits the variety of public debate. It is inconsistent with the First and Fourteenth Amendments.

The constitutional guarantees require, we think, a federal rule that prohibits a public official from recovering damages for a defamatory falsehood relating to his official conduct unless he proves that the statement was made (376 US 254, 280) with "actual malice"—that is, with knowledge that it was false or with reckless disregard of whether it was false or not. An oft cited statement of a like rule, which has been adopted by a number of state courts, 20 is found in the Kansas case of *Coleman v. MacLennan*, 78 Kan. 711, 98 P. 281 (1908). The State Attorney General, a candidate for re-election and a member of the commission charged with the management and control of the state school fund, sued a newspaper publisher for alleged libel in an article purporting to state facts relating to his official conduct in connection with a school-fund transaction. The defendant pleaded privilege and the trial judge, over the plaintiff's objection, instructed the jury that

> where an article is published and circulated among voters for the sole purpose of giving what the defendant (376 US 254, 281) believes to be truthful information concerning a candidate for public office and for the purpose of enabling such voters to cast their ballot more intelligently, and the whole thing is done in good faith and without malice, the article is privileged, although the principal matters contained in the article may be untrue in fact and derogatory to the character of the plaintiff; and in such a case the burden is on the plaintiff to show actual malice in the publication of the article.

In answer to a special question, the jury found that the plaintiff had not proved actual malice, and a general verdict was returned for the defendant. On appeal the Supreme Court of Kansas, in an opinion by Justice Burch, reasoned as follows (78 Kan., at 724, 98 P., at 286):

> It is of the utmost consequence that the people should discuss the character and qualifications of candidates for

their suffrages. The importance to the state and to society of such discussions is so vast, and the advantages derived are so great, that they more than counterbalance the inconvenience of private persons whose conduct may be involved, and occasional injury to the reputations of individuals must yield to the public welfare, although at times such injury may be great. The public benefit from publicity is so great, and the chance of injury to private character so small, that such discussion must be privileged.

The court thus sustained the trial court's instruction as a correct statement of the law, saying:

In such a case the occasion gives rise to a privilege, qualified to this extent: any one claiming to be defamed by the communication must show actual malice or go remediless. This privilege extends to a great variety of subjects, and includes matters of (376 US 254, 282) public concern, public men, and candidates for office" (78 Kan., at 723, 98 P, at 285).

Such a privilege for criticism of official conduct is appropriately analogous to the protection accorded a public official when he is sued for libel by a private citizen. In *Barr v. Matteo*, 360 US 564, 575, this Court held the utterance of a federal official to be absolutely privileged if made "within the outer perimeter" of his duties. The States accord the same immunity to statements of their highest officers, although some differentiate their lesser officials and qualify the privilege they enjoy. But all hold that all officials are protected unless actual malice can be proved. The reason for the official privilege is said to be that the threat of damage suits would otherwise "inhibit the fearless, vigorous, and effective administration of policies of government" and "dampen the ardor of all but the most resolute, or the most irresponsible, in the unflinching discharge of their duties" (*Barr v. Matteo*, supra, 360 US, at 571). Analogous considerations support the privilege for the citizen-critic of government. It is as much his duty to criticize as it is the official's duty to administer (see *Whitney v. California*, 274 US 357, 375 (concurring opinion of Mr. Justice Brandeis), quoted supra, p.270). As Madison said, (see supra, p.275) "the censorial power is in the people over the Government, and not in the Government over the people." It would give public servants an unjustified preference over the public they serve, if critics of official conduct (376 US 254, 283) did not

have a fair equivalent of the immunity granted to the officials themselves.

We conclude that such a privilege is required by the First and Fourteenth Amendments.

III

We hold today that the Constitution delimits a State's power to award damages for libel in actions brought by public officials against critics of their official conduct. Since this is such an action, the rule requiring proof of actual malice Is applicable. While Alabama law apparently requires proof of actual malice for an award of punitive damages, where general damages are concerned malice is "presumed." Such a presumption is inconsistent (376 US 254, 284) with the federal rule. "The power to create presumptions is not a means of escape from constitutional restrictions," (*Bailey v. Alabama*, 219 US 219, 239); "the showing of malice required for the forfeiture of the privilege is not presumed but is a matter for proof by the plaintiff ..." (*Lawrence v. Fox*, 357 Mich. 134, 146, 97 NW2d 719, 725 (1959)). Since the trial judge did not instruct the jury to differentiate between general and punitive damages, it may be that the verdict was wholly an award of one or the other.

But it is impossible to know, in view of the general verdict returned. Because of this uncertainty, the judgment must be reversed and the case remanded (*Stromberg v. California*, 283 US 359, 367–368; *Williams v. North Carolina*, 317 US 287, 291–292; see *Yates v. United States*, 354 US 298, 311–312; *Cramer v. United States*, 325 US 1, 36, n.45).

Since respondent may seek a new trial, we deem that considerations of effective judicial administration require us to review the evidence in the present record to determine (376 US 254, 285) whether it could constitutionally support a judgment for respondent. This Court's duty is not limited to the elaboration of constitutional principles; we must also in proper cases review the evidence to make certain that those principles have been constitutionally applied. This is such a case, particularly since the question is one of alleged trespass across "the line between speech unconditionally guaranteed and speech which may legitimately be regulated" (*Speiser v. Randall*, 357 US 513, 525). In cases where that line must be drawn, the rule is that we "examine for ourselves the statements in issue and the circumstances under which they were made to see

... whether they are of a character which the principles of the First Amendment, as adopted by the Due Process Clause of the Fourteenth Amendment, protect" (*Pennekamp v. Florida*, 328 US 331, 335; see also *One, Inc., v. Olesen*, 355 US 371; *Sunshine Book Co. v. Summerfield*, 355 US 372). We must "make an independent examination of the whole record," (*Edwards v. South Carolina*, 372 US 229, 235), so as to assure ourselves that the judgment does not constitute a forbidden intrusion on the field of free expression.

Applying these standards, we consider that the proof presented to show actual malice lacks the convincing clarity which the constitutional standard demands, and hence that it would not constitutionally sustain the judgment for respondent under the proper rule of law. The case of the individual petitioners requires little discussion. Even assuming that they could constitutionally be found to have authorized the use of their names on the advertisement, there was no evidence whatever that they were aware of any erroneous statements or were in any way reckless in that regard. The judgment against them is thus without constitutional support.

As to the *Times*, we similarly conclude that the facts do not support a finding of actual malice. The statement by the *Times'* Secretary that, apart from the padlocking allegation, he thought the advertisement was "substantially correct," affords no constitutional warrant for the Alabama Supreme Court's conclusion that it was a "cavalier ignoring of the falsity of the advertisement [from which] the jury could not have but been impressed with the bad faith of the *Times*, and its maliciousness inferable therefrom." The statement does not indicate malice at the time of the publication; even if the advertisement was not "substantially correct"—although respondent's own proofs tend to show that it was—that opinion was at least a reasonable one, and there was no evidence to impeach the witness' good faith in holding it. The *Times'* failure to retract upon respondent's demand, although it later retracted upon the demand of Governor Patterson, is likewise not adequate evidence of malice for constitutional purposes. Whether or not a failure to retract may ever constitute such evidence, there are two reasons why it does not here. First, the letter written by the *Times* reflected a reasonable doubt on its part as to whether the advertisement could reasonably be taken to refer to respondent at all. Second, it was not a final refusal, since it asked for an explanation on this point—a request that respondent chose to ignore. Nor does the retraction upon the demand of the Governor supply the necessary proof. It may be doubted that a failure to retract, which is not itself evidence of malice, can retroactively become such by virtue of a retraction subsequently made to another party. But, in any event, that did not happen here, since the explanation given by the *Times'* Secretary for the distinction drawn between respondent and the Governor was a reasonable one, the good faith of which was not impeached.

Finally, there is evidence that the *Times* published the advertisement without checking its accuracy against the news stories in the *Times'* own files. The mere presence of the stories in the files does not, of course, establish that the *Times* "knew" the advertisement was false, since the state of mind required for actual malice would have to be brought home to the persons in the *Times'* organization having responsibility for the publication of the advertisement. With respect to the failure of those persons to make the check, the record shows that they relied upon their knowledge of the good reputation of many of those whose names were listed as sponsors of the advertisement, and upon the letter from A. Philip Randolph, known to them as a responsible individual, certifying that the use of the names was authorized. There was testimony that the persons handling the advertisement saw nothing in it that would render it unacceptable under the *Times'* policy of rejecting advertisements containing "attacks of a personal character"; their failure to reject it on this ground was not unreasonable. We think the evidence against the *Times* supports, at most, a finding of negligence in failing to discover the misstatements, and is constitutionally insufficient to show the recklessness that is required for a finding of actual malice (Cf. *Charles Parker Co. v. Silver City Crystal Co.*, 142 Conn. 605, 618, 116 A2d 440, 446 (1955); *Phoenix Newspapers, Inc., v. Choisser*, 82 Ariz. 271, 277–278, 312 P2d 150, 154–155 (1957)).

We also think the evidence was constitutionally defective in another respect: it was incapable of supporting the jury's finding that the allegedly libelous statements were made "of and concerning" respondent. Respondent relies on the words of the advertisement and the testimony of six witnesses to establish a connection between it and himself. Thus, in his brief to this Court, he states:

> The reference to respondent as police commissioner is clear from the ad. In addition, the jury heard the testimony of a newspaper editor ...; a real estate and insurance man ...; the sales manager of a men's clothing store ...; a food equipment man ...; a service station operator ...; and the operator of a truck line for whom respondent had formerly worked ... . Each of these witnesses stated that he associated the statements with respondent ... ." (Citations to record omitted.)

There was no reference to respondent in the advertisement, either by name or official position. A number of the allegedly libelous statements—the charges that the dining hall was padlocked and that Dr. King's home was bombed, his person assaulted, and a perjury prosecution instituted against him—did not even concern the police; despite the ingenuity of the arguments which would attach this significance to the word "They," it is plain that these statements could not reasonably be read as accusing respondent of personal involvement in the acts (376 US 254, 289) in question. The statements upon which respondent principally relies as referring to him are the two allegations that did concern the police or police functions: that "truckloads of police ... ringed the Alabama State College Campus" after the demonstration on the State Capitol steps, and that Dr. King had been "arrested ... seven times." These statements were false only in that the police had been "deployed near" the campus but had not actually "ringed" it and had not gone there in connection with the State Capitol demonstration, and in that Dr. King had been arrested only four times. The ruling that these discrepancies between what was true and what was asserted were sufficient to injure respondent's reputation may itself raise constitutional problems, but we need not consider them here. Although the statements may be taken as referring to the police, they did not on their face make even an oblique reference to respondent as an individual. Support for the asserted reference must, therefore, be sought in the testimony of respondent's witnesses. But none of them suggested any basis for the belief that respondent himself was attacked in the advertisement beyond the bare fact that he was in overall charge of the Police Department and thus bore

official responsibility for police conduct; to the extent that some of the witnesses thought respondent to have been charged with ordering or approving the conduct or otherwise being personally involved in it, they based this notion not on any statements in the advertisement, and not on any evidence that he had in fact been so involved, but solely on the unsupported assumption that, because of his official position, he must have been. This reliance on the bare (376 US 254, 290) fact of respondent's official position was made explicit by the Supreme Court of Alabama. That court, in holding that the trial court "did not err in overruling the demurrer [of the *Times*] in the aspect that the libelous (376 US 254, 291) matter was not of and concerning the [plaintiff,]" based its ruling on the proposition that:

> We think it common knowledge that the average person knows that municipal agents, such as police and firemen, and others, are under the control and direction of the city governing body, and more particularly under the direction and control of a single commissioner. In measuring the performance or deficiencies of such groups, praise or criticism is usually attached to the official in complete control of the body (273 Ala., at 674–675, 144 So2d at 39).

This proposition has disquieting implications for criticism of governmental conduct. For good reason, "no court of last resort in this country has ever held, or even suggested, that prosecutions for libel on government have any place in the American system of jurisprudence" (*City of Chicago v. Tribune Co.*, 307 Ill. 595, 601, 139 NE [376 US 254, 292] 86, 88 (1923)). The present proposition would sidestep this obstacle by transmuting criticism of government, however impersonal it may seem on its face, into personal criticism, and hence potential libel, of the officials of whom the government is composed. There is no legal alchemy by which a State may thus create the cause of action that would otherwise be denied for a publication which, as respondent himself said of the advertisement. "reflects not only on me but on the other Commissioners and the community." Raising as it does the possibility that a good-faith critic of government will be penalized for his criticism, the proposition relied on by the Alabama courts strikes at the very center of the constitutionally protected area of free expression. We hold that such a proposition may not constitutionally be utilized to establish that an otherwise impersonal attack on governmental operations was a libel of an official responsible for those operations. Since it was relied on exclusively here, and there was no other evidence to connect the statements with respondent, the evidence was constitutionally insufficient to support a finding that the statements referred to respondent.

The judgment of the Supreme Court of Alabama is reversed and the case is remanded to that court for further proceedings not inconsistent with this opinion. Reversed and remanded.

KEY TERMS

common law	libel
consent	likeness
constitutional law	name
defamation	negligence
defamation per se	obscene
estoppel	permanent publication
express waiver	right of publicity
false attribution	slander
freedom of speech	strict liability
implied waiver	tort

EXERCISES

1. A motion picture allegedly depicting Christ as a homosexual is about to be distributed in the United States. The movie was filmed in Europe with an international cast and the producer is a British national. At Kennedy airport, the film is seized by customs officials claiming that the film is obscene. Argue for the American distributor.

2. Give three examples of situations in which the private details of a person's life have been exploited by the media.

3. A woman received a lot of notoriety when she became sexually involved with a married politician. As a result of her publicity, she was able to negotiate a profitable book deal two years ago. Recently, television has produced a docudrama loosely based on this affair and has displayed the woman in an unfavorable light. The woman now wishes to sue for defamation. What are the arguments for and against her prevailing in a lawsuit against the station?

4. Why should certain types of speech not be afforded constitutional protections? Discuss.

5. The estate of a well-known performer has been making a fortune by selling objects with the performer's image printed on them. These items are classified as "authorized" by the deceased performer's estate. A small printing company has decided to print T-shirts with the performer's likeness on them and to market them to foreign fans. Can the performer's estate stop such printing and dissemination? Explain.

6. Read *Roth v. United States*, 354 US 26. How does this case expound on the concept of obscenity in relation to freedom of speech? Do you agree with the majority or the dissent? Discuss.

7. Indicate how a performer or artist could prove to a court that he or she suffered an economic loss because of a defamatory statement. Would the proof be different for a non-public figure?

8. Research the ordinances of your own town to determine whether there are laws that define community standards for obscenity.

9. Explain the circumstances under which a person could lose his or her expectation of privacy other than those discussed in the text.

10. How would you attempt to protect a client's image from being exploited? Explain in detail.

Exhibit

> Congress shall make no law respecting an establishment of religion, or prohibiting the free exercise thereof; or abridging the freedom of speech, or of the press; or the right of the people peaceably to assemble, and to petition the government for a redress of grievances.

EXHIBIT 1-1 First Amendment

CHAPTER

FEDERAL REGULATION OF INTELLECTUAL PROPERTY

CHAPTER OVERVIEW

In addition to the constitutional questions involved with entertainment law, the Congress has further enacted specific statutes that have a direct impact on the entertainment industry. These federal statutes create a framework within which all entertainment law must fit in order to meet these congressional mandates. This chapter will examine four aspects of federal regulation that govern the entertainment field:

- Copyrights
- Trademarks
- Trade names
- Antitrust

copyright
Right of exclusive use of a writing or a work of art.

A **copyright** is a property right that is distinct from any other in that it is not ownership of a material object. A copyright is a governmental grant of exclusive use of a creative work of art or literature that is assigned to the creator. It may be owned, transferred, or bequeathed and has a determined life. This right is dependent on the type of work that is copyrighted and provides the creator with protection against any unauthorized use or change in the work so copyrighted.

trademark
Word, symbol, or group of words that distinguishes a good.

A **trademark** is a word, group of words, or a symbol that distinguishes a particular good from similar goods in the marketplace. Trademarks are registered under the Trademark Act of 1946 (15 USC section 15501, *et. seq.*) and, like copyrights, are property rights for which the government grants exclusive use to the person who registers the mark with the United States Patent and Trademark Office. An example of a trademark would be "CBS."

antitrust laws
Statutes designed to prohibit unfair trade or the lessening of competition.

Antitrust laws are designed to protect consumers and the economy by prohibiting actions that may harm competition. For the entertainer, most antitrust litigation occurs in the areas of restraint of labor or contracts to keep players associated with a particular team, discussed further in chapter 9. Antitrust laws protect an artistic creator from misappropriated use of his or her rights through restraint of trade. If entertainers and artists were not protected by these laws, they would not be able to profit from their art because these rights could be infringed upon.

COPYRIGHTS

Ownership and Transfer

vests
Having a legally enforceable right.

work for hire
Intellectual property that was created to be owned by someone other than the creator.

collective work
Work owned by a group.

Ownership of a protected copyrighted work initially **vests** in, or belongs to, the author or creator. However, there are exceptions to this general rule. For example, if a work is a **work for hire**—a work made by an artist for someone else—then ownership in that work vests in the person for whom the work was made. When works are **collective works**, meaning that several people have contributed their efforts to the work, then ownership may vest in all of the contributing artists.

— *Example* ————

Mandy was hired to write a textbook for a publisher. She entered into a work-for-hire contract. If approached by third parties wishing to use a portion of the text in another book, she must refer them to the publisher in whom the copyright is vested.

exclusive right
The owner is the only person who holds the right.

The owner of a copyrighted work has an **exclusive right** to the use of the copyrighted work. Such exclusive use includes the right to:

1. Reproduce the work
2. Prepare subsequent works using the original work

3. Distribute copies of the work

4. Perform the work

5. Display the work

6. Display the work by means of a digital audio transmission.

Even though the owner of the right has an exclusive right to reproduce his or her work, if the use falls under what is referred to as a **fair use**, then reproduction may be possible. Fair use is use for the purpose of criticism, comment, news reporting, scholarship, or research. The test for whether something falls into the realm of fair use or whether it constitutes a copyright infringement is determined by evaluating the following factors:

fair use
Use for the purpose of criticism, comment, news reporting, parody, scholarship, or research.

1. The purpose and character of the use

2. The nature of the copyrighted work

3. The amount and substantiality of the portion used in relation to the work as a whole

4. The economic effect of the use in the potential market for the work.

── *Example* ─────────────────

A public library wishes to decorate its walls with art. It hangs reproductions of some well-known paintings, indicating that they are reproduced versions of copyrighted works. Such use by a library that is open to the public is not an infringement of the copyright.

Ownership of a copyright may be transferred in whole or in part. It may also be **bequeathed**—left to someone in a will—or transferred through **intestate succession**—passed along through the bloodline of a deceased person who dies without a valid will. Copyright transfer of material that was first **fixed**, or permanently established, in a material object does not convey rights in the copyrighted work.

bequeathed
Personal property left to someone in a will.

intestate succession
Passed along though the blood line of a deceased person by statute.

fixed
Permanently established.

── *Example* ─────────────────

Mandy owns the copyright to her song, "Yuck." It is on an album put out by a major record distributor. When the label conveys the right to use the song to someone else, Mandy will not lose her copyright in the song.

The grant of the use of copyrighted material to someone other than the author or creator is usually effectuated by means of a **license**, a contract that authorizes an individual, group, or entity to use the work in consideration for a payment to the copyright holder. This payment is known as a **royalty**. The license may be terminated if the holder, or anyone authorized to act on behalf of the author or creator, exercises that right. Proper notice, in writing, must be given and must be signed by all parties with interests in the work. At such time

license
An authorization to use.

royalty
Payment for an authorized use of a copyrighted work.

that the termination of a grant of right occurs, the right reverts back to the original author or other party owning the newly terminated interests.

── ***Example*** ──────────────────────────

Prior to dying, the author of a book grants his rights to the novel to a publisher so as to have it published. In this event, his next of kin may be entitled to exercise a termination of the grant of such right in the same manner that the author would have been entitled to terminate it.

─────────────────────────────

constructive notice
Notice not directly given.

non-exclusive license
The right to license a copyright to more than one person.

agent
Someone expressly authorized to act on another's behalf.

good faith
Without prior knowledge or malice.

notice
Warning or indication.

public domain
Intellectual property that anyone has the right to use.

This transfer of copyright should be filed in the United States Copyright Office. The record of transfer gives people **constructive notice**, which is a means by which they can determine that a transfer has occurred. This notice is important because when a conflict arises between two people who claim grants of copyright, the one who executed the grant of right first will prevail if the grant is properly recorded. However, a **non-exclusive license**, or the right to license a copyright to more than one person concurrently, whether it has been recorded or not, will prevail over an existing transfer if such non-exclusive license is in writing and signed by the copyright owner or his or her **agent** (someone expressly authorized to act on his or her behalf). This is true if the rights are granted before the execution of the transfer and only if the license was granted in **good faith**—without prior knowledge or malice—before the transfer was recorded and there was no **notice**, or warning or indication, of it.

Duration of Copyright

Generally, works created after January 1, 1978, exist for the life of the author or creator and seventy years after that person's death. After this date, the material becomes **public domain**, meaning that anyone has the right to use it if the copyright has not been renewed. The length and term of copyright renewals are determined by section 304 of the Copyright Act. The following exceptions to renewal exist:

1. For joint works—works prepared by two or more creators—the copyright lasts for seventy years after the death of the last surviving author.

2. For anonymous works, pseudonymous works, and works made for hire, the copyright lasts for ninety-five years after the date of first publication or one-hundred-and-twenty years from the date of creation, whichever expires first. If the creator is revealed, then the general rules apply pending a proper recording of this change of status.

── ***Example*** ──────────────────────────

A well-known piece of art, the painter of which is unknown, hangs in the Museum of Modern Art. On it is the date 1980. If a person would like to reprint the painting for a greeting card, he or she would have to wait one-hundred-and-twenty years from the date it was created to do so.

Example

The artist in the previous example comes forward. He is determined to be the acknowledged artist and files a change in copyright. The greeting-card designer would now have to wait seventy years after the death of the artist to reprint the painting without the artist's permission.

The death of an author or creator can be determined by the recording of a statement to the fact with the Copyright Office by an interested party. If no statement is filed, the author is presumed dead ninety-five years after the publication of the work or one-hundred-and-twenty years after its creation, whichever expires first.

— *Example*

The card designer from the previous examples wants to use a painting for one of his greeting cards. The painting is signed by the artist, but no one knows if the artist is living or deceased. The date of publication is January 1, 1900; thus, the designer would be free to use it January 1, 1995—ninety-five years after the date of publication.

Notice of Copyright

A notice that a work is copyrighted may appear on the work. Notice is a tangible mark that appears on something to alert the public that it is a protected piece of intellectual property. The notice must conform to the following:

1. The appropriate wording or symbol should be on the work
2. The year of the first publication or, in the case of a compilation, the year of the first publication of the compilation, must appear on the work
3. The name of the owner or a recognizable abbreviation must appear on the work.

The notice should appear on the work in a location that would give reasonable notice to an individual that the work is copyrighted. This notice serves to protect the individual from claims that his or her copyright was innocently infringed. Again, specific types of works require special forms of notice, but omission on certain types of works will not necessarily invalidate the copyright in a work.

— *Example*

Proper notice on a musical composition would protect the composer from subsequent artists claiming that they wrote the song and were entitled to perform the song without compensating the original author.

An application for copyright registration must include the following:

1. The name and address of the copyright claimant

2. The name and nationality or domicile of the author or authors and, if one or more of the authors is dead, the dates of their deaths

3. If the work is anonymous or pseudonymous, the nationality or domicile of the author or authors

4. In the case of a work made for hire, a statement to this effect

5. If the copyright claimant is not the author, a brief statement articulating how the claimant obtained ownership of the copyright

6. The title of the work, together with any previous or alternative titles under which the work can be identified

7. The year the creation of the work was completed

8. If the work has been published, the date and nation of its first publication

9. In the case of a compilation or derivative work, an identification of any preexisting work or works that it is based upon or incorporates and a brief, general statement of the additional material covered by the copyright claim being registered

10. In the case of a work containing material of which copies are required, the names of the persons or organizations who performed the processes and the places where those processes were performed

11. Any other information regarded by the Register of Copyrights as bearing upon the preparation or identification of the work or the existence, ownership, or duration of the copyright.

Infringements and Remedies

The exclusive owner of a properly registered copyrighted work may institute an action for infringement of that right. The copyright exists from the time of creation, but registration affords the benefit of infringement action. An action is instituted by properly filing papers alleging the infringement with the appropriate court. An **injunction**, or an order to stop the alleged infringement, may be issued by the court. The injunction initially may be ordered on a temporary basis, though it may ultimately be deemed permanent.

injunction
Court order to stop doing something.

— *Example*

If the owner of a script that has been properly copyrighted hears that a major movie studio is releasing a movie that he believes is based on his plot, he may ask the court to enjoin the studio from releasing the movie. The court may issue an injunction if it is found that the studio infringed on the author's copyright in the script.

damages
Financial repayment for monetary loss.

actual damages
An award of money for an amount actually lost.

statutory damages
A financial amount set by statute usually when loss of profit would be difficult to determine.

The owner may file for **damages**, or reimbursement in the form of financial repayment, for the infringement on his or her right. The owner may file for **actual damages**, what he or she has actually lost in the form of profit, or **statutory damages**, which is a financial amount set by statute when a determination of loss of profit would be difficult to determine.

— Example

In a case involving the unauthorized reproduction of works of a photographer on T-shirts, the photographer was awarded $20,000 in statutory damages even though the person who improperly used the photographs made only $1,200 in profit from the sales of the shirts.

Example

The major performing rights licensing societies, ASCAP, SESAC and BMI, contact a bar regarding the purchase of a "blanket license." A blanket license allows the licensee access to the licensor's entire catalogue of music for the purpose of public performance of the work for a year at a set fee. The failure to purchase a license is a violation of the right to perform the material in public. If the bar refuses to obtain a license, the performance-rights licensing society would then initiate a lawsuit for copyright infringement requesting statutory damages. These suits are almost always successful and the bar would be charged about $2,500 per song played.

Additionally, depending on the type of infringement, the court may impose criminal sanctions.

MARKS

Trademarks

United States Patent and Trademark Office
The office responsible for registering and issuing patents and trademarks.

The United States trademark laws, under the administration of the **United States Patent and Trademark Office**, protect goods that are natural, manufactured, or produced and that are sold, transferred, or delivered. A trademark is any distinct name, word, symbol, or device used by a person who has a real intent to sell it through interstate commerce and who applies to register it. It is important to register for the correct mark because a failure to do so may result in a cancellation of the mark. A mark can only be found to have trademark significance if the mark is "distinctive." To register a mark, it must fall into one of the following categories:

1. *Coined.* In existence and used for the product.
2. *Arbitrary or fanciful.* Words in the dictionary but not related to the product or not in the dictionary at all, such as *XEROX*®.

3. *Suggestive.* These trademarks suggest a characteristic, quality, or trait of the product but do not describe the goods and services; for example, *FindLaw*™.

4. *Descriptive.* These marks describe the goods and services, such as *National Wholesale Liquidators*™, but must also have a secondary meaning.

5. *Generic marks.* These marks are a common name for a good or service such as *White Bread Crackers*™.

Federal registration is not required to establish rights in a mark. However, as with copyrights, federal registration can secure protections beyond the rights acquired by mere use by allowing the holder to bring infringement actions.

Trademark rights arise from either actual use of the mark, or the filing of a proper application to register a mark.

Unlike copyrights, trademark rights can last indefinitely if the owner continues to use the mark to identify its goods or services. The term of a federal trademark registration is ten years, with renewable ten-year terms. Between the fifth and sixth year after the date of initial registration, the registrant must file an affidavit of continuing use that sets forth certain information to keep the registration alive. If no affidavit is filed between the ninth and tenth year, then the registration is canceled.

— *Example* —

An entertainment company creates a T-shirt emblazoned with its name. The T-shirt is considered to be a good that goes from venue to venue. The name, which the owner hopes to profit from, may be marked, thus putting others on notice that it is owned by someone else. If a competitor wishes to come along and use the name once it has been trademarked, then he must get a grant of license to make use of and profit from the name.

Service Marks

services
Intangible things performed by one person for the benefit of another.

service mark
Word, symbol, or group of words that distinguish a service.

Service marks are used to identify **services**—intangible things performed by one person for the benefit of another. A **service mark** is defined as any name, symbol, device, or combination thereof used by a person who has a real intent to sell it and applies to have it registered.

— *Example* —

Television or radio programs that are of a distinct nature may be service marked. Titles and characters may also be registered under the act if they indicate a service; otherwise, they are trademarks.

Collective Marks

As with copyrights, a trade or service mark may be the product of either a collaborative or a collective work that many people have had a hand in developing. Collective marks are used for membership organizations such as the American Bar Association or the National Association of Realtors. With a collective mark, each member organization of the group has the right to use the mark to identify it is a member of the parent organization. This is distinguishable from a group mark where several persons collaborate to create the entity holding the mark. For example, a three-woman singing group may own the mark to the group name, but no one singer may use the mark alone. With a collective mark, each member may use the mark because it identifies the member as part of the group, which is the purpose for obtaining the mark.

Certification Marks

Similar to typical trademarks and service marks, certification marks are a type of trademark that do not indicate the origin of the goods or services. They are not used by the owner of the mark on the owner's goods or with the owner's services. Therefore, who the user of the word, name, symbol, or device distinguishes a certification mark.

The same standards are used to register a certification mark as are used for other types of marks. The same standards generally applicable to trademarks and service marks are used in considering issues such as descriptiveness, disclaimers, and the likelihood of confusion of the mark for the purposes of registration.

The application must contain a statement of the characteristic, standard, or other feature that is certified, or intended to be certified, by the mark. The statement may begin with the wording, "The certification mark, as used by authorized persons, certifies ..." All of the characteristics or features that the mark certifies should be included. A mark need not be limited to certifying a single characteristic or feature.

Trade Names

The name of a business or company is a trade name. It is used to identify a business or job. If something is used solely as a trade name, there are no provisions for it under the Trademark Act for registration.

___ *Example* _____

Subway is the registered trade name of a store that sells submarine sandwiches.

ANTITRUST

Antitrust laws are designed to protect the economy and apply to all industries, including the entertainment industry. Antitrust laws may be applicable to all areas of the entertainment industry from the manufacturing, distribution, and marketing of an album to the salary limits of athletes. Violations of antitrust laws may result in criminal suits against the violating party.

The United States district courts have authority to determine whether there are violations of the antitrust laws. Proceedings are initiated by filing a **petition**, a legal paper requesting a court hear a claim. The petition asks that the party violating the statutes be **enjoined**, or stopped, from continuing the violation.

For the purpose of antitrust law, the **Federal Trade Commission**, the federal agency that regulates trade, and the United States Department of Justice, through its Antitrust Division, promote and protect the competitive process and the American economy by means of the enforcement of the antitrust laws. The two most commonly known statutes that regulate the competitive aspects of commercial operations are the Sherman Antitrust Act and the Clayton Antitrust Act.

The **Sherman Antitrust Act** is a federal statute regulating the operations of corporate trusts. The act declared "every contract, combination in the form of trust or otherwise, or conspiracy, in restraint of trade or commerce among the several States, or with foreign nations" illegal. The **Clayton Antitrust Act** prohibited monopolies among certain practices that were then common in finance, industry, and trade. It was designed to deal with corporate activities, remedies for reform, and labor disputes.

petition
Legal paper requesting a court hear a claim.

enjoined
Stopped.

Federal Trade Commission
Federal agency that regulates trade.

Sherman Antitrust Act
First federal statute mandating free competition.

Clayton Antitrust Act
A federal statute prohibiting monopolies.

Sports and Antitrust Laws

There are many antitrust issues faced by professional sports leagues. Most litigation is in the area of **restraint of labor**, or contracts to keep players associated with a particular team. The three most affected entities are the National Basketball Association (NBA), the National Football League (NFL), and Major League Baseball (MLB).

restraint of labor
Contracts that prohibit persons from working for others.

— Example

The NBA requires that each team have a limit on the total amount of money it can pay out in salary to its players. This limit also affects the salary that a drafted or renewal player can receive. These limitations, although seemingly restrictive of trade, are not in violation of the antitrust statutes because they are part of collective bargaining agreements between union and management that are recognized exceptions.

Example

The NFL had a provision that stated that "a drafted player who does not sign with the NFL club drafting him and who chooses to play for another professional football team cannot sign with any NFL club other than the drafting team for four years." When brought before a court of competent jurisdiction, it was determined that the short period of time that a player can play football made such a provision too prohibitive—it basically terminated a player's career and violated the provisions of the antitrust laws because it prohibited the player from playing for any other team. The result of this lawsuit was the creation of a form of free agency.

Example

A high school or college baseball player subject to a Major League draft is restricted to bargaining with only the drafting team for a period of one year. This is an exception similar to the exception for the NBA.

For a more detailed discussion of this topic, see chapter 9.

CHAPTER REVIEW

Intellectual property laws protect an artist from misappropriated use of his or her rights. If entertainers and artists were not protected by these laws, they would not be able to profit from their art because others could infringe on their rights. If artists cannot protect the ownership of their works, there would be little incentive to create. If they did not create, there would be no art or entertainment, and the world would be quite dull. Further, antitrust laws protect consumers and the economy by prohibiting actions that may harm competition.

To understand the implications of federal regulation of intellectual property, the legal professional involved in the entertainment field should apply the following principles:

1. Intellectual property is a constitutionally created property right under Articles 1 and 8.
2. The government regards all intellectual property as comparable to other forms of property.
3. The government presumes that intellectual property creates market power in the antitrust context.

JUDICIAL DECISION

The following decision concerns copyright protections for material shown over the public airwaves.

Sony Corporation of America v. Universal City Studios, Inc.
464 US 417 (1984)

Petitioners manufacture and sell home video tape recorders. Respondents own the copyrights on some of the television programs that are broadcast on the public airwaves. Some members of the general public use video tape recorders sold by petitioners to record some of these broadcasts, as well as a large number of other broadcasts. The question presented is whether the sale of petitioners' copying equipment to the general public violates any of the rights conferred upon respondents by the Copyright Act.

Respondents commenced this copyright infringement action against petitioners in the United States District Court for the Central District of California in 1976. Respondents alleged that some individuals had used Betamax video tape recorders (VTR's) to record some of respondents' copyrighted works which had been exhibited on commercially sponsored television and contended that these individuals had thereby infringed respondents' copyrights. Respondents further maintained that petitioners were liable for the copyright infringement allegedly committed by Betamax consumers because of petitioners' marketing of the Betamax VTR's. Respondents sought no relief against any Betamax consumer. Instead, they sought money damages and an equitable accounting of profits from petitioners, as well as an injunction against the manufacture and marketing of Betamax VTR's.

After a lengthy trial, the District Court denied respondents all the relief they sought and entered judgment for petitioners (480 F.Supp. 429 (1979)). The United States Court of Appeals for the Ninth Circuit reversed the District Court's judgment on respondents' copyright claim, holding petitioners liable for contributory infringement and ordering the District Court to fashion appropriate relief (659 F2d 963 (1981)). We granted certiorari (457 US 1116 (1982)); since we had not completed our study of the case last Term, we ordered reargument (463 US 1226 (1983)). We now reverse.

An explanation of our rejection of respondents' unprecedented attempt to impose copyright liability upon the distributors of copying equipment requires a quite detailed recitation of the findings of the District Court. In summary, those findings reveal that the average member of the public uses a VTR principally to record a program he cannot view as it is being televised and then to watch it once at a later time. This practice, known as "time-shifting," enlarges the television viewing audience. For that reason, a significant amount of television programming may be used in this manner without objection from the owners of the copyrights on the programs. For the same reason, even the two respondents in this case, who do assert objections to time-shifting in this litigation, were unable to prove that the practice has impaired the commercial value of their copyrights or has created any likelihood of future harm. Given these findings, there is no basis in the Copyright Act upon which respondents can hold petitioners liable for distributing VTR's to the general public. The Court of Appeals' holding that respondents are entitled to enjoin the distribution of VTR's, to collect royalties on the sale of such equipment, or to obtain other relief, if affirmed, would enlarge the scope of respondents' statutory monopolies to encompass control over an article of commerce that is not the subject of copyright protection. Such an expansion of the copyright privilege is beyond the limits of the grants authorized by Congress.

I

The two respondents in this action, Universal City Studios, Inc., and Walt Disney Productions, produce and hold the copyrights on a substantial number of motion pictures and other audiovisual works. In the current marketplace, they can exploit their rights in these works in a number of ways: by authorizing theatrical exhibitions, by licensing limited showings on cable and network television, by selling syndication rights for repeated airings on local television stations, and by marketing programs on prerecorded videotapes or videodiscs. Some works are suitable for exploitation through all of these avenues, while the market for other works is more limited.

Petitioner Sony manufactures millions of Betamax video tape recorders and markets these devices through numerous retail establishments, some of which are also petitioners in this action. Sony's Betamax VTR is a mechanism consisting of three basic components: (1) a tuner, which receives electromagnetic signals transmitted over the television band of the public airwaves and separates them into audio and visual signals; (2) a recorder, which records such signals on a magnetic tape; and (3) an adapter, which converts the audio and visual signals on the tape into a composite signal that can be received by a television set.

Several capabilities of the machine are noteworthy. The separate tuner in the Betamax enables it to record a broadcast off one station while the television set is tuned to another channel, permitting the viewer, for example, to watch two simultaneous news broadcasts by watching one "live" and recording the other for later viewing. Tapes may be reused, and programs that have been recorded may be erased either before or after viewing. A timer in the Betamax can be used to activate and deactivate the equipment at predetermined times, enabling an intended viewer to record programs that are transmitted when he or she is not at home. Thus a person may watch a program at home in the evening even though it was broadcast while the viewer was at work during the afternoon. The Betamax is also equipped with a pause button and a fast-forward control. The pause button, when depressed, deactivates the recorder until it is released, thus enabling a viewer to omit a commercial advertisement from the recording, provided, of course, that the viewer is present when the program is recorded. The fast-forward control enables the viewer of a previously recorded program to run the tape rapidly when a segment he or she does not desire to see is being played back on the television screen.

The respondents and Sony both conducted surveys of the way the Betamax machine was used by several hundred owners during a sample period in 1978. Although there were some differences in the surveys, they both showed that the primary use of the machine for most owners was "time-shifting"—the practice of recording a program to view it once at a later time, and thereafter erasing it. Time-shifting

enables viewers to see programs they otherwise would miss because they are not at home, are occupied with other tasks, or are viewing a program on another station at the time of a broadcast that they desire to watch. Both surveys also showed, however, that a substantial number of interviewees had accumulated libraries of tapes. Sony's survey indicated that over 80% of the interviewees watched at least as much regular television as they had before owning a Betamax. Respondents offered no evidence of decreased television viewing by Betamax owners.

Sony introduced considerable evidence describing television programs that could be copied without objection from any copyright holder, with special emphasis on sports, religious, and educational programming. For example, their survey indicated that 7.3% of all Betamax use is to record sports events, and representatives of professional baseball, football, basketball, and hockey testified that they had no objection to the recording of their televised events for home use.

Respondents offered opinion evidence concerning the future impact of the unrestricted sale of VTR's on the commercial value of their copyrights. The District Court found, however, that they had failed to prove any likelihood of future harm from the use of VTR's for time-shifting (480 F.Supp. at 469).

The District Court's Decision

The lengthy trial of the case in the District Court concerned the private, home use of VTR's for recording programs broadcast on the public airwaves without charge to the viewer. No issue concerning the transfer of tapes to other persons, the use of home-recorded tapes for public performances, or the copying of programs transmitted on pay or cable television systems was raised (see *id.*, at 432–433, 442).

The District Court concluded that noncommercial home use recording of material broadcast over the public airwaves was a fair use of copyrighted works and did not constitute copyright infringement. It emphasized the fact that the material was broadcast free to the public at large, the noncommercial character of the use, and the private character of the activity conducted entirely within the home. Moreover, the court found that the purpose of this use served the public interest in increasing access to television programming, an interest that "is consistent with the First Amendment policy of providing the fullest possible access to information through the public airwaves (*Columbia Broadcasting System, Inc. v. Democratic National Committee*, 412 US 94, 102)." (*Id.*, at 454.) Even when an entire copyrighted work was recorded, the District Court regarded the copying as fair use "because there is no accompanying reduction in the market for 'plaintiff's original work'" (*Ibid.*).

As an independent ground of decision, the District Court also concluded that Sony could not be held liable as a contributory infringer even if the home use of a VTR was considered an infringing use. The District Court noted that Sony had no direct involvement with any Betamax purchasers who recorded copyrighted works off the air. Sony's advertising was silent on the subject of possible copyright infringement, but its instruction booklet contained the following statement:

> Television programs, films, videotapes and other materials may be copyrighted. Unauthorized recording of such material may be contrary to the provisions of the United States copyright laws (*Id.*, at 436).

The District Court assumed that Sony had constructive knowledge of the probability that the Betamax machine would be used to record copyrighted programs, but found that Sony merely sold a "product capable of a variety of uses, some of them allegedly infringing" (*Id.*, at 461). It reasoned:

> Selling a staple article of commerce—e. g., a typewriter, a recorder, a camera, a photocopying machine—technically contributes to any infringing use subsequently made thereof, but this kind of 'contribution,' if deemed sufficient as a basis for liability, would expand the theory beyond precedent and arguably beyond judicial management.

> * * *

> ... Commerce would indeed be hampered if manufacturers of staple items were held liable as contributory infringers whenever they 'constructively' knew that some purchasers on some occasions would use their product for a purpose which a court later deemed, as a matter of first impression, to be an infringement" (*Ibid*).

Finally, the District Court discussed the respondents' prayer for injunctive relief, noting that they had asked for an injunction either preventing the future sale of

Betamax machines, or requiring that the machines be rendered incapable of recording copyrighted works off the air. The court stated that it had "found no case in which the manufacturers, distributors, retailers and advertisers of the instrument enabling the infringement were sued by the copyright holders," and that the request for relief in this case "is unique" (*Id.*, at 465).

It concluded that an injunction was wholly inappropriate because any possible harm to respondents was outweighed by the fact that "the Betamax could still legally be used to record noncopyrighted material or material whose owners consented to the copying. An injunction would deprive the public of the ability to use the Betamax for this noninfringing off-the-air recording" (*Id.*, at 468).

The Court of Appeals' Decision

The Court of Appeals reversed the District Court's judgment on respondents' copyright claim. It did not set aside any of the District Court's findings of fact. Rather, it concluded as a matter of law that the home use of a VTR was not a fair use because it was not a "productive use." It therefore held that it was unnecessary for plaintiffs to prove any harm to the potential market for the copyrighted works, but then observed that it seemed clear that the cumulative effect of mass reproduction made possible by VTR's would tend to diminish the potential market for respondents' works (659 F2d at 974).

On the issue of contributory infringement, the Court of Appeals first rejected the analogy to staple articles of commerce such as tape recorders or photocopying machines. It noted that such machines "may have substantial benefit for some purposes" and do not "even remotely raise copyright problems" (*Id.*, at 975). VTR's, however, are sold "for the primary purpose of reproducing television programming" and "[virtually] all" such programming is copyrighted material (*Ibid*). The Court of Appeals concluded, therefore, that VTR's were not suitable for any substantial noninfringing use even if some copyright owners elect not to enforce their rights.

The Court of Appeals also rejected the District Court's reliance on Sony's lack of knowledge that home use constituted infringement. Assuming that the statutory provisions defining the remedies for infringement applied also to the nonstatutory tort of contributory infringement, the court stated that a defendant's good faith would merely reduce his damages liability but would not excuse the infringing conduct. It held that Sony was chargeable with knowledge of the home-owner's infringing activity because the reproduction of copyrighted materials was either "the most conspicuous use" or "the major use" of the Betamax product (*Ibid*).

On the matter of relief, the Court of Appeals concluded that "statutory damages may be appropriate" and that the District Court should reconsider its determination that an injunction would not be an appropriate remedy; and, referring to "the analogous photocopying area," suggested that a continuing royalty pursuant to a judicially created compulsory license may very well be an acceptable resolution of the relief issue (*Id.*, at 976).

II

Article I, sec. 8, of the Constitution provides:

The Congress shall have Power ... To Promote the Progress of Science and useful Arts, by securing for limited Times to Authors and Inventors the exclusive Right to their respective Writings and Discoveries.

The monopoly privileges that Congress may authorize are neither unlimited nor primarily designed to provide a special private benefit. Rather, the limited grant is a means by which an important public purpose may be achieved. It is intended to motivate the creative activity of authors and inventors by the provision of a special reward, and to allow the public access to the products of their genius after the limited period of exclusive control has expired.

The copyright law, like the patent statutes, makes reward to the owner a secondary consideration. In *Fox Film Corp. v. Doyal*, 286 US 123, 127, Chief Justice Hughes spoke as follows respecting the copyright monopoly granted by Congress, 'The sole interest of the United States and the primary object in conferring the monopoly lie in the general benefits derived by the public from the labors of authors.' It is said that reward to the author or artist serves to induce release to the public of the products of his creative genius. (*United States v. Paramount Pictures, Inc.*, 334 US 131, 158 (1948)).

As the text of the Constitution makes plain, it is Congress that has been assigned the task of defining the scope of the limited monopoly that should be granted to authors or to inventors in order to give the public appropriate access to their work product. Because this task involves a difficult balance between the interests of authors and inventors in the control and exploitation of their writings and discoveries on the one hand, and society's competing interest in the free flow of ideas, information, and commerce on the other hand, our patent and copyright statutes have been amended repeatedly.

From its beginning, the law of copyright has developed in response to significant changes in technology. Indeed, it was the invention of a new form of copying equipment—the printing press—that gave rise to the original need for copyright protection. Repeatedly, as new developments have occurred in this country, it has been the Congress that has fashioned the new rules that new technology made necessary. Thus, long before the enactment of the Copyright Act of 1909, 35 Stat. 1075, it was settled that the protection given to copyrights is wholly statutory (*Wheaton v. Peters*, 8 Pet. 591, 661–662 (1834)). The remedies for infringement "are only those prescribed by Congress" (*Thompson v. Hubbard*, 131 US 123, 151 (1889)).

The judiciary's reluctance to expand the protections afforded by the copyright without explicit legislative guidance is a recurring theme. (See, e.g., *Teleprompter Corp. v. Columbia Broadcasting System, Inc.*, 415 US 394 (1974); *Fortnightly Corp. v. United Artists Television, Inc.*, 392 US 390 (1968); *White-Smith Music Publishing Co. v. Apollo Co.*, 209 US 1 (1908); *Williams & Wilkins Co. v. United States*, 203 Ct. Cl. 74, 487 F2d 1345 (1973), aff'd by an equally divided Court, 420 US 376 (1975)). Sound policy, as well as history, supports our consistent deference to Congress when major technological innovations alter the market for copyrighted materials. Congress has the constitutional authority and the institutional ability to accommodate fully the varied permutations of competing interests that are inevitably implicated by such new technology.

In a case like this, in which Congress has not plainly marked our course, we must be circumspect in construing the scope of rights created by a legislative enactment which never contemplated such a calculus of interests. In doing so, we are guided by Justice Stewart's exposition of the correct approach to ambiguities in the law of copyright:

The limited scope of the copyright holder's statutory monopoly, like the limited copyright duration required by the Constitution, reflects a balance of competing claims upon the public interest: Creative work is to be encouraged and rewarded, but private motivation must ultimately serve the cause of promoting broad public availability of literature, music, and the other arts.

The immediate effect of our copyright law is to secure a fair return for an 'author's' creative labor. But the ultimate aim is, by this incentive, to stimulate artistic creativity for the general public good. 'The sole interest of the United States and the primary object in conferring the monopoly,' this Court has said, 'lie in the general benefits derived by the public from the labors of authors.' (*Fox Film Corp. v. Doyal*, 286 US 123, 127. See *Kendall v. Winsor*, 21 How. 322, 327–328; *Grant v. Raymond*, 6 Pet. 218, 241–242.) When technological change has rendered its literal terms ambiguous, the Copyright Act must be construed in light of this basic purpose" (*Twentieth Century Music Corp. v. Aiken*, 422 US 151, 156 (1975)).

Copyright protection "subsists … in original works of authorship fixed in any tangible medium of expression" (17 USC § 102(a) (1982 ed)). This protection has never accorded the copyright owner complete control over all possible uses of his work. Rather, the Copyright Act grants the copyright holder "exclusive" rights to use and to authorize the use of his work in five qualified ways, including reproduction of the copyrighted work in copies (§ 106). All reproductions of the work, however, are not within the exclusive domain of the copyright owner; some are in the public domain. Any individual may reproduce a copyrighted work for a "fair use"; the copyright owner does not possess the exclusive right to such a use (compare § 106 with § 107).

"Anyone who violates any of the exclusive rights of the copyright owner," that is, anyone who trespasses into his exclusive domain by using or authorizing the use of the copyrighted work in one of the five ways set forth in the statute, "is an infringer of the copyright" (§ 501(a)). Conversely, anyone who is authorized by the copyright owner to use the copyrighted work in a way specified in the statute or who makes a fair use of the work is not an infringer of the copyright with respect to such use.

The Copyright Act provides the owner of a copyright with a potent arsenal of remedies against an infringer of his work, including an injunction to restrain the infringer from violating his rights, the impoundment and destruction of all reproductions of his work made in violation of his rights, a recovery of his actual damages and any additional profits realized by the infringer or a recovery of statutory damages, and attorney's fees (§§ 502–505).

The two respondents in this case do not seek relief against the Betamax users who have allegedly infringed their copyrights. Moreover, this is not a class action on behalf of all copyright owners who license their works for television broadcast, and respondents have no right to invoke whatever rights other copyright holders may have to bring infringement actions based on Betamax copying of their works. As was made clear by their own evidence, the copying of the respondents' programs represents a small portion of the total use of VTR's. It is, however, the taping of respondents' own copyrighted programs that provides them with standing to charge Sony with contributory infringement. To prevail, they have the burden of proving that users of the Betamax have infringed their copyrights and that Sony should be held responsible for that infringement.

III

The Copyright Act does not expressly render anyone liable for infringement committed by another. In contrast, the Patent Act expressly brands anyone who "actively induces infringement of a patent" as an infringer (35 USC § 271(b)), and further imposes liability on certain individuals labeled "contributory" infringers (§ 271(c)). The absence of such express language in the copyright statute does not preclude the imposition of liability for copyright infringements on certain parties who have not themselves engaged in the infringing activity. For vicarious liability is imposed in virtually all areas of the law, and the concept of contributory infringement is merely a species of the broader problem of identifying the circumstances in which it is just to hold one individual accountable for the actions of another.

Such circumstances were plainly present in *Kalem Co. v. Harper Brothers*, 222 US 55 (1911), the copyright decision of this Court on which respondents place their principal reliance. In *Kalem*, the Court held that the producer of an unauthorized film dramatization of the copyrighted book *Ben Hur* was liable for his sale of the motion picture to jobbers, who in turn arranged for the commercial exhibition of the film. Justice Holmes, writing for the Court, explained:

> The defendant not only expected but invoked by advertisement the use of its films for dramatic reproduction of the story. That was the most conspicuous purpose for which they could be used, and the one for which especially they were made. If the defendant did not contribute to the infringement it is impossible to do so except by taking part in the final act. It is liable on principles recognized in every part of the law" (*Id.*, at 62–63).

The use for which the item sold in *Kalem* had been "especially" made was, of course, to display the performance that had already been recorded upon it. The producer had personally appropriated the copyright owner's protected work and, as the owner of the tangible medium of expression upon which the protected work was recorded, authorized that use by his sale of the film to jobbers. But that use of the film was not his to authorize: the copyright owner possessed the exclusive right to authorize public performances of his work. Further, the producer personally advertised the unauthorized public performances, dispelling any possible doubt as to the use of the film which he had authorized.

Respondents argue that *Kalem* stands for the proposition that supplying the "means" to accomplish an infringing activity and encouraging that activity through advertisement are sufficient to establish liability for copyright infringement. This argument rests on a gross generalization that cannot withstand scrutiny. The producer in *Kalem* did not merely provide the "means" to accomplish an infringing activity; the producer supplied the work itself, albeit in a new medium of expression. Sony in the instant case does not supply Betamax consumers with respondents' works; respondents do. Sony supplies a piece of equipment that is generally capable of copying the entire range of programs that may be televised: those that are uncopyrighted, those that are copyrighted but may be copied without objection from the copyright holder, and those that the copyright holder would prefer not to have copied. The Betamax can be used to make authorized or unauthorized uses of copyrighted works, but the range of its potential use is much broader than the particular infringing use of the film *Ben Hur* involved in *Kalem*. *Kalem* does not support respondents' novel theory of liability.

Justice Holmes stated that the producer had "contributed" to the infringement of the copyright, and the label "contributory infringement" has been applied in a number of lower court copyright cases involving an ongoing relationship between the direct infringer and the contributory infringer at the time the infringing conduct occurred. In such cases, as in other situations in which the imposition of vicarious liability is manifestly just, the "contributory" infringer was in a position to control the use of copyrighted works by others and had authorized the use without permission from the copyright owner. This case, however, plainly does not fall in that category. The only contact between Sony and the users of the Betamax that is disclosed by this record occurred at the moment of sale. The District Court expressly found that "no employee of Sony, Sonam or DDBI had either direct involvement with the allegedly infringing activity or direct contact with purchasers of Betamax who recorded copyrighted works off-the-air" (480 F.Supp. at 460). And it further found that "there was no evidence that any of the copies made by Griffiths or the other individual witnesses in this suit were influenced or encouraged by [Sony's] advertisements" (*Ibid*).

If vicarious liability is to be imposed on Sony in this case, it must rest on the fact that it has sold equipment with constructive knowledge of the fact that its customers may use that equipment to make unauthorized copies of copyrighted material. There is no precedent in the law of copyright for the imposition of vicarious liability on such a theory. The closest analogy is provided by the patent law cases to which it is appropriate to refer because of the historic kinship between patent law and copyright law.

In the Patent Act both the concept of infringement and the concept of contributory infringement are expressly defined by statute. The prohibition against contributory infringement is confined to the knowing sale of a component especially made for use in connection with a particular patent. There is no suggestion in the statute that one patentee may object to the sale of a product that might be used in connection with other patents. Moreover, the Act expressly provides that the sale of a "staple article or commodity of commerce suitable for substantial noninfringing use" is not contributory infringement (35 USC § 271(c)).

When a charge of contributory infringement is predicated entirely on the sale of an article of commerce that is used by the purchaser to infringe a patent, the public interest in access to that article of commerce is necessarily implicated. A finding of contributory infringement does not, of course, remove the article from the market altogether; it does, however, give the patentee effective control over the sale of that item. Indeed, a finding of contributory infringement is normally the functional equivalent of holding that the disputed article is within the monopoly granted to the patentee.

For that reason, in contributory infringement cases arising under the patent laws the Court has always recognized the critical importance of not allowing the patentee to extend his monopoly beyond the limits of his specific grant. These cases deny the patentee any right to control the distribution of unpatented articles unless they are "unsuited for any commercial noninfringing use" *Dawson Chemical Co. v. Rohm & Hass Co.*, 448 US 176, 198 (1980)). Unless a commodity "has no use except through practice of the patented method," (*id.*, at 199) the patentee has no right to claim that its distribution constitutes contributory infringement. "To form the basis for contributory infringement the item must almost be uniquely suited as a component of the patented invention" (P. Rosenberg, *Patent Law Fundamentals* § 17.02[2] (2d ed 1982)). "[A] sale of an article which though adapted to an infringing use is also adapted to other and lawful uses, is not enough to make the seller a contributory infringer. Such a rule would block the wheels of commerce" (*Henry v. A. B. Dick Co.*, 224 US 1, 48 (1912), overruled on other grounds, *Motion Picture Patents Co. v. Universal Film Mfg. Co.*, 243 US 502, 517(1917)).

We recognize there are substantial differences between the patent and copyright laws. But in both areas the contributory infringement doctrine is grounded on the recognition that adequate protection of a monopoly may require the courts to look beyond actual duplication of a device or publication to the products or activities that make such duplication possible. The staple article of commerce doctrine must strike a balance between a copyright holder's legitimate demand for effective—not merely symbolic—protection of the statutory monopoly, and the rights of others freely to engage in substantially unrelated areas of commerce. Accordingly, the sale of copying equipment, like the sale of other articles of commerce, does not constitute contributory infringement if the product is widely used for legitimate, unobjectionable purposes. Indeed, it need merely be capable of substantial noninfringing uses.

IV

The question is thus whether the Betamax is capable of commercially significant noninfringing uses. In order to resolve that question, we need not explore all the different potential uses of the machine and determine whether or not they would constitute infringement. Rather, we need only consider whether on the basis of the facts as found by the District Court a significant number of them would be noninfringing. Moreover, in order to resolve this case we need not give precise content to the question of how much use is commercially significant. For one potential use of the Betamax plainly satisfies this standard, however it is understood: private, noncommercial time-shifting in the home. It does so both (A) because respondents have no right to prevent other copyright holders from authorizing it for their programs, and (B) because the District Court's factual findings reveal that even the unauthorized home time-shifting of respondents' programs is legitimate fair use.

A. Authorized Time-Shifting

Each of the respondents owns a large inventory of valuable copyrights, but in the total spectrum of television programming their combined market share is small. The exact percentage is not specified, but it is well below 10%. If they were to prevail, the outcome of this litigation would have a significant impact on both the producers and the viewers of the remaining 90% of the programming in the Nation. No doubt, many other producers share respondents' concern about the possible consequences of unrestricted copying. Nevertheless the findings of the District Court make it clear that time-shifting may enlarge the total viewing audience and that many producers are willing to allow private time-shifting to continue, at least for an experimental time period.

The District Court found:

Even if it were deemed that home-use recording of copyrighted material constituted infringement, the Betamax could still legally be used to record noncopyrighted material or material whose owners consented to the copying. An injunction would deprive the public of the ability to use the Betamax for this noninfringing off-the-air recording.

Defendants introduced considerable testimony at trial about the potential for such copying of sports, religious, educational and other programming. This included testimony from representatives of the Offices of the Commissioners of the National Football, Basketball, Baseball and Hockey Leagues and Associations, the Executive Director of National Religious Broadcasters and various educational communications agencies. Plaintiffs attack the weight of the testimony offered and also contend that an injunction is warranted because infringing uses outweigh noninfringing uses.

Whatever the future percentage of legal versus illegal home-use recording might be, an injunction which seeks to deprive the public of the very tool or article of commerce capable of some noninfringing use would be an extremely harsh remedy, as well as one unprecedented in copyright law (480 F.Supp. at 468).

Although the District Court made these statements in the context of considering the propriety of injunctive relief, the statements constitute a finding that the evidence concerning "sports, religious, educational and other programming" was sufficient to establish a significant quantity of broadcasting whose copying is now authorized, and a significant potential for future authorized copying. That finding is amply supported by the record. In addition to the religious and sports officials identified explicitly by the District Court, two items in the record deserve specific mention.

First is the testimony of John Kenaston, the station manager of Channel 58, an educational station in Los Angeles affiliated with the Public Broadcasting Service. He explained and authenticated the station's published guide to its programs. For each program, the guide tells whether unlimited home taping is authorized, home taping is authorized subject to certain restrictions (such as erasure within seven days), or home taping is not authorized at all. The Spring 1978 edition of the guide described 107 programs. Sixty-two of those programs or 58% authorize some home taping. Twenty-one of them or almost 20% authorize unrestricted home taping.

Second is the testimony of Fred Rogers, president of the corporation that produces and owns the copyright on Mister Rogers' Neighborhood. The program is carried by more public television stations than any other program. Its audience numbers over 3,000,000

families a day. He testified that he had absolutely no objection to home taping for noncommercial use and expressed the opinion that it is a real service to families to be able to record children's programs and to show them at appropriate times.

If there are millions of owners of VTR's who make copies of televised sports events, religious broadcasts, and educational programs such as Mister Rogers' Neighborhood, and if the proprietors of those programs welcome the practice, the business of supplying the equipment that makes such copying feasible should not be stifled simply because the equipment is used by some individuals to make unauthorized reproductions of respondents' works. The respondents do not represent a class composed of all copyright holders. Yet a finding of contributory infringement would inevitably frustrate the interests of broadcasters in reaching the portion of their audience that is available only through time-shifting.

Of course, the fact that other copyright holders may welcome the practice of time-shifting does not mean that respondents should be deemed to have granted a license to copy their programs. Third-party conduct would be wholly irrelevant in an action for direct infringement of respondents' copyrights. But in an action for contributory infringement against the seller of copying equipment, the copyright holder may not prevail unless the relief that he seeks affects only his programs, or unless he speaks for virtually all copyright holders with an interest in the outcome. In this case, the record makes it perfectly clear that there are many important producers of national and local television programs who find nothing objectionable about the enlargement in the size of the television audience that results from the practice of time-shifting for private home use. The seller of the equipment that expands those producers' audiences cannot be a contributory infringer if, as is true in this case, it has had no direct involvement with any infringing activity.

B. Unauthorized Time-Shifting

Even unauthorized uses of a copyrighted work are not necessarily infringing. An unlicensed use of the copyright is not an infringement unless it conflicts with one of the specific exclusive rights conferred by the copyright statute (*Twentieth Century Music Corp. v. Aiken*, 422 US, at 154–155). Moreover, the definition of exclusive rights in sec. 106 of the present Act is prefaced by the words "subject to sections 107 through 118." Those sections describe a variety of uses of copyrighted material that "are not infringements of copyright" "notwithstanding the provisions of section 106." The most pertinent in this case is sec. 107, the legislative endorsement of the doctrine of "fair use."

That section identifies various factors that enable a court to apply an "equitable rule of reason" analysis to particular claims of infringement. Although not conclusive, the first factor requires that "the commercial or nonprofit character of an activity" be weighed in any fair use decision. If the Betamax were used to make copies for a commercial or profit-making purpose, such use would presumptively be unfair. The contrary presumption is appropriate here, however, because the District Court's findings plainly establish that time-shifting for private home use must be characterized as a noncommercial, nonprofit activity. Moreover, when one considers the nature of a televised copyrighted audiovisual work (see 17 USC § 107(2) (1982 ed.)), and that time-shifting merely enables a viewer to see such a work which he had been invited to witness in its entirety free of charge, the fact that the entire work is reproduced (see § 107(3)) does not have its ordinary effect of militating against a finding of fair use.

This is not, however, the end of the inquiry because Congress has also directed us to consider "the effect of the use upon the potential market for or value of the copyrighted work" (§ 107(4)). The purpose of copyright is to create incentives for creative effort. Even copying for noncommercial purposes may impair the copyright holder's ability to obtain the rewards that Congress intended him to have. But a use that has no demonstrable effect upon the potential market for, or the value of, the copyrighted work need not be prohibited in order to protect the author's incentive to create. The prohibition of such noncommercial uses would merely inhibit access to ideas without any countervailing benefit.

Thus, although every commercial use of copyrighted material is presumptively an unfair exploitation of the monopoly privilege that belongs to the owner of the copyright, noncommercial uses are a different matter. A challenge to a noncommercial use of a copyrighted work requires proof either that the particular use is harmful, or that if it should become

widespread, it would adversely affect the potential market for the copyrighted work. Actual present harm need not be shown; such a requirement would leave the copyright holder with no defense against predictable damage. Nor is it necessary to show with certainty that future harm will result. What is necessary is a showing by a preponderance of the evidence that some meaningful likelihood of future harm exists. If the intended use is for commercial gain, that likelihood may be presumed. But if it is for a noncommercial purpose, the likelihood must be demonstrated.

In this case, respondents failed to carry their burden with regard to home time-shifting. The District Court described respondents' evidence as follows:

> Plaintiffs' experts admitted at several points in the trial that the time-shifting without librarying would result in 'not a great deal of harm.' Plaintiffs' greatest concern about time-shifting is with 'a point of important philosophy that transcends even commercial judgment.' They fear that with any Betamax usage, 'invisible boundaries' are passed: 'the copyright owner has lost control over his program' (480 F.Supp. at 467).

Later in its opinion, the District Court observed:

> Most of plaintiffs' predictions of harm hinge on speculation about audience viewing patterns and ratings, a measurement system which Sidney Sheinberg, MCA's president, calls a 'black art' because of the significant level of imprecision involved in the calculations" (Id., at 469).

There was no need for the District Court to say much about past harm. "Plaintiffs have admitted that no actual harm to their copyrights has occurred to date" (Id., at 451).

On the question of potential future harm from time-shifting, the District Court offered a more detailed analysis of the evidence. It rejected respondents' "fear that persons 'watching' the original telecast of a program will not be measured in the live audience and the ratings and revenues will decrease," by observing that current measurement technology allows the Betamax audience to be reflected (Id., at 466). It rejected respondents' prediction "that live television or movie audiences will decrease as more people watch Betamax tapes as an alternative," with the observation that "[there] is no factual basis for [the underlying] assumption" (Ibid). It rejected respondents' "fear that time-shifting will reduce audiences for telecast reruns," and concluded instead that "given current market practices, this should aid plaintiffs rather than harm them" (*Ibid*). And it declared that respondents' suggestion that "theater or film rental exhibition of a program will suffer because of time-shift recording of that program" "lacks merit" (*Id.*, at 467).

After completing that review, the District Court restated its overall conclusion several times, in several different ways. "Harm from time-shifting is speculative and, at best, minimal" (*Ibid*). "The audience benefits from the time-shifting capability have already been discussed. It is not implausible that benefits could also accrue to plaintiffs, broadcasters, and advertisers, as the Betamax makes it possible for more persons to view their broadcasts" (*Ibid*). "No likelihood of harm was shown at trial, and plaintiffs admitted that there had been no actual harm to date" (*Id.*, at 468–469). "Testimony at trial suggested that Betamax may require adjustments in marketing strategy, but it did not establish even a likelihood of harm" (*Id.*, at 469). "Television production by plaintiffs today is more profitable than it has ever been, and, in five weeks of trial, there was no concrete evidence to suggest that the Betamax will change the studios' financial picture" (*Ibid*). The District Court's conclusions are buttressed by the fact that to the extent time-shifting expands public access to freely broadcast television programs, it yields societal benefits. In *Community Television of Southern California v. Gottfried*, 459 US 498, 508, n.12 (1983), we acknowledged the public interest in making television broadcasting more available. Concededly, that interest is not unlimited. But it supports an interpretation of the concept of "fair use" that requires the copyright holder to demonstrate some likelihood of harm before he may condemn a private act of time-shifting as a violation of federal law.

When these factors are all weighed in the "equitable rule of reason" balance, we must conclude that this record amply supports the District Court's conclusion that home time-shifting is fair use. In light of the findings of the District Court regarding the state of the empirical data, it is clear that the Court of Appeals erred in holding that the statute as presently written bars such conduct. In summary, the record and findings of the District Court lead us to two conclusions. First, Sony demonstrated a significant likelihood that substantial numbers of copyright holders who license their works for broadcast on free television would not object to having their broadcasts time-shifted by private viewers. And second, respondents failed to demonstrate that time-shifting would cause any likelihood of harm to the potential market for, or the value of, their copyrighted works. The Betamax is, therefore, capable of substantial noninfringing uses. Sony's sale of such equipment to the general public does not constitute contributory infringement of respondents' copyrights.

V

> The direction of Art. I is that *Congress* shall have the power to promote the progress of science and the useful arts. When, as here, the Constitution is permissive, the sign of how far Congress has chosen to go can come only from Congress" (*Deepsouth Packing Co. v. Laitram Corp.*, 406 US 518, 530 (1972)).

One may search the Copyright Act in vain for any sign that the elected representatives of the millions of people who watch television every day have made it unlawful to copy a program for later viewing at home, or have enacted a flat prohibition against the sale of machines that make such copying possible.

It may well be that Congress will take a fresh look at this new technology, just as it so often has examined other innovations in the past. But it is not our job to apply laws that have not yet been written. Applying the copyright statute, as it now reads, to the facts as they have been developed in this case, the judgment of the Court of Appeals must be reversed.

It is so ordered.

KEY TERMS

actual damages	license
agent	non-exclusive license
antitrust laws	notice
bequeathed	petition
Clayton Antitrust Act	public domain
collective work	restraint of labor
constructive notice	royalty
copyright	service mark
damages	services
enjoined	Sherman Antitrust Act
exclusive right	statutory damages
fair use	trademark
Federal Trade Commission	United States Patent and
fixed	Trademark Office
good faith	vests
injunction	work for hire
intestate succession	

EXERCISES

1. Locate the copyright notice on three different types of mediums.
2. Go to the United States Patent and Trademark Office Web site and review the on-line application.
3. Other than in sports, explain how antitrust laws affect the entertainment industry.
4. Indicate three trademarks on entertainment products.
5. Go to ASCAP or BMI's Web site and determine how royalties are determined based on copyright (ASCAP: http://www.ascap.com; BMI: http://www.bmi.com).
6. How would a person register a mark on your state's registry? Indicate the circumstances under which a person would use this approach rather than the federal register.
7. What is the current fee to register a trademark?
8. Using a computer-assisted legal research program, locate a judicial decision concerning collective marks.
9. Of the various remedies available for copyright infringement, which do you believe is the most effective? Explain.
10. Should a notice of copyright appear on works that are designed to be placed on the Internet? Discuss.

Exhibit

APPLICATION FOR REGISTRATION OF TRADEMARK / SERVICE MARK

State Form 44436 (R3 / 6-97)
Approved by the State Board of Accounts, 1994

INSTRUCTIONS: See reverse side

Filing Fee: $10.00

IC 24-2-1-4

Todd Rokita
Secretary of State
TRADEMARKS DIVISION
302 W. Washington St., Rm. E111
Indianapolis, IN 46204
Telephone: (317) 232-6540

APPLICANT: INDIVIDUAL, ASSOCIATION, PARTNERSHIP, CORPORATION, OTHER

1. Name of applicant

2. Address (street and number; city, state, ZIP code)

Applicant telephone number ( )

3. Contact Person (Name and address of contact if correspondence about this application should go to a party other than the signatory.)

Contact telephone number ( )

4. The Applicant is ONE of the following: (check the)
☐ Individual ☐ Association ☐ Partnership of any type (Attach name and address of
☐ Corporation (State of ☐ Other

TRADEMARK / SERVICE MARK INFORMATION

5. Trademark / Service Mark: (Include all words to be registered.)

6. Does the Mark involve a symbol, design or any nonstandard type face? If "yes," then briefly describe, in words, major feature(s) of design.
☐ Yes ☐ No

7. DISCLAIMER: Disclaim words, phrases, and pictorial features which are merely descriptive of the goods or services or are primarily geographic. Names of cities, states, and designation of corporate status are normally considered descriptive; e.g., Inc., company, Indiana, USA, etc. No claim is made to the exclusive right to use the symbol / word(s) apart from the Mark as shown.

8. Class number (Select only ONE class per form — see reverse for class) ➡ ☐

9. Describe specific goods (classes 1-52) or services (classes 53-60) used in connection with the Mark. The Mark is used on, or in connection with:

10. Date the Mark was first used in commerce in Indiana by applicant or predecessor. Date the Mark was first used in commerce anywhere in USA, including (m,d,y)

11. If the Mark is used in selected classes, check all boxes that apply to how the Mark is used:
(a) Classes 1-52 (By applying it)
☐ Directly to goods ☐ to the containers for the goods ☐ to tags or labels affixed to the goods ☐ to tags or labels affixed to the containers for the goods
☐ by displaying the mark in physical association with the goods in the sale or distribution thereof ☐ Other (please specify)
(b) Classes 53-60 (By displaying it)
☐ in advertisements of the service
☐ on documents, wrappers, or articles delivered in connection with the service rendered ☐ Other (please specify)
12. If either of the above first uses of the Mark were by a predecessor in business; give name, address, and specify which use(s) of the Mark were by predecessor.

VERIFICATION STATEMENT

I, _____ affirm under penalty of perjury that (1) I am (check box that applies) ☐ the individual owner, ☐ a partner, or ☐ an officer (title) _____ of applicant; (2) I have read this application and its contents / specimens are true and complete to the best of my knowledge; (3) The Mark is now in use in commerce; (4) (i) I am the owner of the applied for Mark and no other person or organization has the right to use this trademark / service mark in Indiana either in identical form or in a form so resembling it as might be calculated to deceive or be mistaken for it, or (ii) written consent by the registrant to applicant's use has been filed with the Secretary of State.

Signature

Date

EXHIBIT 2-1 Trademark/Service Mark Application

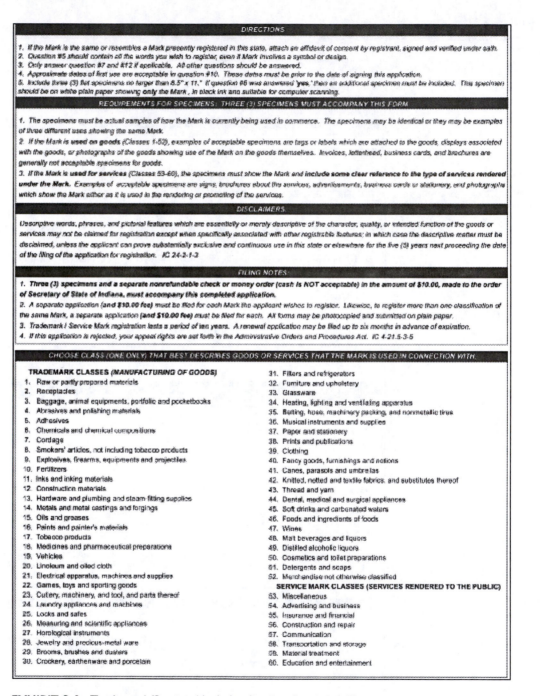

DIRECTIONS

1. If the Mark is the same or resembles a Mark presently registered in this state, attach an affidavit of consent by registrant, signed and verified under oath.
2. Question #5 should contain all the words you wish to register, even if Mark involves a symbol or design.
3. Only answer question #7 and #12 if applicable. All other questions should be answered.
4. Approximate dates of first use are acceptable in question #10. These dates must be prior to the date of signing this application.
5. Include three (3) flat specimens no larger than 8.5" x 11." If question #6 was answered 'yes,' then an additional specimen must be included. This specimen should be on white plain paper showing only the Mark, in black ink and suitable for computer scanning.

REQUIREMENTS FOR SPECIMENS: THREE (3) SPECIMENS MUST ACCOMPANY THIS FORM

1. The specimens must be actual samples of how the Mark is currently being used in commerce. The specimens may be identical or they may be examples of three different uses showing the same Mark.
2. If the Mark is used on goods (Classes 1-52), examples of acceptable specimens are tags or labels which are attached to the goods, displays associated with the goods, or photographs of the goods showing use of the Mark on the goods themselves. Invoices, letterhead, business cards, and brochures are generally not acceptable specimens for goods.
3. If the Mark is **used for services** (Classes 53-60), the specimens must show the Mark and **include some clear reference to the type of services rendered under the Mark.** Examples of acceptable specimens are signs, brochures about the services, advertisements, business cards or stationery, and photographs which show the Mark either as it is used in the rendering or promoting of the services.

DISCLAIMERS

Descriptive words, phrases, and pictorial features which are essentially or merely descriptive of the character, quality, or intended function of the goods or services may not be claimed for registration except when specifically associated with other registrable features; in which case the descriptive matter must be disclaimed, unless the applicant can prove substantially exclusive and continuous use in this state or elsewhere for the five (5) years next proceeding the date of the filing of the application for registration. IC 24-2-1-3

FILING NOTES

1. **Three (3) specimens and a separate nonrefundable check or money order (cash is NOT acceptable) in the amount of $10.00, made to the order of Secretary of State of Indiana, must accompany this completed application.**
2. A separate application (and $10.00 fee) must be filed for each Mark the applicant wishes to register. Likewise, to register more than one classification of the same Mark, a separate application (and $10.00 fee) must be filed for each. All forms may be photocopied and submitted on plain paper.
3. Trademark / Service Mark registration lasts a period of ten years. A renewal application may be filed up to six months in advance of expiration.
4. If this application is rejected, your appeal rights are set forth in the Administrative Orders and Procedures Act. IC 4-21.5-3-5

CHOOSE CLASS (ONE ONLY) THAT BEST DESCRIBES GOODS OR SERVICES THAT THE MARK IS USED IN CONNECTION WITH

TRADEMARK CLASSES (MANUFACTURING OF GOODS)

1. Raw or partly prepared materials
2. Receptacles
3. Baggage, animal equipments, portfolio and pocketbooks
4. Abrasives and polishing materials
5. Adhesives
6. Chemicals and chemical compositions
7. Cordage
8. Smokers' articles, not including tobacco products
9. Explosives, firearms, equipments and projectiles
10. Fertilizers
11. Inks and inking materials
12. Construction materials
13. Hardware and plumbing and steam-fitting supplies
14. Metals and metal castings and forgings
15. Oils and greases
16. Paints and painter's materials
17. Tobacco products
18. Medicines and pharmaceutical preparations
19. Vehicles
20. Linoleum and oiled cloth
21. Electrical apparatus, machines and supplies
22. Games, toys and sporting goods
23. Cutlery, machinery, and tool, and parts thereof
24. Laundry appliances and machines
25. Locks and safes
26. Measuring and scientific appliances
27. Horological instruments
28. Jewelry and precious-metal ware
29. Brooms, brushes and dusters
30. Crockery, earthenware and porcelain

31. Filters and refrigerators
32. Furniture and upholstery
33. Glassware
34. Heating, lighting and ventilating apparatus
35. Belting, hose, machinery packing, and nonmetallic tires
36. Musical instruments and supplies
37. Paper and stationery
38. Prints and publications
39. Clothing
40. Fancy goods, furnishings and notions
41. Canes, parasols and umbrellas
42. Knitted, netted and textile fabrics, and substitutes thereof
43. Thread and yarn
44. Dental, medical and surgical appliances
45. Soft drinks and carbonated waters
46. Foods and ingredients of foods
47. Wines
48. Malt beverages and liquors
49. Distilled alcoholic liquors
50. Cosmetics and toilet preparations
51. Detergents and soaps
52. Merchandise not otherwise classified

SERVICE MARK CLASSES (SERVICES RENDERED TO THE PUBLIC)

53. Miscellaneous
54. Advertising and business
55. Insurance and financial
56. Construction and repair
57. Communication
58. Transportation and storage
59. Material treatment
60. Education and entertainment

EXHIBIT 2-1 Trademark/Service Mark Application (*continued*)

CHAPTER

LEGAL STRUCTURES OF THE ENTERTAINMENT INDUSTRY

CHAPTER OVERVIEW

Before the more glamorous aspects of the entertainment industry materialize, every entertainment enterprise must determine the appropriate legal structure for its organization. This structure, or format, can determine the ultimate success or failure of the venture. A particular legal format has a direct effect on the financing of the venture, the liability of the participants, the tax implications of its success or failure, and its capacity to capitalize by means of marketing and distributing products emanating from its operations. Consequently, the creation of the legal structure is as important as the creativity of the artistic endeavor.

This chapter will explore the most typical formats used to establish the legal structure of an entertainment enterprise, the income-tax implications of that selection, and the nature of the standard contracts that such ventures should employ. Also, there will be some discussion of the types of insurance policies that the venture might consider in order to protect itself against unforeseen catastrophes. Regardless of the high profile of the entertainment field, it must always be borne in mind that it is no more or less than a group of businesses engaged in a specialized area of endeavor.

THE BUSINESS STRUCTURE

In determining a particular structure for an entertainment-oriented enterprise, the creator must focus on the implications of using each format. These concerns can be summed up as the

- Ability of the enterprise to attract backers, both individuals and traditional financial institutions, to finance the enterprise
- Potential financial liability of the persons involved in the enterprise
- Amount of control—financial, artistic, and managerial—that the parties wish to retain or are willing to forego
- Income-tax implications implicit in each given legal structure
- Ease of creating and operating the venture
- Ability to dissolve the enterprise at a natural termination point or because of unforeseen difficulties
- Ability to merchandise and distribute its products
- Ability to sue or defend if the enterprise is legally injured by an outsider or a member of the organization
- Ability of the enterprise to hold title to its property and to transfer that same title
- Ability to operate the enterprise in multiple venues, states, and countries simultaneously or sequentially.

As can be seen, the factors involved in the initial organizational decision have far-reaching effects, and the list presented above only represents *some* of the most commonly encountered factors. The entertainment enterprise must be alert to all of the business aspects of the given industry prior to selecting a particular legal format for the venture.

Before discussing the most prevalent legal formats used to operate an entertainment enterprise, it must be noted that there are other alternatives available to the creative entrepreneur, but the ones selected for discussion are the most commonly used. Further, although many similarities exist among all of the states' laws, each format is governed by the particularities of the state in which the enterprise is organized, and so each jurisdiction's specific law must be analyzed for any variations that may exist.

The Sole Proprietorship

sole proprietorship
Business owned and
managed by one person.

The **sole proprietorship** is possibly the most prevalent business format currently in use in the United States. Simply stated, a sole proprietorship is a business that is owned and operated by just one person. Sole proprietorships exist in every state and are the easiest business formats to create, as no jurisdiction imposes any formal requirements for creation on the **sole proprietor,** the owner of the sole proprietorship. As soon as the individual decides to begin the enterprise, the sole proprietorship is formed.

sole proprietor
Owner of a sole
proprietorship.

— *Example*

An actress has semi-retired in order to raise a family. To generate some income, she decides to offer acting classes for aspiring actors. She can do this from her own home so as not to interfere with familial responsibilities. As soon as the actress decides on this course of action, the sole proprietorship has officially been formed.

The sole proprietorship has several distinct advantages in its formation and operation. First, the sole proprietorship is easy to form because no formalities in creation are required. Second, because there is only one owner, there is only one manager, meaning that management decisions may be made and implemented automatically because the sole proprietor does not have to seek the approval of anyone else.

— *Example*

The actress from the previous example decides that, in addition to acting classes, she will also offer courses in theatrical makeup and stage movement. This decision has changed the curriculum, but it is effectuated immediately because the actress does not need anyone else's approval in order to make this management decision.

Schedule C
Federal tax attachment
for sole proprietors.

Third, there may be certain income-tax advantages to operating a sole proprietorship. A sole proprietorship is not considered to be a taxable entity separate from its owner, meaning that it is not responsible for any income taxes that may be due on profit it generates. A sole proprietorship is deemed to be an extension of its owner; therefore, all revenues and expenses are passed through directly to the owner. To report this income, a sole proprietor is required to attach a **Schedule C**—an addendum to one's own personal income-tax return. Once the sole proprietor reports all revenues derived from the operation of the sole proprietorship, he or she is permitted to subtract from these revenues certain items of expense, such as rent, utilities, supplies, postage, wages, and so forth, that are attributed to the operation of the business, and the owner's income tax liability rests only on the profits left after all expenses have been deducted. This profit is taxed as ordinary income to the sole proprietor, along with any other income the proprietor has generated. If the business operates at a loss, the proprietor may be able to use that loss to offset other income, thereby reducing his or her total tax liability.

— *Example*

A man owns a theater that he operates as a sole proprietorship. In the current tax year, his total income from the theater was $85,000, including all ticket sales. During this same year, his expenses in operating the theater have been $43,000. These figures are reported on Schedule C of his income-tax return. Based on these numbers, the man must pay income tax on an income of $42,000 ($85,000 − $43,000 = $42,000).

estimated income tax
Quarterly tax filing required for a business.

As a tax consequence of operating a sole proprietorship, because no income taxes are withheld, the sole proprietor is required to file **estimated income taxes** on a quarterly basis if any taxes are due to assure the government that the taxes will be paid on income generated. This creates certain additional operating expenses; for example, the cost of filing the returns if the owner employs an accountant or bookkeeper to prepare the returns.

However, despite these advantages, there are several negative consequences of operating an entertainment enterprise as a sole proprietorship:

1. The sole proprietorship is difficult to finance. Because the sole proprietorship is deemed to be no more than an extension of the owner, all financing for the enterprise must come from the sole proprietor, either directly or by means of loans he or she takes out based on personal credit-worthiness. By definition, a sole proprietor cannot have a partner or backer with an ownership interest for the business, as that would mean that there is more than one owner.

— *Example*

A woman has written a play and wants to produce it. If she decides to create the production company as a sole proprietorship, she must raise all of the capital herself, including loans. If she takes out a loan to finance the play and the play loses money, she must repay the loan from her own resources.

2. The sole proprietor has unlimited personal liability for the obligations of the enterprise. Again, because of the singular identity of the owner with the enterprise, the sole proprietor remains personally liable for all obligations of the business, which not only include contracts but may also involve personal-injury liability for persons who are injured on the enterprise's premises.

—— Example ——————————————————

A woman operates a small experimental-film theater as a sole proprietorship. One day, one of her patrons is injured when the chandelier in the lobby collapses. As the sole owner, the woman is personally responsible for all injuries the customer suffered. If the theater is valued at $180,000, and the patron suffers injuries valued at $1,500,000, the woman is responsible for the entire amount of the injury; the liability is not limited to the value of the theater.

This unlimited personal-liability aspect of a sole proprietorship is probably its most detrimental factor.

3. A sole proprietorship has no life independent from its owner; therefore, the business terminates at the death, disability, or bankruptcy of the sole proprietor. For many entertainment enterprises, this could mean that the enterprise could end at the owner's death if provisions are not set in place to provide for the enterprise's continuation. As discussed in the previous chapter, because copyrights and marks exist beyond the death of the creator, some estate planning must be effectuated while the sole proprietor is alive to ensure the continuation of the venture.

—— Example ——————————————————

Agatha Christie owned many valuable copyrights. At her death, all of the copyrights passed to her grandson according to the provisions of her will, and her grandson is now able to see that Ms. Christie's works continue to be published, produced, and enjoyed.

4. Although there generally are no formalities required to create the sole proprietorship, the sole proprietor may be responsible for several regulatory filings with respect to the operation of the enterprise. Most jurisdictions require a sole proprietor to file an assumed name form, also referred to as a **DBA form** ("doing business as") if the owner is going to operate under a name other than his or her own name, and that assumed name must be unique in the area of its operations. Also, many jurisdictions require licensing for various types of enterprises, many of which fall into the broad category of entertainment law, such as theatrical agents, educational institutions, theaters, and so forth. Consequently, although it may be simple to form the sole proprietorship, there may be numerous formalities to comply with in order to operate the enterprise.

DBA form
Form used to operate a business under an assumed name.

—— Example ——————————————————

A dedicated runner wants to promote a road race as a sole proprietor and decides to call the race the *Roadrunners' Challenge*. He files a DBA form at his county clerk's office. Unfortunately, the name *Roadrunner* has been copyrighted by another organization, and this precludes him from using this name for his event.

Example

A woman wants to become a literary agent. In order to operate such an agency in her state, she must first be licensed by her state under the provisions of her state's statutes.

5. If the sole proprietor employs people to help operate the business, the sole proprietor must meet all legal requirements for employers. Remember that a sole proprietorship is owned and managed by one person, but that person may employ others to assist in the enterprise's day-to-day operation. These employees do not become owners. However, the sole proprietor must obtain an **employer identification number** (EIN) from the Internal Revenue Service in order to withhold income taxes from his or her employees' wages and **workers' compensation insurance** to protect the worker if the employee is injured on the job. Further, depending upon the number of employees, the sole proprietor may become liable under state and federal anti-discrimination employment laws, a topic too broad for the scope of this text, though a brief discussion appears in chapter 9.

employer identification number (EIN)
Number assigned by the IRS that serves as a kind of Social Security Number for a business.

workers' compensation insurance
Insurance to cover employees injured on the job.

Example

A small publishing house is operated as a sole proprietorship. The owner employs twenty-five people. The owner must obtain an EIN from the Internal Revenue Service, must withhold taxes from the employees' wages, must obtain workers' compensation insurance, and because of the number of employees, is subject to federal and state anti-discrimination laws.

6. Sole proprietorships may be subject to certain municipal regulations. A local government may impose a **business tax** on all businesses that rent commercial space within its jurisdiction, and municipalities **zone** geographic areas for specific types of use, such as residential or commercial. The sole proprietor, in selecting a particular location for operation, must be sure that the area is zoned for such proposed activity.

business tax
Tax imposed by certain municipalities on businesses that rent commercial property.

zoning
Government regulation of the use of geographic areas.

Example

A man wants to convert his garage into a small theater; however, his neighborhood is zoned only for residential use. Such use of the garage will not be permitted by the local authorities.

As can be seen, sole proprietorships are probably not the most desirable format to select to operate an entertainment enterprise because of the unlimited personal liability for the owner and the difficulties in financing and longevity. Typically, sole proprietorships are used to operate entertainment enterprises, not by design, but by default because the creator of the enterprise had failed to anticipate the realities of operating a business. Although an entertainment enterprise may start its life as a sole proprietorship, it may be worthwhile for the enterprise to convert to one of the following formats.

The General Partnership

general partnership
Association of two or more persons engaged in business as co-owners for profit.

Uniform Partnership Act (UPA)
Statute that regulates general partnerships.

Statute of Frauds
Law requiring certain contracts to be in writing to be enforceable.

A **general partnership** is an association of two or more persons engaged in business for profit as co-owners. General partnerships are governed by the provisions of the **Uniform Partnership Act (UPA),** a version of which has been adopted in every jurisdiction.

Pursuant to the provisions of the UPA, unless the parties have an agreement to the contrary, all partners are deemed to be equal partners with equal rights and obligations. However, this uniformity of equality may be varied (and usually is) by a valid partnership agreement. Further, the UPA does not specify any requisite formalities to create a general partnership. Similar to a sole proprietorship, once two or more persons agree to form a partnership, the partnership comes into existence. In order for the agreement to be enforceable in a court of law, the provisions of the agreement must be in writing if the intent of the parties is to continue the partnership for more than one year. This requirement emanates from the **Statute of Frauds**, a law that mandates that certain types of agreements be in writing to be enforceable.

The primary factor in the determination of whether or not a partnership exists is the intent of the parties. As specified in its definition, the concept of "association" means a voluntary meeting of the minds, and once this mutuality of intent is evidenced, the partnership is formed.

partnership rights (interests)
Basic rights granted to partners engaged in a business enterprise.

Once formed, all the partners are entitled to participate in what are considered to be the **partnership rights (interests),** which are:

1. The right to the physical assets of the enterprise
2. The right to manage and control the enterprise
3. The right to receive the income and profits from the enterprise.

Partnership Property

tenancy in partnership
Form of multiple ownership of property for partners.

As a general rule, most partnership property is owned by the partners as a **tenancy in partnership,** a form of multiple ownership of property that was developed exclusively for business partners. If the partners do not specify a different type of title to the enterprise's property, the law will assume title as a tenancy in partnership. With this form of ownership, the partners are deemed to have equal rights to the property with the following restrictions:

1. No one partner may possess the property for other than partnership purposes without the other partner's consent.

— *Example* —————————————————————

Three friends operate a movie theater as a general partnership. None of the partners has the right to take home the projector for a private screening without the consent of the other partners.

———————————————————————————————

2. No one partner may sell the property, excluding inventory, without the other partner's consent.

— *Example* —————————————————————

Four friends form a band as a partnership. One day, someone offers one of the members a large sum of money for the band's amplifier, which is partnership property. The band member may not sell the equipment without the other members' consent.

———————————————————————————————

3. The partnership property may not be attached by the personal creditors of the partners.

— *Example* —————————————————————

Two women operate a small publishing house as a general partnership. One of the women goes into debt in remodeling her house. Her creditor cannot attach the assets of the publishing company to satisfy her personal obligation.

———————————————————————————————

4. The heirs of a deceased partner are only entitled to the value of that partner's interest in the property; the title to the property passes automatically to the surviving partners, absent an agreement to the contrary.

— *Example* —————————————————————

The Hubert brothers own a chain of theaters as a partnership. The older brother dies, and his widow claims a share of the business. The surviving brother must pay the widow the value of the deceased brother's interest, but the widow has no right to the theaters themselves.

———————————————————————————————

assignment
Transfer of contractual rights.

The right to the partnership property is a personal right of the partners, and the partners cannot **assign** (legally transfer) that right.

Management and Control

The right to manage and control the partnership is a right shared equally by all of the partners, absent an agreement to the contrary. Therefore, unlike a sole proprietorship in which the sole proprietor may make management decisions without restriction, with a general partnership a partner may be required to obtain the consent of other partners prior to acting. Also, under general-partnership law, each partner is considered to be an agent of the partnership, meaning that each partner can bind all the other partners to contracts entered into on behalf of the joint enterprise. This can engender certain financial liabilities for the partners.

--- *Example* ---

Three friends own a publishing house as a general partnership. One of the partners enters into a contract with a well-known celebrity, offering the celebrity several million dollars to write her autobiography. If the book does not sell, the other two partners are equally bound to pay the contract price to the celebrity because the individual who entered into the agreement had the legal ability to bind the enterprise.

However, the UPA recognizes five types of agreements that require the consent of all of the partners in order for the partnership to be bound. These agreements are

1. An agreement in which partnership property is used as collateral for a loan
2. An agreement in which the goodwill and reputation of the enterprise is sold, such as endorsing a product
3. An agreement to arbitrate a partnership claim because such an agreement precludes the partners from having a day in court
4. An agreement whereby the partnership agrees to accept liability without a judicial determination
5. Any agreement that would make it impossible to continue the business of partnership.

As with rights to the partnership property, the right to manage and control is also considered to be personal and is therefore non-assignable.

Income and Profits

Absent an agreement to the contrary, each partner is entitled to an equal share of the income and profits generated by the partnership business. Further, if any losses arise, each partner may use his or her proportionate share of the loss to offset other personal income.

Pursuant to the provisions of the UPA, a general partnership may terminate its operations and existence in one of the following ways:

1. By agreement of the partners
2. By the expulsion or withdrawal of a partner for any reason

3. By operation of law, meaning that the partnership will be deemed automatically terminated if the partners engage in an unlawful activity, if one of the partners dies, or if one of the partners is declared bankrupt

4. By court order if the court finds it inequitable to allow the partnership to continue.

Take note of the fact that because a general partnership is based on the agreement of the parties, if one of the parties, for *any* reason, is no longer involved with the enterprise, the partnership dissolves. If the remaining partners continue the venture, it is legally considered to be a new partnership by operation of law.

There are several advantages to forming an entertainment enterprise as a general partnership rather than a sole proprietorship. Some of these benefits are

1. The enterprise can raise capital by having several owners contribute funds as well as by borrowing money based on the credit-worthiness of all of the owners, not just one person

2. The enterprise may be more efficient by having persons involved with different areas of expertise rather than having all decisions based on just one person's knowledge and experience

3. The business losses may be shared

4. The taxes are passed through to the owners in the same fashion as with a sole proprietorship.

Of course, certain disadvantages are associated with general partnerships as well:

1. Each partner retains unlimited personal liability for the obligations of the enterprise. This is the same disadvantage as operating a sole proprietorship, but at least with a partnership there are other persons who are required to share in this obligation.

— *Example*

A patron is injured in a theater and sues the theater, which is operated as a general partnership. The patron is awarded a $1,000,000 judgment. If the theater were operated as a sole proprietorship, the one owner would be liable for the full amount. As a partnership, each of the partners is obligated for his or her proportionate share.

joint liability
Contract liability for partnerships.

joint and several liability
Tort liability for partnerships.

contribution
Partner's obligation to pay his or her proportionate share of an award granted to a third person injured by the partnership.

It should be noted that the liability for a partner in a general partnership is **joint liability** in a contract dispute, meaning that all the partners must be sued if the basis of the lawsuit is a breach of contract, and **joint and several liability** in tort, meaning that if the basis of the suit is personal injury, the injured party need only sue one partner. That partner must then seek **contribution** from the other partners for their share of the ultimate award that the sued partner must pay.

2. There is a potential loss of control over the management of the business because of the multiple owners whose consent must be acquired.

3. The potential liability for each partner is increased because each partner may act as an agent for the others, thereby increasing their potential liability.

Despite potential disadvantages, many successful entertainment enterprises are operated as general partnerships because of the advantages in funding and greater expertise of multiple owners. It should be noted that most of the operational requirements associated with a sole proprietorship apply equally to general partnerships as well as to almost all business operations. These would include licensing, zoning, DBA forms, and so forth.

The Limited Partnership

limited partnership
Association of two or more persons engaged in business for profit as co-owners, with one or more general partners and one or more limited partners.

Uniform Limited Partnership Act (ULPA)
Statute that regulates limited partnerships.

general partner
Co-owner of a business with unlimited personal liability.

limited partner
Investor in a limited partnership.

security
Attachable interest used to satisfy a debt.

certificate of limited partnership
Document filed to create a limited partnership.

limited partnership agreement
Contract between limited partners.

For many entertainment enterprises, such as theatrical productions and professional athletic teams, the limited partnership has been a favored legal format. By definition, a **limited partnership** is an association of two or more persons engaged in business for profit as co-owners, with one or more general partners and one or more limited partners.

Limited partnerships were historically governed by the provisions of the **Uniform Limited Partnership Act (ULPA)**, a version of which was adopted by every jurisdiction. Over the past several decades, many states have enacted revisions of this statute, and so the peculiarities of each jurisdiction's law must be scrutinized. However, universally, limited partnerships share certain common characteristics:

1. The **general partner** is the person who retains the power to manage and control the enterprise and also who retains unlimited personal liability for the obligations of the enterprise.

2. The **limited partner** is deemed to be an investor in the enterprise, meaning that he or she is not financially responsible for the enterprise beyond the capital he or she originally contributed to become a limited partner. Because limited partners are investors, limited partnerships, depending on the number of limited partners, may be considered a **security**, mandating regulation under state and federal securities laws.

3. There are certain formalities required to create a limited partnership, which may include filing a **certificate of limited partnership** and a **limited partnership agreement** with the state or county government where it is formed.

As indicated above, management and control of the limited partnership rests with the general partner who retains unlimited personal liability for the obligations of the enterprise as a corollary to the right of control. However, this right of control is not unfettered, and the general partner must acquire the approval of the limited partners to bind the enterprise in the following circumstances:

1. Any action that goes against the agreed-upon provisions of the limited partnership agreement

2. An agreement wherein the limited partnership agrees to contract liability without a judicial determination

3. Possessing partnership property for other than partnership purposes—limited partnership property, like general partnership property, is held in tenancy in partnership unless otherwise specified

4. Any agreement that would interfere with the operation of the enterprise

5. Admission of a new or additional general partner, as such a person would have a direct impact on the limited partner's interest because of the ability of the general partner to manage and control the business. Note, however, that a new limited partner may be added without consent, subject to the limited partnership agreement.

With respect to the operation of a limited partnership, all of the general operational requirements for businesses, as previously discussed, would apply. Limited partnerships can terminate their existence in one of the following manners:

1. At the time or happening specified in the limited partnership agreement

2. By the written consent of all of the general partners and a statutory percentage of the limited partners

3. At the withdrawal of the general partner if there are no surviving general partners.

Limited partnerships historically have been a favored format for entertainment enterprises for the following reasons:

limited partnership share
Evidence of the limited partner's ownership interest.

1. The ability to attract financing by the sale of **limited partnership shares** to persons who do not want to have any say in management

2. The tax treatment of having profits and losses pass directly through to the partners because, like sole proprietorships and general partnerships, a limited partnership is not considered to be a separate taxable entity

3. The ability of a person to acquire a financial stake in an enterprise without engendering unlimited personal liability by virtue of being a limited partner.

However, there are certain drawbacks to operating an entertainment enterprise as a limited partnership:

1. There are requisite formalities in creating the enterprise, as well as potential securities regulation

2. There are increased operating costs occasioned by the greater number of formalities

3. The loss of control over the enterprise if one is only a limited partner.

Of the limited partnerships in the entertainment industry, one of the most famous is the New York Yankees.

The Corporation

corporation
Artificial business entity.

shareholder
Stockholder; owner of a corporation.

director
Corporate manager.

board of directors
Managers of a corporation.

certificate of incorporation
Document filed to create a corporation.

bylaws
Day-to-day rules of a corporation.

officers
Senior managers of a corporation.

One of the most favored formats used to create an entertainment enterprise is the corporation. Briefly defined, a **corporation** is a legal entity, separate and distinct from its owners, who are called **shareholders** or **stockholders**. Corporations are managed by persons elected by the shareholders, called **directors**. Every corporation formed in the United States is required to have at least one director to manage its affairs. Multiple directors manage collectively as a group and are called the **board of directors**.

Corporations are formed pursuant to the provisions of individual state laws; there is no federal law that creates a corporation. (There are certain exceptions for certain federal corporations that are not in the entertainment field, and therefore are not relevant to this text). Once formed in a given state, the corporation is required to register in every other state in which it plans to operate.

Corporations have certain requirements with respect to their formation. For instance, to form a corporation a document referred to as the **certificate of incorporation** must be filed in the secretary of state's office for the state in which the entity is being formed. All corporations are further required to adopt **bylaws**, a statement of rules and regulations used to establish the parameters of the entity's day-to-day operations. To oversee the operation, the board of directors appoints **officers**, usually a president, vice-president, treasurer, and secretary, who act on behalf of and for the corporation. Because the corporation is an artificial entity, its operational aspect is controlled by directors, officers, and other persons hired by these individuals.

Corporations historically have been formed for entertainment enterprises because of many distinct advantages over the other formats previously discussed. Some of these advantages are:

1. *Perpetual life.* In most jurisdictions, corporations may exist forever; however, they may also voluntarily select to exist for a shorter duration.

resolution
Agreement of the board of directors.

2. *Centralized management.* The managerial decisions must be made by means of a board of director **resolution**, thereby avoiding a partnership situation in which one partner's actions may unwittingly bind the other partners.

3. *Limited liability for the owners.* Shareholders are generally not personally liable for the obligations of the corporation, but are deemed merely to be investors, similar to limited partners who only lose the money they paid to acquire their shares.

fiduciary
Person in a position of trust.

4. *Limited liability for the directors.* Directors, as a general rule, are not held to be personally liable for the obligations of the corporation, provided that they fulfill their fiduciary obligations. A **fiduciary** is a person who is

in a position of trust with respect to another and who is held to a higher standard of care than ordinary care. The directors are fiduciaries to the shareholder-owners of the corporation. Provided that the directors exercise due care in making their managerial decisions, they will not be personally responsible for bad business decisions. This fiduciary standard for the corporate director is called the **business judgment rule**.

5. *Ability to fund the operations.* A corporation may capitalize itself in one of two ways. First, it can acquire capital by selling additional shares, thereby acquiring additional owners who have limited liability. Second, the corporation, as a legal entity, may borrow funds based on its own credit-worthiness. If the corporation defaults, the lenders can only go after corporate assets, not the personal assets of the director or shareholders, unless they have engaged in some activity that would give rise to personal liability, such as not adhering to the standards of the business judgment rule.

However, there are several detriments to operating an entertainment enterprise as a corporation:

1. *Taxation.* The corporation, as a legal entity, is responsible for its own income taxes on any profits, and the shareholders, who receive the corporations' after-tax profits as **dividends**, must report and pay income taxes on the dividends they receive. Further, if the corporation suffers a loss, the loss cannot be passed through to the shareholders as with a partnership. (There is an exception for subchapter S corporations, discussed later in the chapter.)

2. *Securities regulation.* Because all shareholders are considered investors, corporations may be required to fulfill certain securities law requirements on both the state and federal level.

3. *Administrative burdens.* In addition to the organizational filing requirements to create the corporation, the corporation must also file quarterly income-tax returns, be professionally audited, and may be required to make yearly securities filings. All of these formalities increase the entity's administrative burden.

4. *Loss of ownership and/or control.* Because the corporation may continue to sell shares, the original shareholder-owners may lose control of the corporation due to their decreasing ability to elect the directors.

Despite these drawbacks, most entertainment enterprises utilize this legal format for their operation because of its universal appeal and funding possibilities.

The Limited Liability Company

In the 1980s, many jurisdictions began enacting statutes to create a legal entity called a *limited liability company.* As of 2003, every jurisdiction has enacted laws to permit such entities.

---

business judgment rule
Fiduciary standard for corporate directors.

dividend
Shareholder's return on investment.

limited liability company (LLC)
Company that gives limited liability to its owners but lets them manage the business.

articles of organization
Document filed to establish a limited liability company.

operating agreement
Document used to indicate how an LLC is to function.

members
Owners of an LLC.

managers
Persons who manage an LLC.

membership shares
Evidence of ownership in an LLC.

A **limited liability company (LLC)** is an association of one or more persons who are operating a business that provides limited liability for its owners and that is not a corporation. Basically, the LLC combines aspects of the sole proprietorship, the limited partnership, and the corporation. Also, take careful note that in many jurisdictions the LLC must have at least two owners.

To create an LLC, the entity must file **articles of organization** with the secretary of state in the jurisdiction in which it wishes to form, similar to a corporation. Further, the LLC must adopt an **operating agreement**, similar to a limited partnership agreement, to define the rights and obligations of the parties.

The owners of an LLC are referred to as **members**, and the operating agreement indicates whether the LLC is managed by its members or by **managers**—persons elected by the members who are similar to a corporation's board of directors.

As its name would imply, the LLC provides limited personal liability for its members, meaning that they generally are not personally liable for the business obligations and may only lose the amount they contributed to acquire their **membership shares**, the evidence of their percentage ownership of the company. As with limited partnerships and sole proprietorships, taxes are directly passed through to the owners.

Many entertainment enterprises have opted to form as LLCs because legal requirements to create the entity are slightly less burdensome than those of a corporation; further, there are certain tax advantages of the pass-through, especially for theatrical enterprises that may initially lose money. However, as of 2003, LLCs are so new that there has been little judicial interpretation of this format; as a result, legal problems that may be encountered in operating an LLC have yet to be fully articulated.

These business formats—the sole proprietorship, the general partnership, the limited partnership, the corporation, and the limited liability company—provide the legal structures under which entertainment enterprises may operate. The importance of these structures cannot be too strongly stressed. Because of the advantages and disadvantages associated with each format, this initial legal decision can have a far-reaching impact on the success or failure of the enterprise, especially with respect to its ability to fund its operations and to continue its operations after the death of the initial owners. Further, because of the financial risk involved in any business, but especially in the entertainment field, the potential for unlimited personal liability on the part of the owners can be avoided or minimized by the appropriate selection of a legal format.

CONTRACTS

Once the entertainment enterprise has been formed in keeping with the appropriate laws, one of its first legal tasks should be to create several standard contracts that can be used in its day-to-day operations. It is beyond the scope of this text to provide a detailed and comprehensive analysis of contract law, but a few basic contract-law principles must be discussed so as to understand the basic legal operations of an enterprise. The specific contractual concerns of each type of entity will be discussed later in the text in the chapter devoted to that specific type of endeavor.

Overview

contract
Legally enforceable agreement.

Uniform Commercial Code (UCC)
Law that regulates contracts for the sale of goods valued at over $500 and contracts between merchants.

A **contract** is an agreement between two or more persons that, if it meets certain legal requirements, establishes legal rights and obligations between the parties. Contracts for services are governed by the general common law, whereas contracts for the sale of goods either valued at over $500 or between merchants, regardless of the amount, are governed under the provisos of a statute called the **Uniform Commercial Code (UCC)**. Entertainment-law contracts can involve both types of agreements.

To form a valid contract, six elements must coalesce:

1. Offer
2. Acceptance
3. Consideration
4. Capacity of the parties
5. Legality of the subject matter
6. Contractual intent.

Offer

offer
Proposal to enter into a valid contract.

offeror
Person who makes an offer.

merchants
Persons who regularly trade in a particular good or goods.

An **offer** is a proposal by one party to another indicating an intent to enter into a valid contract. All valid contracts begin with an offer that defines the boundaries of the relationship between the parties. To meet legal requirements, an offer must be certain and definite with respect to its essential terms, such as price, quantity, parties to the agreement, and the time of performance. For contracts governed by the common law, the failure of the party making the proposal, the **offeror**, to be certain and definite with respect to these items will cause the contract to fail. For contracts between **merchants**, persons who regularly trade in the type of goods that form the subject matter of the contract, the UCC only requires that the offer specify the quantity; all other items may be completed by the parties at a later date without invalidating the agreement.

── **Example** ──────────────────

A major opera house wants to hire a world-renowned soprano to perform *Aida*. The manager of the opera house writes to the soprano proposing that she perform the opera at a certain specified date and time for a specified fee plus reasonable expenses. This offer for the personal services of the singer has met all of the common-law requirements for a valid offer.

Example

A retail music-store chain wants to purchase a new CD by a famous rap artist for its outlets. The chain owner writes to the CD distributor offering to purchase 10,000 of the CDs. Because the chain owner and the distributor can be considered merchants under the UCC, this proposal constitutes a valid offer for goods (the CDs).

Acceptance

acceptance
Manifestation of assent to an offer.

offeree
Person to whom an offer is made.

counteroffer
Cross-offer.

mirror-image rule
Acceptance must exactly match the terms of the offer.

An **acceptance** is the manifestation of assent to the offer. For contracts governed by common law, the **offeree**, the one to whom the offer is made, is required to accept the offer according to its exact terms. If the offeree makes any variation in the terms of the offer, it is considered a rejection of the offer and constitutes a **counteroffer** (cross-offer) to the original offeror, reversing the roles of the parties. This legal requirement is called the **mirror-image rule**, requiring that the acceptance match the exact terms of the offer. However, for contracts formed under the provisions of the UCC, the offeree may vary the terms of the offer and a contract will still be formed according to the variance unless the offeror objects to the variance within ten days.

— Example

A man receives an offer to coach a hockey team for an annual salary of $100,000. The man attempts to accept the offer by writing back that he agrees to work for the team for a salary of $120,000 a year. Because the contract is for personal services, the mirror-image rule applies, and the man's "acceptance" acts as a rejection of the initial offer and creates a counteroffer because of the variation in the terms of the original offer.

Example

A theater owner contacts a furniture manufacturer offering to buy chairs for her theater at a price of $300 per chair for 300 chairs. The furniture manufacturer agrees to sell the chairs at $325 per chair. If the theater owner does not object to this change in price, the contract will be for the sale of 300 chairs at a price of $325 per chair because both parties can be deemed merchants. The mirror-image rule does not apply because this agreement is covered by the provisions of the UCC.

Consideration

consideration
The bargain element of a contract.

Consideration is the subject matter of the contract—it is the goods or services that have been bargained for by the parties. In order for a contract to be deemed

mutuality of consideration
Contract requirement that both sides give and receive something of legal value.

valid, both parties to the agreement must give and receive something of legal value. This requirement is referred to as **mutuality of consideration**, and applies to all types of contracts. However, the essential element of consideration is the bargain, meaning that it must be shown that the parties actually bargained for the consideration. If one or both of the parties makes a bad bargain, the court will not invalidate the agreement, provided that the party did receive exactly what was bargained for.

— Example

An author agrees to write a book for a publisher as a work for hire (see chapter 2) for a fee of $7,500. Two days later, he receives an offer from a competitor to write the same book for $12,500. The author cannot void his contract with the first publisher simply because he made a bad bargain.

Capacity of the Parties

contractual capacity
Legal ability to enter into a contract.

minor
Person between the ages of 14 and 18.

The legal ability of a person to enter into a valid contract is called **contractual capacity,** and it falls into two categories: age and mental ability. As a general rule, anyone over the age of 18 has met the age requirement for contractual capacity. Persons between the ages of 14 and 18 are deemed to be **minors,** andcan avoid contractual obligations they enter into provided they disavow them before their eighteenth birthday or, in some jurisdictions, within a reasonable time after their eighteenth birthday (except for contracts to provide them with necessaries such as food, clothing, shelter, education, and so forth). Note, however, that the law makes an exception for contracts entered into with minors who are performers, provided that the contracts are signed by the minors' legal guardians and are approved by the court.

The person's mental ability refers to his or her capacity to understand the nature and extent of the contract and is generally a very low standard of comprehension.

— Example

A twelve-year-old girl is hired to play Helen Keller in a remake of "The Miracle Worker." The contract is signed by the girl, her parents, and her agent and is approved by the court. Because the contract meets the legal requirements for such agreements, the contract is deemed valid.

Legality of the Subject Matter

To be legally enforceable, all valid contracts must be formed for a legal purpose. The court cannot enforce an illegal contract.

Contractual Intent

Contractual intent refers to a meeting of the minds of the parties to the agreement. This requires that both parties be conversant with all of the essential details of the contract, and that neither party was fraudulently induced or forced into the agreement. Intent is a very subjective element, and whereas all of the other requirements will typically appear within the provisions of the agreement itself, intent generally must be proven by extrinsic evidence. This is an extremely complex area of contract law, and a detailed discussion of this element is beyond the scope of this text.

— Example

To induce a famous actress to appear in a play, a producer tells her that he has already secured the services of a director with whom the actress wants to work. Based on this statement, the actress signs the contract. In fact, the director has previously refused to direct the play. The actress was lied to by the producer. Under these circumstances, if the producer's oral representation can be proven, the actress may be able to avoid the contract.

In drafting a form contract to be used by an entertainment enterprise, the enterprise must make sure that all of the above elements are met.

Creation of a Form Contract

All entertainment enterprises should maintain a file of standard, formalized contracts for the various agreements into which they regularly enter. Examples would be standard distribution agreements for television ventures (chapter 4), licensing agreements for film companies (chapter 5), equity employment contracts for live stage performances (chapter 6), collaboration agreements for the recording industry (chapter 7), publishing agreements (chapter 8), and so forth. Examples of such agreements will appear later in this text. At this point, a general overview of how these contracts are created will be useful for anyone who may need to draft, analyze, or modify such agreements.

At the outset, it must be stated that, with certain exceptions, contracts that meet the six requisite elements discussed in the previous section are valid regardless of whether they are oral or in writing. The law makes no distinction between oral and written agreements, except that the proof of the provisions of an oral agreement is more difficult to obtain than the actual paper trail of a written contract. However, pursuant to the Statute of Frauds, in order to be enforceable in a court of law, the following types of contracts must be in writing:

1. Contracts that cannot be performed within one year
2. Contracts concerning an interest in realty
3. Contracts in consideration of marriage

4. Contracts to assume the obligations of another

5. Contracts for the sale of goods valued at over $500

6. Executors' promises to pay a decedent's debts.

Because entertainment entities, to one extent or another, involve property rights, all of these exceptions may be involved in an entertainment-law practice.

— *Example* —

1. A contract to perform a play with a road company for two years

2. A contract to purchase a parcel of land to build a sports stadium

3. A prenuptial agreement that divides the spouses' property rights, which include copyrights

4. A contract to finance a television network where the loan is guaranteed by specific individuals

5. A contract for the sale of 20,000 CDs

6. A contract for licensing entered into by a person who then dies.

Since this section concerns the development of a file of standard agreements, all of these contracts, by implication, will be in writing.

Contracts are composed of various clauses, or paragraphs, that specify each party's promises, which form the contours of the agreement. The clauses that delineate the specific promises are known as **covenants**, and they represent the parties' enforceable rights and/or obligations.

The other provisions of a contract are referred to as **conditions**—clauses that affect the time of the performance of the covenants, specific dates, or events that trigger the parties' obligation to perform.

Most contracts follow a fairly standard format, and typically include the following provisions:

covenant
Contractual promise; obligation.

condition
Timing element of a contract.

Description of the Parties

The introductory clause of every contract includes a statement of the legal names of the parties, the type of legal entity the party is, and the names by which the parties will be referred to throughout the contract. This clause serves the purpose of identifying the parties in case of an eventual legal dispute.

— *Example* —

This publishing agreement is made this _____ day of 200___, between Jones Publishing, Inc., a Delaware corporation (hereinafter "Publisher") and Colin Price, an individual, residing in the State of Iowa (hereinafter "Author").

Description of the Consideration

As previously discussed, to be valid, every contract must be supported by consideration. This clause indicates the basis of the agreement.

—— *Example* ——

In consideration of Three Thousand Dollars ($3000), Homeowner agrees to permit Producer to film the exterior of her house on November 13, 2003, said photographs to be used in a film entitled "Hysteria."

Security Agreement

If the contract is one in which one party is putting up some property that the other party may attach in case of a default of the agreement, the contract must specify that it is creating a security agreement.

Warranties

warranties
Guarantees.

In the case of a contract for the sale of goods, the seller may be called upon to make certain guarantees, known as **warranties**, with respect to the quality of the goods being sold. Any express guarantees made by the seller should appear in a clause in the contract.

—— *Example* ——

Seller warrants that the helmets provided for buyer's football team are able to withstand an impact of 500 pounds and meet all federal safety standards.

Title

title
Right to own and/or possess property.

installment sale
Purchase in which purchase price is paid over time.

Once again, if the contract concerns the sale of goods, the **title**, or right of ownership and/or possession, to the property will be transferred from the seller to the buyer. If the contract calls for the purchase price and the goods to be exchanged simultaneously, title will transfer at that time. However, if payment for the goods is to be made over time (an **installment sale**), the seller may wish to retain title to the property until a specified percentage of the total purchase price has been paid. The timing element of the transfer should be specified in this type of agreement.

—— *Example* ——

When the buyer has paid to the seller an amount equal to 80% of the full purchase price specified above, seller will transfer title to the buyer.

Risk of Loss

In every agreement there exists the possibility that the subject matter of the contract may be destroyed, damaged, or die. The contract should specify which party is to be liable for the risk of the loss of the subject matter, which also gives that person an "insurable interest," so that he or she can acquire insurance to cover such risk.

Waivers

waiver
Relinquishment of a
contract right.

breach of contract
Failure to fulfill a
contractual obligation.

A **waiver** is a surrender of a contract right. Contracts that are intended to exist over many years may provide the parties with certain waivable rights. If a given contractual right is not performed when due, the party to whom the right is owed may view such failure as a **breach of contract** or may forego the right by waiver. Most contracts include some form of a standard waiver provision.

— *Example*

The waiver of one provision of this agreement shall not be considered a continuing waiver of that provision.

Assignment

promisee
A person to whom a
right is owed.

An assignment is a transfer of a contractual right from the original **promisee** (the person to whom the right is owed) to a third person. As a general rule, all contracts except for those involving personal services are assignable, provided that they do not unduly increase the other party's obligations. However, by contract, the parties may agree that the contract is non-assignable.

Terminology

All terms appearing in a contract are construed by the court according to their ordinary meanings. If the parties wish to have a given term interpreted in a specific manner, the parties should include a section on terminology in which such terms are defined.

Special Provisions

Every industry has its own special concepts that are unique to that industry. Throughout the remainder of this text, as each area of the entertainment industry is discussed, provisions particular to that enterprise will be analyzed and should be included in a standard contract. In each of the following chapters, a standard contract for the industry is provided as an exhibit.

Boilerplate Provisions

boilerplate
Standard clause.

Boilerplate refers to clauses that are usually included in all contracts, regardless of the contract's individual application. These clauses include provisions dealing with arbitration, selection of jurisdiction, controlling state law, use of pronouns, and so forth. See the Exhibits in each chapter for examples of these clauses.

Remedies

remedies
Method of legally compensating an injured party.

legal remedies
Monetary awards.

limitation of damages
Agreement to have a ceiling on potential damages.

liquidated damages
Contract provision that provides a specified dollar award in case of breach.

The term **remedies** refers to the award a party may receive if he or she is injured by a contractual obligation not being fulfilled. Remedies fall into two broad categories: legal remedies and equitable remedies. **Legal remedies** are monetary awards known as damages that are designed to provide financial compensation for a monetary loss occasioned by a breach of contract. However, the parties themselves may agree to impose a cap, or ceiling, on the amount of the recoverable damages by inserting a clause called a **limitation of damages** provision. In this instance, the non-breaching party may recover his or her loss up to a specified amount. Also, the parties may insert a **liquidated damages** clause that provides for a set dollar amount to which the injured party may be entitled regardless of actual financial loss. Liquidated-damage provisions are only permitted if, when the contract is formed, it would be difficult or impossible to determine actual damages.

— Example

A woman writes a novel and has it copyrighted. If she arranges to have it published, it is possible that the work will never sell, so the amount of her potential loss may not be calculable. In this instance, prior to publication and sale, the court may permit a liquidated-damages provision.

mitigation of damages
Duty of the injured party to lessen the amount of the damages the wrongdoer must pay.

equitable remedies
Non-monetary awards.

specific performance
Court order to fulfill a contractual obligation.

It must be noted that, when seeking damages, the injured party is under a legal obligation to **mitigate**, or lessen, the damages by attempting to find a contract in substitution for the one that is breached. In the entertainment industry, such mitigation may be difficult because one role may not be considered equivalent to the one that was lost. See the Judicial Decision on page 81.

Equitable remedies are non-monetary awards that are permitted when damages would be insufficient to compensate the injured party. Examples of equitable remedies are **specific performance**, in which the breaching party is compelled to do something, or an injunction, in which the breaching party is compelled not to do something. Such remedies may not be used for personal services to force someone to perform, but it may be used to forestall someone from providing those services to someone else.

— Example

A famous actress has agreed to act in a play, but at the last moment she backs out to work for a competing play being produced across the street. The producer of the first play can enjoin the actress from competing with him, but he cannot force her to play the original role.

Signatures

At the end of the contract, the contracting parties must sign the agreement, inserting the parties' legal capacity (title), such as vice-president of the contracting company.

Most entertainment enterprises maintain banks of standard contracts, and simply fill in the names, amounts, and negotiated clauses as the need arises.

TAXATION

After personal financial liability and management and control, the tax implications of a legal format have the greatest impact on the actual selection of that format. Although a complete discussion of federal taxation is beyond the scope of this text, it is important to highlight certain federal-tax aspects of the various business formats previously discussed.

The Sole Proprietorship

As indicated earlier in this chapter, a sole proprietorship is not considered to be an entity separate from the sole proprietor. As a consequence, all income attributed to the operation of the entertainment enterprise is deemed to be ordinary income to the sole proprietor. However, unlike salaries and wages, this type of income is generated by means of the taxpayer operating a business, and therefore the taxpayer is entitled to **deduct**, or subtract, from the total income generated by the enterprise all expenses reasonably related to the production of that income. To this end, the Internal Revenue Service, the federal agency that oversees federal income taxation, provides the taxpayer with a document called a Schedule C, which is an attachment to his or her regular income-tax return, the **Form 1040**.

On the Schedule C, the taxpayer includes all of the expenses associated with the entertainment enterprise, such as:

- Rent
- Advertising
- Utilities
- Telephone
- Travel and entertainment
- Insurance
- Equipment
- Salaries and wages of employees
- Professional fees
- Supplies.

deduction
Subtraction from gross income.

Form 1040
Federal individual income-tax return.

After all of these items are totaled, they are deducted from the income generated by the enterprise; the difference is the amount on which the taxes are determined.

— *Example* ———————————————————————

A man writes a screenplay that he sells for $100,000. In order to create that screenplay, the man had the following expenses:

Rent, at $300/month for 9 months	$2700.00
Utilities, 9 months	875.00
Telephone	435.00
Supplies (paper, pens, ink, and so forth)	510.00
Dues (Screen Writers Guild)	300.00
Total	$4920.00

The screenwriter's taxable income for the year is $95,180 ($100,000 – $4920)

If the expenses exceed the income for the year, the loss may be carried over to the following year to reduce the following year's taxable income.

See Exhibit 3-1 on page 89 for the 2002 Schedule C.

General and Limited Partnerships

Partnerships, like sole proprietorships, are not considered to be taxable entities separate from the partners; therefore, the partners are taxed in the same manner as the sole proprietor. The partnership files an informational return with the IRS indicating its income and expenses and indicating the proportion of ownership attributable to each partner. A copy of this form, shown in Exhibit 3-2 on page 91, is given to each partner to attach to his or her individual tax return.

Corporations and LLCs

As previously stated, a corporation is a legal entity separate and distinct from its shareholders. As a consequence, corporations are taxable entities and are responsible for paying income tax on all income generated by the operation of the business. Of course, as a business, they are entitled to deduct all expenses reasonably related to the operation of the enterprise.

After all income taxes of the corporation are paid, if there is any profit remaining, this profit is distributed to the shareholders as a dividend, a return on their investment in the corporation. This dividend income is then taxed as income to the shareholder, but the shareholder may not deduct any business expenses attributable to the generation of this income.

subchapter S corporation
Tax election for qualifying corporations to be taxed as a partnership.

collapsible corporation
Corporation formed for one purpose that dissolves when that purpose is completed for tax benefits.

dissolved
Terminated.

capital gain
Increase in the value of an asset between the time it is bought and the time it is sold.

Certain types of corporations, those that are owned by a small number of shareholders, may elect to be taxed as a **Subchapter S corporation**, a tax treatment in which the corporation is taxed like a partnership, meaning that all profit and losses are passed through to the shareholders. In this instance, the corporation is treated, for tax purposes, as a general partnership.

Many years ago, a special type of corporation came about exclusively for entertainment enterprises, known as a **collapsible corporation**. With this type of corporation, the entity was created exclusively to produce *one* film or *one* play. When that particular production was completed, the corporation **dissolved**, or terminated, and the assets of the corporation were distributed to the shareholders. Because these assets, upon dissolution, are not considered income, but rather a return of capital on the shareholder's investment, this money was treated as a **capital gain** that is afforded a favorable tax rate. However, the government has subsequently changed the law, and so-called collapsible corporations are now not afforded this favorable treatment.

It should be noted that, unlike a sole proprietorship or a partnership, any losses suffered by the corporation are not passed on to the shareholders.

See Exhibit 3-3 on page 93 for a sample corporate return.

All of these legal formats are required to file estimated income-tax returns on a quarterly basis to assure the government that it will receive the taxes to which it is entitled. Any over or underpayment can be corrected on the final tax return.

It must be noted that not all entertainment entities are subject to income taxation. Many such enterprises may be exempt from federal (and state) income taxes if they qualify as a tax-exempt organization under § 501(c) of the Internal Revenue Code. Certain types of enterprises, such as opera companies, dance troupes, sports leagues, and other entities specializing in the arts, by submitting an application to the IRS, may be deemed tax exempt. The specifics of such exemption are dependent upon the exact nature of the entity in question and must be analyzed on a case-by-case basis.

INSURANCE

insurance
Contract used to indemnify against loss.

premium
Consideration to support an insurance contract.

Because of the potential liability associated with operating a business enterprise in the entertainment field, most businesses acquire some form of insurance to minimize or eradicate such liability. **Insurance** is simply a contractual relationship in which one party, in consideration of annual payments made to it called **premiums**, agrees to reimburse the other party for any losses specified in the contract. For businesses that employ workers, most states require that they at least maintain workers' compensation and liability insurance to protect the workers and patrons from injuries sustained on the job or at the workplace. Although not governmentally mandated, many businesses also provide some form of health and/or life insurance for their employees as a form of an employee benefit. The cost of maintaining such insurance is a deductible expense for all businesses on their federal income-tax returns.

Key Man Insurance

In many industries, but especially in the entertainment field, particular individuals play a crucial part in the success or failure of a given activity. For example, a film may be financed simply because a particular actor has agreed to be part of the film. However, what happens if that actor dies or becomes seriously injured prior to completion of the project? The project may have to be cancelled, and any completed work will have to be jettisoned.

key man insurance
Insurance used to protect against loss occasioned by injury or death of a principal.

Many entertainment enterprises, to protect themselves from such loss, acquire what is referred to as **key man insurance**, a form of life and health insurance that provides the enterprise with funds to compensate it for any loss it suffers because of the death or injury of its key (most important) participants.

— *Example* —

A hockey team has just signed a goalie for a multimillion-dollar contract. To protect itself in the event the goalie is severely injured or dies during the term of the agreement, the team takes out key man insurance on the player to compensate for the loss such injury or death would cost the team (not the player).

Some famous examples of key man insurance are
- Jimmy Durante's nose was insured against injury
- Betty Grable's legs were insured against injury
- Barbra Streisand's nose was insured against injury.

In any situation in which one person, or a small group of individuals, plays a significant and unique role in an enterprise's operations, the enterprise should consider obtaining key man insurance on such persons to mitigate against potential loss. Remember, the insurance provides funds to the enterprise, not the individual or the individual's family.

CHAPTER REVIEW

Before the entertainment entrepreneur actually begins operation of the enterprise, he, she, or they must carefully prepare the appropriate legal format that the enterprise will take. This decision is significant to the success or failure of the entity because of the potential personal liability such decision may engender for the entrepreneur.

Most entertainment enterprises choose to operate by means of a sole proprietorship, a general or limited partnership, a corporation, or a limited liability company. Each format provides certain benefits and detriments for its owners.

A sole proprietorship is easy to form, and management rests exclusively with the owner. However, sole proprietorships are not considered to be entities separate from the sole proprietor; therefore, the owner has unlimited personal liability for the obligations of the business. Further, the business can only be funded by means of personal contributions of the owner or loans guaranteed by the owner.

General partnerships are also easy to form and provide greater opportunities for funding because funds are contributed by more than just one person. However, the partners retain unlimited personal liability, and that liability may be increased due to the actions of the other partners. Also, management decisions must be shared among all the partners.

A limited partnership is more complex to create because all of the states have enacted specific rules dealing with the creation of limited partnerships. Also, because the limited partners are considered investors, limited partnerships, depending upon their size, may be regulated by various state and/or federal securities laws.

The general partners in a limited partnership retain unlimited personal liability for the obligations of the business, whereas the limited partners' liability is limited to the extent of their contribution to the venture. However, to gain this limited liability, the limited partner foregoes almost all management decisions.

The corporation is one of the most favored legal formats selected to operate an entertainment enterprise. To form the corporation, the founders must fulfill all of the specific state requirements of the jurisdiction in which the corporation will be formed and has to file certain documents in every other state in which they plan to operate. The owners, called shareholders, have limited liability, only liable to the extent of their contribution to the corporation. Owners exercise management by electing the board of directors. The board makes all management decisions for the corporation; however, provided that they adhere to their fiduciary obligations, they are not held personally liable for the corporation's liabilities.

The most recent legal format to be used to create entertainment enterprises is the limited liability company. LLCs combine aspects of sole proprietorships, partnerships, and corporations, and provide a format whereby the owner may manage the business while retaining limited personal liability. However, there are specific requirements mandated to create an LLC, and because this format is relatively new, there is little judicial interpretation of their operations.

In order to limit liability and reduce costs, many entertainment enterprises create form contracts that can be used when the enterprise becomes operational. By having form contracts already prepared, the entity can reduce its legal fees and speed up negotiations. However, the entrepreneur must always review such formats to make sure that they are appropriate to a given situation.

Insurance is another agreement used by entertainment enterprises to limit potential liability, especially with the use of key man insurance to protect against any losses occasioned by the injury, illness, or death of a key player in the organization.

Finally, as an important consequence of the legal format selected to operate the enterprise, the entertainment entrepreneur must be cognizant of the tax implications of that selection, which can have a dramatic affect on the enterprise's profitability and ability to be funded.

JUDICIAL DECISION

The following case concerns compensation in a theatrical contract.

Shirley MacLaine Parker

v.

Twentieth Century-Fox Film Corporation

3 Cal3d 176, 474 P2d 689 (1970)

Defendant Twentieth Century-Fox Film Corporation appeals from a summary judgment granting to plaintiff the recovery of agreed compensation under a written contract for her services as an actress in a motion picture. As will appear, we have concluded that the trial court correctly ruled in plaintiff's favor and that the judgment should be affirmed.

Plaintiff is well known as an actress, and in the contract between plaintiff and defendant is sometimes referred to as the "Artist." Under the contract, dated August 6, 1965, plaintiff was to play the female lead in defendant's contemplated production of a motion picture entitled "Bloomer Girl." The contract provided that defendant would pay plaintiff a minimum "guaranteed compensation" of $53,571.42 per week for 14 weeks commencing May 23, 1966, for a total of $750,000. Prior to May 1966 defendant decided not to produce the picture and by a letter dated April 4, 1966, it notified plaintiff of that decision and that it would not "comply with our obligations to you under" the written contract.

By the same letter and with the professed purpose "to avoid any damage to you," defendant instead offered to employ plaintiff as the leading actress in another film tentatively entitled "Big Country, Big Man" (hereinafter, "Big Country"). The compensation offered was identical, as were 31 of the 34 numbered provisions or articles of the original contract. Unlike "Bloomer Girl," however, which was to have been a musical production, "Big Country" was a dramatic "western type" movie. "Bloomer Girl" was to have been filmed in California; "Big Country" was to be produced in Australia. Also, certain terms in the proffered contract varied from those of the original. Plaintiff was given one week within which to accept; she did not and the offer lapsed. Plaintiff then commenced this action seeking recovery of the agreed guaranteed compensation.

The complaint sets forth two causes of action. The first is for money due under the contract; the second, based upon the same allegations as the first, is for damages resulting from defendant's breach of contract. Defendant in its answer admits the existence and validity of the contract, that plaintiff complied with all the conditions, covenants and promises and stood ready to complete the performance, and that defendant breached and "anticipatorily repudiated" the contract. It denies, however, that any money is due to plaintiff either under the contract or as a result of its breach, and pleads as an affirmative defense to both causes of action plaintiff's allegedly deliberate failure to mitigate damages, asserting that she unreasonably refused to accept its offer of the leading role in "Big Country."

Plaintiff moved for summary judgment under Code of Civil Procedure section 437c, the motion was granted, and summary judgment for $750,000 plus interest was entered in plaintiff's favor. This appeal by defendant followed.

The familiar rules are that the matter to be determined by the trial court on a motion for summary judgment is whether facts have been presented which give rise to a triable factual issue. The court may not pass upon the issue itself. Summary judgment is proper only if the affidavits or declarations in support of the moving party would be sufficient to sustain a judgment in his favor and his opponent does not by affidavit show facts sufficient to present a triable issue of fact. The affidavits of the moving party are strictly construed, and doubts as to the propriety of summary judgment should be resolved against granting the motion. Such summary procedure is drastic and should be used with caution so that it does not become a substitute for the open trial method of determining facts. The moving party cannot depend upon allegations in his own pleadings to cure deficient affidavits, nor can his adversary rely upon his own pleadings in lieu or in support of affidavits in opposition to a motion; however, a party can rely on his adversary's pleadings to establish facts not contained in his own affidavits (*Slobojan v. Western Travelers Life Ins. Co.* 70 Cal2d 432, 436–437 (74 CalRptr 895, 450 P2d 271)(1969); and cases cited). Also, the court may consider facts stipulated to by the parties and facts which are properly the subject of judicial notice (*Ahmanson Bank & Trust Co. v. Tepper* 269 CalApp2d 333, 342 (74 CalRptr 774)(1969)).

As stated, defendant's sole defense to this action which resulted from its deliberate breach of contract is that in rejecting defendant's substitute offer of employment plaintiff unreasonably refused to mitigate damages.

The general rule is that the measure of recovery by a wrongfully discharged employee is the amount of salary agreed upon for the period of service, less the amount which the employer affirmatively proves the employee has earned or with reasonable effort might have earned from other employment (*W.F. Boardman Co. v. Petch* 186 Cal 476, 484 (199 P 1047)(1921); *De Angeles v. Roos Bros., Inc.* 244 CalApp2d 434, 441–442 (52 CalRptr 783)(1966); *de la Falaise v. Gaumont-British Picture Corp.* 39 CalApp2d 461, 469 (103 P.2d 447)(1940), and cases cited; see also *Wise v. Southern Pac. Co.* 1 Cal3d 600, 607–608 (83 CalRptr 202, 463 P2d 426)(1970)). However, before

projected earnings from other employment opportunities not sought or accepted by the discharged employee can be applied in mitigation, the employer must show that the other employment was comparable, or substantially similar, to that of which the employee has been deprived; the employee's rejection of or failure to seek other available employment of a different or inferior kind may not be resorted to in order to mitigate damages.

In the present case defendant has raised no issue of reasonableness of efforts by plaintiffs to obtain other employment; the sole issue is whether plaintiff's refusal of defendant's substitute offer of "Big Country" may be used in mitigation. Nor, if the "Big Country" offer was of employment different or inferior when compared with the original "Bloomer Girl" employment, is there an issue as to whether or not plaintiff acted reasonably in refusing the substitute offer. Despite defendant's arguments to the contrary, no case cited or which our research has discovered holds or suggests that reasonableness is an element of a wrongfully discharged employee's option to reject, or fail to seek, different or inferior employment lest the possible earnings therefrom be charged against him in mitigation of damages.

Applying the foregoing rules to the record in the present case, with all intendments in favor of the party opposing the summary judgment motion—here, defendant—it is clear that the trial court correctly ruled that plaintiff's failure to accept defendant's tendered substitute employment could not be applied in mitigation of damages because the offer of the "Big Country" lead was of employment both different and inferior, and that no factual dispute was presented on that issue. The mere circumstance that "Bloomer Girl" was to be a musical review calling upon plaintiff's talents as a dancer as well as an actress, and was to be produced in the City of Los Angeles, whereas "Big Country" was a straight dramatic role in a "Western Type" story taking place in an opal mine in Australia, demonstrates the difference in kind between the two employments; the female lead as a dramatic actress in a western style motion picture can by no stretch of imagination be considered the equivalent of or substantially similar to the lead in a song-and-dance production.

Additionally, the substitute "Big Country" offer proposed to eliminate or impair the director and screenplay approvals accorded to plaintiff under the original "Bloomer Girl" contract , and thus constituted an offer of inferior employment. No expertise or judicial notice is required in order to hold that the deprivation or infringement of an employee's rights held under an original employment contract converts the available "other employment" relied upon by the employer to mitigate damages, into inferior employment which the employee need not seek or accept (see *Gonzales v. Internat. Assn. of Machinists*, supra, 213 CalApp2d 817, 823–824).

Statements found in affidavits submitted by defendant in opposition to plaintiff's summary judgment motion, to the effect that the "Big County" offer was not of employment different from or inferior to that under the "Bloomer Girl" contract, merely repeat the allegations of defendant's answer to the complaint in this action, constitute only conclusionary assertions with respect to undisputed facts, and do not give rise to a triable factual issue so as to defeat the motion for summary judgment.

In view of the determination that defendant failed to present any facts showing the existence of a factual issue with respect to its sole defense—plaintiff's rejection of its substitute employment offer in mitigation of damages—we need not consider plaintiff's further contention that for various reasons, including the provisions of the original contract, plaintiff was excused from attempting to mitigate damages.

The judgment is affirmed.

DISSENT: The basic question in this case is whether or not plaintiff acted reasonably in rejecting defendant's offer of alternate employment. The answer depends upon whether that offer (starring in "Big Country, Big Man") was an offer of work that was substantially similar to her former employment (starring in "Bloomer Girl") or of work that was of a different or inferior kind. To my mind this is a factual issue which the trial court should not have determined on a motion for summary judgment. The majority have not only repeated this error but have compounded it by applying the rules governing mitigation of damages in the employer-employee context in a misleading fashion. Accordingly, I respectfully dissent.

The familiar rule requiring a plaintiff in a tort or contract action to mitigate damages embodies notions of fairness and socially responsible behavior which are fundamental to our jurisprudence. Most broadly stated, it precludes the recovery of damages which, through the exercise of due diligence, could have been avoided. Thus, in essence, it is a rule requiring reasonable conduct in commercial affairs. This general principle governs the obligations of an employee after his employer has wrongfully repudiated or terminated the employment contract. Rather than permitting the employee simply to remain idle during the balance of the contract period, the law requires him to make a reasonable effort to secure other employment. He is not obliged, however, to seek or accept any and all types of work which may be available. Only work which is in the same field and which is of the same quality need be accepted.

Over the years the courts have employed various phrases to define the type of employment which the employee, upon his wrongful discharge, is under an obligation to accept. Thus in California alone it has been held that he must accept employment which is "substantially similar" (*Lewis v. Protective Security Life Ins. Co.* 208 CalApp2d 582, 584 (25 CalRptr 213)(1962); *de la Falaise v. Gaumont-British Picture Corp.* 39 CalApp2d 461, 469 (103 P2d 447)(1940)); "comparable employment" (*Erler v. Five Points Motors, Inc.* 249 CalApp2d 560, 562 (57 CalRptr 516)(1967); *Harris v. Nat. Union etc. Cooks, Stewards* 116 Cal App2d 759, 761 (254 P2d 673)(1953)); employment "in the same general line of the first employment" (*Rotter v. Stationers Corp.* 186 CalApp2d 170, 172 (8 CalRptr 690)(1960)); "equivalent to his prior position" (*De Angeles v. Roos Bros., Inc.* 244 CalApp2d 434, 443 (52 CalRptr 783)(1966)); "employment in a similar capacity" (*Silva v. McCoy* 259 CalApp2d 256, 260 (66 CalRptr 364)(1968)); employment which is "not ... of a different or inferior kind. ..." (*Gonzales v. Internat. Assn. Of Machinists* 213 CalApp2d 817, 822 (29 CalRptr 190)(1963)).

For reasons which are unexplained, the majority cite several of these cases yet select from among the various judicial formulations which they contain one particular phrase, "Not of a different or inferior kind," with which to analyze this case. I have discovered no historical or theoretical reason to adopt this phrase, which is simply a negative restatement of the affirmative standards set out in the above cases, as the exclusive standard. Indeed, its emergence is an example of the dubious phenomenon of the law responding not to rational judicial choice or changing social conditions, but to unrecognized changes in the language of opinions or legal treatises. However, the phrase is a serviceable one and my concern is not with its use as the standard but rather with what I consider its distortion.

The relevant language excuses acceptance only of employment which is of a different kind (*Gonzales v. Internat. Assn. of Machinists*, supra, 213 CalApp2d 817, 822; *Harris v. Nat. Union etc. Cooks, Stewards*, supra, 116 CalApp2d 759, 761; *de la Falaise v. Gaumont-British Picture Corp.*, supra, 39 CalApp2d 461, 469). It has never been the law that the mere existence of differences between two jobs in the same field is sufficient, as a matter of law, to excuse an employee wrongfully discharged from one from accepting the other in order to mitigate damages. Such an approach would effectively eliminate any obligation of an employee to attempt to minimize damage arising from a wrongful discharge. The only alternative job offer an employee would be required to accept would be an offer of his former job by his former employer.

Although the majority appear to hold that there was a difference "in kind" between the employment offered plaintiff in "Bloomer Girl" and that offered in "Big Country," an examination of the opinion makes crystal clear that the majority merely point out differences between the two films (an obvious circumstance) and then apodically assert that these constitute a difference in the kind of employment. The entire rationale of the majority boils down to this: that the "mere circumstances" that "Bloomer Girl" was to be a musical review while "Big Country" was a straight drama "demonstrates the difference in kind" since a female lead in a western is not "the equivalent of or substantially similar to" a lead in a musical. This is merely attempting to prove the proposition by repeating it. It shows that the vehicles for the display of the star's talents are different but it does not prove that her employment as a star in such vehicles is of necessity different in kind and either inferior or superior.

I believe that the approach taken by the majority (a superficial listing of differences with no attempt to assess their significance) may subvert a valuable legal doctrine. The inquiry in cases such as this should not be whether differences between the two jobs exist (there will always be differences) but whether the differences which are present are substantial enough to constitute differences in the kind of employment or, alternatively, whether they render the substitute work employment of an inferior kind.

It seems to me that this inquiry involves, in the instant case at least, factual determinations which are improper on a motion for summary judgment. Resolving whether or not one job is substantially similar to another or whether, on the other hand, it is of a different or inferior kind, will often (as here) require a critical appraisal of the similarities and differences between them in light of the importance of these differences to the employee. This necessitates a weighing of the evidence, and it is precisely this undertaking which is forbidden on summary judgment (*Garlock v. Cole* 199 CalApp2d 11, 14 (18 CalRptr 393)(1962)).

This is not to say that summary judgment would never be available in an action by an employee in which the employer raises the defense of failure to mitigate damages. No case has come to my attention, however, in which summary judgment has been granted on the issue of whether an employee was obliged to accept available alternate employment. Nevertheless, there may well be cases in which the substitute employment is so manifestly of a dissimilar or inferior sort, the declarations of the plaintiff so complete and those of the defendant so conclusionary and inadequate that no factual issues exist for which a trial is required. This, however, is not such a case.

It is not intuitively obvious, to me at least, that the leading female role in a dramatic motion picture is a radically different endeavor from the leading female role in a musical comedy film. Nor is it plain to me that the rather qualified rights of director and screenplay approval contained in the first contract are highly significant matters either in the entertainment industry in general or to this plaintiff in particular. Certainly, none of the declarations introduced by plaintiff in support of her motion shed any light on these issues. Nor do they attempt to explain why she declined the offer of starring in "Big Country, Big Man." Nevertheless, the trial court granted the motion, declaring that these approval rights were "critical" and that their elimination altered "the essential nature of the employment."

The plaintiff's declarations were of no assistance to the trial court in its effort to justify reaching this conclusion on summary judgment. Instead, it was forced to rely on judicial notice of the definitions of "motion picture," "screenplay" and "director" (Evid. Code, § 451, subd.(e)) and then on judicial notice of practices in the film industry which were purportedly of "common knowledge" (Evid. Code, § 451, subd.(f) or § 452, subd.(g)). This use of judicial notice was error. Evidence Code § 451, subdivision (e) was never intended to authorize resort to the dictionary to solve essentially factual questions which do not turn upon conventional linguistic usage. More important, however, the trial court's notice of "facts commonly known" violated Evidence Code § 455, subdivision (a). Before this section was enacted there were no procedural safeguards affording litigants an opportunity to be heard as to the propriety of taking judicial notice of a matter or as to the tenor of the matter to be noticed. Section 455 makes such an opportunity (which may be an element of due process, *see* Evid. Code, § 455, Law Revision Com. Comment (a)) mandatory and its provisions should be scrupulously adhered to. "[Judicial] notice can be a valuable tool in the adversary system for the lawyer as well as the court" (*Kongsgaard*, Judicial Notice (1966) 18 Hastings LJ 117, 140) and its use is appropriate on motions for summary judgment. Its use in this case, however, to determine on summary judgment issues fundamental to the litigation without complying with statutory requirements of notice and hearing is a highly improper effort to "cut the Gordion knot of involved litigation" (*Silver Land & Dev. Co. v. California Land Title Co.* 248 CalApp2d 241, 242 (56 CalRptr 178)(1967)).

The majority do not confront the trial court's misuse of judicial notice. They avoid this issue through the expedient of declaring that neither judicial notice nor expert opinion (such as that contained in the declarations in opposition to the motion) is necessary to reach the trial court's conclusion. Something, however, clearly is needed to support this conclusion. Nevertheless, the majority make no effort to justify the judgment through an examination of the plaintiff's declarations. Ignoring the obvious insufficiency of these declarations, the majority announce that "the

deprivation or infringement of an employee's rights held under an original employment contract" changes the alternate employment offered or available into employment of an inferior kind.

I cannot accept the proposition that an offer which eliminates any contract right, regardless of its significance, is, as a matter of law, an offer of employment of an inferior kind. Such an absolute rule seems no more sensible than the majority's earlier suggestion that the mere existence of differences between two jobs is sufficient to render them employment of different kinds. Application of such per se rules will severely undermine the principle of mitigation of damages in the employer-employee context.

I remain convinced that the relevant question in such cases is whether or not a particular contract provision is so significant that its omission creates employment of an inferior kind. This question is, of course, intimately bound up in what I consider the ultimate issue: whether or not the employee acted reasonably. This will generally involve a factual inquiry to ascertain the importance of the particular contract term and a process of weighing the absence of that term against the countervailing advantages of the alternate employment. In the typical case, this will mean that summary judgment must be withheld.

In the instant case, there was nothing properly before the trial court by which the importance of the approval rights could be ascertained, much less evaluated. Thus, in order to grant the motion for summary judgment, the trial court misused judicial notice. In upholding the summary judgment, the majority here rely upon per se rules which distort the process of determining whether or not an employee is obliged to accept particular employment in mitigation of damages.

I believe that the judgment should be reversed so that the issue of whether or not the offer of the lead role in "Big Country, Big Man" was of employment comparable to that of the lead role in "Bloomer Girl" may be determined at trial.

KEY TERMS

acceptance

articles of organization

assignment

board of directors

boilerplate

breach of contract

business judgment rule

business tax

by-laws

capital gain

certificate of incorporation

certificate of limited partnership

collapsible corporation

condition

consideration

contract

contractual capacity

contribution

corporation

counteroffer

covenant

DBA form

deduction

director

dissolved

dividend

employer identification number
   (EIN)

equitable remedies

estimated income tax

fiduciary

Form 1040

general partner

general partnership

insurance

installment sale

joint and several liability

joint liability

key man insurance

legal remedies

limitation of damages

limited liability company (LLC)

limited partner

limited partnership

limited partnership agreement

limited partnership share

liquidated damages

managers

members

membership shares

merchants

minor

mirror-image rule

mitigation of damages

mutuality of consideration

offer

offeree

offeror

officers

operating agreement

partnership rights (interests)

premium

promisee

remedies

resolution

Schedule C

security

shareholder

sole proprietor

sole proprietorship

specific performance

statute of frauds

subchapter s corporation

tenancy in partnership

title

Uniform Commercial Code (UCC)

Uniform Limited Partnership Act (ULPA)

Uniform Partnership Act (UPA)

waiver

warranties

workers' compensation insurance

zoning

EXERCISES

1. Obtain a copy of a form contract from the Internet or the library that can be used to hire a performer.

2. Briefly discuss the benefits and detriments of operating an entertainment enterprise as a limited partnership, a corporation, or an LLC.

3. Who would be considered a "key man" in the following endeavors?
   A. Producing a film
   B. Producing a CD
   C. A baseball team

4. Obtain a copy of a key man insurance policy from an insurance company and analyze its provisions.

5. Discuss why a personal services contract would not be subject to specific performance.

6. Read *Majeski et al. v. Balcor Entertainment Co. et al.*, 893 FSupp 1397. What does this case have to say about securities fraud and the offering of investments in the entertainment industry? Discuss.

7. Obtain a contract from the Internet or the library that can be used to mount a stage production.

8. Which business structure discussed in this chapter do you feel would be most appropriate as the format for each of the following?
   A. A stage production
   B. A motion picture
   C. A publishing house

9. What are the requirements for forming an LLC in your state?

10. Briefly discuss the tax implications of selecting a particular business format. How might this impact obtaining investors and creditors? Discuss.

EXHIBITS

Following are sample tax forms and business documents.

SCHEDULE C (Form 1040)	**Profit or Loss From Business** (Sole Proprietorship)	OMB No. 1545-0074
Department of the Treasury Internal Revenue Service (99)	▶ Partnerships, joint ventures, etc., must file Form 1065 or 1065-B. ▶ Attach to Form 1040 or 1041. ▶ See Instructions for Schedule C (Form 1040).	**2002** Attachment Sequence No. **09**

Name of proprietor | Social security number (SSN)

A Principal business or profession, including product or service (see page C-1 of the instructions) | **B** Enter code from pages C-7, 8, & 9 ▶

C Business name. If no separate business name, leave blank. | **D** Employer ID number (EIN), if any

E Business address (including suite or room no.) ▶ ....
City, town or post office, state, and ZIP code

F Accounting method: (1) ☐ Cash (2) ☐ Accrual (3) ☐ Other (specify) ▶ ....

G Did you "materially participate" in the operation of this business during 2002? If "No," see page C-3 for limit on losses . ☐ Yes ☐ No

H If you started or acquired this business during 2002, check here . . . . ▶ ☐

Part I   Income

1	Gross receipts or sales. **Caution.** If this income was reported to you on Form W-2 and the "Statutory employee" box on that form was checked, see page C-3 and check here . . . . . ▶ ☐	1	
2	Returns and allowances	2	
3	Subtract line 2 from line 1	3	
4	Cost of goods sold (from line 42 on page 2)	4	
5	**Gross profit.** Subtract line 4 from line 3	5	
6	Other income, including Federal and state gasoline or fuel tax credit or refund (see page C-3) . . .	6	
7	**Gross income.** Add lines 5 and 6 . . . . ▶	7	

Part II   Expenses. Enter expenses for business use of your home **only** on line 30.

8	Advertising	8			19	Pension and profit-sharing plans	19	
9	Bad debts from sales or services (see page C-3) . .	9			20	Rent or lease (see page C-5):		
					a	Vehicles, machinery, and equipment .	20a	
10	Car and truck expenses (see page C-3)	10			b	Other business property . .	20b	
11	Commissions and fees . .	11			21	Repairs and maintenance . .	21	
12	Depletion	12			22	Supplies (not included in Part III) .	22	
13	Depreciation and section 179 expense deduction (not included in Part III) (see page C-4) .	13			23	Taxes and licenses	23	
					24	Travel, meals, and entertainment:		
					a	Travel	24a	
14	Employee benefit programs (other than on line 19) . . .	14			b	Meals and entertainment		
15	Insurance (other than health) .	15			c	Enter nondeductible amount included on line 24b (see page C-5)		
16	Interest:							
a	Mortgage (paid to banks, etc.) .	16a			d	Subtract line 24c from line 24b .	24d	
b	Other	16b			25	Utilities	25	
17	Legal and professional services	17			26	Wages (less employment credits) .	26	
18	Office expense	18			27	Other expenses (from line 48 on page 2)	27	

28	**Total expenses** before expenses for business use of home. Add lines 8 through 27 in columns . . . ▶	28	
29	Tentative profit (loss). Subtract line 28 from line 7	29	
30	Expenses for business use of your home. Attach **Form 8829**	30	
31	**Net profit or (loss).** Subtract line 30 from line 29.
• If a profit, enter on **Form 1040, line 12,** and **also** on **Schedule SE, line 2** (statutory employees, see page C-6). Estates and trusts, enter on **Form 1041, line 3.**
• If a loss, you **must** go to line 32.	31	
32	If you have a loss, check the box that describes your investment in this activity (see page C-6).
• If you checked 32a, enter the loss on **Form 1040, line 12,** and **also** on **Schedule SE, line 2** (statutory employees, see page C-6). Estates and trusts, enter on **Form 1041, line 3.**
• If you checked 32b, you must attach **Form 6198.**	32a ☐ All investment is at risk. 32b ☐ Some investment is not at risk.	

For Paperwork Reduction Act Notice, see Form 1040 instructions. Cat. No. 11334P **Schedule C (Form 1040) 2002**

EXHIBIT 3-1 Schedule C (Form 1040)

Schedule C (Form 1040) 2002   Page **2**

Part III   Cost of Goods Sold (see page C-6)

33   Method(s) used to value closing inventory: **a** ☐ Cost   **b** ☐ Lower of cost or market   **c** ☐ Other (attach explanation)

34   Was there any change in determining quantities, costs, or valuations between opening and closing inventory? If "Yes," attach explanation . . . . ☐ Yes ☐ No

35   Inventory at beginning of year. If different from last year's closing inventory, attach explanation . . .   **35**

36   Purchases less cost of items withdrawn for personal use **36**

37   Cost of labor. Do not include any amounts paid to yourself **37**

38   Materials and supplies **38**

39   Other costs **39**

40   Add lines 35 through 39 . . . .   **40**

41   Inventory at end of year **41**

42   **Cost of goods sold.** Subtract line 41 from line 40. Enter the result here and on page 1, line 4 . .   **42**

Part IV   **Information on Your Vehicle.** Complete this part **only** if you are claiming car or truck expenses on line 10 and are not required to file Form 4562 for this business. See the instructions for line 13 on page C-4 to find out if you must file.

43   When did you place your vehicle in service for business purposes? (month, day, year) ▶ _____ / _____ / _____ .

44   Of the total number of miles you drove your vehicle during 2002, enter the number of miles you used your vehicle for:

a Business _____   **b** Commuting _____   **c** Other _____

45   Do you (or your spouse) have another vehicle available for personal use? . . . . ☐ Yes ☐ No

46   Was your vehicle available for personal use during off-duty hours? . . . . ☐ Yes ☐ No

47a   Do you have evidence to support your deduction? . . . . ☐ Yes ☐ No

   b If "Yes," is the evidence written? . . . . ☐ Yes ☐ No

Part V   **Other Expenses.** List below business expenses not included on lines 8–26 or line 30.

48   Total other expenses. Enter here and on page 1, line 27 . . . .   **48**

Schedule C (Form 1040) 2002

EXHIBIT 3-1 Schedule C (Form 1040) *(continued)*

For office use only

New York State Department of Taxation and Finance

Partnership Return

2002

IT-204

For calendar year 2002 or fiscal year beginning **0 2** and ending

Read the instructions, Form IT-204-I, before completing this return.

Print or type

Legal name

Trade name of business if different from legal name above

Address (number and street or rural route)

City, village, or post office   State   ZIP code

▼ Employer identification number

Principal business activity

Principal product or service

NAICS business code (see instructions)   Date business started

If you do not need forms mailed to you next year, mark an **X** in the box ....

A Mark an **X** in the box that applies to your entity:
- Regular partnership
- Limited liability partnership (LLP)
- Portfolio investment partnership
- Limited liability company (LLC - including limited liability investment company and a limited liability trust company)

B 1) Did the partnership have any income gain, loss, or deduction derived from New York sources during the tax year? **B1** Yes ☐ No ☐

2) If No, enter the number of resident partners ... **B2**

C Mark applicable box(es): ► ☐ Change of address ► ☐ Initial return ► ☐ Amended return ☐ Final return (attach explanation)

D Is this return the result of federal audit changes? **D** Yes ☐ No ☐

If Yes: 1) Enter date of final federal determination ... **D1** ►

2) Do you concede the federal audit changes? (see instructions for amended return or federal changes) ... **D2** Yes ☐ No ☐

E Did you file a New York State partnership return for: .... 2000 Yes ☐ No ☐   2001 Yes ☐ No ☐
If No, state reason:

F Total number of partners required to be listed on Form IT-204-ATT (see instructions) **F**

G Does the partnership currently have tax accounts with New York State for the following taxes?
1. Sales and use tax ■ • Yes ☐ ■ No ☐   If Yes, enter ID number **G1**
2. Withholding tax ■ • Yes ☐ ■ No ☐   **G2**

Schedule A

Part I — List all places, both in and out of New York State, where the partnership carries on business (attach additional sheets if necessary)

Street address	City and state	Description (see instructions)

Part II — Formula basis allocation of income if books do not reflect income earned in New York

Items used as factors	A Totals - in and out of New York State Dollars	B New York State amounts Dollars	C Percent column B is of column A
Property percentage (see instructions)			
1 Real property owned .... 1.		1.	
2 Real property rented from others ...... 2.		2.	
3 Tangible personal property owned ..... 3.		3.	
4 Property percentage (add lines 1, 2, and 3; see inst.) 4.		4.	4. %
5 Payroll percentage (see instructions) ... 5.		5.	5. %
6 Gross income percentage (see inst.) ...... 6.		6.	6. %
7 Total of percentages (add column C, lines 4, 5, and 6) ...			7. %
8 Business allocation percentage (divide line 7 by three or by actual number of percentages if less than three)			8. %

Third - party designee	Do you want to allow another person to discuss this return with the Tax Dept? (see instructions) ■ Yes ☐ (complete the following) ■ No ☐		
	Designee's name	Designee's phone number ( )	Personal identification number (PIN)

Paid preparer's use only	Preparer's signature	▼ Preparer's SSN or PTIN		Signature of general partner
	Firm's name (or yours, if self-employed)	● Employer identification number	**Sign here**	
	Address	Date	Mark X if self-employed ☐	Date Daytime phone number (optional) ( )

Partnership must attach federal Form 1065 or Form 1065-B and all schedules to this Form IT-204 (see instructions for Penalties).
Mail your return to: STATE PROCESSING CENTER, PO BOX 61000, ALBANY, NY 12261-0001.

311292   This is a scannable form: please file this original return with the Tax Department.   IT-204   2002

EXHIBIT 3-2 Partnership Return

IT-204 (2002) (back)

Schedule B — Partners' New York modifications, credits, etc.

Part I — Partners' New York modifications to federal items

			Total
9	New York State additions (attach schedule; see instructions)	9.	
10	New York State subtractions (attach schedule; see instructions)	10.	
11	Additions to federal itemized deductions	11.	
12	Subtractions from federal itemized deductions	12.	
13	Amount of interest expense incurred to carry tax-exempt obligations	13.	
14	New York adjustments to federal tax preference items (see instructions)	14.	

Part II — Partners' credit information

			Total
15	Manufacturing and production, retail enterprise, waste treatment and pollution control property - investment credit (attach Form IT-212)	15.	
16	Research and development property - investment credit (attach Form IT-212)	16.	
17	Add-back of investment credit on early dispositions (attach Form IT-212)	17.	
18	Defibrillator credit (attach Form IT-250)	18.	
19	Investment credit for the financial services industry (attach Form IT-252)	19.	
20	Add-back of investment credit on early dispositions for the financial services industry (attach Form IT-252)	20.	
21	Credit for employment of persons with disabilities (attach Form IT-251)	21.	
22	Alternative fuels credit (attach Form IT-253)	22.	
23	Add-back of alternative fuels credit on early dispositions (attach Form IT-253)	23.	
24	Fuel oil storage tank credit (attach Form IT-254)	24.	
25	Industrial or manufacturing business (IMB) credit (attach Form DTF-623)	25.	
26	Low-income housing credit (attach Form DTF-624)	26.	
27	Green building credit (attach Form DTF-630)	27.	
28	Long-term care insurance credit (attach Form IT-249)	28.	
29	EZ wage tax credit (attach Form IT-601)	29.	
30	ZEA wage tax credit (attach Form IT-601.1)	30.	
31	EZ capital tax credit for investments in and donations to EZ capital corporations (from Form IT-602, Schedule A, line 2; attach form)	31.	
32	EZ capital tax credit for investments in certified EZ businesses (from Form IT-602, Schedule B, line 9; attach form)	32.	
33	EZ capital tax credit for monetary contributions to EZ development projects (from Form IT-602, Schedule C, line 13; attach form)	33.	
34	EZ investment tax credit and EZ employment incentive credit (attach Form IT-603)	34.	
35	QEZE credit for real property taxes (attach Form IT-604)	35.	
36	QEZE employment increase factor (see instructions)	36.	
37	QEZE zone allocation factor (see instructions)	37.	
38	QEZE benefit period factor (see instructions)	38.	
39	Add-back of QEZE credit for real property taxes (attach Form IT-604)	39.	
40	EZ investment tax credit and EZ employment incentive credit for the financial services industry (attach Form IT-605)	40.	
41	Add-back of EZ capital tax credit, EZ investment tax credit, and EZ employment incentive credit (attach Forms IT-602 and IT-603)	41.	
42	Add-back of EZ investment tax credit and EZ employment incentive credit for the financial services industry (attach Form IT-605)	42.	
43	QETC employment credit (attach Form DTF-621)	43.	
44	QETC capital tax credit (attach Form DTF-622)	44.	
45	Add-back of QETC capital tax credit on early dispositions (attach Form DTF-622)	45.	
46	Total acres of qualified agricultural property	46.	
47	Total acres of qualified conservation property	47.	
48	Total amount of eligible taxes paid	48.	
49	Total acres of qualified agricultural property converted to nonqualified use	49.	

Part III — Income and deductions allocated to New York (see instructions)

			Allocated NY amounts
50	Ordinary income (loss) from trade or business activities	50.	
51	Net income or loss from New York rental real estate activities	51.	
52	Net income or loss from other rental activities	52.	
53	Portfolio income (loss)	53.	
54	Guaranteed payments to partners	54.	
55	Net gain (loss) under IRC section 1231 (other than due to casualty or theft)	55.	
56	Other income	56.	
57	Expense deduction for property under IRC section 179	57.	
58	Deductions related to portfolio income (do not include investment interest expense)	58.	
59	Other deductions (see instructions)	59.	
60	Tax preference items for minimum tax (see instructions)	60.	
61	New York adjustments to federal tax preference items (see instructions)	61.	
62	Investment interest expense (see instructions)	62.	
63	Other items not included above that are required to be reported separately to partners	63.	

312292   This is a scannable form; please file this original return with the Tax Department.   IT-204   2002

EXHIBIT 3-2 Partnership Return (*continued*)

Form **1120**	U.S. Corporation Income Tax Return	OMB No. 1545-0123
Department of the Treasury Internal Revenue Service	For calendar year 2002 or tax year beginning .... , 2002, ending .... , 20 ..... ► Instructions are separate. See page 20 for Paperwork Reduction Act Notice.	**2002**

A Check if a:				
1 Consolidated return (attach Form 851) ☐	Use IRS label. Other- wise, print or type.	**Name**	B Employer identification number	
2 Personal holding co. (attach Sch. PH) ☐		Number, street, and room or suite no. (If a P.O. box, see page 7 of instructions.)	C Date incorporated	
3 Personal service corp. (as defined in Regulations sec. 1.441-3(c)— see instructions) ☐		City or town, state, and ZIP code	D Total assets (see page 8 of instructions) $	

E Check applicable boxes: (1) ☐ Initial return (2) ☐ Final return (3) ☐ Name change (4) ☐ Address change

Income	**1a** Gross receipts or sales	**b** Less returns and allowances	c Bal ►	**1c**
	2 Cost of goods sold (Schedule A, line 8)			**2**
	3 Gross profit. Subtract line 2 from line 1c			**3**
	4 Dividends (Schedule C, line 19)			**4**
	5 Interest			**5**
	6 Gross rents			**6**
	7 Gross royalties			**7**
	8 Capital gain net income (attach Schedule D (Form 1120))			**8**
	9 Net gain or (loss) from Form 4797, Part II, line 18 (attach Form 4797)			**9**
	10 Other income (see page 9 of instructions—attach schedule)			**10**
	11 Total income. Add lines 3 through 10		►	**11**
Deductions (See instructions for limitations on deductions.)	**12** Compensation of officers (Schedule E, line 4)			**12**
	13 Salaries and wages (less employment credits)			**13**
	14 Repairs and maintenance			**14**
	15 Bad debts			**15**
	16 Rents			**16**
	17 Taxes and licenses			**17**
	18 Interest			**18**
	19 Charitable contributions (see page 11 of instructions for 10% limitation)			**19**
	20 Depreciation (attach Form 4562)	**20**		
	21 Less depreciation claimed on Schedule A and elsewhere on return	**21a**		**21b**
	22 Depletion			**22**
	23 Advertising			**23**
	24 Pension, profit-sharing, etc., plans			**24**
	25 Employee benefit programs			**25**
	26 Other deductions (attach schedule)			**26**
	27 Total deductions. Add lines 12 through 26		►	**27**
	28 Taxable income before net operating loss deduction and special deductions. Subtract line 27 from line 11			**28**
	29 Less: **a** Net operating loss (NOL) deduction (see page 13 of instructions)	**29a**		
	b Special deductions (Schedule C, line 20)	**29b**		**29c**
Tax and Payments	**30** Taxable income. Subtract line 29c from line 28			**30**
	31 Total tax (Schedule J, line 11)			**31**
	32 Payments: **a** 2001 overpayment credited to 2002	**32a**		
	b 2002 estimated tax payments	**32b**		
	c Less 2002 refund applied for on Form 4466	**32c** ( )	d Bal ►	**32d**
	e Tax deposited with Form 7004			**32e**
	f Credit for tax paid on undistributed capital gains (attach Form 2439)			**32f**
	g Credit for Federal tax on fuels (attach Form 4136). See instructions	**32g**		**32h**
	33 Estimated tax penalty (see page 14 of instructions). Check if Form 2220 is attached ► ☐			**33**
	34 Tax due. If line 32h is smaller than the total of lines 31 and 33, enter amount owed			**34**
	35 Overpayment. If line 32h is larger than the total of lines 31 and 33, enter amount overpaid			**35**
	36 Enter amount of line 35 you want: Credited to 2003 estimated tax ► Refunded ►			**36**

Sign Here	Under penalties of perjury, I declare that I have examined this return, including accompanying schedules and statements, and to the best of my knowledge and belief, it is true, correct, and complete. Declaration of preparer (other than taxpayer) is based on all information of which preparer has any knowledge.		May the IRS discuss this return with the preparer shown below (see instructions)? ☐ Yes ☐ No
	► Signature of officer Date Title		

Paid Preparer's Use Only	Preparer's signature ►	Date	Check if self-employed ☐	Preparer's SSN or PTIN
	Firm's name (or yours if self-employed), address, and ZIP code ►		EIN	
			Phone no. ( )	

Cat. No. 11450Q   Form **1120** (2002)

EXHIBIT 3-3 Corporate Tax Return

Form 1120 (2002)   Page **4**

Note: *The corporation is not required to complete Schedules L, M-1, and M-2 if Question 13 on Schedule K is answered "Yes."*

Schedule L	Balance Sheets per Books	Beginning of tax year		End of tax year	
	Assets	(a)	(b)	(c)	(d)
1	Cash				
2a	Trade notes and accounts receivable . . .				
b	Less allowance for bad debts	( )		( )	
3	Inventories				
4	U.S. government obligations				
5	Tax-exempt securities (see instructions) . .				
6	Other current assets (attach schedule) . .				
7	Loans to shareholders				
8	Mortgage and real estate loans				
9	Other investments (attach schedule) . . .				
10a	Buildings and other depreciable assets . .				
b	Less accumulated depreciation	( )		( )	
11a	Depletable assets				
b	Less accumulated depletion	( )		( )	
12	Land (net of any amortization)				
13a	Intangible assets (amortizable only) . . .				
b	Less accumulated amortization	( )		( )	
14	Other assets (attach schedule)				
15	Total assets				
	Liabilities and Shareholders' Equity				
16	Accounts payable				
17	Mortgages, notes, bonds payable in less than 1 year				
18	Other current liabilities (attach schedule) . .				
19	Loans from shareholders				
20	Mortgages, notes, bonds payable in 1 year or more				
21	Other liabilities (attach schedule)				
22	Capital stock: a Preferred stock . . .				
	b Common stock . . .				
23	Additional paid-in capital				
24	Retained earnings—Appropriated (attach schedule)				
25	Retained earnings—Unappropriated . . .				
26	Adjustments to shareholders' equity (attach schedule)				
27	Less cost of treasury stock		( )		( )
28	Total liabilities and shareholders' equity . .				

Schedule M-1	Reconciliation of Income (Loss) per Books With Income per Return (see page 20 of instructions)

1	Net income (loss) per books		7	Income recorded on books this year not included on this return (itemize):
2	Federal income tax per books			Tax-exempt interest $ ....
3	Excess of capital losses over capital gains .			....
4	Income subject to tax not recorded on books this year (itemize):		8	Deductions on this return not charged against book income this year (itemize):
	....		a	Depreciation . . . . $............
5	Expenses recorded on books this year not deducted on this return (itemize):		b	Charitable contributions $............
a	Depreciation . . . . $............			....
b	Charitable contributions $............		9	Add lines 7 and 8 . . . .
c	Travel and entertainment $............		10	Income (line 28, page 1)—line 6 less line 9
6	Add lines 1 through 5			

Schedule M-2	Analysis of Unappropriated Retained Earnings per Books (Line 25, Schedule L)

1	Balance at beginning of year		5	Distributions: a Cash . . .
2	Net income (loss) per books			b Stock . . . .
3	Other increases (itemize):			c Property . . . .
	....		6	Other decreases (itemize): ....
	....		7	Add lines 5 and 6 . . . .
4	Add lines 1, 2, and 3		8	Balance at end of year (line 4 less line 7)

Form **1120** (2002)

EXHIBIT 3-3 Corporate Tax Return (*continued*)

Form 1120 (2002) Page **3**

Schedule J   Tax Computation (see page 17 of instructions)

1 Check if the corporation is a member of a controlled group (see sections 1561 and 1563) . . . . ▶ ☐
   Important: Members of a controlled group, see instructions on page 17.

2a If the box on line 1 is checked, enter the corporation's share of the $50,000, $25,000, and $9,925,000 taxable income brackets (in that order):
   (1) ☐ $ |_____| (2) $ |_____| (3) $ |_____|

b Enter the corporation's share of: (1) Additional 5% tax (not more than $11,750) $ |_____|
   (2) Additional 3% tax (not more than $100,000) $ |_____|

3 Income tax. Check if a qualified personal service corporation under section 448(d)(2) (see page 17) . . ▶ ☐ **3**

4 Alternative minimum tax (attach Form 4626) **4**

5 Add lines 3 and 4 . . . . **5**

6a Foreign tax credit (attach Form 1118) **6a**

b Possessions tax credit (attach Form 5735) **6b**

c Check: ☐ Nonconventional source fuel credit ☐ QEV credit (attach Form 8834) **6c**

d General business credit. Check box(es) and indicate which forms are attached.
   ☐ Form 3800 ☐ Form(s) (specify) ▶ **6d**

e Credit for prior year minimum tax (attach Form 8827) **6e**

f Qualified zone academy bond credit (attach Form 8860) **6f**

7 **Total credits.** Add lines 6a through 6f **7**

8 Subtract line 7 from line 5 . . . . **8**

9 Personal holding company tax (attach Schedule PH (Form 1120)) **9**

10 Other taxes. Check if from: ☐ Form 4255 ☐ Form 8611 ☐ Form 8697
    ☐ Form 8866 ☐ Other (attach schedule) **10**

11 **Total tax.** Add lines 8 through 10. Enter here and on line 31, page 1 . . . . **11**

Schedule K   Other Information (see page 19 of instructions)

		Yes	No
1	Check method of accounting: a ☐ Cash b ☐ Accrual c ☐ Other (specify) ▶		
2	See page 21 of the instructions and enter the:		
a	Business activity code no. ▶		
b	Business activity ▶		
c	Product or service ▶		
3	At the end of the tax year, did the corporation own, directly or indirectly, 50% or more of the voting stock of a domestic corporation? (For rules of attribution, see section 267(c).)		
	If "Yes," attach a schedule showing: (a) name and employer identification number (EIN), (b) percentage owned, and (c) taxable income or (loss) before NOL and special deductions of such corporation for the tax year ending with or within your tax year.		
4	Is the corporation a subsidiary in an affiliated group or a parent-subsidiary controlled group?		
	If "Yes," enter name and EIN of the parent corporation ▶		
5	At the end of the tax year, did any individual, partnership, corporation, estate, or trust own, directly or indirectly, 50% or more of the corporation's voting stock? (For rules of attribution, see section 267(c).)		
	If "Yes," attach a schedule showing name and identifying number. (Do not include any information already entered in 4 above.) Enter percentage owned ▶		
6	During this tax year, did the corporation pay dividends (other than stock dividends and distributions in exchange for stock) in excess of the corporation's current and accumulated earnings and profits? (See sections 301 and 316.) . . .		
	If "Yes," file **Form 5452,** Corporate Report of Nondividend Distributions.		
	If this is a consolidated return, answer here for the parent corporation and on **Form 851,** Affiliations Schedule, for each subsidiary.		

		Yes	No
7	At any time during the tax year, did one foreign person own, directly or indirectly, at least 25% of (a) the total voting power of all classes of stock of the corporation entitled to vote or (b) the total value of all classes of stock of the corporation?		
	If "Yes," enter: (a) Percentage owned ▶ .... and (b) Owner's country ▶		
c	The corporation may have to file **Form 5472,** Information Return of a 25% Foreign-Owned U.S. Corporation or a Foreign Corporation Engaged in a U.S. Trade or Business. Enter number of Forms 5472 attached ▶		
8	Check this box if the corporation issued publicly offered debt instruments with original issue discount . . ▶ ☐		
	If checked, the corporation may have to file **Form 8281,** Information Return for Publicly Offered Original Issue Discount Instruments.		
9	Enter the amount of tax-exempt interest received or accrued during the tax year ▶ $		
10	Enter the number of shareholders at the end of the tax year (if 75 or fewer) ▶		
11	If the corporation has an NOL for the tax year and is electing to forego the carryback period, check here ▶ ☐		
	If the corporation is filing a consolidated return, the statement required by Regulations section 1.1502-21(b)(3)(i) or (ii) must be attached or the election will not be valid.		
12	Enter the available NOL carryover from prior tax years (Do not reduce it by any deduction on line 29a.) ▶ $		
13	Are the corporation's total receipts (line 1a plus lines 4 through 10 on page 1) for the tax year **and** its total assets at the end of the tax year less than $250,000?		
	If "Yes," the corporation is not required to complete Schedules L, M-1, and M-2 on page 4. Instead, enter the total amount of cash distributions and the book value of property distributions (other than cash) made during the tax year. ▶ $		

Note: If the corporation, at any time during the tax year, had assets or operated a business in a foreign country or U.S. possession, it may be required to attach **Schedule N (Form 1120),** Foreign Operations of U.S. Corporations, to this return. See Schedule N for details.

Form **1120** (2002)

EXHIBIT 3-3 Corporate Tax Return (*continued*)

Form 1120 (2002)   Page **2**

Schedule A   Cost of Goods Sold (see page 14 of instructions)

1	Inventory at beginning of year	1
2	Purchases	2
3	Cost of labor	3
4	Additional section 263A costs (attach schedule)	4
5	Other costs (attach schedule)	5
6	**Total.** Add lines 1 through 5	6
7	Inventory at end of year	7
8	**Cost of goods sold.** Subtract line 7 from line 6. Enter here and on line 2, page 1	8

9a Check all methods used for valuing closing inventory:
- (i) ☐ Cost as described in Regulations section 1.471-3
- (ii) ☐ Lower of cost or market as described in Regulations section 1.471-4
- (iii) ☐ Other (Specify method used and attach explanation.) ▶ ....

b Check if there was a writedown of subnormal goods as described in Regulations section 1.471-2(c) . . . . ▶ ☐

c Check if the LIFO inventory method was adopted this tax year for any goods (if checked, attach Form 970) . . . . . ▶ ☐

d If the LIFO inventory method was used for this tax year, enter percentage (or amounts) of closing inventory computed under LIFO   9d

e If property is produced or acquired for resale, do the rules of section 263A apply to the corporation? . . . . . ☐ Yes ☐ No

f Was there any change in determining quantities, cost, or valuations between opening and closing inventory? If "Yes," attach explanation . . . . . ☐ Yes ☐ No

Schedule C   Dividends and Special Deductions (see instructions beginning on page 15)

		(a) Dividends received	(b) %	(c) Special deductions (a) × (b)
1	Dividends from less-than-20%-owned domestic corporations that are subject to the 70% deduction (other than debt-financed stock)		70	
2	Dividends from 20%-or-more-owned domestic corporations that are subject to the 80% deduction (other than debt-financed stock)		80	
3	Dividends on debt-financed stock of domestic and foreign corporations (section 246A)		instructions	
4	Dividends on certain preferred stock of less-than-20%-owned public utilities		42	
5	Dividends on certain preferred stock of 20%-or-more-owned public utilities		48	
6	Dividends from less-than-20%-owned foreign corporations and certain FSCs that are subject to the 70% deduction		70	
7	Dividends from 20%-or-more-owned foreign corporations and certain FSCs that are subject to the 80% deduction		80	
8	Dividends from wholly owned foreign subsidiaries subject to the 100% deduction (section 245(b))		100	
9	**Total.** Add lines 1 through 8. See page 16 of instructions for limitation			
10	Dividends from domestic corporations received by a small business investment company operating under the Small Business Investment Act of 1958		100	
11	Dividends from certain FSCs that are subject to the 100% deduction (section 245(c)(1))		100	
12	Dividends from affiliated group members subject to the 100% deduction (section 243(a)(3))		100	
13	Other dividends from foreign corporations not included on lines 3, 6, 7, 8, or 11			
14	Income from controlled foreign corporations under subpart F (attach Form(s) 5471)			
15	Foreign dividend gross-up (section 78)			
16	IC-DISC and former DISC dividends not included on lines 1, 2, or 3 (section 246(d))			
17	Other dividends			
18	Deduction for dividends paid on certain preferred stock of public utilities			
19	**Total dividends.** Add lines 1 through 17. Enter here and on line 4, page 1 ▶			
20	**Total special deductions.** Add lines 9, 10, 11, 12, and 18. Enter here and on line 29b, page 1 ▶			

Schedule E   Compensation of Officers (see instructions for line 12, page 1, on page 10 of instructions)

Note: Complete Schedule E only if total receipts (line 1a plus lines 4 through 10 on page 1) are $500,000 or more.

(a) Name of officer	(b) Social security number	(c) Percent of time devoted to business	(d) Common	(e) Preferred	(f) Amount of compensation
1		%	%	%	
		%	%	%	
		%	%	%	
		%	%	%	
		%	%	%	

2 Total compensation of officers

3 Compensation of officers claimed on Schedule A and elsewhere on return

4 Subtract line 3 from line 2. Enter the result here and on line 12, page 1

Form **1120** (2002)

EXHIBIT 3-3 Corporate Tax Return (*continued*)

Limited Partnership Agreement

Agreement of Limited Partnership (the Agreement) of _____ (the Partnership), entered into this day of _____ 20____, by and among _____, Inc. (the General Partner), and each of the persons executing this Agreement (the Limited Partners). Reference herein to "Partners" without designation to "General" or "Limited" includes the General Partner and the Limited Partners except as the context otherwise requires.

PREAMBLE

The Partnership has been organized as a Limited Partnership under the laws of the State of _____ for the purpose of _____.

NOW THEREFORE, in consideration of the promises and mutual covenants hereinafter set forth, the parties hereto do hereby agree and certify as follows:

Article I

Definitions

1.0 Whenever used in this Agreement, the following terms shall have the following meanings:

(a) "Affiliate" shall mean (i) any person directly or indirectly controlling, controlled by or under common control with another person, (ii) a person owning or controlling ten percent (10%) or more of the outstanding voting securities of such other person, (iii) any officer, director, or partner of such person, and (iv) if such other person is an officer, director, or partner, any company for which such person acts in any such capacity.

(b) "Capital Account" means with respect to each partner his Capital Contribution, to the extent contributed, *increased* by: (i) any additional contributions and (ii) his distributive share of Partnership income and gains, and *decreased* by (i) cash and the Partnership's adjusted basis of property distributed to him and (ii) his distributive share of Partnership losses.

(c) "Capital Contribution" means the capital contributed by the General Partner and Limited Partners as set forth in Article IV and as hereinafter contributed to the Partnership by any Partner.

(d) "Cash Flow" means cash from revenues to the Partnership available for distribution after payment of Partnership expenses, advances made by the General Partner and others, and after amounts reserved to meet future contingencies as determined in the sole discretion of the General Partner.

(e) "Closing Date" shall mean the date the offering of the Units is complete.

EXHIBIT 3-4 Limited Partnership Agreement

(f) "Code" shall mean the Internal Revenue Code of 1986, as amended.

(g) "General Partner's Contribution" shall mean the contribution of the General Partner pursuant to Section 4.2 hereof.

(h) "Interest" shall mean the individual interest of each Partner in the Partnership.

(i) "Limited Partners' Contributions" shall mean the aggregate cash contributions of the Limited Partners.

(j) "Original Limited Partner" shall mean the Limited Partner who executed the original Certificate of Limited Partnership of the Partnership.

(k) "P&L Percentage" shall mean the percent of Profits and Losses allocable to each Partner.

(l) "Partnership Property" or "Partnership Properties" shall mean all interest, properties and rights of any type owned or leased by the Partnership.

(m) "Permitted Transfer" shall mean a transfer by a Limited Partner of his Interest to: (i) his spouse, unless legally separated, child, parent, or grandparent; or (ii) a corporation, partnership, trust or other entity, fifty-one percent (51%) of the equity interest of which is owned by such Limited Partner individually or with any of the persons specified in subparagraph (i) hereof.

(n) "Profits and Losses" shall mean the Profits and Losses of the Partnership as reflected on its Federal Partnership Income Tax Return.

(o) "Unit" shall have the same meaning ascribed to such a term in a Private Placement Memorandum of the Partnership and any and all amendments thereto (the Memorandum).

Article II

Organization

2.1 *Addition of Limited Partners.* Promptly following the execution hereof, the General Partner, on behalf of the Partnership, shall execute or cause to be executed an Amended Certificate of Limited Partnership reflecting the withdrawal of the Original Limited Partner and the addition of the Limited Partners to the Partnership and all such other certificates and documents conforming thereto and shall do all such filing, recording, publishing and other acts, as may be necessary or appropriate from time to time to comply with all requirements for the operation of a limited partnership in the State of _____ and all other jurisdictions where the Partnership shall desire to conduct business. The General Partner shall cause the Partnership to comply with all requirements for the qualification of the Partnership as a Limited Partnership (of a partnership in which the Limited Partners have limited liability) in any jurisdiction before the Partnership shall conduct any business in such jurisdiction.

2.2 *Withdrawal of Original Limited Partner.* Upon execution of this Agreement by the Limited Partners, the Original Limited Partner shall withdraw as a Limited Partner and acknowledge that

EXHIBIT 3-4 Limited Partnership Agreement (*continued*)

he shall have no interest in the Partnership as a Limited Partner and no rights to any of the profits, losses, or other distributions of the Partnership from the inception of the Partnership.

2.3 *Partnership Name.* The name of the Partnership shall be _____.

2.4 *Purposes of the Partnership.* The purposes of the Partnership shall be to acquire, own and continue to acquire, own, lease, and deal in or with real and personal property, securities, and investments of every kind, nature and description consistent with the best interests of the Limited Partners.

2.5 *Principal Place of Business and Address.* The principal office of the Partnership shall be maintained as _____, or such other address or addresses as the General Partner may designate by notice to Limited Partners. The Partnership may maintain offices and other facilities from time to time at such locations, within or without the State of _____, as may be deemed necessary or advisable by the General Partner.

2.6 *Term.* The Partnership shall dissolve on December 31, 20____ unless sooner terminated or dissolved under the provisions of this Agreement.

Article III

Operation of the Partnership

3.1 *Powers and Duties of the General Partner.* Except as set forth in Section 3.2 below, the General Partner (if more than one, then such General Partners shall act by any one of the General Partners with the consent of the majority of the General Partners) shall have full, exclusive, and irrevocable authority to manage and control the Partnership and the Partnership Properties, and to do all reasonable and prudent things on behalf of the Partnership including, but not limited to, the following:

(a) To acquire any additional Partnership Property, including all property ancillary thereto and obtain rights to enable the Partnership to renovate, construct, alter, equip, staff, operate, manage, lease, maintain, and promote the Partnership Property, as well as all of the equipment and any other personal or mixed property connected therewith, including, but not limited to, the financial arrangements, development, improvement, maintenance, exchange, trade, or sale of such Property (including, but not limited to, all real or personal property connected therewith) at such price or amount for cash, securities, or other property, and upon such terms as it deems in its absolute discretion to be in the best interests of the Partnership;

(b) To sell or otherwise dispose of the Partnership Property and terminate the Partnership;

(c) To borrow or lend money for operation and/or for any other Partnership purpose, and, if security is required therefor, to mortgage or subject to any other security device any portion of the Partnership Property, to obtain replacements of any mortgage or other security device, and to prepay, in whole or in part, refinance, increase, modify, consolidate, or extend any mortgage or

EXHIBIT 3-4 Limited Partnership Agreement (*continued*)

other security device, all of the foregoing at such terms and in such amounts as it deems, in its absolute discretion, to be in the best interest of the Partnership;

(d)   To enter into contracts with various contractors and subcontractors for the maintenance of the Property;

(e)   To enter into employment or other agreements to provide for the management and operation of the Partnership Property (including the right to contract with affiliates of the General Partner on behalf of the Partnership for such services);

(f)   To place record title to, or the right to use, Partnership assets in the name or names of a nominee or nominees for any purpose convenient or beneficial to the Partnership;

(g)   To acquire and enter into any contract of insurance that the General Partner deems necessary and proper for the protection of the Partnership, for the conservation of its assets, or for any other purpose, convenience, or benefit of the Partnership;

(h)   To employ persons in the operation and management of the Partnership business, including, but not limited to, supervisory managing agents, consultants, insurance brokers, and loan brokers on such terms and for such compensation as the General Partner shall determine,

(i)   To employ attorneys and accountants to represent the Partnership in connection with Partnership business;

(j)   To pay or not pay rentals and other payments to lessors;

(k)   To sell, trade, release, surrender, or abandon any or all of the Partnership Properties, or any portion thereof, or other assets of the Partnership;

(l)   To settle claims, prosecute, defend, and settle and handle all matters with governmental agencies;

(m)   To purchase or acquire, lease, construct, and/or operate equipment and any other type of tangible, real or personal property;

(n)   To open bank accounts for the partnership and to designate and change signatories on such accounts;

(o)   To invest the funds of the Partnership in certificates of deposit or evidence of debt of the United States of America or any state, or commonwealth thereof, or any instrumentality of either;

(p)   To enter into any other partnership agreement whether general or limited, or any joint venture or other similar agreement; and

(q)   Without in any manner being limited by the foregoing, to execute any and all other agreements, conveyances, and other documents and to take any and all other action which the General Partner in its sole discretion deems to be necessary, useful, or convenient in connection with the Partnership Properties or business.

In accomplishing all of the foregoing, the General Partner may, in its sole discretion, but shall not be required to, use its own personnel, properties, and equipment, and may employ on a temporary or continuing basis outside accountants, attorneys, brokers, consultants, and others on such terms as he deems advisable. Any or all of the Partnership Properties, and any or all of the

EXHIBIT 3-4   Limited Partnership Agreement (*continued*)

other Partnership assets, may be held from time to time, at the General Partner's sole discretion, in the name of the General Partner, the Partnership, or one or more nominees; and any and all of the powers of the General Partner may be exercised from time to time, at the General Partner's sole discretion, in the name of any one or more of the foregoing.

3.2 *Limitations of the Powers of the General Partner.* The General Partner may not act for or bind the Partnership without the prior consent of the holders of fifty-one percent (51%) of Limited Partnership Interests on the following matters:

(i) Amendment of the Partnership Agreement (except as set forth in Section 12.4); or

(ii) A change in the general character or nature of the Partnership's business.

3.3 *Powers and Liabilities of the Limited Partners.* No Limited Partner shall have any personal liability or obligation for any liability or obligation of the Partnership or be required to lend or advance funds to the Partnership for any purpose. No Limited Partner shall be responsible for the obligations of any other Limited Partner. No Limited Partner shall take part in the management of the business of the Partnership or transact any business for the Partnership, and no Limited Partner shall have power to sign for or bind the Partnership. No Limited Partner shall have a drawing account. No Limited Partner shall be entitled to the return of his capital contribution, except to the extent, if any, that distributions are deemed to be made to such Limited Partner otherwise than out of Profits pursuant to this Agreement. No Limited Partner shall receive any interest on his capital account. Upon the consent of fifty-one percent (51%) in interest of the Limited Partners, the Limited Partners shall have a right to call a meeting of the Partnership upon written notice to all of the Partners of the time, date, and place of such meeting. Upon the written request of twenty-five percent (25%) in interest of the nonaffiliated Limited Partners, the General Partner shall promptly call an informational meeting of the Partnership upon written notice to all of the Partners of the time, date, and place of such meeting.

3.4 *Exculpation and Indemnification of the General Partner.* (a) The Limited Partners recognize that there are substantial risks involved in the Partnership's business. The General Partner is willing to continue to serve as General Partner only because the Limited Partners hereby accept the speculative character of the Partnership business and the uncertainties and hazards which may be involved, and only because the Limited Partners hereby agree, that despite the broad authority granted to the General Partner by Section 3.1, the General Partner shall have no liability to the Partnership or to the Limited Partners because of the failure of the General Partner to act as a prudent operator, or based upon errors in judgment, negligence, or other fault of the General Partner in connection with its management of the Partnership, so long as the General Partner is acting in good faith. Accordingly, the Limited Partners, for themselves, their heirs, distributees, legal representatives, successors, and assigns, covenant not to assert or attempt to assert any claim or liability as against the General Partner for any reason whatsoever except for gross negligence, fraud, bad faith, or willful misconduct in connection with the operation of the Partnership. It shall be deemed conclusively established that the General Partner is acting in good faith with respect to

EXHIBIT 3-4 Limited Partnership Agreement (*continued*)

action taken by him on the advice of the independent accountants, legal counsel, or independent consultants of the partnership.

(b)   In the event of any action, suit, or other legal proceeding, including arbitration, instituted or threatened against the General Partner or in which he (or if more than one, any of them) may be a party, whether such suit, action, or proceeding is brought on behalf of third parties or Limited Partners, individually or as a class, or in a derivative or representative capacity, the General Partner shall have the right to obtain legal counsel and other expert counsel at the expense of the Partnership and to defend or participate in any such suit, action, or proceeding at the expense of the Partnership, and he shall be reimbursed, indemnified against, and saved harmless by the Partnership for and with respect to any liabilities, costs, and expenses incurred in connection therewith. It is understood and agreed that the reimbursement and indemnification herein provided for shall include and extend to any suit, action, or proceeding based upon a claim of misrepresentation or omission to reveal any act of substance in any document pursuant to which the Limited Partnership Interests have been offered. It is expressly agreed that any claim of the nature referred to in the preceding sentences is and shall be subject to the provisions of this Subsection 3.4(b), other provisions of this Section, and other provisions of this Agreement relating to the nonliability, reimbursement, and indemnification of the General Partner. This Agreement is part of the consideration inducing the General Partner to accept the Limited Partners as members of the Partnership. The foregoing provisions for the indemnification and reimbursement of the General Partner shall apply in every case except in which it is affirmative determined in any proceeding that the General Partner shall not be entitled to have indemnification or reimbursement by reason of his having been guilty of gross negligence, fraud, bad faith, or willful misconduct.

(c)   Nothing herein shall be deemed to constitute a representation or warranty by the General Partner with respect to the title to or value of any Partnership Property or with respect to the existence or nonexistence of any contracts or other encumbrances with regard thereto, whether as against its own acts in the normal course of business or otherwise.

3.5   *Power of Attorney*. (a) Each Limited Partner by the execution of this Agreement does irrevocably constitute and appoint the General Partner or any one of them, if more than one, with full power of substitution, as his true and lawful attorney in his name, place, and stead to execute, acknowledge, deliver, file, and record all documents in connection with the Partnership, including but not limited to (i) the original Certificate of Limited Partnership and all amendments thereto required by law or the provisions of this Agreement, (ii) all certificates and other instruments necessary to qualify or continue the Partnership as a limited partnership or partnership wherein the Limited Partners have limited liability in the states or provinces where the partnership may be doing its business, (iii) all instruments necessary to effect a change or modification of the Partnership in accordance with this Agreement, (iv) all conveyances and other instruments necessary to effect the dissolution and termination of the Partnership, and (v) all election under

EXHIBIT 3-4 Limited Partnership Agreement (*continued*)

the Internal Revenue Code governing the taxation of the Partnership. Each Limited Partner agrees to be bound by any representations of the attorney-in-fact under this power of attorney, and hereby ratifies and confirms all acts which the said attorney-in-fact may take as attorney-in-fact hereunder in all respects as though performed by the Limited Partner.

(b)   The power of attorney granted herein shall be deemed to be coupled with an interest and shall be irrevocable and survive the death of a Limited Partner. In the event of any conflict between this Agreement and any instruments filed by such attorney-in-fact pursuant to the power of attorney granted in this Section, this Agreement shall control, and no power granted herein shall be used to create any personal liabilities on the part of the Limited Partners.

(c)   By virtue of the power of attorney granted herein, the General Partner, or any one of them, if more than one, shall execute the Certificate of Limited Partnership and any amendments thereto by listing all of the Limited Partners and executing any instrument with the signature of the General Partner(s) acting as attorney-in-fact for all of them. Each Limited Partner agrees to execute with acknowledgement of affidavit, if required, any further documents and writings which may be necessary to effectively grant the foregoing power of attorney to the General Partner(s).

Article IV

Capitalization and Capital Contribution

4.1   *Capitalization.* The total initial capital of the Partnership shall be a minimum of _____ ($_____) and a maximum of _____ ($_____), exclusive of any capital contribution by the General Partner.

4.2   *General Partner's Contribution.* The General Partner has contributed _____ ($_____) in cash to the capital of the Partnership and will be reimbursed at Closing for amounts that he has expended on behalf of the Partnership prior to Closing.

4.3   *Limited Partner's Contribution.* Each Limited Partner has made the contribution of capital to the Partnership in the amount set forth on Schedule A annexed hereto. Subscription for a Unit shall be made upon the execution hereof by the payment of _____ ($_____) in cash on subscription.

4.4   *Capital Accounts.* A separate Capital Account shall be maintained for each Partner and shall be credited with his Capital Contribution and his allocable share of all revenues, income, or gain and shall be debited with his allocable share of costs, expenses, deductions, and losses of the Partnership and any distributions made to him.

EXHIBIT 3-4 Limited Partnership Agreement (*continued*)

Article V

Fees and Compensation

In consideration of various services to be rendered to the Partnership by the General Partner, the General Partner will receive the compensation and fees as described in the Memorandum.

In furtherance of the provisions of Article III hereof, the General Partner may contract with any person, firm, or corporation (whether or not affiliated with the General Partner) for fair value and at reasonable competitive rates of compensation, for the performance of any and all services which may at any time be necessary, proper, convenient, or advisable to carry on the business of the Partnership.

Article VI

Distribution of Proceeds from Operations and Profit and Loss Allocations

6.1 *Distribution of Cash Flow.* Subject to the right of the General Partner to retain all or any portion of the annual cash flow for the anticipated needs of the Partnership, the net annual cash flow of the Partnership available for distribution from operations will be allocated ninety-nine percent (99%) to the Limited Partners (pro rata among them in the proportion that each Unit owned by a Limited Partner bears to the total number of Units owned by all Limited Partners) and one percent (1%) to the General Partner, until such time as the Limited Partners shall have received their capital contributions (Payout) and thereafter, fifty percent (50%) to the Limited Partners, pro rata, and fifty percent (50%) to the General Partner.

6.2 *Allocation of Profits and Losses.* Profits and losses of the Partnership from operation will be allocated ninety-nine percent (99%) to the Limited Partners (pro rata among them in proportion that each Unit owned by a Limited Partner bears to the total number of Units owned by all Limited Partners) and one percent (1%) to the General Partner until Payout. After Payout, profits and losses will be allocated fifty percent (50%) to the Limited Partners, pro rata, and fifty percent (50%) to the General Partner.

6.3 *Allocation of Income for Certain Tax Purposes.* (a) Anything contained in this Agreement to the contrary notwithstanding, in the event an allocation of income in any calendar year pursuant to Section 6.2 above would cause the General Partner to have a positive Capital Account at the end of such year at a time when the Limited Partners have negative Capital Accounts, the amount of such income which would have been allocated to the General Partner pursuant to Section 6.2 in excess of the aggregate negative Capital Accounts of the Limited Partners shall instead be allocated to the Capital Accounts of the Limited Partners on a pro rata basis. For purposes of computing what a Partner's Capital Account would be at the end of a year, any cash available for distribution at such

EXHIBIT 3-4 Limited Partnership Agreement (*continued*)

time which is intended to be distributed shall be deemed to have been distributed to such Partner on the last day of such year.

(b)   Anything contained in this Agreement to the contrary notwithstanding, a Partner or Partners with deficit Capital Account balances resulting, in whole or in part, from an interest or other expense accrual, shall be allocated income resulting from the forgiveness of indebtedness of such deficit Capital Account balances no later than the time at which the accrual is reduced below the sum of such deficit Capital Account balances.

(c)   If any Partner is, for income tax purposes, allocated additional income or denied a loss because of Section 6.3(b) above, a compensating allocation shall be made, for income tax purposes, at the first time such an allocation would be permissible thereunder.

Article VII

Allocation of Profits and Losses on a Sale or Other Taxable Disposition of
Partnership Property

7.1   Any gain realized by the Partnership in connection with the sale or other taxable disposition of the Partnership Property shall be allocated to the Partners in the following order of priority:

(a)   If any Partner has a negative Capital Account, any gain from the sale or other disposition of the Partnership Property shall be allocated to such Partners in the amount of their respective negative account balances, until the balance of each such Partner's Capital Account is equal to zero; and

(b)   Any remaining gains shall be allocated ninety-nine percent (99%) to the Limited Partners, pro rata, and one percent (1%) to the General Partner until Payout, and thereafter fifty percent (50%) to the Limited Partners, pro rata, and fifty percent (50%) to the General Partner.

7.2   Any loss realized by the Partnership in connection with the sale or other taxable disposition of the Partnership Property shall be allocated to the Partners in the following order of priority:

(a)   If any of the Partners has a positive Capital Account, any loss from the sale or other disposition of the Partnership Property shall be allocated to such Partners in the amount of their respective positive account balances, until the balance of each such Partner's Capital Account is equal to zero; and

(b)   Any remaining losses shall be allocated to the Partners as set forth in Section 7.1(b) above.

7.3   It is the intention of the General Partner that the allocation set forth herein have "substantial economic effect" within the meaning of regulations promulgated under Internal Revenue Code Section 704. In the event such allocations are deemed by the Internal Revenue

EXHIBIT 3-4 Limited Partnership Agreement (*continued*)

Service or the courts not to have substantial economic effect, the General Partner reserves the right to modify allocations of profits and losses, after consulting with counsel, to achieve substantial economic effect. Nothing herein shall be construed to require the General Partner to so modify the allocation as set forth herein.

Article VIII

Limited Partners' Covenants and Representation with Respect to Securities Act

8.1 *Investment Representations.* Each of the Limited Partners, by signing this Agreement, represents and warrants to the General Partner and to the Partnership that he (a) is acquiring his Interest in the partnership for his own personal account for investment purposes only and without any intention of selling or distributing all or any part of the same; (b) has no reason to anticipate any change in personal circumstances, financial or otherwise, which would cause him to sell or distribute, or necessitate or require any sale or distribution of such Interest; (c) is familiar with the nature of and risks attending investments in securities and the particular financial, legal, and tax implications of the business to be conducted by the Partnership, and has determined on his own or on the basis of consultation with his own financial and tax advisors that the purchase of such Interest is consistent with his own investment objectives and income prospects; (d) has received a copy of the Private Placement Memorandum, to which a copy of this Agreement is attached as Exhibit A, and has had access to any and all information concerning the Partnership which he and his financial, tax, and legal advisors requested or considered necessary to make proper evaluation of this investment; (e) is aware that no trading market for Interests in the Partnership will exist at any time and that his Interest will at no time be freely transferable or be transferable with potential adverse tax consequences; and (f) is aware that there is a substantial risk that the federal partnership tax returns will be audited by the Internal Revenue Service and that, upon such audit, a part of the deductions allocated to the Limited Partners could be disallowed, thereby reducing the tax benefits of investing in the Partnership.

8.2 *Covenant Against Resale.* Each of the Limited Partners agrees hereby that he will, in no event, sell or distribute his Interest in the Partnership or any portion thereof unless, in the opinion of counsel to the Partnership, such Interest may be legally sold or distributed without registration under the Securities Act of 1933, as amended, or registration or qualification under then applicable state or federal statutes, or such Interest shall have been so registered or qualified and an appropriate prospectus shall then be in effect. *Notwithstanding the foregoing, no Limited Partner will be permitted to sell, distribute, or otherwise transfer his Interest in the Partnership or any portion thereof without the written consent of the General Partner (except as otherwise provided in Paragraph 9.1(b) below), the granting of which consent is in the absolute discretion of the General Partner.*

EXHIBIT 3-4 Limited Partnership Agreement (*continued*)

8.3 *Reliance on Private Offering Exemption.* Each of the Limited Partners represents and warrants hereby that he is fully aware that his Interest in the Partnership is being issued and sold to him by the Partnership in reliance upon the exemption provided for by Section 4(2) of the Securities Act of 1933, as amended, and Regulation D promulgated under such Act, and exemptions available under state securities laws, on the grounds that no public offering is involved, and upon the representations1 warranties, and agreements set forth in this Article VIII.

Article IX

Transfer of Partnership Interests

9.1 *Limited Partnership Interest.* (a) No transfer of all or any part of a Limited Partner's Interest (including a transferee by death or operation of law and including a transferee in a Permitted Transfer) shall be admitted to the Partnership as a Limited Partner without the written consent of the General Partner, which consent may be withheld in the complete discretion of the General Partner. In no event shall the General Partner consent to the admission of the transferee as a Limited Partner unless the transferee executes this Agreement and such other instruments as may be required by law, or as the General Partner shall deem necessary or desirable to confirm the undertaking of such transferee to: (i) be bound by all the terms and provisions of this Agreement; and (ii) pay all reasonable expenses incurred by the Partnership in conjunction with the transfer, including, but not limited to, the cost of preparation, filing, and publishing such amendments to the Certificate as may be required by law of such other instruments as the General Partner may deem necessary and desirable.

A sale, assignment, or transfer of a Limited Partner's Interest will be recognized by the Partnership when it has received written notice of such sale or assignment, signed by both parties, containing the purchaser's or assignee's acceptance of the terms of the Partnership Agreement and a representation by the parties that the sale or assignment was lawful. Such sale or assignment will be recognized as of the date of such notice, except that if such date is more than thirty (30) days prior to the time of filing of such notice, such sale or assignment will be recognized as of the time the notice was filed with the Partnership. For purposes of allocating Profits and Losses, the assignee will be treated as having become a Limited Partner as of the date of which the sale, assignment, or transfer was recognized by the Partnership.

(b) Except for: (i) a Permitted Transfer and/or transfer by operation of law other than transfers in excess of the "forty" percent (40%) limitation" (see subsection (c) below); or (ii) a transfer by gift, bequest, or inheritance, no Limited Partner may transfer all or any part of his Interest without first giving written notice of the proposed transfer to the General Partner (setting forth the terms thereof and the name and address of the proposed transferee) and obtaining the

EXHIBIT 3-4 Limited Partnership Agreement (*continued*)

written consent of the General Partner to such transfer. Such consent shall be within the complete discretion of the General Partner and subject to such conditions, if any, as it shall determine.

(c)   Anything else to the contrary contained herein notwithstanding:

(i)   in any period of twelve (12) consecutive months, no transfer of an Interest may be made which would result in increasing the aggregate Profit and Loss Percentages of Partnership Interests previously transferred in such period above forty percent (40%). This limitation is herein referred to as the "forty percent (40%) limitation";

(ii)   a Permitted Transfer is fully subject to the forty percent (40%) limitation;

(iii)   subparagraph (i) hereof shall not apply to a transfer by gift, bequest, or inheritance, or a transfer to the Partnership, and for the purposes of the forty percent (40%) limitation, any such transfer shall not be treated as such;

(iv)   if, after the forty percent (40%) limitation is reached in any consecutive twelve- (12-) month period, a transfer of a Partnership Interest would otherwise take place by operation of law (but not including any transfer referred to in subparagraph (ii) hereof), then such Partnership Interest shall be deemed sold by the transferor to the Partnership immediately prior to such transfer for a price equal to the fair market value of such interest on the date of transfer. The price shall be paid within ninety (90) days after the date of the sale out of the assets of the Partnership and the General Partner. If the Partnership and the transferor do not agree upon the fair market value of the Partnership Interest, then the purchase price shall be determined in accordance with Section 9.3. The purchase price shall be paid by the Partnership out of its assets in cash within ten (10) days after such determination.

9.2   *Events Requiring Sale of Partnership Interest.* (a) The Interest of a Limited Partner shall be deemed offered for sale to a person designated by the General Partner upon the happening of any of the following events:

(i)   a petition in bankruptcy having been filed by or against a Limited Partner and not discharged within ninety (90) days from the date of such filing; or

(ii)   a receiver or committee having been appointed to manage a Limited Partner's property; or

(iii)   a creditor of a Limited Partner having attached his Interest and such attachment not being discharged or vacated within ninety (90) days from the date it became effective.

The General Partner shall have ninety (90) days after the occurrence of any of the foregoing within which to accept such offer, designate such a purchaser (including the General Partner), and transmit written notice thereof to such Limited Partner. If the General Partner fails to make such designation within ninety (90) days as aforesaid, the offer shall be deemed withdrawn. The purchase price for such Interest shall be its appraised value as determined in accordance with Section 9.3. The purchaser shall pay over to the selling Limited Partner the purchase price in cash within ten (10) days after such determination. Upon payment of the purchase price to the selling Limited Partner, his Interest shall be deemed transferred to the aforesaid designated person.

EXHIBIT 3-4 Limited Partnership Agreement (*continued*)

(b)   If any of the events described in Subsection 10.1(a)(v) should occur to the General Partner, or any one of them if more than one, and the Partnership shall not thereafter be dissolved but shall continue as a successor Limited Partnership with a successor General Partner, then upon the happening of any of such events the Interest of such General Partner shall be deemed offered for sale to the successor General Partner at its appraised value determined in accordance with Section 9.3 (except in the case of a voluntary withdrawal by a General Partner, in which event the value shall be determined by the withdrawing General Partner and the proposed successor General Partner, as selected by the withdrawing General Partner). The successor General Partner shall not become a General Partner of the Partnership until such former General Partner's Interest has been paid for in full in cash.

9.3   *Appraisal.* For the purpose of this Agreement, the appraised value of an Interest shall be the average of the values determined by three appraisers who are experts in evaluating property similar to the Partnership Property selected at the request of the General Partner. The appraisal made by such appraisers shall be binding and conclusive as between the selling Partner or Partners and the persons purchasing such Interest. The cost of such appraisal shall be borne equally by the selling and purchasing parties, and by each set of parties, among themselves, in proportion to their respective shares.

9.4   *Death, Bankruptcy, Incompetence, or Dissolution of a Limited Partner.*

(a)   Upon the death, bankruptcy, or legal incompetency of an individual Limited Partner, his legally authorized personal representative shall have all of the rights of a Limited Partner for the purpose of settling or managing his estate, and shall have such power as the decedent, bankrupt, or incompetent possessed to make an assignment of his Interest in the Partnership in accordance with the terms hereof and to join with such assignee in making application to substitute such assignee as a Limited Partner.

(b)   Upon bankruptcy, insolvency, dissolution, or other cessation to exist as a legal entity of any Limited Partner which is not an individual, the authorized representative of such entity shall have all of the rights of the Limited Partner for the purpose of effecting the orderly winding up and disposition of the business of such entity, and such power as such entity possessed to make an assignment of its Interest in the Partnership in accordance with the terms hereof and to join with such assignee in making application to substitute such assignee as a Limited Partner.

9.5   *Voluntary Withdrawal or Transfer by a General Partner.* (a) A General Partner may resign as General Partner at any time, but only upon compliance with the following procedures:

(i)   The General Partner shall give notification to all Limited Partners that he proposes to withdraw and that he proposes that there be substituted in his place a person designated and described in such notification.

(ii)   Enclosed with such notification shall be (a) an opinion of counsel to the Partnership that the proposed General Partner qualifies to serve as a General Partner under federal law, and (b) a certificate, duly executed by or on behalf of such proposed successor General Partner, to the effect

EXHIBIT 3-4 Limited Partnership Agreement (*continued*)

that he is experienced in performing (or employs sufficient personnel who are experienced in performing) functions of the type then being performed by the resigning General Partner.

(iii)   The consent of the remaining General Partner and the holders of at least fifty-one percent (51%) in interest of the Limited Partner shall be required for the appointment of the proposed successor General Partner pursuant to this Section 9.5(a). If the proposed successor General Partner shall not receive such consent within sixty (60) days after the date of the withdrawing General Partner's notification, then, at the sole option of the General Partner seeking to withdraw, the Partnership may be terminated and dissolved and its assets liquidated in accordance with Article VIII of this Agreement.

(iv)   The General Partner who has withdrawn pursuant to this Section shall cooperate fully with the successor General Partner so that the responsibilities of such withdrawn General Partner may be transferred to such successor General Partner with as little disruption of the Partnership's business and affairs as is practicable.

(b)   Except as part of a transfer to a successor General Partner pursuant to Section 9.5(a), the General Partner shall not have the right to retire or to transfer or assign his General Partner's Interest.

9.6   *Removal of a General Partner.* (a) A General Partner may be removed as General Partner only without his consent or the consent of the other General Partners only for cause upon the consent of 51% in Interest of the Limited Partners, such removal to be effective upon the service of written notice upon the General Partner to be removed by posting said notice in the United States mails. Upon such removal, the Partnership shall continue and the remaining General Partners shall continue the Partnership. If all the General Partners are removed, then the Partnership shall be dissolved unless 51% in Interest of the Limited Partners vote to continue the Partnership as a successor limited partnership and appoint a successor General Partner who (i) in the opinion of counsel to the Partnership qualifies to serve as General Partner under federal law, and (ii) agrees to purchase the Interest of the other General Partners in accordance with Sections 9.2(b) and 9.3 hereof.

(b)   Any successor General Partner appointed by the Limited Partners to replace the General Partner shall, beginning on the effective date of such replacement, have the same rights and obligations under this Agreement as the General Partner would have had subsequent to such date if the General Partner continued to act as General Partner.

9.7   *Death, Retirement, Bankruptcy, Legal Incapacity, etc. of a General Partner.* Upon the death, retirement, or legal incapacity of a General Partner, or the filing by or against a General Partner of a petition in bankruptcy, the adjudication of the General Partner as a bankrupt, or the making by the General Partner of an assignment for the benefit of creditors, the remaining General Partners shall continue the Partnership unless all of the General Partners are subject to the foregoing events, in which case the Partnership shall terminate unless fifty-one percent (51%) in Interest of the Limited Partners (or one hundred percent (100%) in the case of the death, retirement, or

EXHIBIT 3-4 Limited Partnership Agreement (*continued*)

insanity of a General Partner) vote to continue the Partnership as a successor Limited Partnership and appoint a successor General Partner, who (i) in the opinion of counsel to the Partnership qualifies to serve as General Partner under federal law, and (ii) agrees to purchase the Interest of the General Partner in accordance with Sections 9.2(b) and 9.3 hereof.

9.8 *Admission of a Successor General Partner.* The admission of a successor General Partner shall be effective only if the Interests of the Limited Partners shall not be affected by the admission of such successor General Partner.

9.9 *Liability and Rights of Replaced General Partner.* Any General Partner who shall be replaced as General Partner shall remain liable for his portion of any obligation and liabilities incurred by him as General Partner prior to the time such replacement shall have become effective. He shall be free of any obligation or liability incurred on account of the activities of the Partnership from and after such time. Such replacement shall not affect any rights of the General Partner which shall mature prior to the effective date of such replacement.

Article X

Dissolution, Liquidation, and Termination

10.1 *Dissolution.* (a) The Partnership shall be dissolved upon the earliest of:

(i) the expiration of its term as provided in this Agreement;

(ii) the sale of all or substantially all of the Partnership Property;

(iii) the occurrence of any event which causes the dissolution of a limited partnership under the laws of the State of _____

(iv) the written election of Limited Partners owning eighty percent (80%) of the Limited Partnership Interests; or

(v) except as otherwise provided herein, the withdrawal or removal of, the death, retirement, or legal incapacity of, or the filing of a petition in bankruptcy, the adjudication as a bankrupt, or the making of an assignment for the benefit of creditors by the last remaining General Partner, unless fifty-one percent (51%) in Interest of the Limited Partners (or one hundred percent (100%) in the case of the death, retirement, or legal incapacity of the General Partner) appoint a successor General Partner and vote to continue the Partnership as a successor Limited Partnership.

(b) The Partnership shall not be dissolved upon the death of a Limited Partner.

(c) In the event of such dissolution, the assets of the Partnership shall be liquidated and the proceeds thereof distributed in accordance with Section 7.1 hereof.

10.2 *Liquidating Trustee.* Upon the dissolution of the Partnership, the liquidating trustee (which shall be those General Partners which are not subject to any of the events set forth in subparagraph 10.1(a)(v), or, in the event all General Partners are subject to such events, a trustee appointed by the Limited Partners representing a majority in interest of the profit and loss

EXHIBIT 3-4 Limited Partnership Agreement (*continued*)

percentages of the Limited Partners), shall proceed diligently to wind up the affairs of the Partnership and distribute its assets in accordance with Section 7.1 hereof. All saleable assets of the Partnership may be sold in connection with any liquidation at public or private sale, at such price and upon such terms as the liquidating trustee in his sole discretion may deem advisable. Any Partner and any partnership, Corporation, or other firm in which any Partner is in any way interested may purchase assets at such sale. Distributions of Partnership assets may be made in cash or in kind, in the sole and absolute discretion of the liquidating trustee. The liquidating trustee shall make a proper accounting to each Limited Partner of his Capital Account and of the net profit or loss of the Partnership from the date of the last previous accounting to the date of dissolution.

Article XI

Accounting, Records, Reports, and Taxes

11.1 *Fiscal Year and Reports.* The fiscal year of the Partnership for both accounting and federal income tax purposes shall be the calendar year. At all times during the continuance of the Partnership, the General Partner shall keep or cause to be kept full and faithful books of account in which shall be entered fully and accurately each transaction of the Partnership. All of the books of account shall be open to the inspection and examination of the Limited Partners or their duly authorized representatives upon reasonable notice during normal business hours. Annual financial statement of the Partnership shall be transmitted by the General Partner to each Limited Partner. The General Partner shall further transmit to each Limited Partner annually, within a reasonable time after the end of each calendar year (but in no event later than seventy-five (75) days after the end of the calendar year or as soon as practicable thereafter), a report setting forth the Limited Partner's share of the Partnership's Profits or Losses for each such year, and such Limited Partner's allocation of cash receipts. The reports and statements delivered in accordance herewith may be changed from time to time to cure errors or omission and to give effect to any retroactive costs or adjustments. All costs and expenses incurred in connection with such reports and statements shall constitute expenses of Partnership operation.

11.2 *Income Tax Elections.* (a) No elections shall be made by the Partnership, the General Partner or any Limited Partner to be excluded from the application of the provision of Subchapter K of Chapter I of Subtitle A of the Code or from the application of any similar provisions of state tax laws.

All other elections required or permitted under the Code shall be made by the General Partner in such manner as will, in the opinion of the Partnership's accountants, be most advantageous to a majority in Interest of the Limited Partners.

EXHIBIT 3-4 Limited Partnership Agreement (*continued*)

11.3   *Tax Matters Partner.* The General Partner shall be designated the tax matters partner of the Partnership pursuant to Section 6231(7) of the Internal Revenue Code.

Article XII

General

12.1   *Notices.* Any notice, communication, or consent required or permitted to be given by any provision of this Agreement shall, except as otherwise expressly provided herein, be deemed to have been sufficiently given or served for any purpose only if in writing, delivered personally, or sent by registered mail, postage and charges prepaid, or by standard prepaid telegram.

12.2   *Further Assurances.* Each of the Partners agrees hereafter to execute, acknowledge, deliver, file, record, and publish such further certificates, instruments, agreements and other documents and to take all such further actions as may be required by law or deemed by the General Partner to be necessary or useful in furtherance of the Partnership's purposes and the objectives and intentions underlying this Agreement and not inconsistent with the terms hereof.

12.3   *Banking.* All funds shall be deposited in the Partnership's name in such checking accounts as shall be designated by the General Partner. All withdrawals therefrom shall be made upon checks signed by the General Partner.

12.4   *Amendment of Certificate of Limited Partnership.* The General Partner may amend the Certificate of Limited Partnership and the Agreement when any one of the following events occur: (a) there is a change in the name of the Partnership, or the amount of character of the contribution of any Limited Partner; (b) a person is substituted as a Limited Partner; or (c) an additional Limited Partner is admitted.

12.5   This Agreement may not be modified or amended in any manner whatsoever except with the written consent of the General Partner and the written consent of Limited Partners whose Profit and Loss percentages at that time are sixty-six and two-thirds percent (66-2/3%) of the total Profit and Loss Percentages of all Limited Partners.

12.6   Any vote of the Limited Partners on any matters upon which Limited Partners are entitled to vote hereunder may be accomplished at a meeting of Limited Partners called for such purposes by the General Partner or by the nonpromoted, nonaffiliated Limited Partners whose Profit and Loss Percentages at that time exceed fifty-one percent (51%) of the total Profit and Loss Percentages of all such Limited Partners, upon not less than ten (10) days' prior notice or, in lieu of a meeting, by the written consent of the required percentage of Limited Partners.

12.7   *Access to Records.* The Limited Partners and their designated representatives shall be permitted access to all records of the Partnership at the office of the Partnership during reasonable hours. The Partnership records shall include a list of the names and addresses of the Limited Partners.

EXHIBIT 3-4 Limited Partnership Agreement (*continued*)

12.8 *Miscellaneous.* (a) Except as otherwise expressly provided herein, the headings in this Agreement are inserted for convenience of reference only and are in no way intended to describe, interpret, define, or limit the scope, extent, or intent of this Agreement or any provision hereof.

(b)   Every provision of this Agreement is intended to be severable. If any term or provision hereof is illegal or invalid for any reason whatsoever, such illegality or invalidity shall not affect the validity of the remainder of this Agreement.

(c)   This Agreement, and the application and interpretation hereof, shall be governed exclusively by the terms hereof and by the laws of the State of _____.

(d)   The rights and remedies provided by this Agreement are cumulative, and the use of any one right or remedy by any party shall not preclude or waive its right to pursue any or all other remedies. Such rights and remedies are given in addition to any other rights the parties may have by law, statute, ordinance, or otherwise.

(e)   This Agreement may be executed in any number of counterparts with the same effect as if the parties had all signed the same instrument. All counterparts shall be construed together and shall constitute one Agreement. Limited Partners may become parties to this Agreement by executing and delivering to the General Partner a signature page hereto in the form approved by the General Partner.

(f)   Time is of the essence hereof.

(g)   Each and all of the covenants, terms, provisions and agreements therein contained shall be binding upon and inure to the benefit of each party and, to the extent permitted by this Agreement, the respective successors and assigns of the parties.

(h)   No person, firm, or corporation dealing with the Partnership shall be required to inquire into the authority of the General Partner to take any action or to make any decision.

(i)   This instrument incorporates the entire agreement between the parties hereto, regardless of anything to the contrary contained in any certificate of limited partnership or other instrument or notice purporting to summarize the terms hereof, whether or not the same shall be recorded or published.

(j)   The General Partner shall prepare or cause to be prepared and shall file on or before the due date (or any extension thereof) any federal, state, or local tax returns required to be filed by the Partnership. The General Partner shall cause the Partnership to pay any taxes payable by the Partnership.

IN WITNESS WHEREOF, the undersigned have executed this Agreement as of the day and year first above written.

General Partner _____

Limited Partner _____

EXHIBIT 3-4 Limited Partnership Agreement (*continued*)

*   234-Certificate of Incorporation.
Business Corporation Law §402.§-6

Blumberg Excelsior, Publisher, NYC 10013
www.blumberg.com

Certificate of Incorporation of

under Section 402 of the Business Corporation Law

IT IS HEREBY CERTIFIED THAT:

(1)   The name of the corporation is

(2)   The purpose or purposes for which this corporation is formed, are as follows, to wit:
To engage in any lawful act or activity for which corporations may be organized under the Business
Corporation Law. The corporation is not formed to engage in any act or activity requiring the consent or
approval of any state official, department, board, agency or other body.*

The corporation, in furtherance of its corporate purposes above set forth, shall have all of the powers enumerated in
Section 202 of the Business Corporation Law, subject to any limitations provided in the Business Corporation Law or any
other statute of the State of New York.

*If specific consent or approval is required delete this paragraph, insert specific purposes and obtain consent or approval prior to filing..

EXHIBIT 3-5 Certificate of Incorporation

(3)   The office of the corporation is to be located in the County of
State of New York.

(4)   The aggregate number of shares which the corporation shall have the authority to issue and a statement of the par
value of each share or a statement that the shares are without par value are

(5)   The Secretary of State is designated as agent of the corporation upon whom process against it may be served. The
post office address to which the Secretary of State shall mail a copy of any process against the corporation served
upon the Secretary of State is

(6)   A director of the corporation shall not be liable to the corporation or its shareholders for damages for any breach of
duty in such capacity except for

(i) liability if a judgment or other final adjudication adverse to a director establishes that his or her acts or
omissions were in bad faith or involved intentional misconduct or a knowing violation of law or that the director
personally gained in fact a financial profit or other advantage to which he or she was not legally entitled or that the
director's acts violated BCL § 7 19, or

(ii) liability for any act or omission prior to the adoption of this provision.

The undersigned incorporator, or each of them if there are more than one, is of the age of eighteen years or over.

IN WITNESS WHEREOF, this certificate has been subscribed on _____ by the undersigned
incorporator(s).

_____	_____
Type name of Incorporator	Signature
_____	
Address	
_____	_____
Type name of Incorporator	Signature
_____	
Address	
_____	_____
Type name of Incorporator	Signature
_____	
Address	

*Publisher's Note: If you wish to grant preemptive rights to shareholders, you may type the following in the blank space:

(7)   The holders of any of the corporation's equity shares shall be entitled to preemptive rights in accordance with the provisions of BCL § 622.

EXHIBIT 3-5   Certificate of Incorporation (*continued*)

Certificate of Incorporation of

under Section 402 of the Business Corporation Law

Filed By:

Office and Post Office Address

EXHIBIT 3-5 Certificate of Incorporation (*continued*)

New York State
Department of State
Division of Corporations, State Records
and Uniform Commercial Code
Albany, NY 12231

(This form must be printed or typed in black ink)

ARTICLES OF ORGANIZATION
OF

_____
(Insert company name)
Under Section 203 of the Limited Liability Company Law

FIRST: The name of the limited liability company is: _____

SECOND: The county within this state in which the office of the limited liability company is to be located is: _____

THIRD: (optional) The latest date on which the limited liability company is to dissolve is:

_____
(month/day/year)

FOURTH: The Secretary of State is designated as agent of the limited liability company upon whom process against it may be served. The address within or without this state to which the Secretary of State shall mail a copy of any process against the limited liability company served upon him or her is:

_____
_____
_____

FIFTH: (optional) The name and street address within this state of the registered agent of the limited liability company upon whom and at which process against the limited liability company may be served is:

_____
_____
_____

SIXTH: (optional) The future effective date of the Articles of Organization, which does not exceed 60 days from the date of filing, is: _____
(month/day/year)

DOS-1336 (Rev. 01/00)

EXHIBIT 3-6 Articles of Organization

SEVENTH: (optional) If all or specified members are to be liable in their capacity as members for all or specified debts, obligations or liabilities of the limited liability company as authorized by Section 609 of the Limited Liability Company Law, an affirmative statement must be made. A statement of such effect is made as follows:

_____

_____

_____

_____   _____
(signature of organizer)   (print or type name of organizer)

<hr/>

ARTICLES OF ORGANIZATION
OF

Under Section 203 of the Limited Liability Company Law

<hr/>

Filed by:

_____
(Name)

_____
(Mailing address)

_____
(City, State and ZIP code)

NOTE: • This form was prepared by the New York State Department of State for articles of organization. It does not contain all optional provisions under the law. You are not required to use this form. You may draft your own form or use forms available at legal supply stores. The Department of State recommends that legal documents be prepared under the guidance of an attorney. The certificate must be submitted with a $200 filing fee made payable to the Department of State.

    • This form may not be accompanied by any riders or attachments except a certificate evidencing reservation of name.

EXHIBIT 3-6 Articles of Organization (continued)

CHAPTER

TELEVISION

CHAPTER OVERVIEW

Federal Communications Commission (FCC)
Federal agency that regulates television.

Communications Act of 1934
First federal statute that established the regulation of the airways.

Without question, the most regulated of the entertainment media discussed in this text is television. Ever since the era of the New Deal in the 1930s, the airways have been monitored and supervised by the **Federal Communications Commission (FCC)** pursuant to the authority detailed in the **Communications Act of 1934**. The airwaves are federally regulated because of their ability to transmit both information and misinformation that directly impact a nation's viewpoint and sensibilities.

Television as a means of communication first came into the general public awareness in the United States after RCA demonstrated a prototype television at the Chicago World's Fair in 1938. Shortly thereafter, the FCC began receiving applications from individuals eager to acquire rights to utilize specific air channels for broadcasting both pictures and sound, despite the fact that the technology had not yet reached the point where such transmissions would be easily or universally available. Even by the end of World War Two, very few people indicated any sustained interest in the concept of television, and most viewed it merely as a fad intended to compete with movies. Of course, television is now recognized as more than just competition to attract the movie audience. It is a distinct and important medium of information and entertainment in its own right.

This chapter will explore the history of federal regulation of the airwaves as well as the new cable access to television, including the role the government and the creative unions play in programming shows, acquiring intellectual property rights, determining news content, and negotiating financial and artistic agreements. Arguably, no other entertainment medium overlaps news and theater to such an immediate extent as does television.

DISTRIBUTION REGULATION

As stated in the Introduction, the governmental organization responsible for the regulation of electronic transmissions is the Federal Communications Commission (FCC). The genesis of the FCC lies in the regulation of radio prior to World War One when radio transmissions were viewed primarily as a communication device for the military and ocean-going vessels. The FCC itself was created pursuant to the Communication Act of 1934, granting it the specific authority to "regulate interstate and foreign commerce in communication by wire and radio so as to make available, so far as possible, to all the people of the United States a rapid, efficient, nationwide and world-wide wire and communication service with adequate facilities at reasonable charges. ..." Pursuant to this statute, the FCC's powers are construed as narrowly as possible, and certain areas are specifically excluded from FCC regulation. The FCC's powers are as follows:

1. Communications governed by international treaty

2. Communications that are owned and operated by the government of the United States

3. Communications that are considered to be in violation of United States antitrust laws

4. Advertising claims made over the airways

5. Establishment of advertising rates

6. Litigation among broadcasters

7. Regulation of closed-circuit television or radio

8. Rates charged for pay television.

spectrum space
Airways and cable
frequencies.

Basically, the function of the FCC is to allocate **spectrum space** (airwaves and cable) among interested broadcasters to ensure that the public receives a wide variety of electronically transmitted communications. Similar to the Interstate Commerce Commission, the purpose of the FCC is to encourage as much free-market participation in electronic communication as possible by making sure that all spectrum space is fairly distributed.

— Example

An entrepreneur in a small town in North Dakota wants to establish a small television station to service that area of the country. She files an application with the FCC (see below) that will determine whether that region is receiving appropriate service and whether there is spectrum space available. The FCC will then determine whether the applicant broadcaster meets its criteria to be granted such spectrum space so that it will be utilized appropriately. If approved, she will receive a license to broadcast in the area.

The FCC is composed of five commissioners who are appointed by the President and approved by the Senate. The commissioners serve for five-year terms. The FCC itself is divided into several departments to regulate specific areas:

1. *Common Carrier Bureau* that regulates wire and radio transmissions and rates for interstate and foreign service
2. *Mass Media Bureau* that governs all commercial broadcasting
3. *Cable Service Bureau* that oversees cable-television carriers pursuant to the Cable Television Consumer Protection and Competition Act of 1992
4. *Private Radio Bureau* that regulates radio transmissions not otherwise regulated, such as police-radio communications.

The FCC began regulating electronic transmissions shortly after it was created because of the perceived scarcity of broadcast frequencies. This section of the chapter will discuss the FCC regulation and allocation policies with respect to the various types of transmissions currently in use.

Broadcast Regulation

VHF
Very-high frequency.

UHF
Ultra-high frequency.

All television stations are designated either **VHF** (very-high frequency) or **UHF** (ultra-high frequency), and are permitted to operate twenty-four hours a day, seven days a week. However, the FCC assigns specific frequencies to particular geographic regions, which are distributed according to FCC rules concerning regional distribution service. The allocation of frequencies is determined on a competitive basis—areas with greater populations are granted more frequencies than less-populated areas.

low-power television service
Exempt category from FCC regulation for facilities with limited broadcasting ranges.

There is an exception to the general FCC allocation rules for what are termed **low-power television service** broadcasters that permits stations that have a maximum power of 100 watts VHF and 1000 watts UHF (broadcast ranges of between ten and fifteen miles) to operate on any available channel. Further, such stations are permitted to broadcast without any interference from the more-powerful broadcasters so as to promote competition.

— *Example*

A low-power television station starts broadcasting on an available channel in its area. Its programming is creative and innovative, and it begins to draw viewers away from the area's larger stations. One of the larger stations starts to cause interference with the small station's transmissions. This is a violation of FCC rules.

A broadcaster acquires the right to use a particular frequency by submitting an application for a license to the FCC. If selected, the FCC will grant the successful applicant a license for a maximum period of eight years, but the license is renewable for eight-year periods. If a license is granted, the licensee (broadcaster) has no vested, or legally enforceable, property right in the specific frequency, and the license may be revoked by the FCC during the eight-year period. If the FCC contemplates revocation of a license due to violations of FCC rules, it must notify the licensee of its proposed action and allow the licensee the opportunity to challenge the proposed revocation. The burden rests with the FCC to prove the grounds that would warrant the revocation of a license.

To qualify for a broadcast license, the applicant must

1. Be a citizen of the United States.
2. Demonstrate good character, although the definition of *good character* does not appear in the FCC's statutes or rules. Generally, convictions of crimes of moral turpitude, drug offenses, and so forth would be considered evidence of "bad" character, thus permitting the FCC to deny the application.
3. Be able to demonstrate financial stability and ability to operate a broadcast facility.
4. Be able to prove that it possesses the technology to utilize the frequency.
5. Meet the FCC program guidelines. Although this guideline has been functionally abandoned, the FCC still mandates adherence to the **Children's Television Act of 1990**.

Children's Television Act of 1990
Federal law regulating broadcasts aimed at children.

Once the applicant has been determined to qualify for a license, the application is open for a public hearing so that those opposed to granting the license may be heard. If several applicants are seeking a license for the same frequency and are deemed to be equally qualified, the FCC will hold an auction for the frequency and award the license to the highest bidder, a practice in use since 1997.

If a current licensee is seeking a renewal license, according to the provisions of the Telecommunications Act of 1996, the licensee will be granted the renewal *unless* it is shown that the renewal applicant has committed a serious violation of FCC rules.

In addition to the above qualifications, the FCC, pursuant to its general mission, is required to make sure that electronic transmissions are not concentrated in the hands of just a few individuals. Consequently, in granting licenses for the various electronic media under its control, the FCC has established three rules to guarantee diversity in media ownership:

duopoly
Ownership of several broadcast facilities in the same community by one person.

multiple ownership
FCC rule dealing with diversity in ownership.

cross ownership
Television and newspaper in the same community owned by one person.

1. The FCC forbids **duopoly**—ownership of several broadcast facilities in the same community.

2. The FCC limits **multiple ownership**—ownership of multiple broadcast facilities by single owners—regardless of where the facilities are located.

3. The FCC forbids **cross ownership**—newspapers owning a television station in the same community in which they print their paper.

— *Example* —

The major daily newspaper in a medium-sized community applies for a license from the FCC to operate a television station in the same area. The FCC will probably deny this application so as to ensure that the media in the area will not be controlled by just one company presenting only one point of view to the public.

Cable Regulation

CATV
Cable television transmission.

Cable television, also referred to as **CATV**, was introduced at the end of World War Two in order to be able to transmit television broadcasts into areas in which regular transmissions were not possible. Unlike regular radio and television transmissions, cable transmits by means of underground wires, just like telephone transmissions. However, at first the FCC was unwilling to regulate the cable television market because the Federal Communication Act of 1934 did not encompass CATV. The FCC originally maintained that it would only exert jurisdiction over CATV if Congress amended its enabling statute. However, in 1962, after several unsuccessful legislative attempts to include CATV under FCC jurisdiction, the FCC itself issued an order in which it indicated its willingness to regulate CATV to a limited extent, and in 1966 it decided to extend its ability to regulate to all cable transmissions, with some regulatory ability left to the individual states.

Cable Act
Amendment to the Communication Act that added cable to the FCC's jurisdiction.

Finally, in 1984, Congress amended the Communications Act by enacting the **Cable Act**, which established specific rules for cable transmissions. The Cable Act further delineated the scope of authority of the FCC and the local state authorities. Under this amendment, the ability to franchise cable channels rested with the local agencies. Pursuant to its provisions, the Cable Act

1. Established a national policy with respect to cable channels
2. Enacted franchise procedures
3. Established regulatory guidelines
4. Mandated diversity in cable broadcasting.

Cable Television Consumer Protection and Competition Act
Statute currently regulating cable television.

preemption
Granting priority to FCC rules that may conflict with local rules.

More recently, in 1990, Congress passed the **Cable Television Consumer Protection and Competition Act**, which forms the basis of current cable regulatory law. The concept behind this statute is that competition between cable licensees would benefit consumers, and to further this end the FCC was granted preemptive authority over local governments. **Preemption** means that if an FCC rule is in conflict with a local policy, the FCC rule will prevail. The 1996 Act

1. Limits the regulatory authority of local governments
2. Precludes municipalities from requiring franchises of fundamental cable operators
3. Eliminates the federal requirement for open cable-system operators to obtain cable franchises.

The present law regarding cable broadcasting falls into three distinct areas: cable ownership, special carrier rules, and program content and copyrighting. The first two areas will be discussed in this section; the third will be addressed starting on page 128.

Cable Ownership

Under the FCC rules and guidelines, in order to be franchised to operate a cable broadcasting system, the applicant must demonstrate the following:

universal service
FCC requirement that a cable operator make its service available to all homeowners in its area.

1. That the franchisee will make service available to all households within the franchised area, known as **universal service**, and will allocate a portion of its broadcasting for educational and public programming.
2. The applicant cannot obtain a cable franchise if it owns a television broadcast license within the same signal coverage area. This provides diversity in broadcasting. However, such dual ownership may be permitted in high-concentration areas with multiple available channels.
3. The applicant must indicate that its rates permit effective competition in the viewing area by showing that
   A. Fewer than thirty percent of the households subscribe to its system
   B. The area is served by at least two multi-channel video-programming distributors
   C. Each multi-channel video-programming distributor offers programming to at least fifty percent of all households in the area
   D. The applicant does not require subscribers to purchase more than the basic tier of service.

Signal Coverage Rules

Signal-coverage rules are designed to guarantee that cable operators carry certain local and long-distance signals to their subscribers so as to avoid limiting broadcast access. These rules are characterized as follows:

must-carry rules
FCC requirement that cable station must carry all local stations.

Must-Carry Rule **Must-carry rules** dictate that the cable operator is required to carry *all* local stations. Cable systems with no more than twelve channels must carry at least three local broadcast signals; larger systems must carry all local commercial stations up to a maximum of one-third of the system's total number of channels.

— *Example*

In a large urban area, the regular television signals provide poor reception because of the tall buildings obstructing transmissions. Many households subscribe to a cable system so that they can receive transmissions without interference. The cable operator must carry the area's local commercial stations so that the cable system does not unduly limit competition.

may-carry rules
FCC requirement for cable stations to carry long-distance broadcast transmissions.

May-Carry Rule **May-carry rules** enable the cable operator to carry syndicated programming emanating from distant stations. However, cable operators are required to black out these distant syndicated programs if local commercial stations own exclusive broadcast rights.

— *Example*

A cable operator is precluded from broadcasting a championship baseball game because a local commercial channel has obtained exclusive broadcast rights from the teams.

Because of the ability of cable transmissions to broadcast without the interference that may occur with transmission by airways, and because of its virtually unlimited frequencies, the impact of CATV to the industry cannot be underestimated. Further, because CATV is subject only to limited regulation, most of the legal concerns center on the contracts into which the operators enter, discussed later in the chapter.

Other Transmissions' Regulation

In addition to transmission by traditional broadcast methods and CATV, there are several other methods that have evolved over the past two decades.

These methods of transmission are also regulated by the FCC, and include the following:

multi-point distribution service (MDS)
Method of television transmission using microwaves.

MMDS
Multi-channel MDS.

1. **Multipoint Distribution Service (MDS)** This method involves transmitting microwave frequencies to an antenna that can receive transmissions up to a range of 20 miles. The antenna converts the microwaves for reception to a subscriber's television. MDS is also capable of broadcasting multi-channel signals, referred to as **MMDS**, which have several advantages over CATV.
   A. Installation is less expensive than cable.
   B. MMDS has no franchising requirement.
   C. MMDS can transmit up to 300 channels.

satellite master antenna television (SMATV)
Satellite transmission for entire buildings or small communities.

direct broadcast satellite (DBS)
Satellite for individual homeowner's reception.

2. **Satellite Master Antenna Television (SMATV)** This is a method of receiving transmissions without using public airways. The purchaser can set up a system for a large building or small community and transmit broadcasts to all televisions in that building or area. As a subset of this form of reception, homeowners can use a satellite antenna to receive direct transmissions, known as a **direct broadcast satellite (DBS)**.

home satellite dish (TVRO)
Small dish used for receiving multiple channels.

3. **Home Satellite Dish (TVRO)** This is a small satellite dish that can be installed in a relatively small space, such as a backyard, and that enables the owner to receive a virtually unlimited number of channels. These systems were originally designed to service remote areas, but have become very popular in urban areas because of their reduced cost compared to cable and their ability to receive a wide range of broadcasts.

PROGRAM REGULATION

Not only is the right to use the airwaves regulated, but the government and private individuals have attempted to regulate television as well. As will be discussed throughout this text, the regulation of the content of artistic work is one of the more often debated and litigated areas of entertainment law. Any attempted regulation of program content must be viewed in the context of free speech, as guaranteed to all citizens by the United States Constitution.

Bill of Rights
The first ten amendments to the Constitution of the United States.

First Amendment
The amendment to the constitution that protects free speech and freedom of the press.

The First Amendment

Under the **Bill of Rights**—the first ten amendments to the Constitution of the United States—Americans have certain freedoms. In particular, the **First Amendment** decrees that "Congress shall make no law respecting an establishment of religion, or prohibiting the free exercise thereof, or abridging the freedom of speech, or of the press; or the right of the people peaceably to assemble, and to petition the Government for a redress of grievances." Television, as a means of disseminating information to the public, is subject to the regulations and privileges of the First Amendment. In fact, the First Amendment, in conjunction with regulations set forth by the television industry itself, regulates what may or may not be shown on television.

While the First Amendment protects speech, it does not permit unfettered programming. For instance, programming cannot defame, or libel or slander an individual. *Defamation* is the dissemination of untrue, or false, programming that causes injury to an individual. Libel is written defamation; slander is spoken defamation. Defamation has several requirements:

1. It must identify, either by name or by description, the individual who is the subject of the defamation.
2. The defamatory statement must be false.
3. The statement must cause injury to the defamed person or to his or her reputation.

— *Example*

WTVV airs a program that depicts a famous actor as an out-of-control alcoholic who cannot show up on the set of a movie he is filming because of his addiction. The actor claims that this statement has caused injury to his reputation, and he cannot get work as a result of the statement. If the statement made in the WTVV program is true and the actor is an alcoholic who cannot show up to work on time because of his addiction, the station cannot be sued for defamation; but, the television depiction of the actor must be verifiable.

As with other aspects of television, material that would otherwise be protected by copyright law is protected within the scope of television programming. For an in-depth discussion of what is protected by copyright, refer to chapter 2.

Newscasting

right to privacy
An inherent right to be left alone.

On the flip side of freedom of speech and freedom of the press is the **right to privacy**. There is an inherent right to be left alone. Some states have even enacted legislation to protect an individual's privacy. New York, for example, in § 50 of its Civil Rights Law, enacted a provision which reads, in pertinent part, that "a person, firm, or corporation that uses for advertising purposes, or for purposes of the trade, the name, portrait, or picture of any living person without having first obtained the written consent of such person, or if a minor of his or her parent or guardian, is guilty of a misdemeanor."

This right to privacy has taken on a new direction lately with the onslaught of newsgathering methods. The courts have attempted to balance the public's right to know and the freedom of the press with an individual's right to privacy.

paparazzi
Zealous photographers
who often freelance.

The **paparazzi**, zealous photographers who often work freelance, have been criticized for the way they work. Further, traditional reporters have had their tactics called into question when they perpetrate a fraud to get their story.

— Example

A television station decides to air a show about the way a large supermarket chain dated and sold its meat. In order to get a reporter into the supermarket, false information is given to the store's personnel when the reporter is interviewed for a position in the butcher's department. Since the reporter fraudulently represented himself to the supermarket, the television station he or she represents would lose a case brought against it.

Other Regulations

Obscenity on television is illegal. In fact, any material considered obscene in other mediums, for example, radio, is considered obscene on television. Statutes concerning obscenity are under the United States Code Title 18. It reads in part, "Whoever utters any obscene, indecent, or profane language by means of radio communication shall be fined under this title or imprisoned not more than two years, or both." Something is considered obscene if the average person applying community standards would find the work as a whole offensive and if the work lacks literary value.

While regulations vary slightly between broadcast television and cable television, the approach to regulation is similar. One difference is that material that is only indecent, and does not rise to the level of obscenity, may be regulated on broadcast television but not on cable television. **Indecency** is not only limited to sexual content, but also includes foul language and nudity that is not sexual in its orientation. Obscenity and indecency laws are affected not only by content, but also the mores of a given era.

indecency
Inappropriate sexual
content, foul language,
and nudity that is not
sexual in its orientation.

— Example

A station airs a program that has several nude scenes. If the program airs after midnight, it may not violate obscenity/indecency regulations because it is believed that most children, or those most affected by the viewing of indecent material, would not view the program because of the late hour; thus, the community of viewers would not be offended.

Other material that may be censored from the public's view includes that which may affect national security, that which may affect an individual's right to a fair trial, and that which would allow criminals to profit from their crimes. Children are afforded additional protection in that they are ensured a certain number of commercial-free air minutes; consequently, they are ensured a certain amount of quality air-time.

To help individuals monitor what they view, a rating system has been developed by the industry. This rating system designates what is acceptable for specific categories of viewers; for example, for children and for mature audiences. Shows with sexual content, violence, coarse language, and suggestive dialogue are also regulated by having rating labels indicated to the audience.

TELEVISION CONTRACTS

Television shows are miniature movies based on stories with music and pictures. Because of the complex make-up of a television show, many different contracts must be entered into before a television broadcast is completed and aired. The following section discusses some general concepts in contract law that relate to the medium of television.

Generally, a contract can be either oral or written. Even though not reduced to a writing, an **oral contract** may be binding unless it violates the Statute of Frauds. The Statute of Frauds requires that certain contracts be reduced to writing in order to be valid. Further, contracts may also be either express or implied. An **express contract** is one that relies on an unambiguous agreement. An **implied contract** is one based on an understanding.

oral contract
Binding contract not reduced to writing.

express contract
A contract that relies on an unambiguous agreement.

implied contract
A contract based on an understanding.

— Example

Bob and Sue go to the movies and order popcorn. Bob gets the popcorn and starts to walk away without paying. It is implied through the act of ordering the popcorn that Bob will pay for the popcorn. This act of agreement may be construed as an oral implied contract.

In fact, every time an author sends a story idea off to studio an implied contract is entered into. Nevertheless, much litigation has arisen out of the belief that a story concept has been stolen. To protect oneself, a person can send a letter along with the story idea and instruct that the story concept is to be held in confidence and, if it is exploited by the studio, then just compensation must be paid.

To protect the studio from financial risk, some studios enter into what is known as an **option contract** depicted in Exhibit 4-1 at the end of this chapter. The studio buys the exclusive right to purchase a story in the future. In other words, a studio can buy the right to exercise its option to purchase a story within a set period of time, generally one year. The studio generally also has a right of renewal, or a right to exercise the option to purchase a story for an additional sum.

option contract
Exclusive right to purchase a story in the future.

— *Example* —————————————

BIG Studio is interested in a story, but due to its sensitive nature it is not sure that it is a financially sound investment. BIG Studio can enter into an option contract with the writer, and if BIG Studio decides within the period of time specified in the contract that the story would make a hit series, the studio can exercise its option and purchase the story. Additionally, if Studio B had been interested in purchasing the story after hearing about it from a disgruntled BIG Studio employee, it would not be allowed to until BIG Studio's option contract and right-of-renewal term had ended.

---

step agreement
Agreement that proceeds after the completion of certain steps.

Another type of agreement frequently entered into is a step agreement. A **step agreement** is one that proceeds after the completion of certain steps. If a studio is unsure about the talent of a writer, it may base the continuance of a contract upon completion of work in various stages.

Other television agreements include contracts similar to those discussed in other chapters.

CHAPTER REVIEW

Both the content of a television show and how that content is distributed are regulated. Such regulation is done by the Federal Communications Commission, some other constitutional provision, or by case law.

Regulations differ as to the format of the medium through which the material is disseminated. For example, regulations for broadcast television differ from regulations for cable television.

The public at large is protected from obscene, indecent, and violent material. They are protected from invasion of privacy by invasive newscasters, and also from censorship of important information by governmental agencies.

JUDICIAL DECISION

The following case concerns the regulation of the television industry.

Schurz Communications, Incorporated
v.

Federal Communications Commission and
United States of America

982 F2d 1043 (7th Cir 1992)

In 1970 the Federal Communications Commission adopted "financial interest and syndication" rules designed to limit the power of the then three television networks—CBS, NBC, and ABC—over television programming (47 CFR § 73.658(j)(1990); see *Network Television Broadcasting*, 23 FCC2d 382, 387 (1970), aff'd under the name of *Mt. Mansfield Television, Inc. v. FCC*, 442 F2d 470 (2d Cir 1971)). Each of the three networks consisted (as they still do) of several television stations, in key markets, owned and operated by the network itself, plus about two hundred independently owned stations electronically connected to the network by cable or satellite. In exchange for a fee paid them by the network, these affiliated stations broadcast programs that the network transmits to them, as well as to its owned and operated stations, over the interconnect system. The networking of programs intended for the early evening hours that are the "prime time" for adult television viewing gives advertisers access to a huge number of American households simultaneously, which in turn enables the networks to charge the high prices for advertising time that are necessary to defray the cost of obtaining the programming most desired by television viewers.

The financial interest and syndication rules adopted in 1970 forbade a network to syndicate (license) programs produced by the network for rebroadcast by independent television stations—that is, stations that were not owned by or affiliated with the network—or to purchase syndication rights to programs that it obtained from outside producers, or otherwise to obtain a financial stake in such programs. If the network itself had produced the program it could sell syndication rights to an independent syndicator but it could not retain an interest in the syndicator's revenues or profits.

Many syndicated programs are reruns, broadcast by independent stations, of successful comedy or dramatic series first shown on network television. Very few series are sufficiently successful in their initial run to be candidates for syndication. Independent stations like to air five episodes each week of a rerun series that originally had aired only once a week or less, so unless a series has a first run of several years—which few series do—it will not generate enough episodes to sustain a rerun of reasonable length. The financial interest and syndication rules thus severely limited the networks' involvement in supplying television programs other than for their own or their affiliated stations.

The concern behind the rules was that the networks, controlling as they did through their owned and operated stations and their affiliates a large part of the system for distributing television programs to

American households, would unless restrained use this control to seize a dominating position in the production of television programs. That is, they would lever their distribution "monopoly" into a production "monopoly." They would, for example, refuse to buy programs for network distribution unless the producers agreed to surrender their syndication rights to the network. For once the networks controlled those rights, the access of independent television stations, that is, stations not owned by or affiliated with one of the networks, to reruns would be at the sufferance of the networks, owners of a competing system of distribution. Market power in buying has the same misallocative effects as the more common market power in selling. The relation is especially close in this case because the networks can just as well be viewed as sellers of a distribution service as they can be as buyers of programs—the less they pay for programs, the more in effect they charge for distributing them.

The Commission hoped the rules would strengthen an alternative source of supply (to the networks) for independent stations—the alternative consisting of television producers not owned by networks. The rules would do this by curtailing the ability of the networks to supply the program market represented by the independent stations, and by protecting the producers for that market against being pressured into giving up potentially valuable syndication rights. And the rules would strengthen the independent stations (and so derivatively the outside producers, for whom the independent stations were an important market along with the networks themselves) by securing them against having to purchase reruns from their competitors the networks.

The basis for this concern that the networks, octopus-like, would use their position in distribution to take over programming, and would use the resulting control of programming to eliminate their remaining competition in distribution, was never very clear. If the networks insisted on buying syndication rights along with the right to exhibit a program on the network itself, they would be paying more for their programming. (So one is not surprised that in the decade before the rules were adopted, the networks had acquired syndication rights to no more than 35 percent of their prime-time series, although they had acquired a stake in the syndicator's profits in a considerably higher percentage of cases.) If the networks then turned around and refused to syndicate independent stations, they would be getting nothing in return for the money they had laid out for syndication rights except a long-shot chance—incidentally, illegal under the antitrust laws—to weaken the already weak competitors of network stations. Nor was it clear just how the financial interest and syndication rules would scotch the networks' nefarious schemes. If forbidden to buy syndication rights, networks would pay less for programs, so the outside producers would not come out clear winners—indeed many would be losers. Production for television is a highly risky undertaking, like wildcat drilling for gas and oil. Most television entertainment programs are money losers. The losses are offset by the occasional hit that makes it into syndication after completing a long first run. The sale of syndication rights to a network would enable a producer to shift risk to a larger, more diversified entity presumptively better able to bear it. The resulting reduction in the risks of production would encourage new entry into production and thus give the independent stations a more competitive supply of programs. Evidence introduced in this proceeding showed that, consistent with this speculation, networks in the pre-1970 era were more likely to purchase syndication rights from small producers than from large ones.

Whatever the pros and cons of the original financial interest and syndication rules, in the years since they were promulgated the structure of the television industry has changed profoundly. The three networks have lost ground, primarily as a result of the expansion of cable television, which now reaches 60 percent of American homes, and videocassette recorders, now found in 70 percent of American homes. Today each of the three networks buys only 7 percent of the total video and film programming sold each year, which is roughly a third of the percentage in 1970. (The inclusion of films in the relevant market is appropriate because videocassettes enable home viewers to substitute a film for a television program.) And each commands only about 12 percent of total television advertising revenues. Where in 1970 the networks had 90 percent of the prime-time audience, today they have 62 percent, and competition among as well as with the three networks is fierce. They are, moreover, challenged today by a fourth network, the

Fox Broadcasting Corporation, which emerged in the late 1980s.

Notwithstanding the fourth network, which might have been expected to reduce the number of independent stations by converting many of them to network—Fox network—stations, the number of independent stations has increased fivefold since 1970. At the same time, contrary to the intention behind the rules yet an expectable result of them because they made television production a riskier business, the production of prime-time programming has become more concentrated. There are 40 percent fewer producers of prime-time programming today than there were two decades ago. And the share of that programming accounted for directly or indirectly by the eight largest producers, primarily Hollywood studios—companies large enough to bear the increased risk resulting from the Commission's prohibition against the sale of syndication rights to networks—has risen from 50 percent to 70 percent.

The original rules had been supported by the Antitrust Division of the Department of Justice. But as the years passed, antitrust thinking changed. The "leverage" theory, which taught that a firm having economic power in one market would use it to acquire a monopoly of another market, was widely discredited. The evolution of the television industry, sketched above, suggested that the rules, if they were having any effect at all, were working perversely from a competitive standpoint. An extensive staff study ordered by the Commission concluded that the rules were obsolete and recommended that they be abandoned (*Final Report of Network Inquiry Special Staff* (1980)). In 1983 the Commission issued a tentative decision agreeing with the staff, proposing radical revisions in the rules leading to their eventual repeal, but inviting further public comments on the details of its proposals (*Tentative Decision and Request for Further Comments in Docket 82-345*, 94 FCC2d 1019 (1983)). The networks, the Commission found in the tentative decision, had lost any significant monopoly or market power that they may once have had. The financial interest and syndication rules were hampering the entry of new firms into production by blocking an important mechanism (the sale of syndication rights) by which new firms might have shifted the extraordinary risks of their undertaking to the networks.

Mainly as a result of congressional pressure, *Hearings before the Subcomm. on Communications of the S. Comm. on Commerce, Science & Transportation on S. 1707,* 98th Cong., 1st Sess. 6, 9 (1984); Henry M. Sooshan III & Erwin G. Krasnow, "New Checks, Balances Affect FCC Policymaking," *Legal Times,* April 8, 1985, at p. 12, there was no follow-up to the tentative decision. The question what to do about the rules remained in limbo until 1990, when the Commission at the request of the Fox network initiated a fresh notice-and-comment rulemaking proceeding. After receiving voluminous submissions from the various segments of the television industry, the Commission held a one-day hearing, after which it issued an opinion, over dissents by two of the five commissioners, including the chairman, promulgating a revised set of financial interest and syndication rules (*In re Evaluation of the Syndication and Financial Interest Rules,* 56 Fed Reg 26242 (May 29, 1991), on reconsideration, *56 Fed Reg 64207* (November 22, 1991)). The new rules (published at 47 CFR §§ 73.658(k), 73.659–73.662, 73.3526(a)(11)(1991)) are different from the old and also more complicated. They define "network" as an entity that supplies at least 15 hours of prime-time programming to interconnected affiliates. They take off all restrictions on nonentertainment programming (that is, news and sports), and most restrictions on nonprime-time programming and on syndication for the foreign as distinct from the domestic market. But in a provision that has no counterpart in the old rules, the new ones provide that no more than 40 percent of a network's own prime-time entertainment schedule may consist of programs produced by the network itself. The new rules unlike the old permit a network to buy domestic syndication rights from outside producers of prime-time entertainment programming—provided, however, that the network does so pursuant to separate negotiations begun at least 30 days after the network and the producer have agreed on the fee for licensing the network to exhibit the program on the network itself. Even then the network may not do the actual syndication; that is, it may not arrange for the distribution of the programming to the independent stations; it must hire an independent syndicator for that. And it may acquire syndication rights only in reruns, not in first-run programs, and thus it may not distribute first-run programming other

than to its network stations. This restriction applies to foreign as well as to domestic syndication unless the program is not intended for exhibition in the US at all. There is more to the new rules—there are provisions designed to prevent networks from discriminating in program supply in favor of their affiliates—but our summary will suffice to indicate the character of the rules.

The Commission's majority opinion describes them as "deregulatory," arguing that they expand the networks' opportunities to participate in the program market and promising to reexamine them in four years to see whether a further relaxation of restrictions might then be justifiable. Although the Commission conceded that the networks may already have lost so much of their market power as no longer to pose a threat to competition as it is understood in antitrust law, it concluded that some restrictions remain necessary to assure adequate diversity of television programming. The Commission's chairman, understandably irate because the majority had ignored most of the points in his long and detailed dissent, predicted that the majority's decision would "produce a milestone case on what constitutes arbitrary and capricious decisionmaking."

The new rules were not stayed, and became effective in May of last year. The networks have petitioned this court to invalidate them as arbitrary and capricious (5 USC § 706(2)(A)). They argue that the only administrative order supportable by the record compiled by the Commission would be a total repeal of the 1970 rules. Coalitions of producers and of independent stations have also filed petitions for review, arguing, though halfheartedly—for on the whole they are content with the new rules—that the Commission should have left the original rules intact.

The Communications Act of 1934, 47 USC §§ 151 *et seq.,* gives the Federal Communications Commission authority over the use of the electromagnetic spectrum to propagate communications signals. With the blessing of the Supreme Court the Commission has used this authority, in much the same fashion that it accuses the networks of wanting to use leverage in the distribution market to gain a stranglehold over programming, to regulate activities by networks that are remote from the concerns with signal interference that first summoned federal regulation of the airwaves into being. The handle is the Commission's control over broadcast licenses, including those held by the networks' owned and operated stations. The Commission has been allowed to condition the renewal of those licenses on the networks' accepting constraints intended to maximize the Commission's conception of the social benefits of broadcasting (*National Broadcasting Co. v. United States*, 319 US 190, 87 LEd 1344, 63 S Ct 997 (1943)). The statute provides no guidance for the exercise of this authority other than that the Commission is to act in accordance with the public interest, convenience, or necessity (*Id.* at 215; 47 USC § 303; *FCC v. WNCN Listeners Guild*, 450 US 582, 593–94, 67 LEd2d 521, 101 S Ct 1266 (1981); *FCC v. National Citizens Committee for Broadcasting*, 436 US 775, 810, 56 LEd2d 697, 98 S Ct 2096 (1978)). So nebulous a mandate invests the Commission with an enormous discretion and correspondingly limits the practical scope of responsible judicial review. The nature of the record compiled in a notice-and-comment rulemaking proceeding—voluminous, largely self-serving commentary uncabined by any principles of reliability, let alone by the rules of evidence—further enlarges the Commission's discretion and further diminishes the capacity of the reviewing court to question the Commission's judgment (Cf. *Morales v. Yeutter*, 952 F2d 954, 958 (7th Cir 1991)).

Although the television industry is less complex than some and its product is well known even to federal judges, there are more than enough technical aspects to the industry, involving such things as the modes of financing and contracting and the effects of market structure and practices on television fare, to enforce judicial diffidence. Moreover, economists do not agree on the relation between monopoly or competition, on the one hand, and the quality or variety of an industry's output, on the other, so that it is difficult to obtain a theoretical perspective from which to evaluate the Commission's claims about that relation. If the Commission were enforcing the antitrust laws, it would not be allowed to trade off a reduction in competition against an increase in an intangible known as "diversity." Since it is enforcing the nebulous public interest standard instead, it is permitted, and maybe even required, to make such a tradeoff—at least we do not understand any of the parties to question the Commission's authority to do so. And although as

an original matter one might doubt that the First Amendment authorized the government to regulate so important a part of the marketplace in ideas and opinions as television broadcasting, the Supreme Court has consistently taken a different view (*FCC v. National Citizens Committee for Broadcasting, supra; FCC v. Pacifica Foundation*, 438 US 726, 57 LEd2d 1073, 98 S Ct 3026 (1978); *National Broadcasting Co. v. United States, supra*, 319 US at 226–27). The challenged rules themselves, finally, are so complicated that it is unclear whether they are more or less restrictive than the rules they modified.

From what we have said so far, it should be apparent that the networks have no hope of proving to our satisfaction that the Commission is without *any* power to restrict the networks' participation in television programming. Even if we were persuaded that it would be irrational to impute to the networks even a smidgen of market power, the Commission could always take the position that it should carve out a portion of the production and distribution markets and protect them against the competition of the networks in order to foster, albeit at a higher cost to advertisers and ultimately to consumers, a diversity of programming sources and outlets that might result in a greater variety of perspectives and imagined forms of life than the free market would provide. That would be a judgment within the Commission's power to make.

The difficult question presented by the petitions to review is not whether the Commission is authorized to restrict the networks' participation in program production and distribution. It is whether the Commission has said enough to justify, in the face of the objections lodged with it, the particular restrictions that it imposed in the order here challenged. One might be tempted as an original matter to treat an administrative rule as courts treat legislation claimed to deny substantive due process, and thus ask whether on any set of hypothesized facts, whether or not mentioned in the statement accompanying the rule, the rule was rational (*United States v. Carolene Products Co.*, 304 US 144, 154, 82 LEd 1234, 58 S Ct 778 (1938); *Williamson v. Lee Optical of Oklahoma, Inc.*, 348 US 483, 487–88, 99 LEd 563, 75 S Ct 461 (1955); *Central States, Southeast & Southwest Areas Pension Fund v. Lady Baltimore Foods, Inc.*, 960 F2d 1339, 1343 (7th Cir 1992)). And then the new financial interest and syndication rules would have to be upheld. But that is not the standard for judicial review of administrative action. It is not enough that a rule might be rational; the statement accompanying its promulgation must show that it is rational—must demonstrate that a reasonable person upon consideration of all the points urged pro and con the rule would conclude that it was a reasonable response to a problem that the agency was charged with solving (*Bowen v. American Hospital Ass'n*, 476 US 610, 626–27, 90 LEd2d 584, 106 S Ct 2101 (1986) (plurality opinion); *Motor Vehicle Mfrs. Ass'n v. State Farm Mutual Automobile Ins. Co.*, 463 US 29, 43, 77 LEd2d 443, 103 S Ct 2856 (1983); *SEC v. Chenery Corp.*, 318 US 80, 87–88, 87 LEd 626, 63 S Ct 454 (1943); *International Union, UAW v. NLRB*, 802 F2d 969, 972 (7th Cir 1986); *Wong Wing Hang v. INS*, 360 F2d 715, 719 (2d Cir 1966)). "The agency must examine the relevant data and articulate a satisfactory explanation for its action including a 'rational connection between the facts found and the choice made'" (*Motor Vehicle Mfrs. Ass'n v. State Farm Mutual Automobile Ins. Co.*, supra, 463 US at 43, quoting *Burlington Truck Lines, Inc. v. United States*, 371 US 156, 168, 9 LEd2d 207, 83 S Ct 239 (1962)).

The new rules flunk this test. The Commission's articulation of its grounds is not adequately reasoned. Key concepts are left unexplained, key evidence is overlooked, arguments that formerly persuaded the Commission and that time has only strengthened are ignored, contradictions within and among Commission decisions are passed over in silence. The impression created is of unprincipled compromises of Rube Goldberg complexity among contending interest groups viewed merely as clamoring suppliants who have somehow to be conciliated. The Commission said that it had been "confronted by alternative views of the television programming world so starkly and fundamentally at odds with each other that they virtually defy *reconciliation*" (emphasis added). The possibility of resolving a conflict in favor of the party with the stronger case, as distinct from throwing up one's hands and splitting the difference, was overlooked. The opinion contains much talk but no demonstration of expertise, and a good deal of hand-wringing over the need for prudence and the desirability of avoiding "convulsive" regulatory reform, yet these unquestioned

goods are never related to the particulars of the rules—rules that could have a substantial impact on an industry that permeates the daily life of this nation and helps shape, for good or ill, our culture and our politics. The Commission must do better in articulating their justification. Perhaps the attempt to do so will result in significant modifications in the rules. Not all remands result in the reinstatement of the original decision with merely a more polished rationalization (*Graphic Communications Int'l Union v. NLRB*, 977 F2d 1168 (7th Cir 1992)).

The Commission's majority opinion (in which we include its opinion on reconsideration) is long, but much of it consists of boilerplate, the recitation of the multitudinous parties' multifarious contentions, and self-congratulatory rhetoric about how careful and thoughtful and measured and balanced the majority has been in evaluating those contentions and carrying out its responsibilities. Stripped of verbiage, the opinion, like a Persian cat with its fur shaved, is alarmingly pale and thin. It can be paraphrased as follows. The television industry has changed since 1970. There is more competition—cable television, the new network, etc. No longer is it clear that the networks have market power in an antitrust sense, which they could use to whipsaw the independent producers and strangle the independent stations. So there should be some "deregulation" of programming—some movement away from the 1970 rules. But not too much, because even in their decline the networks may retain some power to extort programs or program rights from producers. The networks offer advertisers access to 98 percent of American households; no competing system for the distribution of television programming can offer as much. Anyway the Commission's concern, acknowledged to be legitimate, is not just with market power in an antitrust sense but with diversity, and diversity is promoted by measures to assure a critical mass of outside producers and independent stations. So the networks must continue to be restricted—but less so than by the 1970 rules. The new rules will give the networks a greater opportunity to participate in programming than the old ones did, while protecting outside producers and independent stations from too much network competition.

All this is, on its face, plausible enough, but it is plausible only because the Commission, ostrich fashion, did not discuss the most substantial objections to its approach, though the objections were argued vigorously to it, by its own chairman among others. To begin with, the networks object that the new rules do not in fact increase their access to the programming market and may decrease it, in the face of the Commission's stated objective. The 40 percent limitation on the amount of prime-time entertainment that a network can supply from its in-house production is a new restriction on the networks, having no counterpart in the original rules. It does have a counterpart in consent decrees that the networks entered into some years ago, e.g., *United States v. National Broadcasting Co.*, 449 FSupp 1127 (CD Cal 1978), when the Justice Department was still enamored of the leverage theory, but those decrees expired two years ago. The carving out of nonentertainment programming from the restrictions imposed by the new rules is a throwaway, because there is no syndication market for news and sports programs. Also illusory, the networks argue, is the newly granted right to acquire syndication rights from outside producers, given the restrictions with which the new right is hedged about. A producer cannot wait until 30 days after negotiating the network license fee to sell off syndication rights, because the sale of those rights, the networks contend, is critical to obtaining the financing necessary to produce the program in the first place. These arguments may be right or wrong; our point is only that the Commission did not mention them. We are left in the dark about the grounds for its belief that the new rules will give the networks real, not imaginary, new opportunities in programming.

The new rules, like their predecessors, appear to harm rather than to help outside producers as a *whole* (a vital qualification) by reducing their bargaining options. It is difficult to see how taking away a part of a seller's market could help the seller. One of the rights in the bundle of rights that constitutes the ownership of a television program is the right to syndicate the program to nonnetwork stations. The new rules restrict—perhaps, as a practical matter, prevent—the sale of that right to networks. How could it help a producer to be *forbidden* to sell his wares to a class of buyers that may be the high bidders for them? It is not as if anyone supposed that syndication rights, like babies or human freedom or the vital organs of a

living person, should not be salable at all. They are freely salable—except to networks. Since syndication is the riskiest component of a producer's property right—for its value depends on the distinctly low-probability event that the program will be a smash hit on network television—restricting its sale bears most heavily on the smallest, the weakest, the newest, the most experimental producers, for they are likely to be the ones least able to bear risk. It becomes understandable why the existing producers support the financial interest and syndication rules: the rules protect these producers against new competition both from the networks (because of the 40 percent cap) and from new producers. The ranks of the outside producers of prime-time programming have been thinned under the regime of financial interest and syndication rules. The survivors are the beneficiaries of the thinning. They do not want the forest restored to its pristine density. They consent to have their own right to sell syndication rights curtailed as the price of a like restriction on their potential competitors, on whom it is likely to bear more heavily.

This analysis of risk and its bearing on competition in the program industry is speculative, theoretical, and may for all we know be all wet—though it is corroborated by the increasing concentration of the production industry since the rules restricting the sale of syndication rights were first imposed in 1970. The Commission was not required to buy the analysis. But as the analysis was more than plausible and had been pressed upon it by a number of participants in the rulemaking proceeding—including a putatively disinterested Justice Department that in the past had frequently seen the bogeyman of monopoly lurking everywhere, as well as the Commission's own chairman—the Commission majority was not entitled to ignore it. Not even to consider the possibility that the unrestricted sale of syndication rights to networks would strengthen the production industry (the industry—not necessarily its present occupants) and thereby increase programming diversity by enabling a sharing between fledgling producers and the networks of the risks of new production was irresponsible. For if the argument about risk sharing is correct, the rules are perverse; by discouraging the entry of new producers into the high-risk prime-time entertainment market, they are likely to reduce the supply of programs to the independent stations and so reduce diversity both of program sources and of program outlets. The Commission's stated desiderata are competition and diversity. The rules adopted by the Commission in order to achieve these desiderata have the remarkable property—if the risk-sharing argument that the Commission did not deign to address is correct—of disserving them both.

Central to the Commission's decision to continue restricting the networks' participation in programming is its belief that whether or not they have market power in some antitrust sense they have the power to force producers to sell them programs for less than the programs would be worth in a fully competitive market. The networks call this a contradiction: either they have market power, or they don't; there is no middle ground. A rational commission could disagree. Market power is a matter of degree. Some firms have a lot of it, some a little, some none. It is plausible that each network, even when not colluding with the others (there is no evidence that they are colluding), has some market power and thus can drive a harder bargain with producers than it could do if it had none. Even though each of the three major networks has only about 20 percent of the prime-time audience and a producer who does not sell his program to a network can still hope to distribute it to the public via independent stations and cable networks, or for that matter movie theaters and videocassette dealers, network distribution offers advertisers unique simultaneous access to a large fraction of American households and increases the prospects for successful syndication, which apparently is where the real money in the creation of television entertainment is to be made.

The difficulty is that if the networks do have market power, the new rules (in this respect like the old) do not seem rationally designed to prevent its exercise. A rule telling a person he may not do business with some firm believed to have market power is unlikely to make the person better off. Suppose that in a competitive market a network would pay $2 million for first-run rights to some program and $1 million for syndication rights, for a total of $3 million, but that because of the lack of perfect substitutes for using this network to distribute his program the producer is willing to sell each of these rights to the network for half their competitive-market value (i.e., for $1 million

and $500,000 respectively). The producer is made no better off by being forbidden to sell the syndication rights to the network. He gets the same meager first-run license fee ($1 million) and now must cast about for another buyer for the syndication rights. That other buyer is unlikely to pay more than the network would ($500,000); otherwise the producer would have sold the syndication rights to him in the first place. It is no answer that the network would not have given the producer the option of selling it only first-run rights, that it would have insisted on the whole package so that it could control the program supply of the independent stations, which are heavily dependent on reruns and hence on syndication. The producer might indeed be desperate for network distribution, but that desperation would be reflected in the low price at which he was willing to sell the network whatever rights the network wanted. He cannot do better by being forbidden to make such a deal. If he could do better by selling syndication rights to someone else he would not accede to such unfavorable terms as the network offered.

If this is right, the new rules, at least insofar as they restrict network syndication, cannot increase the prices that producers receive. All they can do is increase the costs of production by denying producers the right to share risks with networks.

To this the Commission might (though did not) reply by pointing to the movement for artists' rights statutes (Cal. Civ. Code § 986(a)). Such statutes reserve to an artist a royalty on future sales of his art. They thus force the artist to retain a counterpart to syndication rights. The only intelligible rationale for tying the artist's hands in this way is that artists may be financially unsophisticated and hence at the mercy of crafty, rapacious dealers. No one supposes that producers of television programs are financially unsophisticated. The rationale for the Commission's producers' rights statute is left unilluminated.

Everything that we have said about the effect of forbidding producers to sell syndication rights to networks may be wrong. That we freely grant. But the argument we have sketched—an argument vigorously pressed upon the Commission by the networks—is sufficiently persuasive to have placed a burden of explanation on the Commission. It did not carry the burden. It did not mention the objection.

And we have said nothing as yet of the treatment of the Fox network. That network is built around the production capability and film library of Twentieth Century Fox. At present the network supplies only 12 to 14 hours a week of prime-time programming to its owned and affiliated stations and is therefore exempt from the new rules. Should it reach 15 hours, however, it would be subject to them. Fox argues that, given the importance of program production in its overall corporate activity, the effect of the rules is to limit it to supplying fewer than 15 hours of prime-time programming and therefore to limit its growth as a network. Corroboration of this argument is found in the fact that the Fox network hit 15 hours a week shortly before the rules went into effect, then cut back to the present 12 to 14 hours. By limiting Fox in this way the new financial interest and syndication rules limit competition with the major networks and thus entrench the market power that is the rules' principal rationale. Or so Fox argues; it may be bluffing; maybe the effect of the rules will be to induce Fox to divest its production or network arms, so that the network can grow without constraining Fox's production activities. But once again the Commission failed even to mention the argument that its rules perversely limit competition with the established networks.

More than competition in the economic sense is at stake. Fox's affiliates are for the most part the traditionally weak UHF stations. They do not consider themselves "network" stations in the same sense that a CBS or NBC or ABC affiliate does. Many of them are members of the trade association of independent television stations. Anything that weakens Fox's incentives to furnish prime-time programming weakens them, contrary to the Commission's desire, protectionist though it may be, to strengthen independent stations. This perverse consequence of the rules also went unmentioned.

The Commission's treatment of precedent was also cavalier. An administrative agency is no more straitjacketed by precedent than a court is. It can reject its previous decisions. But it must explain why it is doing so (*Motor Vehicle Mfrs. Ass'n v. State Farm Mutual Automobile Ins. Co., supra; Illinois Bell Tel. Co. v. FCC*, 740 F2d 465, 470–71 (7th Cir 1984); *Continental Web Press, Inc. v. NLRB*, 742 F2d 1087, 1093–94 (7th Cir 1984)). This is an aspect of the duty

mentioned earlier of rational explanation; a rational person acts consistently, and therefore changes course only if something has changed. In 1983, in its tentative decision, the Commission rejected the proposition that the networks had significant market power, found that the financial interest and syndication rules were preventing efficient risk-sharing, and concluded that the rules should be phased out by 1990 (*Tentative Decision and Request for Further Comments in Docket 82-345, supra*, 94 FCC2d at 1063–71, 1101). In the eight years between that decision and the one under review the networks lost still more ground, with the continued rapid growth of cable television and the advent of the Fox network. The Commission majority cited the tentative decision but did not discuss it—did not explain what had happened in eight years to justify the Commission's about face or, if nothing had happened, why the tentative decision had been wrong from the start. The tentative decision had also laid down a general approach to the evaluation of network restrictions: "the Commission should not intervene in the market except where there is evidence of a market failure and a regulatory solution is available that is likely to improve the net welfare of the consuming public" (*Id.* at 1055). That standard went unremarked in the present order.

It is no answer that the 1983 decision had been tentative, and specifically that the Commission had not promulgated a remedy—had not actually abrogated the rules that it had found had outlived their usefulness. The Supreme Court's first decision in *Brown v. Board of Education*, which held that public school segregation was unconstitutional, was not deprived of precedential status by the fact that the Court postponed the issuance of a remedial decree to a subsequent decision. There was nothing tentative about the Commission's conclusion in the 1983 decision that the networks had lost their market power and that the financial interest and syndication rules were unsound and should be phased out. It said, "we are confident that our analysis of the effect of the rules in terms of the network/supplier relationship is correct" (94 FCC2d at 1101). It was unsure only about "the mechanical aspects of whatever form of regulation" was adopted in lieu of the old rules, pending complete repeal in 1990 (*Id.*).

We remarked earlier that even if the networks had zero market power, the Commission might in the discharge of its undefined, uncanalized responsibility to promote the public interest restrict the networks' programming activities in order to create a more diverse programming fare. What it could not do, consistent with the principles of reasoned decision-making, was pretend that it had never found that the networks had lost market power. Imagine just the purely *professional* criticism to which the Supreme Court would have been subjected if in the second *Brown* decision, without so much as discussing the first decision, it had held that public school segregation was constitutional after all.

Finally, while the word diversity appears with incantatory frequency in the Commission's opinion, it is never defined. At argument one of the counsel helpfully distinguished between source diversity and outlet diversity (as had the Commission itself in previous decisions—including *Tentative Decision and Request for Further Comments in Docket 82-345, supra,* 94 FCC2d at 1054). The former refers to programming sources, that is, producers, and the latter to distribution outlets, that is, television stations. The two forms of diversity are related because the station decides what programs to air and therefore affects producers' decisions about what to produce. A third and one might suppose the critical form of diversity is diversity in the programming itself; here "diversity" refers to the variety or heterogeneity of programs. The Commission neither distinguished among the types of diversity nor explained the interrelation among them. As it is very difficult to see how sheer *number* of producers or outlets could be thought a good thing—and anyway the rules seem calculated, however unwittingly, to decrease, or at least to freeze, but certainly not to increase, the number of producers—we assume that the Commission thinks of source diversity and outlet diversity as means to the end of programming diversity.

Are they? It has long been understood that monopoly in broadcasting could actually promote rather than retard programming diversity. If all the television channels in a particular market were owned by a single firm, its optimal programming strategy would be to put on a sufficiently varied menu of programs in each time slot to appeal to every substantial group of potential television viewers in the market, not just the largest group. For that would be the strategy that maximized the size of the station's audience. Suppose, as a simple example, that there were only two television broadcast frequencies (and no cable television), and that 90 percent of the viewers in the market wanted to watch comedy from 7 to 8 P.M. and 10 percent wanted to watch ballet. The monopolist would broadcast comedy over one frequency and ballet over the other, and thus gain 100 percent of the potential audience. If the frequencies were licensed to two competing firms, each firm would broadcast comedy in the 7 to 8 P.M. time slot, because its expected audience share would be 45 percent (one half of 90 percent), which is greater than 10 percent. Each prime-time slot would be filled with "popular" programming targeted on the median viewer, and minority tastes would go unserved. Some critics of television believe that this is a fair description of prime-time network television. Each network vies to put on the most popular programs and as a result minority tastes are ill served.

Well, so what? Almost everyone in this country either now has or soon will have cable television with 50 or 100 or even 200 different channels to choose among. With that many channels, programming for small audiences with specialized tastes becomes entirely feasible. It would not have been surprising, therefore, if the Commission had taken the position that diversity in prime-time television programming, or indeed in over-the-air broadcasting generally, was no longer a value worth promoting. It did not take that position. Instead it defended its restrictions on network participation in programming on the ground that they promote diversity. But it made no attempt to explain how they do this. It could have said, but did not, that independent television stations depend on reruns, which they would prefer to get from sources other than the networks with which they compete, and—since reruns are the antithesis of diversity—they use their revenue from reruns to support programming that enhances programming diversity. It could have said that programs produced by networks' in-house facilities are somehow more uniform than programs produced by Hollywood studios. It didn't say that either. It never drew the link between the rules, which on their face impede the production of television programs—not only by constraining negotiations between networks and outside producers but also by reducing the networks' incentive to produce by limiting the extent to which a network can exhibit its own programs in prime time—and the interest in diverse programming. The Commission may have thought the link obvious, but it is not. The rules appear to handicap the networks and by handicapping them to retard new entry into production; how all this promotes programming diversity is mysterious, and was left unexplained in the Commission's opinion.

That opinion, despite its length, is unreasoned and unreasonable, and therefore, in the jargon of judicial review of administrative action, arbitrary and capricious. The Commission's order is therefore vacated and the matter is returned to the Commission for further proceedings. The Commission may of course reopen the record of the rulemaking proceeding to receive additional comments if that will help it reach an articulate reasoned decision.

There is one loose end. The precise form of our order could be important. The Commission's order both adopted new rules and vacated the old ones, the 1970 rules. If we simply vacate the order, this would seem to imply that the old rules—which the Commission itself believes outmoded—would spring back into effect. One of the networks therefore asks us to leave undisturbed the portion of the Commission's order that vacates the old rules. The other parties have not addressed this issue. It could be important because the Commission may take some time to determine its further course in light of our order. We have therefore decided to stay our order for 30 days to give the parties an opportunity to submit supplementary briefs on the question of its exact scope and terms. Briefs are due within 15 days of today and shall be limited to 10 pages in length; parties aligned on the same side of the case are urged to file a joint brief.

VACATED.

KEY TERMS

Bill of Rights

CATV

Cable Act

Cable Television Consumer Protection and Competition Act

Children's Television Act of 1990

Communications Act of 1934

cross ownership

direct broadcast satellite (DBS)

duopoly

express contract

Federal Communications Commission (FCC)

First Amendment

home satellite dish (TVRO)

implied contract

indecency

low-power television service

MMDS

may-carry rules

multiple ownership

multi-point distribution service (MDS)

must-carry rules

option contract

oral contract

paparazzi

pre-emption

right to privacy

satellite master antenna television
    (SMATV)

spectrum space

step agreement

UHF

universal service

VHF

EXERCISES

1. Briefly explain why television is the most regulated of all of the entertainment media.

2. Analyze the provisions of the option agreement in Exhibit 4-1 on page 144 and compare these provisions to similar contracts used in other media.

3. Contact the FCC and obtain their forms for applying for a broadcast license.

4. Discuss the constitutional implications of news broadcasting.

5. Discuss the impact of television syndication rights on creative artists.

6. Read *Sony Corp. of America et al. v. Universal City Studios, Inc. et al.*, 464 US 467, to see how the United States Supreme Court dealt with the problem of copyrights and VCRs. What is the impact of this case on DVDs today?

7. Discuss what you believe may be the legal impact of television programs being transmitted over the Internet. Do traditional legal theories apply to this type of situation? Explain.

8. What is your opinion of the regulation of airwaves? Does this impact individual rights and liberties? Discuss.

9. Television programming has been blamed for causing violence in society. What is your opinion of this attitude? How could you correct this?

10. Briefly discuss the provisions that you feel would be important to include in a television contract.

EXHIBIT

Exhibit 4-1 depicts a sample option agreement.

Option Agreement

Dear   [Author]:

This letter, when signed by you, will confirm our agreement for an option for us to acquire the exclusive television, film, and allied rights in the work written by you (the 'Work'), and described in the attached Exhibit A, on the following terms:

1. In return for $_____, you are giving us the exclusive option for _____ months from the date of this letter to acquire the exclusive television, video, film, multimedia, and allied rights for the Work, in perpetuity, for exploitation worldwide in all media.

2. Should we exercise our option, we will give you notice and pay you a fee of $_____, less the amount described in Paragraph 1 above.

3. If we exercise our option, we will have the right to produce or co-produce one or more projects based on the Work, adapted as we feel necessary, or to license the production to any other producer, broadcaster, etc. We will have the right to use your name and likeness in publicizing any such production.

4. You do not grant us any literary publishing rights in the Work, other than the right to use customary excerpts and synopses in connection with productions. You warrant that the grant of rights you are making, and our exploitation of those rights as provided herein, will not infringe on the rights of any third party.

5. It is our intention to enter into a longer agreement containing these and other terms customary in the entertainment industry, but unless and until such a longer agreement is fully signed by both you and us, this letter will be the complete agreement between us.

Yours sincerely,
[Production Company]

By:
[Producer]

AGREED TO AND ACCEPTED:

[Author]

[Note: Attach Exhibit A describing the Work]

EXHIBIT 4-1 Option Agreement

CHAPTER

5

FILM

CHAPTER OVERVIEW

For many people of the world, the term *entertainment* means the movies. Arguably, the greatest means of reporting and recording society and culture is the motion picture. No other medium is capable of creating an immediate visual record of a point in time in a manner that is both historical and artistic. Further, for the United States especially, the film industry provides one of the greatest sources of domestic and foreign revenue. For these reasons, the entertainment-law professional should be familiar with the application of American legal principles to the film industry.

Possibly no other entertainment medium has garnered as much attention as motion pictures. From its earliest days, including the period referred to as the "Golden Age of Hollywood" when film production was controlled by a small and select group of studios located primarily on the West Coast, to the present period in which film production is increasingly in the hands of independent producers, the motion picture industry has been fraught with legal problems concerned with constitutionally protected speech and censorship, antitrust violations associated with studio control, copyright infringements, and invasions of privacy regulated by both the Constitution and tort law. Although many of these legal questions have already been addressed, as technology advances new problems and concerns affect the creation and distribution of film. Some of the most intellectually challenging of these questions involve the contractual arrangements that may evolve between the creative participants and the producer of the film, the effect of union involvement in the film industry, the artist's control over his or her end product, and the effect of computer technology on licensing agreements and infringements.

This chapter will examine the law surrounding the contractual clauses involved in producing a motion picture, the conflict between American and European laws with respect to an artist's right to control distortion of his or her creative output (the film) once it is in the hands of the producer, and the impact of the various unions representing the different participants in the creative-film process. Several threshold questions concerning constitutional rights, federal regulation, and the legal structure of the film industry have already been addressed, either directly or by implication, in the preceding chapters.

PROPERTY FOR MOTION PICTURES

The phrase *property for motion pictures* is used to denote the acquisition of all of the personnel and materials that are necessary to create a movie. This property includes the writer, director, and actors and production staff, as well as the completed screenplay.

In order to create the screenplay, the producer, the person in charge of managing all of this property, may either hire a writer to create an original screenplay or may acquire the right to adapt material from a different medium into a screenplay. If the former method is chosen, the writer is considered an employee of the producer and the resulting screenplay is a work for hire (chapters 2 and 7 and Exhibit 5-1 on page 162). If the latter method is used, the producer must obtain rights from the holder of the work's copyright in order to make the adaptation.

— Example —

A producer has an idea for a film based on his own experiences as a child growing up in Indiana. He hires a scriptwriter to create the screenplay. This is an original idea developed directly for film, and the screenplay, in this instance, would probably be considered a work for hire with all rights held by the producer/employer.

Example

A producer reads a novel and feels that it would make an excellent film. He contacts the author, who holds the copyright, to acquire the appropriate permission to develop a screenplay based on the book.

In developing an idea for a screenplay, regardless of whether it is an original idea or an adaptation from a different work, the initial process involves pitching the idea to a potential film producer. **Pitch** simply means presenting the proposal to a producer in a format that can be used as the basis for accepting or rejecting the proposal. In general, this process is identical to the process involved in presenting a proposal for a book to a publisher. For screenplays, the pitch may take one of three forms, all of which are automatically copyrighted under the common law to the writer:

pitch
Proposal used to attract a potential producer.

1. A **step outline** is a detailed outline similar to a Table of Contents, in which the entire project is laid out, not scene-by-scene but only in outline form

step outline
Proposal written in outline format.

2. A **treatment** includes a detailed synopsis of the work, usually between twenty and fifty pages in length

treatment
Proposal written as a short synopsis of the intended work.

3. A **spec script** is a completed first draft of the screenplay; this format is the most time-consuming and financially detrimental for the writer.

spec script
Script written in advance of finding a producer.

If the pitch is successful and a producer is willing to go forward with the project, several contractual provisions specific to the film industry must be addressed. To determine the nature of the particular rights involved in screenplay contracts, the following checklist may prove useful for the entertainment law professional:

- Is the work original or based on another work? This question is especially important if the film is based on a published work that is not yet in the public domain. To produce the work, the film producer and/or writer must obtain the appropriate releases from the holder of the work's copyright.

- Is the writer an employee of the producer or an independent contractor? During the Golden Age of Hollywood, when the film industry was dominated by a few major studios, most screenwriters were under contract to the studio as employees, thus making the screenplay a work for hire. Nowadays, because of the proliferation of independent film companies, many screenplays are created by independent contractors, meaning that copyrights and obligations must be negotiated in the contract.

- How are distribution rights to be allocated? As discussed in chapter 4, distribution rights can form a major source of the income and profits derived from the film. As a consequence, the party who controls distribution can have a tremendous impact on the profitability of the film.

Writers' Guild of America (WGA)
Writers' union.

option
Exclusive right to acquire a work for a set period of time.

option/purchase agreement
Contract used by producers to acquire screenplays by writers.

This checklist must be addressed *prior* to negotiating the terms of the screenwriter's contract. However, the concept of "negotiation" is generally far more limited with respect to screenplays than with other entertainment contracts because of the large financial risk involved in film production and the influence of the industry's labor unions. The **Writers' Guild of America (WGA)** is the major union involved in screenplay contracts, and it mandates specific contract provisions to protect its members. Some of the clauses incorporated into its standard contract will be discussed throughout this chapter, and can be seen in Exhibit 5-1.

In order to acquire the right to a work as a screenplay, the producer may enter into a contract to option the material. An **option** is a legal right that may be exercised only by the holder. Note that an option for the purpose of the film industry is distinct from an option in the music industry, discussed in chapter 7. In this context, the producer would enter into an **option/purchase agreement**, a contract entitling the producer to buy the rights to the material. During the period of the option, the copyright holder may not sell these rights to anyone other than the option holder. In consideration of this agreement, the producer pays the copyright holder a negotiated fee.

The period of the option will depend upon the negotiating skill of the parties; the typical option period at the present time is one year. In the common option/purchase agreement, the following terms and conditions may be found:

1. The price of the option can be applied to the eventual price of purchasing the rights.

--- **Example** ---

Pursuant to the terms of the agreement, a producer pays a writer $25,000 for the option to acquire rights for the writer's novel. The contract states that if the option is exercised, the producer will pay the writer $250,000 for these rights, but the $25,000 option fee will be applied to this sum so that, if the option is exercised, the writer will receive an additional $225,000. Note that if the option is not exercised, the writer gets to keep the option fee.

free option
Price to obtain the option is not applied to the eventual purchase price.

2. The price of the option will belong to the copyright holder without being applied to the eventual purchase price, referred to as a **free option**.

--- **Example** ---

A film company obtains a right to develop a novel into a film. To acquire this right, the film company gives the novelist a free option of $100,000. The total purchase price is $1 million. If the film company exercises its option, it must pay the novelist $1 million in addition to the $100,000 it has already paid the writer.

3. If the material is to be adapted for television rather than as a theatrical release, such use must be specified and, as a general rule, the option price is typically lower.

— *Example* —————————————————————

A television network wants to develop a novel into a made-for-television film. It acquires an option from the novel's author for a price much lower than a film company would have to pay to acquire similar rights to develop the novel into a feature-length film.

—————————————————————————————

4. Pursuant to the Writers' Guild requirements, unless an option contract is in place, the producer is prohibited from shopping the material to a third party. **Shopping** is the practice of sending scripts to studios to see if any interest in the project can be garnered. If a producer shops the material without first having an option agreement with the writer, the writer's material may be rejected without the writer receiving any consideration.

shopping
Sending material to a studio without compensating the writer.

— *Example* —————————————————————

A major film producer convinces a young writer to let him have some of the writer's work for a few weeks. The producer then sends the material to several studios that do not express any interest in the work. The producer tells the writer that he is not interested in the material. If the writer tries to sell the material directly to the studio, the studio records will indicate that they have already viewed and rejected the material. The writer's work has been shopped without the writer receiving any consideration.

—————————————————————————————

Pursuant to the Writers' Guild, if a producer shops material without first having an option/purchase agreement with the author, the producer is required to pay the Guild a fine that the Guild in turn transfers to the writer.

5. The option agreement may be extended in the event of an Act of God, known as a **force majeure**, which will permit the option holder not to make a decision within the original option period. Events such as a labor strike or a studio shutdown have been deemed sufficient forces majeure to trigger this provision.

force majeure
Act of God.

Once the option has been exercised, all other rights with respect to the material come into play. For example, granting the right to adapt a book into a motion picture does not automatically grant the right to merchandise the material (marketing T-shirts, jackets, and so forth). Further, the original writer may still retain the right to adapt the work into other media. In such circumstances, many contracts include **holdback** provisions, a time period during which any rights retained by the parties may not be exercised. This provision affords some

holdback
Period during which certain retained rights cannot be exercised.

guarantee that the producer will be able to maximize his or her profit on the material before it is transferred to another medium.

— *Example* —

A producer has purchased the right to adapt a novel into a feature-length film. The writer has retained television and stage rights. To protect the producer, the author agrees that she will not adapt the work into a stage play for a stated period after the initial release of the film.

Many of these contracts contain fairly standard provisions to delineate the rights and obligations of the parties. Some of the most pertinent of these standard clauses are:

1. *Separation-of-rights clause*, indicating that all rights under the agreement will revert to each party upon the happening of a stated condition within a certain number of years.

— *Example* —

A screenwriter and a producer enter into a contract for the film production of a screenplay prepared by the writer. The contract states that if the producer does not make the film within three years of the date of the execution of the contract, all rights revert to the writer. After three years, if the film has not yet been produced, the writer may then pitch the film to a different producer.

2. *Loan-out provision*, which was much more common in the past, provides for the loan of an employee-writer from one employer-producer to another. If the writer is an employee, this provision permits the writer to work for another producer without being in breach of a covenant not to compete clause, and also evidences that the finished work is a work for hire.

3. *Certificate of authority*, similar to the general warranty clause previously discussed, mandates that the film is either an original work of the screenwriter or that the screenwriter has obtained all necessary releases to avoid potential copyright-infringement litigation.

4. *Editorial rights*, for films, unlike general publishing contracts, enable the writer to retain significant control over the editing of the work. In the United States, such rights are granted pursuant to the **Visual Artists Rights Act of 1990**, 17 USC 106A. It should be noted that in Europe screenwriters have what are termed **moral rights**, which have no direct American counterpart. These European rights permit the writer to have greater control over the use of his or her artistic product.

5. *Termination rights*, under 17 USC 203, allow anyone who pitches a product to terminate the project, for cause, for a thirty-five-year period. These

Visual Artists Rights Act of 1990
Federal statute designed to extend certain rights of control over their works to authors.

moral rights
Rights to retain a work's integrity granted to artists under European laws.

rights do not attach to works for hire, and mandate that the project can be resuscitated only with the original author, and that author can stop any unauthorized use or change to the project. These termination rights have sometimes been viewed as similar to the European moral rights; they are designed to protect the writer from having the work changed in a manner that the author believes destroys the integrity of his or her work.

For the parties involved, probably the most important provision is the financial term of the purchase. The following is a list of some of the standard payment provisions that may be negotiated for the sale of a work:

exercise price
Consideration given to a writer to purchase a screenplay.

- **Exercise price,** a fixed price stated in the agreement. This amount may be paid either in a lump sum when the option is exercised (rare), or divided up over several payments as specified in the agreement (typical).

bonus based on budget
Method of compensating a writer by granting him a payment above the exercise price for a script based on a percentage of the film's operating budget.

- **Bonus based on budget,** the price agreed upon and is stated as a percentage of the actual budget for the film production, usually with a minimum fee indicated. Because budgets for productions may vary from initial estimates, this could provide a greater fee to the copyright holder than just the exercise price.

bonus based on credit
Method of compensating a writer by granting him a payment above the exercise price for a script based on his eventual credit for the film.

- **Bonus based on credit,** an amount above the exercise price that the copyright holder will receive based on the credit he or she gets for the eventual production. For example, if the copyright holder is the one who adapts the material by writing the screenplay, her credit will be more important than that of merely being the author of the work on which the film is based. Also, during production other writers may be called upon to revise the original screenplay. The value of this bonus is dependent upon the value of the credit that may be negotiated in the initial contract (see chapter 8).

contingent payment
Method of purchasing a script by allocating profits and losses rather than having a set price.

net profit
Revenues less expenses.

gross profit
Revenue before expenses.

double add-back
Doubling all costs over the budget as an expense of the film.

- **Contingent payment,** the payment that the original copyright holder receives as a percentage of net or gross profit. **Net profit** reflects all receipts received after deducting all expenses. **Gross profit** reflects all revenue without deducting expenses. The determination of what constitutes an expense can cause the eventual amount the parties will receive to vary a great deal (this concept is further discussed in chapter 7). Further, many such contingent agreements include a **double add-back** provision that operates as a penalty if the production costs exceed the budget. With this provision, the amount of expenses exceeding the budget are doubled and then deducted as an expense against profits.

These financial arrangements, although addressed above in terms of the producer's agreement with the copyright holder, apply equally to all of the other professionals involved in the production. The producer, the director, and the actors may each be compensated in one of the above-indicated fashions. In these instances, the exercise price would be called the contract price for the work. However, with producers and directors, studios may have what is referred to as a

cross-collateralization charge. This charge applies whenever the producer or director is retained by the studio for multiple projects. In these circumstances, the studio may link the costs of all of the projects together to determine the expenses to be deducted in calculating a **contingent fee arrangement**, whereby the eventual fee is determined as a percentage of the profits. This causes a financially unsuccessful film to make money for the studio because its losses are offset against a popular film made by the same director.

The producer of the project, the one who coordinates all of the various parts of the production for the studio, is engaged by being paid a **development fee**, a set sum to guarantee that the producer will be available for a specific project. However, this could create problems for the producer, who basically is being kept on hand until the studio actually begins the project. Consequently, producers often negotiate a **progress-to-production clause**, which vacates the agreement if the project is not begun within a specific period of time. This clause also permits the producer to pursue other projects and may contain a **turnaround provision**, permitting the producer to take the project to a second studio during the progress-to-production period. If the producer does entice a second studio, that studio must reimburse the first studio for all of the first studio's costs expended on the project to date.

Because of the number of creative people involved, in most instances studios and independent producers acquire key man insurance on the principal artists involved in the project. As discussed in chapter 3, this insurance will compensate the studio or producer if the insured is injured or dies prior to completing his or her role with respect to the film, which would potentially cost the producer millions of dollars.

UNIONS

This text is not designed as a treatise on American labor law and unions, but it is virtually impossible to discuss the motion-picture industry without discussing the impact of the various unions on film production. Although almost every category of worker involved in making a film does or may belong to a union, from the electricians and carpenters to the drivers and costume designers, this section of the text will focus on the unions to which the "creative" personnel belong: the **Directors Guild of America (DGA)**, the Writers Guild of America (WGA), and the **Screen Actors Guild (SAG)**.

Since the 1930s, unions and collective bargaining have been recognized and encouraged by the federal government, and the various federal statutory enactments dealing with unions have been determined to apply to the artistic fields. Although studios and production companies are not prohibited from engaging the services of nonunion members, such hiring is, in practice, fairly limited, and even when such nonunion personnel are hired, if the production is a union production these persons may acquire temporary union status for the duration of the filming. However, the question remains as to what benefits are afforded members of these various artistic guilds and what, if any, detriments may ensue from such membership.

As a general statement, all of the artistic guilds promulgate constitutions to define their relationship with their members. When an individual elects to become a member of a particular guild, he or she agrees to be bound by the provisions of its constitution, and the courts have interpreted these constitutions to create contractual relationships between the union and its members.

The benefits associated with guild membership are similar to those benefits afforded to members of all labor unions: The union negotiates, under the doctrines of collective bargaining, standard contracts that dictate minimum wages, credits, insurance benefits, and so forth for its members. Pursuant to general collective-bargaining doctrines, union membership provides for specified grievance procedures to mediate disputes between employers and member artists.

However, there are certain detriments for the artist with respect to membership in the guilds. If the member violates any of the guild's rules, such as working on a nonunion production or working for a studio during a strike, the member is subject to internal disciplinary procedures that could result in fines, suspension from the union, or actual expulsion. Once a member is expelled from a union, he or she may find it difficult to obtain further work.

— *Example*

The Screen Actors Guild has declared a strike in order to force studios to negotiate an increased minimum wage for its members. During the strike an actress, in need of funds, works on a "scab" production (a production being filmed in spite of the strike). When the SAG officials discover her participation, she is subject to an internal hearing, after which SAG suspends her for a six-month period for violating a SAG rule by working during a declared strike.

Any disciplinary action taken by the union may be enforced by means of a lawsuit filed in the appropriate state court.

In order to avoid internal disciplinary actions and to afford greater variety in work, many performers opt to change their status from regular membership to what is termed *financial core status*. **Financial core status** indicates that an artist has resigned from the union but continues to pay all fees and dues in an amount determined to maintain the union's collective bargaining, contract administration, and grievance procedures for the benefit of its members. Financial core status relieves the artist from adherence to the union's constitution, while still allowing him or her to be protected by union benefits. However, financial core status precludes the artist from holding a union office, attending union meetings, and voting on collective-bargaining proposals.

financial core status
Method whereby a union member resigns membership but continues to pay fees.

— *Example*

A writer wants to keep working, even though his union has declared a strike. She opts for financial core status and thereby is permitted to write scripts for studios during the strike without being subject to disciplinary proceedings by the guild.

security clause
Contract provision indicating when a studio may hire nonunion members.

In order to avoid all, or most, problems associated with producing a nonunion production, both SAG and WGA have included **security clauses** in their standard contracts. These contract provisions permit employers to hire nonunion members, provided that the reason that the artist is not a union member is that he or she has failed to pay the appropriate dues. However, despite these clauses, employers may hire any nonunion member, regardless of the reason for the nonmembership under general labor law, *unless* such hiring is an attempt to violate labor law or a collective-bargaining agreement.

— *Example*

A studio wants to hire a foreign actor who does not belong to the Screen Actors Guild. The actor may be hired even though he is not a union member.

hyphenate
Union member performing some supervisory role as well.

Labor unions, including the artists' guilds, represent only members and are generally prohibited from representing employers and supervisors. However, in the film industry certain situations may arise that result in what is referred to as a *hyphenate*. A **hyphenate** is a union member who is also working in a supervisory category. The types of positions that are considered supervisory include producers and editors. Therefore, a writer who is a member of WGA may also be hired to act as a script editor or an assistant producer for a given project. In such situations, whether or not the guild may represent the member, hyphenate is determined on a case-by-case basis.

THE RUNAWAY PRODUCTION

runaway production
Films produced abroad designed for American distribution.

A fairly recent phenomenon in the American film industry is the runaway production. A **runaway production** is a film designed for the American market that is produced overseas. When Hollywood dominated the film industry, such runaway productions represented only a small fraction of United States film distribution. An example would be the "Spaghetti Westerns" filmed in the 1960s in Italy that were designed to be shown in the United States. However, recently such productions have become far more commonplace.

Several factors have been identified to explain this recent growth in runaway productions:

1. The increased global economy, in which more and more companies are segmented internationally in order to maximize profits. One corporation may have branches located all over the world, each branch producing a portion of the company's end product in the locale where that portion can be most inexpensively manufactured.

2. Increased distribution and production costs in the United States, in part resulting from union activity in increasing minimum wages.

3. Technology, which has advanced to such an extent that production standards can be maintained anywhere in the world.

4. Foreign government incentive, such as tax reductions and special reduced fees, used to encourage United States producers to film abroad, as well as foreign-exchange rates that can further reduce estimated expenses.

According to studies performed for the Screen Actors Guild and the Directors Guild of America, in 1998 alone American workers lost over $10 billion to runaway productions. In response to this financial decline in the film industry, California enacted a statute entitled **Film California First**, which is designed to increase California's ability to attract and retain film production within that state. Pursuant to this program, the state grants certain subsidies, such as leasing property at below market rates, to companies that film exclusively in California. It is anticipated that other states will soon follow suit and enact similar statutes to encourage American film production.

Film California First
Statute designed to attract film production in California.

COLORIZATION

Probably one of the most controversial legal problems facing the film industry at the present time concerns the colorization of motion pictures. Colorization refers to the technical process whereby a film that was produced in black and white is transformed into a color version. The legal question surrounding this process is whether this technology so transforms the original aesthetic of the film so as to infringe upon any rights to the film that the artist may have retained.

Exactly what is the colorization process? Colorization of a black-and-white film is accomplished by utilizing one of the following methods:

chromotoid process
A method of colorizing a film based on making prints of a black-and-white film in red, green, and blue and then combining those prints.

1. The **chromotoid process**, whereby a fine-grained black-and-white print is used to create a print in red, green, and blue by means of an optical printer (all colors are combinations of these three hues). These three color prints are then combined to create a new print that gives the impression of being fully colorized.

colorization process
Method of colorizing a film by assigning specific colors to a pixel version of the film.

pixel
Microdot.

2. The **colorization process**, whereby a computer dissects a film into individual frames and each frame is then bleached to create thousands of **pixels**, or microdots, similar to the process used in digital cameras. At this point an artistic director assigns a color to each pixel, which results in a colored version of the film.

The problem with both of these methods is that the ultimate result does not precisely mirror a film that is originally filmed in color, and so the impact on the viewer is slightly off. Proponents of colorization assert that these colored versions are not meant to imitate the original, but rather to be an adaptation of the original work. The opponents claim that these processes destroy the aesthetic integrity of the black-and-white film. These arguments could be seen to have more weight if the black-and-white film were created during a period in which black and white as well as color were available, and the creator selected black and white for artistic reasons.

At the time of this writing, the United States does not have any specific law that protects the integrity of the work the artist has created. Once the copyright to a film has been transferred to a studio or a production company, that copyright holder is free to make any changes to the original that he or she wishes. This is true even if such a change destroys the aesthetic integrity of the work.

However, under European law, creative artists, regardless of any rights to the work that they have transferred, retain what are called moral rights, or **droit moral**, which permit the artist to enjoin any change in his or her work that the artist can prove destroys the artist's original vision. These moral rights apply to all forms of creative endeavor, not just films. As stated above, there is no counterpart in American law, although the United States, as a signatory to the Berne Convention for the Protection of Artistic and Literary Works, may eventually be called upon to enact some form of similar protection because of a provision in the convention calling for the protection of the moral rights of artists.

Under European law, primarily developed in France, artists and authors are granted what is referred to as the **droit d'auteur**, or right of authorship, which is divided into moral rights and **droits patrimoniaux**, property rights. The moral rights grant an artist complete control over the artistic content of his or her work and permit the artist to retain rights to the presentation of the work. The basis of this moral right is the belief that an artist's work represents an extension of the artist's personality, and as such cannot be tarnished with impunity. In keeping with this concept, the *droit moral* affords an artist the following rights:

1. To have his or her name, authorship, and the integrity of the work respected
2. To prevent disclosure of a work the artist feels is incomplete
3. To withhold the work from distribution if the artist feels that the work no longer represents his or her artistic vision
4. To have absolute control over the use of his or her name with respect to the work
5. To enjoin modification of the work
6. To be free from excessive criticism.

These rights are retained by the artist, regardless of who may hold the copyrights on the works. Currently, American artists have been attempting to assert such artistic control over their creations by means of traditional American legal theories, such as unfair competition, defamation, invasion of privacy, and breach of contract.

Pursuant to American copyright law, colorized versions of black-and-white films are eligible for their own copyrights. The studio or producer of the film is

droit moral
European moral rights granted to artists to retain control over their works.

droit d'auteur
European right of authorship.

droits patrimoniaux
European property rights given to an artist over his work.

considered to be the creator, and so is the person who has exclusive rights to make all derivative works from the original. Unless the writer and/or director have retained derivative rights to the film, to protect the film's integrity the writer/director must be able to assert a right based on a different area of law. To date, four specific theories have been proffered by writers and directors to attempt to enjoin colorization:

1. *Contract right* Many creative individuals have started to insert specific provisions in their agreements with producers and studios whereby they retain or limit the right of the producer to make derivative works or they retain the right of final approval on all future depictions of the work. Although this approach would satisfy the artist, unless the artist has a tremendous degree of clout, it would be difficult to negotiate this provision.

— *Example*

A famous filmmaker has agreed to direct a film for a major studio. Because of his reputation, the filmmaker is able to retain the right of final approval over creating, editing, and making derivations of the film. Several years later, when the studio wants to make a colored version of the film for television release, the filmmaker is able to assert his rights under the contract to stop the process.

2. *A right under tort law* The Artist alleges that the change to the film defames the creator. This approach has not generally been found to be successful, because in order to meet the burden of proof, the work must disgrace the artist in the eyes of others. Although many people may oppose the process of colorization, it is virtually impossible to demonstrate that colorization has disgraced the creator of a black-and-white film

3. *Constitutional rights to privacy* These rights generally have not been held to protect the artist. Because the artist has placed the work before the public by distribution of the film, he or she cannot later claim that his or her privacy was invaded when the work is colorized

Lanham Act
Federal statute prohibiting unfair trade practices.

4. *Trademark infringement under the provisions of the **Lanham Act*** The Lanham Act is a federal statute that prohibits deceptive trade practices such as the appropriation of a copyrighted work by a third person. The Lanham Act also prohibits the misrepresentation of an artist's contribution to a literary or artistic work. This statute has been held to extend its protections to both actors and production personnel. To date, most of the litigation invoking the Lanham Act in this regard has only involved adapting films for television in which the original version is cut to fit into the confines of network timing. It has yet been applied to the colorization process, and it does not appear likely that it will provide a sufficient legal basis to enjoin colorization.

Recently, several statutes have been introduced in Congress in an attempt to extend European moral rights to American artists, but all such proposals have failed to be enacted. With the global reach of the film industry, it is likely that lawsuits will be forthcoming when foreign artists attempt to assert their moral rights against changes made for American distribution of their films.

CHAPTER REVIEW

The film industry probably represents the greatest export of entertainment for the United States. It is one of America's foremost industries and, consequently, it demands the attention of anyone involved in entertainment law.

Motion pictures are developed either by studios hiring authors to create original ideas for screenplays or by purchasing film rights to material that appears on other media or is written on speculation for feature films. In the latter instance, a writer typically employs the services of a literary agent who pitches a proposal to a studio or a producer to obtain a contract for the author. As with most areas of entertainment law, this contract forms the basis of the legal relationships involved in creating a film.

Probably the most important provisions of this agreement concern the payment to the creator and the determination of subsidiary rights to the material. In most circumstances, payments may be based on bonuses or contingent fees that are dependent upon the accounting methods used by the studio. For this reason, careful attention must be paid to the definitions of the accounting terms used in the agreement.

Subsidiary rights refer to the ability to market the screenplay to other media, such as television, stage, to sell T-shirts, and so forth. The individual who retains these rights may garner greater financial rewards than the person who only holds the copyright to the film itself.

In the film industry, the various artistic unions play an extremely important role in the development and production process. These unions mandate minimum wages and hours, standard contract provisions, health and insurance benefits, and other associated work procedures for the protection of their members. Although studios are permitted to hire nonunion members, such hiring is fairly uncommon and may result in certain internal disciplinary procedures for union members who participate in nonunion productions.

Recently, the hottest issue facing the film industry is the question of the colorization process, whereby black-and-white films are transformed into colored versions. Many creative artists believe that such transformation destroys their aesthetic visions, and efforts are being made to grant to American artists the same moral rights that European artists enjoy to retain artistic control over their creative work.

JUDICIAL DECISION

The following case discusses legal problems encountered with theatrical agency contracts.

Goldstone-Tobias Agency, Inc.
v.
Barbroo Enterprises Productions, Inc.

237 CalApp2d 720 (1965)

Respondent, (plaintiff) is a theatrical agency. Pursuant to written contracts of agency it solicits and exerts itself to obtain employment in various facets of the entertainment industry for its clients. Appellant (defendant) is a similar agency and at the time of this action and for some time prior thereto, represented Mickey Rooney, an actor.

On August 19, 1960, respondent had entered into an agency contract with Rooney to represent Rooney for one year for which representation respondent was to receive 10 per cent of Rooney's gross income in the entertainment industry. The agency contract was signed by one Red Doff, Rooney's personal manager, acting under a power of attorney from Rooney.

During its representation, respondent, under the 10 per cent arrangement, claimed that it had earned $13,500. In addition, respondent loaned Rooney $1,500, which was evidenced by a promissory note executed on March 8, 1961.The note was signed by Doff for Rooney under the power of attorney. The validity of this note and the indebtedness under it is admitted by appellant.

To collect the note respondent filed an action for $1,500 in the Municipal Court of Beverly Hills Judicial District. To collect its commissions respondent filed a proceeding for $13,500 before the Arbitration Tribunal of the Screen Actors Guild.

To avoid and eliminate the municipal court action and the arbitration proceeding the parties to the action and Rooney did on September 1, 1961, execute a settlement agreement (settlement) whereby appellant and Rooney agreed to pay respondent $9,000 in certain installments and reasonable attorney's fees if any action was brought to enforce the settlement; $650 had been paid on the settlement. No further payments having been made after demand therefor, the present action was filed to recover the balance.

Judgment was for respondent. This appeal is taken from that judgment.

Appellant seeks to avoid the settlement on the theory that it is invalid because Rooney did not personally sign the contract with respondent. He argues that the regulations of the Screen Actors Guild which are incorporated automatically into respondent's agency contract render all such agency contracts void if they are not signed by the actor himself. Forbearance to bring an action on an illegal contract, he asserts, cannot be consideration to support the settlement. This proposition is not sound.

It is settled that unless a claim is advanced in bad faith, or is without foundation, the actual validity of the claim is immaterial in determining whether forbearance from proceeding thereon is sufficient consideration (*Kale v. Bankamerica Agricultural Credit Corp.*, 2 CalApp2d 113, 117 (37 P2d 494); *Khasigian v. Arakelian*, 180 CalApp2d 10, 14 (4 CalRptr 148)).

In *Khasigian* at page 14 the court says: "It has been definitely held in *Union Collection Co. v. Buckman*, 150 Cal 159, 163 (88 P 708, 119 AmStRep 164, 11 AnnCas 609, 9 LRA NS 568):

> … the compromise of a doubtful claim asserted and maintained in good faith constitutes a sufficient consideration for a new promise, even though it may ultimately be found that the claimant could not have prevailed. This is true whether the claim be in suit or not.

…

There is no evidence in the record showing a lack of good faith. On the contrary, the trial court properly found that valid consideration supported the settlement.

Appellant also argues that the court committed error when it found that the settlement was not a guarantee contract based upon an antecedent indebtedness, since without an antecedent indebtedness the settlement would be "utterly valueless." This contention is without merit, for the consideration in a compromise agreement is not the discharge of a prior debt (which, indeed, may not even have existed), but the payment of money in return for forbearance from suit.

The trial court refused to admit a copy of the Screen Actors Guild regulations into evidence. Appellant urges error. The contention is based upon a stipulation contained in the pretrial order that any and all documents which were part of the arbitration file could be introduced into evidence "without foundation proof but subject to all other objections." The record shows that this evidence was rejected because of its immateriality and not for lack of foundation. Since the validity of a claim upon which a compromise agreement is based is not material to a determination of the sufficiency of consideration for that agreement, no error was committed in rejecting the proffered evidence. It could be argued however that the regulations were relevant to the issue of good faith on the part of the respondents in pressing their claim on an allegedly void agency contract. Assuming arguendo that the evidence should have been admitted on this issue, no reversible error resulted since the questionable applicability of the regulations to respondent's claim could show no bad faith on the part of the respondent.

Appellant's final contention is that respondent knew at the time the compromise agreement was signed, that Rooney did not want to go to court on the promissory note or to arbitration on the agency contract because he was just emerging from a "slump" and could not afford the bad publicity. From this, appellant argues that the settlement was entered into by appellant under the pressure of economic compulsion.

The underlying principle of the defense of economic compulsion is the performance of, or threat to perform, some unlawful act under circumstances sufficient to control the actions of a reasonable man (*Young v. Hoagland*, 212 Cal 426, 431 (208 P 996, 75 ALR 654); *Thompson Crane & Trucking Co. v. Eyman*, 123 CalApp2d 904, 908–909 (267 P2d 1043)).

In the case at bench, respondent's only conduct was to press an apparently valid claim using the due process of the law to recover monies which it in good faith believed were owing. It was not required to drop the legal proceedings it had instituted because of Rooney's alleged plight. The exercise of a legal right does not constitute unlawful duress or compulsion under the law of this state (*International Fishermen & Allied Workers of America v. Stemland*, 97 CalApp2d Supp 931, 934 (219 P2d 554)).

The judgment is affirmed.

KEY TERMS

bonus based on budget	*droits partimoniaux*
bonus based on credit	exercise price
chromotoid process	Film California First
colorization process	financial core status
contingent payment	force majeure
cross-collateralization charge	free option
development fee	gross profit
Directors Guild of America (DGA)	holdback
double add-back	hyphenate
droit d'auteur	Lanham Act
droit moral	moral rights

net profit	security clause
option	shopping
option/purchase agreement	spec script
pitch	step outline
pixel	treatment
progress-to-production clause	turnaround provision
runaway production	Visual Artists Rights Act of 1990
Screen Actors Guild (SAG)	Writers Guild of America (WGA)

EXERCISES

1. What is your opinion of the colorization of black-and-white films? Do you believe it destroys the integrity of the original version?

2. Should the concept of an artist's moral right be incorporated into American law? Discuss.

3. Does your state have any laws to promote film production? If so, what is your opinion of their benefits and effectiveness?

4. Briefly discuss the purpose and benefits of financial core status.

5. Discuss the importance of delineating accounting methods in a bonus based fee contract.

6. Read *Stewart v. Abend, dba Authors Research Co.*, 495 US 207. What does this case add to your understanding of the problems involved in producing a film from a derivative work? How does this case relate to chapter 2 of this text? Explain.

7. Analyze the provisions of Exhibit 5-1 on page 162, the Screen Actors' Guild Producer Incentive Media Agreement. Which provisions are most favorable to the producer, and which favor the other artists? How would you use this contract as a form for negotiating a film contract? Discuss.

8. Should artists have unions? Do you feel the unions are beneficial or detrimental to the creation of a motion picture?

9. How does the independent film producer fit into the legal principles discussed in this chapter?

10. How would you develop a pitch to convince a producer to create a film from your favorite novel (assume you have rights to that novel)?

EXHIBIT

Screen Actors' Guild Producer Incentive Media Agreement

AMENDED 1993-1995
SCREEN ACTORS GUILD-PRODUCER
INTERACTIVE MEDIA AGREEMENT

This AGREEMENT is made by and between the SCREEN ACTORS GUILD, INC. (hereinafter sometimes referred to as the "Guild" or "SAG"), and Producer.

ARTICLE I - GENERAL

1. TITLE OF AGREEMENT

This agreement shall be referred to as the AMENDED 1993-1995 SCREEN ACTORS GUILD, INC.-PRODUCER INTERACTIVE MEDIA AGREEMENT ("Agreement"), and includes the Articles I, II and III hereof.

2. RECOGNITION

A. The Guild is recognized as the exclusive bargaining agent for all Principal Performers (throughout the United States) and Extra Performers (only in the zones specified in Section 10 below) in the production of Material for Interactive Media. The term "Performer" as used herein means those persons covered by this Agreement as defined in Section 4.F.

B. The terms and conditions of this Agreement apply to those applicable Interactive Programs produced by Producer in the United States, its commonwealths and possessions, and to Interactive Programs for which Producer engages Performers within the United States, its commonwealths and possessions, wherever such Interactive Programs are produced.

3. APPLICATION
This Agreement shall not apply to the following:

A. Interactive Programs in which (1) part or all of the audio portion replicates a phonograph recording, tape, or disc or portion thereof, as those recordings are known under the AFTRA Phono Code and (2) the video portion consists of concert-type footage which may or may not include performers other than the recording artist(s), and/or other visual information (e.g., lyrics, text, still photos, or biographical information).

EXHIBIT 5-1 Screen Actors' Guild Producer Incentive Media Agreement

B. Interactive Programs consisting of still photographs with or without narration.

C. Any tape production more than half of which is made up of excerpts or whole programs that were produced under an AFTRA agreement.

D. Any tape production more than half of which is made up of news, game shows, quiz panel type shows, or talk shows.

4. DEFINITIONS

A. "Material": includes all products (audio or visual) derived from the recordation of the performances of Performers hereunder, whether or not such performances are incorporated into the final version of the fully-edited Interactive Program produced hereunder by Producer.

B. "Interactive": Interactive describes the attribute of products which enables the viewer to manipulate, affect or alter the presentation of the creative content of such product simultaneous with its use by the viewer.

C.

(i) "Interactive Media" means: any media on which Interactive product operates and through which the user may interact with such product including but not limited to personal computers, games, machines, arcade games, all CD-Interactive machines and any and all analogous, similar or dissimilar microprocessor-based units and the digitized, electronic or any other formats now known or hereinafter invented which may be utilized in connection therewith; and

(ii) "Remote Delivery" means any system by or through which Interactive product may be accessed for use from a location that is remote from the central processing unit on which the product is principally used or stored, such as an on-line service, a delivery service over cable television lines, telephone lines, microwave signals, radio waves, satellite, wireless cable or any other service or method now known or hereinafter invented for the delivery of transmission of such Interactive product.

"Interactive Media" and "Remote Delivery" specifically exclude the Linear transmission of Interactive Programs by: (i) traditional, public or commercially sponsored over-the-air network television (i.e., PBS, NBC, CBS, ABC or Fox), syndicated television broadcasts (UHF or VHF), and cable television transmission (i.e., HBO, TNT, Showtime); and (ii) radio broadcasts, which uses are not included within the subject matter of this Agreement; and any other systems now known or hereafter invented for the transmission of Linear Programs.

EXHIBIT 5-1 Screen Actors' Guild Producer Incentive Media Agreement (*continued*)

D. "Program": A Program refers to the final version of a fully-edited product for presentation to the viewer or user. An "Interactive Program" is the final version of a fully-edited product presented on or through Interactive Media, notwithstanding any variations which may occur between Platforms or Remote Delivery methods. "Program" does not refer to the computer software code utilized in the digitization process, any type of electronic technology, patents, trademarks or any of the intellectual property rights of Producer.

E. "Platform(s)": Platform refers to microprocessor-based hardware including but not limited to SEGA, Nintendo and 3DO machines that utilize the appropriate compatible formats such as cartridges and discs, or any other formats now known or hereinafter invented which memorialize Interactive Programs for viewer use.

F. "Performers": Persons whose performances are used as on or off-camera, including those who speak, act, sing, or in any other manner perform as talent in Material for Interactive Media.

G. "Principal Performer(s)": Principal Performers are: (i) Performers who are used on-camera who speak dialogue or portray a major part in the Interactive Program and are hired as Day Performers, Three-Day or Weekly Performers; (ii) Singers; (iii) Stunt Performers; (iv) Puppeteers, and (v) Voice-Over Performers, and (vi) Choreographed Dancers, Swimmers and Skaters. Principal Performers specifically exclude Extra Performers.

H. "Loan-Out Company": A Loan-Out Company is a corporation which is controlled by a Performer and which furnishes the Performer's services to others.

I. "Qualified Professional Performer": A Qualified Professional Performer is a person who has had prior employment as a Performer at least once during the period of three (3) years preceding the date of proposed employment hereunder.

J. "Day Performer": A Day Performer is a Principal Performer employed by the day.

K. "Three-Day Performer": A Three-Day Performer is a Principal Performer employed for three (3) consecutive days, other than a Singer, Dancer, Stunt Performer or Airplane Pilot.

L. "Weekly Performer": A Weekly Performer is a Principal Performer employed on a weekly basis.

M. "Voice-Over Performer": A Voice-Over Performer is one who provides off-camera narration or other vocal services (except singing) for Interactive Programs.

EXHIBIT 5-1 Screen Actors' Guild Producer Incentive Media Agreement (*continued*)

N. "Looping": Looping services are those audio recording services provided by a Principal Performer in the sound studio to correct, enhance or augment the audio portion of a Performer's performance which was visually recorded during Principal Photography.

O. "Singer(s)": A Singer is a Principal Performer that musically vocalizes either alone, or with other Singer(s), and who may also speak written lines.

(i) A "Specialty Singer" is a professional Singer employed for a solo or employed as part of a "name" group;

(ii) A "Contractor" is a professional Singer who contributes services to Producer in addition to singing by assembling a group of three (3) or more Singers for the production and is entitled to the additional compensation for such services as specified in Sections 16. A. and B. A Singer shall not be deemed a Contractor by assembling a group which is an established group or act.

(iii) "Over-dubbing" or "Multiple Tracking" occurs when a Singer re-records over the Singer's original track containing the same Material as recorded on the original track.

(iv) "Sweetening": occurs when a Singer records a new track containing new or variant Material over the Singer's original track.

(v) "Stepping out" occurs when a Singer is asked by the Producer to sing a solo or duo during a recording session in addition to his/her performance within the group.

P. "Extra Performer": Extra Performers are non-Principal Performers who do not speak any words other than atmospheric words as part of a crowd, commonly known in the industry as "omnies".

(i) A "Qualified Professional Extra Performer" is an Extra Performer who has had prior employment as such at least once during the period of three (3) years preceding the date of proposed employment hereunder.

(ii) A "Special Ability Extra Performer" is an Extra Performer who is directed to and does satisfactorily perform in accordance with such Extra Performer's special talents or abilities.

Q. "Computer animation": Visual characters and graphics based on computer generated art to simulate life-like movement in the characters.

R. "Integration": Integration is the inclusion of any Material from a Principal Performer's performance rendered under the terms of this Agreement in one or more Programs for Interactive

EXHIBIT 5-1 Screen Actors' Guild Producer Incentive Media Agreement (*continued*)

Media produced by Producer for which the Principal Performer is not employed to render services. "Integration" does *not* mean or include: (i) the repetition of segments of any single Interactive Program that may appear to be many different Programs due to the way viewers choose or recall various segments and manipulate the Program, (ii) the reconfiguration or re-formulation of the Material produced hereunder for a single Program for the computer software code to adapt the Interactive Program to different Platforms or Remote Delivery systems, (iii) the use of Material for Interactive Media in Linear Programs.

S. "Linear": Programs which do not possess Interactive qualities are "linear" in nature, and "Linear Program(s)" mean those Programs which are:

(i) produced and memorialized by means of videotape or film photography or any other processes now known or hereafter invented through which photographic images or other visual representations (whether live-action or animated) are used alone, or in conjunction with audio effects, and create life-like images of the characters therein, and are:

(ii) exhibited or transmitted to the viewer by:

(a) television (UHF or VHF over-the-air broadcast, cable, satellite, or any other means or methods which may now be known or hereafter invented for television reception); and/or

(b) video cassettes, video discs or any other devices used in conjunction with corresponding hardware to cause a presentation to be exhibited visually on the screen of a television receiver or any comparable device; and/or

(c) film projection in motion picture theaters.

For example "Linear Program(s)" include theatrically exhibited motion pictures, network and cable television pilots/series and made-for-television films, films on cassettes and discs, "live" television or other traditional, filmed or videotaped, non-Interactive entertainment programming. "Linear Program(s)" do not include any Programs produced hereunder for Interactive Media, notwithstanding any method of delivery to the viewer or venue for exhibition of Interactive Programs which may utilize television cable, wire (or any other means or methods) which heretofore have been utilized to transmit or exhibit Linear Program(s).

T. "Linear Television": The act of broadcasting or transmitting Linear Program(s) to the viewer.

U. "Motion Picture Exhibition": The act of exhibiting Linear Program(s) in motion picture theaters before audiences.

EXHIBIT 5-1 Screen Actors' Guild Producer Incentive Media Agreement (*continued*)

V. "Minimum Applicable Compensation": The Minimum Applicable Compensation is the base amount on which additional fees are calculated to determine payments due Principal Performers for Remote Delivery and/or Integration as specified in Section 15.

W. "Trailer": A short audio and/or visual presentation used to promote the Interactive Program which may include excerpts therefrom.

X. "Overtime" payments are sums paid to Performers in addition to their initial compensation for services as a result of time worked beyond the regular workday.

Y. "Liquidated Damages" are those sums paid to Performer in addition to his/her initial compensation for services as a result of Producer's violation of a working condition hereunder (e.g., meal period violation).

Z. "Reuse" means the incorporation of Material produced hereunder in any Program other than another Interactive Program produced by Producer hereunder.

A.A. "Scale": The minimum compensation payable to Performers for applicable services hereunder.

B.B. "Overscale" is any compensation paid to a Performer for services which is greater than Scale for the applicable services (excluding Overtime and Liquidated Damages).

C.C. "Stunt Coordinator" is a trained, Qualified Professional who plans and supervises the execution of stunts.

D.D. "Principal Photography" refers to the period of production when a Producer is recording Performers in a substantial portion of the creative Material for an Interactive Program. "Principal Photography" does not include tests, auditions, pre-recording of Material occurring before the actual production of an Interactive Program, and any services which are customarily considered ancillary to the primary taping, photography or visual recordation of Material such as Retakes, Added Scenes, etc.

E.E. "Retakes, Added Scenes, Etc.": are on-camera or off-camera services which are required by Producer in addition to Principal Photography in connection with a Performer's performance such as retakes, added scenes, work for soundtracks including looping and dubbing, process shots, transparencies, trick shots, trailers, including changes or additional shots of any of the foregoing to adapt an Interactive Program for Platforms or foreign versions.

EXHIBIT 5-1 Screen Actors' Guild Producer Incentive Media Agreement (continued)

F.F A "Promotional Program": is a specially-produced Program, the subject matter of which is "the making of" the applicable Interactive Program produced hereunder which may include interviews, behind-the-scenes information, segments of the applicable Interactive Program, etc..

G.G. "Choreographed Dancers": Dancers, swimmers and skaters who are professionally trained, doing choreographed routines requiring rehearsals such as ballet, chorus dancing, modern dance, tap dancing, jazz dancing, acrobatic dancing, exhibition-level dancing, or skating.

5. REASON FOR CODE
This Agreement represents the minimum wages and working conditions for Performers in the production and use of Material for Interactive Programs, thus ensuring more stable, harmonious and ethical conditions in the industry for Performers and Producer.

6. TERM OF AGREEMENT
The term of this Agreement shall commence from the date first written above and remain effective through June 30, 1996. In the event either party has not served appropriate timely notice of termination for the expiration date above, the Agreement shall be extended on a day-to-day basis until sixty (60) days after either party serves written notice of termination on the other

7. PRODUCER'S DUTIES

A. Producer will not enter into any agreement with or employ any Performer for the production of Material for Interactive Media upon terms and conditions less favorable to the Performer than those set forth in this Agreement.

B. No waiver by any Performer of any provisions of this Agreement shall be effective unless the written consent of SAG to such waiver is first obtained.

C. Nothing in this Agreement shall be deemed to prevent any Performer from negotiating for and/or obtaining from Producer better terms than the minimum terms provided for herein.

D. Nothing herein shall obligate any person, firm or corporation which may be affiliated with Producer (including but not limited to parent and affiliated corporations) to either comply with, negotiate with or become a signatory to this Guild Agreement or any other Guild agreement or other agreement of a controlled, allied or affiliated union.

EXHIBIT 5-1 Screen Actors' Guild Producer Incentive Media Agreement (*continued*)

8. ADMISSION TO PREMISES

Any authorized representative of the Guild shall be admitted to the premises of the Producer or where the rehearsal or production of Interactive Programs takes place, at any reasonable time to check the performance by the Producer pursuant to this Agreement subject to product security or clearance restrictions; such checking shall be done so as not to interfere with the conduct of Producer's business.

9. UNION SECURITY

Producer agrees to report to the Guild in writing within fifteen (15) days of the first employment of a non-member of the Guild, (or within twenty-five (25) days of the first employment of a non-member of the Guild on an overnight location), giving the non-member's name, address and telephone number, Social Security number and his/her first date of employment. Any inquiry by any Producer to the Guild as to the first date on which a Performer has been employed in the industry shall be answered by the Guild, and its answer shall bind the Guild, and the Producer, if it acts in good faith, shall not be liable for acting on such answer, but the Producer who fails to report shall be liable to the Guild for such failure to report. The inquiry provided for in the preceding sentence may be made before, on or one (1) business day after the date of employment.

As used herein, the term "member of the Guild in good standing" means a person who pays union initiation fees and dues in accordance with the requirements of the National Labor Relations Act.

Until and unless the Union Security provisions of the Labor Management Relations Act, 1947, as amended are repealed or amended so as to permit a stricter Union Security clause, it is agreed that during the term of this Agreement, Producer will employ and maintain in Producer's employ only such Performers covered by this Agreement who are members of Screen Actors Guild in good standing or those who shall make application for membership on the thirtieth (30th) day following the beginning of employment hereunder or the date of execution of this Agreement, whichever is later, and thereafter maintain such membership in good standing as a condition of employment.

In the event that said Act is repealed or amended so as to permit a stricter Union Security clause, the above provision shall be amended accordingly. The provisions of this Section are subject to such Act.

It is understood that it would be impossible to accurately fix the actual damages suffered by SAG by reason of a breach by a Producer of the provisions of this Section 9. It is therefore agreed that Producer will pay to SAG, as Liquidated Damages, the sum of Five Hundred Dollars ($500.00) for each breach by Producer of the provisions of this Section 9. Any breach of the provisions hereof shall be deemed a single breach, regardless of the number of days of employment involved in the hiring; but each separate hiring of the same person in violation hereof shall be deemed a separate breach.

EXHIBIT 5-1 Screen Actors' Guild Producer Incentive Media Agreement (*continued*)

10. PREFERENCE OF EMPLOYMENT

A. In recognition of the services performed by professional Performers, Producer agrees that in the hiring of Weekly Performers, Three-Day Performers, Day Performers, Singers, Dancers, Stunt Performers, Puppeteers, and Extra Performers employed for the day for work to be performed within the 300-mile, 75-mile or 50-mile zone as the case may be, referred to in Subsection C. of this Section 10 ("preference zone"), preference will be given to Qualified Professional Performers in each such preference zone who are reasonably and readily available in such zone.

B. The obligation of the Producer to give preference to Qualified Professional Performers shall require the employment of a Qualified Professional Performer in the hiring of a Performer employed as a Day Performer, Weekly and Three-Day Performers, unless no Qualified Professional Performer of the type required is reasonably and readily available to the Producer through the use of the present hiring practices generally and customarily followed by the Interactive Media industry. If a Qualified Professional Performer is reasonably and readily available to the Producer for employment in the locality where the Producer's production facility is based, he/she shall be deemed available regardless of the place within the 300-mile, 75-mile or 50-mile preference zone, as the case may be, at which the services are to be performed.

C. For the purpose of this Section 10, the preference zones are:

CITY ZONE
1. Atlanta 75
2. Boston 75
3. Chicago 300
4. Cincinnati 75
5. Cleveland 75
6. Columbus/Dayton 75
7. Dallas/Fort Worth 75
8. Denver 75
9. Detroit 300
10. Hawaii/The state of Hawaii
11. Houston 75
12. Indianapolis 75
13. Kansas City/Omaha 75
14. Kissimmee 75
15. Las Vegas 75
16. Los Angeles 300

EXHIBIT 5-1 Screen Actors' Guild Producer Incentive Media Agreement (*continued*)

17. Louisville 75
18. Miami 75
19. Nashville 75
20. New Orleans 75
21. New York 300
22. Philadelphia 75
23. Phoenix/Tucson 75
24. Pittsburgh 75
25. Portland 75
26. Rochester 75
27. San Diego 75
28. San Francisco 75
29. Seattle 75
30. St. Louis 75
31. Twin Cities 75
32. Washington/Baltimore 300
33. 75 Miles from any new Local Office of SAG
34. 50 Miles from any production location site utilized by Producer in the United States

For purposes of this Section 10, the above Los Angeles zone is the area within the radius of 300 miles from the intersection of Beverly Boulevard and La Cienega Boulevard in Los Angeles, California; the above New York 300-mile zone is the area within a radius of 300 miles from the center of Columbus Circle in New York; the above 75-mile zones are the areas within the radius of 75 miles from the center of the designated city or the location of the Guild's local office, whichever the case may be; and the 50-mile zone is the area within the radius of 50 miles from such applicable production location site.

D. There shall be automatically excluded from the provisions of this Section 10, the following:

1. Members of a group which is recognized in the trade or by a significant segment of the public as a "name" specialty group;

2. A person portraying himself/herself, or persons portraying themselves; the exception will apply in effect to important, famous, well-known or unique persons of special skills or ability who portray themselves;

EXHIBIT 5-1 Screen Actors' Guild Producer Incentive Media Agreement (*continued*)

3. Military or other governmental personnel, where restrictions prevent use of non-military or non-governmental personnel, as the case may be, in restricted areas or in the handling of governmental property or equipment; however, the use of military or other governmental pilots or aircraft shall not be the subject of an automatic waiver, but the facts shall be presented to the Guild and waivers will be granted in accordance with the previously established custom in the Interactive and entertainment industries;

4. Persons having special skills or abilities, or special or unusual physical appearances, where such Performers having such required skills or abilities or physical appearances are not reasonably or readily available to the Producer through the use of hiring practices generally and customarily followed by the industry in the employment of such Performers;

5. The first employment within the studio zone of a person with respect to whom the producer presents in writing to the Guild facts showing that the employee: (i) has had a sufficient training and/or experience so as to qualify for a career as a professional Performer, and (ii) that such employee intends to pursue the career of a Performer and intends to be currently available for employment in the industry;

6. Children under the age of eighteen (18); and

7. The owner of special or unique vehicles or equipment, or an operator appointed by the owner if such vehicle or equipment is not available to the Producer without the employment of the owner or such operator.

If a Performer is employed under one or more of the exceptions provided for in Subsection 10.D, above, the obligation of the Producer to give preference to Qualified Professional Performers in the cases provided in Subsection 10.A, above, shall nevertheless be applicable to any subsequent employment of such Performer by Producer. Producer agrees to promptly report to the Guild each hiring under the provision of this Subsection D together with the reasons why the person employed comes within such provision. A joint Producer-Guild Committee shall be appointed to resolve claims arising under this Section 10 between Producer and the Guild.

E. Nothing contained in this Section 10 shall alter or modify Producer's exclusive right to cast any and all Performers performing services for Producer.

F. It is understood that it would be impossible to accurately fix the actual damages suffered by the Guild by reason of a breach by Producer of the provisions of this Section 10. It is therefore agreed

EXHIBIT 5-1 Screen Actors' Guild Producer Incentive Media Agreement (*continued*)

that the Producer will pay to the Guild, as Liquidated Damages, the sum of Five Hundred Dollars ($500.00) for each breach by the Producer of the provisions of this Section 10. The hiring by Producer of a Performer in violation of the provisions hereof shall be deemed a single breach, regardless of the number of days of employment involved in the hiring; but each separate hiring of the same person in violation hereof shall be deemed a separate breach.

G. A breach of this Section 10 is subject to arbitration between the Guild and Producer.

11. PEOPLE COVERED

No services of any Performer are excluded from the scope of this Agreement unless specifically waived by the Guild, however, excluded from this provision are skilled technicians when the context of the script requires special understanding and expertise which cannot be realistically portrayed or narrated by the Performer. The Guild reserves the right to review these exceptions in the event utilization becomes excessive.

12. RIGHTS

A. In consideration of the initial compensation paid hereunder, Producer may exploit the results and proceeds of Principal Performers' services in the Interactive Programs for which the Performer was employed in all Interactive Media as defined in Subsection 4.C (i) including the right to adapt such Interactive Programs for any and all Platforms and, if Producer pays the additional compensation specified in Subsection 15.C, Producer's rights shall include Remote Delivery and/or Integration as defined in Subsection 4.C (ii) and 4.R, respectively, above. It is understood and agreed that Producer will have all of the foregoing rights, without payment of any additional compensation, with respect to the results and proceeds of the services of Performers who are not Principal Performers.

B. Producer also will have the right, without payment of any additional compensation except as provided in Section 14 below, to: (i) use Interactive Material for reference, file, private audition purposes, and for customary industry promotional purposes within the "trade" (i.e., at sales conventions and other events within the Interactive and entertainment industries); (ii) use and give publicity to the Performer's name and likeness, photographic or otherwise (including the use of stills and lifts in product packaging and in print) to advertise and promote the applicable Interactive Program including the use of excerpts of Interactive Programs at point-of-purchase to promote the sales of Interactive Programs.

EXHIBIT 5-1 Screen Actors' Guild Producer Incentive Media Agreement (*continued*)

13. REUSE OF MATERIAL

A. Producer shall not re-use any part of the photography or soundtrack of an Interactive Program produced hereunder containing the results and proceeds of a Principal Performer's performance ("Reuse") without separately bargaining with the individual Principal Performer appearing therein and reaching an agreement therefor. The foregoing requirements shall be applicable to a Principal Performer only if the Principal Performer is recognizable and to stunts only if the stunt is identifiable. The foregoing requirements shall not be applicable to Extra Performers and shall not limit Producer's right to acquire Integration rights from Performers or to utilize Interactive Material in any manner otherwise authorized under the terms of this Agreement.

B. The Day Performer rate for the field in which the Interactive Material is re-used (i.e., broadcast television, radio, etc.) shall be the minimum for purposes of the bargaining referred to above with respect to such Reuse of Interactive Material in accordance with the applicable Guild agreement unless compensation for such other use is provided for herein.

SAG may, at its discretion, grant waivers of the requirements of this Section 13 with respect to the Reuse of Interactive Material containing a Performer's performance in public service, educational and like Linear Programs, and will follow a liberal policy in granting such waivers.

C. If Producer fails to bargain separately with the Performer as provided herein, or if Producer and the Performer bargain but are unable to reach an agreement, consent for such Reuse shall not be deemed to have been given by the Performer. In the case of violation of the foregoing, the Performer shall be entitled to damages for such unauthorized Reuse of his/her performance equivalent to three (3) times the amount originally paid the Performer for the number of days of work covered by the Material actually re-used as well as the minimum fees, if any, applicable to the field in which the Material is exploited (i.e., broadcast television, radio, etc.). In lieu of accepting such damages, however, the Performer may elect to arbitrate the claim as provided hereunder.

D. If Producer is unable to find a Performer within a reasonable time for the purpose of the bargaining pursuant to this Section 13, Producer shall notify the Guild within a reasonable period of time to allow the Guild the opportunity to locate such Performer. If the Guild thereafter is unable to notify Producer of a telephone number or an address at which the Performer may be contacted within a reasonable time to allow the Producer to comply with deadlines, Producer may re-use the Material without penalty.

EXHIBIT 5-1   Screen Actors' Guild Producer Incentive Media Agreement (*continued*)

14. TRAILERS; PROMOTIONS

A. Producer shall have the right to make (or cause to be made) trailers and/or Promotional Programs for the purpose of advertising and promoting the Interactive Program. A Performer's services in any such Trailer (and/or Promotional Programs) shall not require the payment of additional compensation (other than compensation for services; Overtime or any compensation otherwise due hereunder) if the recordation of such Trailer (and/or Promotional Program) occurs during the Performer's term of employment in connection with the applicable Interactive Program hereunder. Otherwise, the applicable Scale set forth in this Agreement shall be the minimum compensation for services in connection with such Trailers. No additional compensation shall be payable for the use of any portion of an Interactive Program in a Trailer when such Trailer is utilized to promote such Interactive Program.

B. No use of a Performer's services in a Trailer as herein defined may be used as an endorsement of any service or product other than the Interactive Program(s) for which the Performer was employed to render services. References to the hardware, Platforms or Remote Delivery systems upon which the Interactive Program operates or references to other Interactive Programs shall not be deemed an endorsement of a service or product in violation of this Subsection 14.B if the Interactive Program is clearly identified by its title in such promotion to the consumer.

C. Performer may, at his/her sole discretion, also agree to provide additional services without additional compensation (other than the compensation for services, Overtime or any compensation otherwise due hereunder) during the production of an Interactive Program for such Promotional Program. If any Promotional Program is a Linear Program exhibited or transmitted to the viewer as specified in Section 4.S.(ii). (a) - (c), Producer shall pay all recognizable Principal Performers therein an additional payment equal to the Day Performer minimum hereunder for such use.

D. In the interest of promoting this young industry, the Guild agrees that Producer may utilize the results and proceeds of a Principal Performer's services hereunder in a Promotional Program (of up to thirty (30) minutes), as defined in Subsection 4.F.F., without additional compensation to such Performer. This provision will automatically terminate on July 1, 1996, unless the parties hereto specifically agreed otherwise.

EXHIBIT 5-1 Screen Actors' Guild Producer Incentive Media Agreement (*continued*)

15. COMPENSATION
MINIMUM SCALE FOR PRINCIPAL PERFORMERS:

01/01/02 to 12/31/04

A. On-Camera Performers:

1. Day Performers $ 556.20
(including Solo/Duo Singers)

2. Three-Day Performers $1,408.00
(including Solo/Duo Singers)

3. Weekly Performers $1,932.30
(including Solo/Duo Singers)
6-day
Overnight Location $2,125.90

4. Group Singers
3–8 $ 483.00
9 or more $ 429.50
Contractor (3–8) +50%
Contractor (9 or more) +100%

(a) Over-Dubbing
Thirty-three and one third percent (33 1/3%) of above applicable rate without limitation as to the number of tracks.

(b) Sweetening
One hundred percent (100%) of the applicable rate (with or without over-dubbing), without limitation as to the number of tracks.

(c) Stepping-Out

(i) If a Singer is called upon to step-out of a group to sing up to fifteen (15) cumulative bars during a session, the Singer shall be paid an adjustment of fifty percent (50%) of the solo/duo rate in addition to the appropriate group rate for that day.

EXHIBIT 5-1 Screen Actors' Guild Producer Incentive Media Agreement (*continued*)

(ii) If a Singer is called upon to step-out of a group to sing sixteen (16) or more cumulative bars, or remain more than one (1) hour after the group has been released, to perform a solo or duo of any length, the Singer shall be paid the full solo/duo rate in addition to the appropriate group rate for that day.

(iii) Any member of a group who steps-out to perform as part of a smaller group to sing over four (4) consecutive bars shall be paid at the smaller group fee for that day. Such re-classification shall not operate to reduce the size of the overall group with respect to fees payable to the remainder of the group.

5. Choreographed Dancers, Swimmers, Skaters, etc.
Rehearsal Days only $ 327.55

Work Days
Solo/Duo $ 556.20
3–8 $ 487.20
9 or more $ 426.40

Weekly Option
(includes rehearsals)
Solo/Duo $1,789.10
3–8 $1,640.80
9 or more $1,491.45

B. *Off-Camera Performers:*

6. Voice-Over Performer $ 556.20
(Up to 3 voices/4 hour day)
Additional Voices (each) $ 185.40
6+ Voices/8 hour day $1,112.40
One character voice/1 hour or less $278.10

Voice-Over Performer Retakes
(within 3 months)
3 voices/2 hour or less session $ 278.10
3 voices/more than 2 hour session $ 556.20

7. Singers
Solo/Duo $ 556.20

EXHIBIT 5-1 Screen Actors' Guild Producer Incentive Media Agreement (*continued*)

Hourly Rate* $ 276.05

3–8 $294.60

9 or more $ 255.45

Contractor (3–8) +50% +50%

Contractor (9 or more) +100% +100%

Group Hourly Rate* $ 164.80

Over-Dubbing, Sweetening and Stepping-Out for off-camera Singers (same as on-camera rates, see Subsections A.4.(a) - (c) above).

(*Once Producer engages Singers at hourly rate, no conversion to Day Performer rates is permitted.)

C. Additional Compensation for Remote Delivery and Integration

1. Producer shall pay Principal Performers the following for Remote Delivery and Integration rights in an Interactive Program:

A. Remote Delivery:
If acquired not later than one (1) year after initial release of the applicable Program in Interactive Media, one hundred percent (100%) of the Minimum Applicable Compensation as specified below; otherwise, plus ten percent (10%) thereof.

B. Integration:
If acquired not later than one (1) year after initial release of the applicable Program in Interactive Media, one hundred percent (100%) of the Minimum Applicable Compensation as specified below; otherwise, plus ten percent (10%) thereof.
The "Minimum Applicable Compensation" shall be the Performer's actual salary for the total number of days or weeks employed, up to one hundred fifty percent (150%) of the minimum daily or weekly Scale, as detailed in Subsection A. or B., above, for the total employment period, excluding Overtime and Liquidated Damages, if any.

D. Half-Day Employment (Rehearsals)
Producer may engage a Performer (except Dancers, Extra Performers and Stunt Performers) once per Program for up to four (4) consecutive hours of rehearsal time at sixty-five percent (65%) of the Day Performer rate pro-rata, or sixty-five percent (65%) of the Performer's pro-rata single day rate, whichever is higher, as follows:

EXHIBIT 5-1   Screen Actors' Guild Producer Incentive Media Agreement (*continued*)

(1) Rehearsal time (no recordation of Performers) of four (4) consecutive hours or less, provided a firm date for the subsequent workday(s) is given at the time of booking.

(2) Call times, except for travel, are restricted to:

(a) Morning Call - no later than 8:00 a.m.

(b) Afternoon Call - no earlier than 1:00 p.m.

(c) Evening Call - any four (4) consecutive hours provided work ends by 12:00 a.m. Any extension of the half-day rehearsal beyond four (4) hours is subject to the Performer's consent at the time of extension and shall require payment of an additional thirty-five percent (35%) of the daily rate for such day, whether four (4) additional hours or less are worked. Any Overtime beyond eight (8) hours of work will then be computed at time and one-half or double time in hourly units, as specified in Article II, Section 6. All required meal periods will be observed.

For Three-Day Performers or Weekly Performers, Producer may use the half-day rehearsal rate based only on the Day Performer minimum.

E. Extra Performer Rates:
General Extra Performers $110.20
Special Ability Extra Performers $135.00
Choreographed Simmers and Skaters, etc. $330.65

A. The weekly salary for Extra Performers employed by the week shall be five (5) times the minimum daily rates as specifically set forth above. Extra Performers employed by the week are guaranteed a minimum employment of five (5) consecutive days, provided that a Saturday work day shall be included in such five (5) consecutive days.

B. Any Extra Performer who speaks atmospheric words, commonly known in the industry as "omnies", is entitled to the basic wage for the particular call.

C. Whenever Producer employs more than ten (10) registered Extra Performers for general Extra Performer work in an Interactive Program on any day, Producer may employ any number of non-registered persons to perform crowd work.

EXHIBIT 5-1 Screen Actors' Guild Producer Incentive Media Agreement (*continued*)

16. NON-DISCRIMINATION POLICY

A. The parties hereto reaffirm their commitment to a policy of non-discrimination and fair employment in connection with the engagement and treatment of Performers on the basis of sex, race, color, creed, national origin, age, or disability, in accordance with applicable state and federal law; no inquiry shall be made with respect to a Performer's marital status, sexual preference or national origin, creed, age or disability.

B. Producer shall cast Performers in accordance with the above policy in all types of roles, having due regard for the requirements of and the suitability for the role so that, for example, the American scene may be portrayed realistically. To that end, due regard shall be given to women, minorities, Performers with disabilities and seniors in all aspects of society. The parties agree that the Producer shall retain its exclusive creative prerogatives.

In furtherance of the foregoing, the Producer shall make good faith efforts to seek out and provide audition opportunities for women, minorities, Performers with disabilities and seniors in the casting of each production thereby creating fair, equal and non-stereotyped employment opportunities. Producer agrees to provide equal employment opportunities (including auditions) for women and men for Voice-Over roles having due regard for the requirements of and suitability for such roles.

C. When applicable, and with due regard to the safety of cast, crew and other persons, women and minorities shall be considered for stunt doubling roles and for scripted and unscripted stunts on a functional non-discriminatory basis.

Producer shall make every effort to cast Performers with physical disabilities for scripted and unscripted stunts for which they are qualified and with due regard to safety, in roles portraying their particular disability such as wheelchair stunts or stunts involving the use of other adaptive devices, e.g., crutches, prostheses, etc.. Where the Stunt Performer doubles for a role which is identifiable as female and/or Black, Latin-Hispanic, Asian-Pacific or Native American and the race and/or sex of the double is also identifiable, Producer shall make every effort to cast qualified persons of the same sex and/or race involved. The Stunt Coordinator shall make every effort to identify and recruit qualified minority and female Stunt Performers and Stunt Performers with disabilities prior to the commencement of production.

D. *Special Considerations:* All facilities under the control of or used on behalf of Producer in connection with the casting or production of Material for Interactive Programs, including but not limited to dressing rooms, lodging, studios, locations (where feasible), sets, and transportation and

EXHIBIT 5-1 Screen Actors' Guild Producer Incentive Media Agreement *(continued)*

access thereto, shall provide reasonable accommodations for Performers with disabilities and shall be suitable for the special needs and requirements of any Performers whether by reason of age or disability. For any role in which a deaf Performer is sought or cast, Producer shall provide, during the audition or throughout the engagement, a certified or a qualified interpreter(s) for the deaf (i.e., interpreter(s) qualified or certified in sign language or oral interpretation). With regard to Performers who are blind or visually impaired, Producer and such Performers shall make mutually acceptable provisions to make the script and/or sites available to the Performer in advance of auditions.

17. CONTRACTS WITH PERFORMERS

Every contract (whether written or oral) between Producer and any Performer shall be deemed to contain the following clauses:

"Notwithstanding any provision in this contract to the contrary, it is specifically understood and agreed by all parties hereto:

A. That they are bound by all the terms and provisions of the Amended 1993 - 1995 Screen Actors Guild, Inc.- Producer Interactive Media Agreement.

B. That should there be any inconsistency between said contract and the Agreement or the valid rules and regulations enacted by the Guild not in derogation thereof, the Agreement and the rules and regulations of the Guild shall prevail; but nothing in this provision shall affect terms, compensation or conditions provided for in this contract which are more favorable to members of the Guild than the terms, compensation and conditions provided for in said Agreement.

C. If the term of this contract is of longer duration than the term of the Agreement between the Guild and the Producer, this contract shall be modified to conform to any agreements or modifications negotiated or agreed to in said Agreement, and the existence of this contract shall not prevent the Performer from engaging in any strike or obeying any of the lawful rules and regulations of the Guild without penalty by way of damage or otherwise, subject to mutual cancellation or termination of this contract without penalty on either side.

D. Performer is a member of the Guild in good standing subject to and in accordance with Section 9 of this Article I and is subject to the rules and regulations of the Guild.

E. That the Performer is covered by the provisions governing the Screen Actors Guild Pension and Health Plans.

EXHIBIT 5-1 Screen Actors' Guild Producer Incentive Media Agreement (*continued*)

F. All disputes and controversies of every kind and nature arising out of or in connection with this contract shall be determined by arbitration in accordance with the procedure and provisions of said Agreement."

18. EXISTING CONTRACTS

The parties acknowledge that existing contracts between Performers and Producer entered into prior to the date of execution of this Agreement shall not be subject to the terms and conditions hereof.

19. INDIVIDUAL CONTRACTS

Except as otherwise herein expressly provided, the minimum terms and conditions hereof shall be deemed incorporated into all individual contracts of employment in effect on the effective date hereof or thereafter executed, with respect to all services rendered on or after such effective date.

20. MINIMUM SCALE/TERMS

Producer agrees that it will make no contract with any Performer at terms less favorable to such Performer than those contained in this Agreement, and no waiver of any of the terms hereof shall be effective without the written consent of the Guild. All Performers, whether employed at Scale or in excess of the minimum rates set forth herein, shall have the protection and benefits of the provisions and conditions set forth in this Agreement. Nothing herein shall prevent an individual Performer from bargaining for more favorable terms and conditions in his/her individual contract than those accorded Performers hereunder.

21. PROHIBITION AGAINST CREDITING

No compensation paid to a Performer for his/her services in excess of the minimum may be credited against Overtime, Liquidated Damages or any other compensation otherwise due the Performer; however, nothing herein shall prevent Producer from bargaining with the Principal Performer to allocate compensation payable to a Principal Performer (other than Overtime and Liquidated Damages) which is greater than two hundred percent (200%) of Scale to sums which may be otherwise due the Principal Performer hereunder.

22. SAG MEMBER REPORTS; PERFORMER CONTRACTS

Producer shall have the option of utilizing SAG Member Reports at the time of hiring of Principal Performers and/or Extra Performers in connection with Interactive Programs on a form similar to that authorized by SAG, or to employ the same pursuant to individual contracts in forms approved by the Guild. If Producer utilizes such Member Reports, it will be the duty and responsibility of each Performer to deliver a form initialed by the Producer to the local SAG office.

EXHIBIT 5-1 Screen Actors' Guild Producer Incentive Media Agreement (*continued*)

If Producer does not utilize Member Reports, Producer shall employ Scale Performers pursuant to individual contracts on a form approved by the Guild which guarantees the Performers the minimum terms and conditions of this Agreement. No changes, alterations or additions may be made in such form except such changes as are more favorable to the Performer and as to which changes both Performer and Producer have given written approval on the contract. Copies of all such employment contracts shall be filed with the appropriate Guild office.

23. EVASION OF RESPONSIBILITY
Producer agrees that Producer will not knowingly, for the purpose of evading performance under this Agreement:

(1) sublet or transfer responsibility hereunder to any third person;

(2) transfer operations to any other place of origin or territory solely for the purpose of defeating or evading this Agreement;

(3) use, lease or authorize others to use Material for Interactive Media for any purpose or in any manner other than as permitted by this Agreement.

24. WAIVERS
The Guild recognizes that the production, distribution and exhibition of Programs in Interactive Media is in its formative stages, and there may be uses of a nature not contemplated at the time the parties enter into this Agreement. The Guild agrees to consider any special circumstances which warrant modification of any of the terms of this Agreement and to grant waivers to accommodate such productions, which waivers shall not be unreasonably withheld. Any request by a producer for consideration for changes or waiver by the Guild hereunder must be made in writing by advance notice to the Guild to afford sufficient time to give proper consideration to such request. The parties acknowledge that fifteen (15) business days notice prior to the scheduled production of any Interactive Program shall be deemed sufficient time for purposes of evaluating such request.

25. WAIVER OF RIGHTS BY MEMBERS
The acceptance of consideration by a member of the Guild under this Agreement shall not be deemed sufficient consideration to effect a waiver, release or discharge by such Guild member of such Guild member's contractual rights under this or any other Guild agreement. Releases, discharges, notations on checks, cancellations, etc., and similar devices which may operate as waivers or releases shall be null and void to the extent provided for above without the Guild's prior written approval.

EXHIBIT 5-1 Screen Actors' Guild Producer Incentive Media Agreement (*continued*)

26. PRODUCTION STAFF

A. Producer shall not utilize persons employed as members of Producer's casting or production staff as Performers in any Interactive Program on which they also render other services without the express consent of the Guild, however, the Guild shall grant waivers on a reasonable basis in good faith to accommodate the legitimate production necessities of Producer.

B. The following are exceptions to the above: (1) Animal handlers (appearing in a scene in which they handle animals); (2) Actor/directors, actor/writers, or actor/producers engaged by written contract prior to the commencement of Principal Photography of the Program; (3) an "emergency" in the production which requires immediate response. Emergency is defined as a situation on location in which a member of the cast cannot perform or fails to report for work ready, willing and able to perform the duties assigned to such Performer hereunder.

C. Violations of the foregoing prohibition shall require payment of Liquidated Damages, as follows:
Day Performer $300.00
Three Day Performer 400.00
Weekly Performer 600.00

27. PAYMENTS

A. Performers shall be paid not less than the minimum applicable fees due hereunder, in the legal tender of the United States not later than thirty (30) calendar days after the time specified for payment. All fees shall be due as of the date of the last day of production in which such Performer's services are utilized.

B. Liquidated Damages for Late Payment
The following cumulative payments shall be added to the compensation due and payable to the Performer for each day, beginning with the day following the day of default: Two Dollars and Fifty Cents ($2.50) for each day's delinquency up to thirty (30) days (excluding Saturday, Sunday, and holidays which the Producer observes). Thereafter, the accrual of damages shall cease unless either the Guild or the member gives written notice to the Producer of the non-payment. In the event such notice is given and full payment including accrued Liquidated Damages is not made within twelve (12) working days thereafter, the Producer shall be liable for an immediate payment of Seventy-Five Dollars ($75.00) plus further payments at the rate of Five Dollars ($5.00) per day from the date of receipt of notice of non-payment which shall continue without limitation as to time until the delinquent payment together with all Liquidated Damages are fully paid. Such Liquidated

EXHIBIT 5-1 **Screen Actors' Guild Producer Incentive Media Agreement** (*continued*)

Damages shall be in addition to any and all other remedies which the Guild may have against Producer under this Agreement.

The above cumulative payments shall not apply in the following case:

(1) Where a bona fide dispute exists as to the amount due and payable concerning which the Guild has been notified promptly;

(2) When force majeure intervenes;

(3) Where Performer's services are provided by a Loan-Out Company, and he/she has failed to furnish to the Producer pertinent information required and all W-4 forms (provided, however, that Producer has made such forms available at the production site);

(4) Where there is no Loan-Out Company and a Performer has failed to furnish the Producer his/her W-4 form (provided, however, that Producer has made such forms available at the production site); and

(5) Where the Performer, having been furnished his/her contract on or before the day of his/her performance, fails to return the signed engagement contract promptly.

C. All Fees are Net

The minimum fees specified in this Agreement shall be net to the Performer. No deductions whatsoever may be made by Producer from Performer's compensation except for deductions and withholding that are required by law, including but not limited to the Social Security and withholding taxes as specified below.

28. SOCIAL SECURITY, WITHHOLDING, UNEMPLOYMENT AND DISABILITY INSURANCE TAXES

All compensation paid to Performers covered by the Agreement for and in connection with the making and use of Programs for Interactive Media constitute wages and as such is subject to Social Security, withholding, unemployment insurance taxes and disability insurance taxes. Producer and any others who assume the obligation to make such payments shall also make the required payments, reports and withholdings with respect to such taxes.

Employers must honor a Performer's request that taxes be withheld over a longer payroll period (i.e., by a more favorable tax withholding schedule) to the extent Producer can do so without incurring liability therefrom as determined by Producer in accordance with its standard customary practices. Producer shall attach appropriate forms for this purpose to Performer's contract.

EXHIBIT 5-1 Screen Actors' Guild Producer Incentive Media Agreement (*continued*)

A W-4 form or an alternative form with appropriate IRS tax information for withholding purposes will be included in the standard union employment contract form.

29. SAFEGUARDS AGAINST VIOLATION

Producer shall furnish the Guild written reports, under the same cover as checks for Performers' services, specifying: the details relevant to the Interactive Program produced; time of the production sessions; the title of the Interactive Program; names of Performers; complete time in rehearsal and shooting; gross fees payable to Performers.

30. SAG PENSION AND HEALTH PLANS

A. Producer shall become a party to the "Screen Actors Guild-Producers Pension Plan for Motion Picture Actors" and "Screen Actors Guild-Producer Health Plan for Motion Picture Actors" and shall contribute to the Plans amounts equal to 13.3% of all gross compensation as herein defined with respect to Interactive Programs produced under this Agreement.

The term "Gross Compensation" as used in this Section means all salaries, fees, and other compensation or remuneration; excluding, however, payments for meal period violations, rest period violations, traveling, lodging or living expenses, Liquidated Damages for late payments, flight insurance allowance, reimbursements for special hair dress or for wardrobe maintenance or damage, but without any other deductions whatsoever. Such terms also include amounts paid to any employee with respect to services as a Performer (including compensation paid as salary settlements) whether or not any services were performed.

B. All contributions shall be allocated between the Pension and Health Plans as determined by the Plan Trustees, and will be subject to reallocation from time to time in accordance with the determination of the Trustees based on actuarial studies.

C. It is understood that the Pension and Health contributions are industry-wide and open to all Producers and advertising agencies signatory to any of the Guild's collective bargaining agreements or Letters of Adherence thereto which provide for payments to the Plans as above set forth. By signing a Letter of Adherence to the Trust Agreement hereinafter referred to and upon acceptance by the Trustees, Producers and advertising agencies shall be deemed bound by the terms and conditions of the Plans and to have appointed the Producers, Trustees and alternative Trustees previously appointed.

D. The funds contributed to the Pension Plan and the Health Plan shall be trust funds and shall be administered under the Screen Actors Guild-Producers Pension Plan Trust Agreement and the

EXHIBIT 5-1 Screen Actors' Guild Producer Incentive Media Agreement (*continued*)

Screen Actors Guild-Producers Health Plan Trust Agreement, both dated February 1, 1960, which Agreements and Declarations of Trust shall become part of the collective bargaining contract. The Trust Fund for the Pension Plan shall be used solely for the purpose of providing pension benefits for employees covered by the Guild's collective bargaining contracts in the motion picture industry who are eligible for benefits under the Pension Plan, and for expenses in connection with the establishment and administration of such Pension Plan. The Trust Fund for the Health Plan shall be used solely for the purposes of providing welfare benefits for employees covered by the Guild's collective bargaining contracts in the motion picture industry who are eligible for benefits under the Health Plan and, in the discretion of the Trustees, for their families and for expenses in connection with the establishment and administration of such Health Plan.

The Trustees shall determine the form, nature and amount of pension and health benefits, respectively, the rule of eligibility for such benefits, and the effective dates of such benefits.

E. The Plan of pension benefits shall be subject to the approval of the Internal Revenue Service as a qualified Plan. If any part of the Plan is not approved, the Plan shall be modified by the Trustees to such form as is approved by the Internal Revenue Service.

F. The Declarations of Trust shall provide that no portion of the contributions thereof may be paid or revert to any Producer.

G. Producers and advertising agencies shall furnish the Trustees to each Plan, upon request, with the required information pertaining to the names, job classifications, Social Security numbers and wage information for all persons covered by the agreement together with such information as may be reasonably required for the proper

and efficient administration of the Pension Plan and the Health Plan, respectively. Upon the written request of the Guild to the Producer, such information shall also be made available to the Guild.

H. No part of the Producer's contributions to such Plans may be credited against the Principal Performer's compensation over Scale or against any other remuneration that the Performer may be entitled to no matter what form such other remuneration may take nor shall such contributions constitute or be deemed to be wages due to the individual employees subject to this Agreement, nor in any manner to be liable for or subject to the debts, contracts, liabilities, or torts of such employees.

EXHIBIT 5-1 Screen Actors' Guild Producer Incentive Media Agreement (*continued*)

I. LOAN OUTS

Where the Producer borrows acting services from a signatory Loan-Out Company, or enters into a contract with a Performer under which covered services and non-covered services are to be provided, the following shall apply:

1. There will be a separate provision in the Principal Performer's agreement or loan-out agreement covering only acting services. Where other services are involved, and there is a dispute over the portion of the compensation allocated to acting services, the Principal Performer's "customary salary" shall be given substantial consideration in resolving such dispute.

2. Contributions shall be payable on the amount allocated to covered services.

3. The Producer shall have the obligation to make the contributions directly to the Plans whether the agreement is with the Performer or with the Performer's Loan-Out Company.

4. If, prior to the date on which Producer assumed the obligation to make the contributions directly to the Plans, a Loan-Out Company has failed to make the applicable pension and health contributions on behalf of the loan-out Performer pursuant to the provisions of the applicable SAG Contract, Producer shall not be liable for such contribution.

5. Claims against the Producer for pension and health contributions on behalf of Performers borrowed from a Loan-Out Company, or claims against the Producer on behalf of Performers employed directly by the Producer must be brought within four (4) years from the date of filing of the compensation remittance report covering such Performers.

6. Any claim for contribution not brought within the four (4) year period referred to in Subsection I.(5) above shall be barred.

J. AUDITS

Claims against the Producer pursuant to Subsection I, above, for pension and health contributions on behalf of Performers borrowed from a Loan-Out Company, or claims against Producer pursuant to this Section 30 must be brought within four (4) years from the date of filing of the compensation remittance covering such Performers.

K. ADHERENCE TO THE PLANS

By signing this Agreement, Producer thereby applies to become a party to and agrees to be bound by the Screen Actors Guild-Producers Pension Plan Trust Agreement and the Pension Plan adopted

EXHIBIT 5-1 Screen Actors' Guild Producer Incentive Media Agreement (*continued*)

thereunder; and the Screen Actors Guild-Producers Health Plan Trust Agreement and the Health Plan adopted thereunder, if the Producer is not already a party to said Agreements and Plans.

Producer further hereby accepts and agrees to be bound by all amendments and supplements heretofore and hereafter made to the foregoing Agreements and documents. Producer hereby accepts the Producer Plan Trustees under said Trust Agreements and their successors designated as provided herein

31. RIGHT TO RESPECT PICKET LINES

The Producer will not discriminate against any individual Guild Performer for refusal to cross a lawful picket line which is established at the premises of Producer as the result of a lawful strike, authorized by responsible Guild officers having the right to do so (at the appropriate local or national level).

32. SEPARABILITY

If any clause, sentence, paragraph or part of this Agreement or the application thereof to any person or circumstances, shall be adjudged by a court of competent jurisdiction to be invalid, such judgment shall not affect, impair, or invalidate the remainder of this Agreement or the application thereof to any other person or circumstances, but shall be confined in its operation to the clause, sentence, paragraph or part thereof directly involved in the controversy in which such judgment shall have been rendered and to the person or circumstances involved. It is hereby declared to be the intent that this Agreement would have been accepted even if such invalid provision had not been included.

33. PRODUCTION PROSECUTED

In the event that the Material in which the Performer has performed hereunder is the subject of any civil or criminal prosecution, Producer agrees to defend the Performer and to pay all expenses, charges and judgments so incurred. This Section does not apply to a case where the prosecution results from Material furnished by the Performer or acts done by the Performer without authorization of the Producer or beyond the scope of his/her employment.

34. NO STRIKE - NO LOCKOUT

So long as the Producer performs this Agreement, the Guild will not strike against the Producer, as to Performers covered by this Agreement in the field covered by this Agreement. To the extent the Guild has agreed not to strike, it will order its members to perform their contracts with the Producer. This and the following paragraph shall apply only to companies who sign this Agreement. Producer and the Guild agree that there will be no stoppage of work pending any arbitration and award, and the parties agree that all judgments rendered pursuant to arbitration brought in accordance with the procedures specified hereunder will be binding upon them.

EXHIBIT 5-1   Screen Actors' Guild Producer Incentive Media Agreement (*continued*)

35. TRANSFER OF RIGHTS - ASSUMPTION AGREEMENT

A. Upon the sale, transfer, assignment or other disposition by Producer of any Interactive Program produced by it hereunder, the Producer shall not be responsible to the Guild or to any Guild members for any payments thereafter due with respect to the use of such Programs or for a breach or violation of this Agreement by such transferees, if the Guild approves the financial responsibility of such transferee in writing (which consent shall not be unreasonably withheld), and if the Producer in its agreement with such transferee has included a provision substantially in the following form:

"("Transferee") hereby agrees with ("Producer") that all Programs covered by this agreement are subject to the Amended 1993-1995 Screen Actors Guild Inc. - Producer Interactive Media Agreement. Transferee hereby agrees expressly for the benefit of the Guild and its members affected thereby to make all payments of fees as provided in said Agreement and all Social Security, withholding, unemployment insurance and disability insurance payments and all appropriate contributions to the SAG Pension and Health Plans required under the provisions of said Agreement with respect to any and all such payments and to comply with the provision of said Agreement with respect to the use of such Program and required records and reports. It is expressly understood and agreed that the rights of Transferee to use such Program shall be subject to and conditioned upon the prompt payment to the Performers involved of all compensation as provided in said Agreement, and the Guild, on behalf of the Performers involved, shall be entitled to injunctive relief in the event such payments are not made."

The Producer agrees to give written notice by mail to the Guild of each sale, transfer, assignment or other disposition of any Program which is subject to this Agreement within thirty (30) days after the consummation of each sale, etc., and such notice shall specify the name and address of the purchaser, transferee or assignee.

36. UNION STANDARDS

A. Producer will neither engage in the production of an Interactive Program or any part thereof as to which one (1) or more Performers are employed by a person not a signatory to this Agreement or a Letter of Adherence herein (a "non-signatory"), nor acquire an Interactive Program or any part thereof as to which one or more Performers were employed by a non-signatory unless, in each case, the Producer determines after reasonable investigation that such Performers have been and will be either (1) afforded the wages, hours, working conditions and other economic benefits provided in the Agreement; or (2) afforded wages, hours, working conditions and other economic benefits having substantially equivalent economic cost to such non-signatory. The Producer shall upon written request from the Guild, report to the Guild the name of such non-signatory, the number of

EXHIBIT 5-1 Screen Actors' Guild Producer Incentive Media Agreement (*continued*)

Interactive Programs to be recorded and other pertinent data to enable the Guild to administer this Agreement. Notwithstanding anything in the foregoing to the contrary, this Section 36 shall not apply to Interactive Programs or parts thereof which exist prior to the execution hereof.

B. If the Producer obtains an agreement substantially in the form below from such non-signatory, Producer shall be deemed to have observed the provisions of Subsection 36.A.:

"It is hereby agreed by [Name of Non-Signatory Employer] that all Performers as defined in the Amended 1993-1995 SAG - Producer Interactive Media Agreement be afforded either (1) the wages, hours, working conditions and other economic benefits provided in said Agreement; or (2) wages, hours, working conditions and other economic benefits having a substantially equivalent economic cost to [Name of Non Signatory Employer]."

C. In addition to any other remedies at law or under this Agreement, the Guild reserves the right to terminate its agreement with any Producer who fails to observe the provisions of Subsection 36.A, unless such failure is isolated or inadvertent.

37. ARBITRATION

In the event of any controversy or dispute arising with respect to this Agreement or the interpretation or breach thereof between the Guild and the Producer or a Performer and the Producer, the Guild and the Producer agree, in good faith, to promptly attempt to settle such dispute amicably by conciliation. In the event that they are unable to do so, any such controversy or dispute shall be settled in accordance with the voluntary Labor Arbitration Rules then prevailing of the American Arbitration Association located with the State of California by a single Arbitrator chosen in accordance with such rules and as specified below.

A. Conciliation Procedures:

1. Whenever any dispute arises which is arbitrable under this Agreement, a representative of the Guild and a representative of Producer shall meet within ten (10) business days after a written request is made for conciliation by either party to the other. The filing of a formal claim by the Guild or Producer for arbitration shall be deemed an automatic request for prior conciliation. If the parties are not able to reach agreement by conciliation after such good faith attempts, a claim for arbitration may be filed. Claims for arbitration hereunder shall be filed not later than the later of: (I) six (6) months after the occurrence of the facts upon which the claim is based; or (ii) within six (6) months after the employee or the Union, or the Producer, as the case may be, has had a reasonable opportunity to become aware of the occurrence. Otherwise, such claims shall be deemed waived.

EXHIBIT 5-1 Screen Actors' Guild Producer Incentive Media Agreement (*continued*)

2. The time period for filing claims shall be tolled while conciliation discussions are taking place between the Producer and the Guild, and/or the Producer and a Performer's agent or representative, as the case may be.

B. Arbitration:

1. If the parties fail to settle the dispute by conciliation or if one party fails or refuses to meet after a request for conciliation, then either the Guild or Producer shall deliver to the other a written demand for arbitration setting forth the material facts concerning the dispute. The demand for arbitration shall be served upon the other party by first class mail addressed to the representative of the Guild or the Producer designated to receive such service at such party's last known address or by personal service within the state where the proceeding is to take place. A request for arbitration shall be filed with the American Arbitration Association office in a locale within the preference zone in which the Producer has its primary place of business.

2. The arbitrator shall be selected within fifteen (15) days of the date the arbitration demand is served in accordance with the procedures of the American Arbitration Association in effect at such time. The arbitration hearing will be commenced within sixty (60) days of the date that the arbitrator is selected. The arbitration award will be issued within thirty (30) days of the date of submission. All time periods herein may be extended in any particular case upon the written agreement of the parties.

3. All arbitrations hereunder which are not instituted by Producer, shall be brought by and in the name of the Guild, whether such arbitration is on its own behalf or on behalf of a Performer and, in the latter case, the Guild may, but shall not be required to, represent the Performer. The Guild may, however, in its discretion, permit a Performer to bring an arbitration in the name of the Performer. It shall, however, be solely within the discretion of the Guild whether a claim of a Performer shall be brought to arbitration.

4. The cost and expenses of the arbitrator shall be shared equally by the Guild and the Producer.

5. The award of the arbitrator shall be final and binding upon all parties to the proceeding, and judgment upon such award may be entered by any party in the highest court of the forum, state or federal, of competent jurisdiction.

6. The Guild shall be an ex officio party for all arbitration proceedings hereunder in which any Performer is involved, and the Guild may do anything which any Performer named in such proceeding might do. Copies of all notices, demands and other papers filed by any party in

EXHIBIT 5-1 Screen Actors' Guild Producer Incentive Media Agreement (*continued*)

arbitration proceedings, and copies of all motions, actions or proceedings in court following the award shall be promptly filed with the Guild. The Guild agrees to aid the enforcement of awards against its members by appropriate disciplinary action.

7. The Guild agrees that there will be no stoppage of work during an arbitration or prior to the rendition of the award.

8. Disputes involving or relating to injunctive relief are not arbitrable hereunder.

38. SERVICES/RATE NOT SPECIFIED

The only services Performers contracted for are those specified in this collective bargaining agreement. This paragraph is not intended to prevent a Performer from contracting for services of a kind not covered by this Agreement by individual contract at such rates of pay and under such conditions as Producer and the Performer shall agree, subject only to the requirement that it shall not be in conflict with this collective bargaining agreement. Producer shall not require a Performer to include such services as a part of his or her employment under this Agreement but must bargain separately therefor.

If Producer wishes to employ a Performer to perform work for which there is no specified compensation within this Agreement, the parties agree that a Qualified Professional Performer's established rate (which is the rate actually paid within the prior twelve (12) months by a third party producer for similar services), shall be deemed a fair and reasonable rate of compensation for which no waiver need be obtained from the Guild. If Producer wishes to employ such a Performer on terms other than his/her established rate, Producer shall seek a waiver therefor from the Guild.

39. RIGHT TO TERMINATE; UNFAIR LIST

Nothing in this Agreement shall preclude the right of the Guild to terminate this Agreement (on reasonable notice, taking into account in particular any productions already underway or about to begin at such time) and declare a Producer unfair when such Producer, knowingly and intentionally, materially breaches its obligations under the Agreement such as, by way of example and not by way of limitation, where a Producer fails to pay compensation owing to Performers employed by Producer where there is no bona fide controversy arising out of employment under the Agreement. This provision only has effect when Producer refuses to arbitrate or refuses to recognize arbitrator's decision.

40. NOTICES TO PERFORMERS

All notices which the Producer desires or is required to send a Performer shall be sent to not more than two (2) addresses which the Performer may designate, one of which shall be the address which Performer designates for the sending of payments on his or her standard employment contract.

EXHIBIT 5-1 Screen Actors' Guild Producer Incentive Media Agreement (*continued*)

41. FORCE MAJEURE

If a production for which the Performer is engaged is necessarily prevented, suspended or postponed during the course thereof, by reason of fire, accident, strike, riot, act of God, or the public enemy, or by any executive or judicial order or by reason of the illness of any other member of the cast or of the director (herein an event of "Force Majeure"), the following provisions shall apply:

A. Day Performers: Producer shall have the right to terminate the services of Day Performers without further liability, except for compensation for services previously rendered, provided however, that: (i) if such termination occurs before the Performer is used or (ii) if the Performer is subsequently replaced (other than because of his/her unavailability), the Performer shall be entitled to one day's salary in addition to compensation for services previously rendered. Producer shall have the right to recall the Performer after such termination without compensation for intervening time, when production is resumed at the same rate as that previously applicable, subject to the Performer's professional availability.

B. Three-Day and Weekly Performers: Producer has the right to suspend Performers' services and place Performers on one-half (1/2) salary during the period of Force Majeure, subject to the Producer's right to terminate the Performers' employment at any time during the event of Force Majeure. The Weekly Performer shall have the right to terminate employment effective at the end of the third week of suspension at one-half (1/2) salary or, in the case of a Three-Day Performer, effective at the end of the second week of suspension at one-half (1/2) salary, or at any time thereafter unless the Producer commences and continues thereafter to pay Performer his/her full compensation upon receipt of Performer's notice of termination.

Notwithstanding the foregoing, at any time after the commencement of an event of Force Majeure and prior to any resumption by the Performer of his/her services, the Producer may terminate the services of the Performer without further liability except for compensation for services previously rendered. Producer shall have the right at any time during the next three (3) weeks (or, in the case of a Three-Day Performer, after two (2) weeks), to recall the Performer without compensation for intervening time at the same rate as that specified in the Performer's contract, subject only to the Performer's professional availability.

C. Any guaranteed employment hereunder may be extended by the period of any suspension for Force Majeure hereunder by giving written notice to such effect not later than the date of resumption of production following such suspension.

42. ENTIRE AGREEMENT

This Agreement represents the entire understanding between the parties and supersedes all previous

EXHIBIT 5-1 Screen Actors' Guild Producer Incentive Media Agreement (*continued*)

agreements, written or oral, which may have been entered into prior to the date of execution hereof. This Agreement shall not be altered except by written agreement executed by both parties hereto. This Agreement will be governed by the laws of the State of California, as applied to agreements made and performed entirely within California.

ARTICLE II

WORKING CONDITIONS

PRINCIPAL PERFORMERS

1. CASTING AND AUDITIONS

A. If Performers are requested to audition prior to an engagement, Producer shall provide the Performers (or his/her representatives) comprehensive information regarding the audition such as a specific time therefore, the nature of the role(s) available (whether Day Performer, Three-Day Performer, etc.), the nature of the performance desired and any unusual working conditions (work involving animals, stunts, hazards, improvisations, or nudity). An ample supply of segments of the script ("sides") and/or story boards for the particular role(s) which are the subject of the audition shall be available at the location of the audition at the time of the Performers' sign-in. Cue cards may be used by Producer instead of sides or story boards if Producer determines that script Material must be kept confidential.

B. If, at either a first or second audition, the Performer is required to remain for more than one (1) hour from the time of call or arrival, whichever is later, he/she shall be compensated for all time on said call in excess of one (1) hour, at straight time, in one-half (1/2) hour units, at the rate of one-sixteenth (1/16) of the Day

Performer rate. For the third and each subsequent audition, the Performer shall be paid a minimum of one-eighth (1/8) of the Day Performer rate. For all time in excess of one (1) hour, the Performer shall be paid at straight time in one-half (1/2) hour units, at a rate of one-sixteenth (1/16) of the Day Performer rate per unit. Pension and Health contributions shall be paid on all compensation payable to the Performer hereunder for the third and all subsequent audition calls. If the Performer is required to memorize lines for an audition which he/she has been given to learn outside the studio, he/she shall be compensated at one (1) hour of straight time or actual time required for such audition, whichever is greater. If there has been no agreed salary before the auditions, and if the

EXHIBIT 5-1 Screen Actors' Guild Producer Incentive Media Agreement (*continued*)

Performer and Producer cannot agree, the salary rate at which he/she shall be compensated for such excess time shall be one-sixteenth (1/16) of the Day Performer rate.

C. Auditions shall be conducted before Producer and authorized representatives thereof and not in public; mass auditions shall be prohibited. If an audition is recorded, it is agreed that such audition Material shall be used only to determine the suitability of a Performer for a specific project.

D. Adequate seating shall be provided at all auditions.

2. CONSECUTIVE EMPLOYMENT

A. Employment of Three-Day or Weekly Performers shall be for consecutive days from the beginning of the engagement. Such Three-Day and Weekly Performers may agree that consecutive employment is not applicable to a certain engagement provided that such agreement is in writing and Producer provides the firm work dates in writing no later than the first day of work. Additional days of work shall be subject to the professional availability of such performer. Three-Day and Weekly Performers must be engaged in units, throughout their engagement, of not less than three days or weeks, respectively.

B. The requirement of paid consecutive employment is not applicable to: Day Performers; Extra Performers (who are subject to the call back provisions of Article III, Section 9); Singers; Dancers; Stunt Performers; and Three-Day or Weekly Performers engaged at a rate greater than $45,000 for the Interactive Program.

C. Any Principal Performer who has been recalled to render services (other than Retakes, Added Scenes, Etc.) and completes such services, and is then later required for additional Principal Photography ("spillover") by Producer, shall render such spillover services shall be rendered to Producer on a first-call basis on the same terms and conditions as the original employment (except for the term), subject to the Performer's professional availability.

D. The Producer may not agree with any Singer that the Singer will hold himself/herself available for any day after the termination of an original period of employment (which may be as short as one (1) day) unless the Producer agrees at the same time to employ the Singer for such day. It is agreed, however, that the Singer may be recalled by the Producer and will report, at any time prior to the completion of production of the Interactive Program for which he/she was originally employed on the same terms and conditions (except for the term), provided that he/she is not then otherwise professionally employed.

EXHIBIT 5-1 Screen Actors' Guild Producer Incentive Media Agreement (*continued*)

E. Notwithstanding any of the above, all Performers shall be paid for intervening days on an overnight location when required to remain at such location by Producer.

3. RETAKES, ADDED SCENES, ETC.
Compensation for services in connection with retakes, added scenes, soundtrack (including Looping), process shots, transparencies, trick shots, trailers, changes in foreign versions, shall be paid only for the days on which the Performer is actually so employed subject to the individual Performer's availability.

If such services are commenced within three (3) months after the prior termination of employment, compensation therefor shall be at the daily rate or the prorated three day or weekly rate originally agreed upon. In the case of conversion from a Day Performer to a Three Day or Weekly Performer, the compensation shall be based on the prorated three day or weekly rate. A Three Day or Weekly Performer recalled to loop after completion of Principal Photography shall be paid one half (1/2) day's pay (one sixth (1/6) or one tenth (1/10) of the Performer's three day or weekly base rate, respectively) for a four (4) hour Looping session. If the session exceeds four (4) hours, a full day's pay shall be payable. A Voice Over Performer may be recalled for retakes for one half of the performer's original four hour day rate for no more than a two hour session. If the session exceeds two (2) hours, the performer's full four hour day rate shall be payable.

An on-camera performer recalled to perform looping services may loop his/her on-camera performance for the payment detailed above. Performance of additional voices requires compensation at rates not less than Article I, Section 15.B.

4. CONVERSION OF DAY PERFORMERS
Producer shall have the right to convert the engagement of a Day Performer to a Three-Day or Weekly Performer at any time, but such conversion shall commence not earlier than the date Producer gives such Performer (or his/her representative) written notice of such conversion in person or by telegraphing or mailing the same to the address furnished the Producer by the Performer. If the notice is delivered personally to the Performer by noon, or if a telegraphic or facsimile notice is delivered to the office transmitting such messages to the Guild by noon, then the conversion shall be effective commencing with that day. If notice is delivered personally to the Performer or to the telegraph office after noon, or if sent by mail, then in each of the instances as mentioned the conversion shall be effective on the Performer's next work day.

EXHIBIT 5-1 Screen Actors' Guild Producer Incentive Media Agreement (*continued*)

5. WORK TIME - DEFINITION AND EXCEPTIONS

A. For the purpose of ascertaining and computing hours of work, the rest period and Overtime, the period from the time the Performer is required to report to work by Producer ("call") and does actually report ready, willing and able to work without interruption, until the time such Performer is finally dismissed for the day, shall constitute work time, except as follows:

1. Allowable meal periods, as provided by Section 13;

2. Casting or audition calls, as provided by Section 1;

3. Story, song and production conferences, as provided by Section 14;

4. Study of lines or scripts, as provided by Section 15;

5. Publicity interviews and stills, as provided by Section 16;

6. Fittings, Wardrobe Tests and Makeup Tests, as provided by Sections 10 and 11; or

7. Travel time, to the extent provided by Section 30.

B. After the starting date of employment, none of the events referenced in Subsection 5.A., above, shall break the consecutive employment of such Performer.

C. Any period during which the Performer fails, refuses, or is unable because of disability to render services, and any period during which the Performer at his/her own request is excused from rendering services, shall not be work time for any purpose.

6. OVERTIME

A. For the purpose of computing Overtime, a Performer's day is computed from the time of first call to dismissal, excluding meal periods.

1. Overtime payments for all on-camera Performers shall begin with the ninth hour of any given day; the ninth and tenth hours shall be paid at time and one-half; the eleventh hour and beyond shall be paid at double-time. If the Performer is working at midnight of any day, then his/her hours of work for such day shall be computed until the Performer has been dismissed subsequent to midnight.

EXHIBIT 5-1 Screen Actors' Guild Producer Incentive Media Agreement (*continued*)

2. Overtime, payments for Voice-Over Performers are calculated as follows:
The Overtime rates are based on the Voice-Over Performer's daily wage divided by eight (8). All Voice-Over Performers are entitled to double time in hourly units for work in the eleventh hour and thereafter.

A Performer engaged to perform three (3) or less voices shall be entitled to Overtime after four (4) hours on each day of work. The fifth through the tenth hours shall be paid at time and one half.

A Performer engaged to perform four (4) voices shall be entitled to Overtime after five (5) hours on each day of work. The sixth through the tenth hours shall be paid at time and one half.

A Performer engaged to perform five (5) voices shall be entitled to Overtime after six (6) hours on each day of work. The seventh through the tenth hours shall be paid at time and one half.

A Performer engaged to perform six (6) or more voices shall be entitled to Overtime after eight (8) hours on each day of work. The ninth and tenth hours shall be paid at time and one half.

B. Rate Maximums:

1. Day Performers compensated more than $1,149.00 per day are payable for work beyond eight (8) hours based on the rate of $1,149.00.

2. Three-Day Performers compensated more than $2,531.00 are payable for work beyond eight (8) hours based on the rate of $2,531.00.

3. Weekly Performers compensated more than $4,285.00 per week are payable for work beyond eight (8) hours based on the rate of $4,285.00.

C. Payment of Overtime shall not be deemed to reduce a Performer's guaranteed employment or compensation. Except as otherwise herein provided in Sections 10 and 11, makeup, hair dress, wardrobe, or fittings shall be considered work time for all purposes including Overtime.

7. ENGAGEMENT; NON-USE OF SERVICES AFTER ENGAGEMENT

A. A Performer shall be considered definitely engaged by a Producer in any of the following events:

1. When the Performer is given written notice of acceptance by the Producer;

EXHIBIT 5-1 Screen Actors' Guild Producer Incentive Media Agreement (*continued*)

2. When a form contract signed by the Producer is delivered to a Performer;

3. When a form contract unsigned by the Producer is delivered to a Performer and is executed by a Performer and returned to Producer within forty-eight (48) hours;

4. When the Performer is fitted; however, this shall not apply to wardrobe tests;

5. When the Performer is given an oral call which the Performer accepts; or

6. When a Day Performer is given oral notice by the Producer and agrees to report on the commencement date for which the call is given; however, until noon of the day preceding such commencement date, either the Producer or the Performer may cancel such employment. If the Producer is unable to reach the Performer personally, either by telephone or otherwise, notice of such cancellation may be given to the Performer by telegraph or fax, in which event the time when such telegram is given by the Producer to the telegraph company, addressed to the Performer at his/her address or sent via facsimile at the appropriate fax number last known to the Producer, shall be the time of such cancellation.

B. Neither auditions nor interviews shall constitute an engagement.

C. When a Performer is engaged and not used for any reasons other his/her default, illness or other incapacity, he/she shall be entitled to a day's pay or his/her guarantee, whichever is greater. If the Performer who is selected is unavailable when called to render actual services, he/she shall not be entitled to a day's pay.

D. A Performer who is replaced in a production after commencement of his/her services pursuant to his/her engagement and before the completion of the engagement, for reasons other than his/her default, illness, or other incapacity, shall receive his/her guarantee, or a day's pay in addition to payment for services rendered to that time, whichever is greater.

E. A Performer shall be notified by Producer at the time of engagement whether the engagement requires overnight location work and, if so, the approximate time and duration of such location work to the extent such information is then known.

8. PROMPTING DEVICES; DESCRIPTION OF ROLE; SCRIPTS

A. A full and forthright description of the role to be played must be given at the time of audition or interview or, if none, at the time of booking. Such description should include length of Performer's

---

EXHIBIT 5-1 Screen Actors' Guild Producer Incentive Media Agreement (*continued*)

role, use of unusual terminology, whether memorization is required, and whether cue cards or other prompting devices will be used.

B. When an on-camera Performer is required to deliver unusual terminology, Producer will make every effort to have a prompting device or cue cards. If the script is not made available to the on-camera Performer at least twenty-four (24) hours prior to the shooting date, Producer must have cue cards or a prompting device.

C. If the Performer's services will include development of a script through so called "ad-lib" work or substantial embellishment of an existing script through such work, Producer must so inform Performer or Performer's representative at the time of audition or interview.

9. ADVANCE INFORMATION

Producer shall inform a Performer (or his/her representative) at the time of audition or interview for a job, or at the time of hiring (if there is no audition or interview), whether the employment is to be as a Principal Performer, Extra Performer, or otherwise.

10. FITTINGS, WARDROBE TESTS, AND MAKEUP TESTS

A. Fittings: Time spent by a Performer in fittings shall be paid as follows:

1. Fittings on the same day that the Performer works:

a. Time spent in such fittings shall be work time and part of the Performer's continuous day.

b. If four (4) hours or more intervene between the end of the fitting call and the beginning of the work call and the Performer is dismissed in the interim, the fitting shall be paid for as though it were on a prior day on which the Performer did not work.

2. Fittings on a day prior to work:

a. Day Performer: Where a Day Performer is fitted on a day prior to the day on which he/she works, he/she shall be entitled to one (1) hour pay for each call. Additional time shall be paid for in fifteen (15) minute units. Day Performers receiving more than two (2) times Scale shall not be entitled to any compensation for such fittings.

b. Three-Day Performers: Producer shall be entitled to two (2) hours free fitting time. Additional fitting time shall be payable at the compensation rate specified in the Performer's contract, in fifteen (15) minute units, with a one (1) hour minimum call.

EXHIBIT 5-1 Screen Actors' Guild Producer Incentive Media Agreement (continued)

c. Weekly Performers: Producer shall be entitled to four (4) hours free fitting time on no more than two (2) days for each week the Performer works on the Program. Additional fitting time shall be payable at the compensation rate specified in the Performer's contract, in fifteen (15) minute units, with one (1) hour minimum call period.

3. A call to determine whether a Performer's own wardrobe is appropriate shall be deemed a "fitting" covered by the provisions of this Section 10.

B. Wardrobe and Makeup Tests

1. If a Performer is given a makeup or wardrobe test and not used in the Program for which he/she was tested, he/she shall receive one half (1/2) day's pay at Scale for each day on which he/she is given such tests.

2. If a Performer is given a makeup or wardrobe test and is used in the Program for which he/she was tested, he/she shall be paid as follows:

a. Tests on the same day that the Performer works: Time spent in such tests shall be work time and part of the Performer's continuous day.

b. Test on a day prior to work: Where a Day Performer is given a makeup or wardrobe test on a day prior to the day on which he/she works, he/she shall be entitled to (1) hour minimum pay for each call. Additional time shall be paid for in fifteen (15) minute units. A Day Performer receiving more than two (2) times Scale per day shall not be entitled to any compensation for such tests.

3. Producer shall be entitled to one (1) day's free fitting time for a test of each Three-Day or Weekly Performer on the Program. The Performer shall be entitled to a half (1/2) day's pay, pro-rata for each additional day tested in excess of such free time.

11. MAKEUP, HAIR DRESS, WARDROBE ALLOWANCE

A. Exception to Work Time: Producer may require a Performer to report ready for work made-up with hair dress and/or in wardrobe without assistance from the Producer. In such cases, any time spent by the Performer therein prior to the Performer's first call shall not be work time for any purpose, but the Producer may not have a Performer do any such preparation at any place designated by the Producer. The mere fact that a dressing room is available to Performers on the work site, to which he/she is not directed to report, is not the designation of a place for preparation by Producer. In the case of wardrobe, if the Performer is allowed to take home wardrobe or is

EXHIBIT 5-1 Screen Actors' Guild Producer Incentive Media Agreement (continued)

furnished a dressing room with the wardrobe available in the dressing room, the time spent by such Performer in wardrobe shall not be considered work time.

B. Except as specifically designated in the foregoing Subsection 11.A., any call by Producer for makeup, hair dress, or wardrobe is a call to work. Any Performer to whom Producer supplies the services of a makeup artist for makeup, or hairdresser for hairdressing, shall be considered to have a call for makeup or hair dress. When the Performer has reported pursuant to a call for makeup, hair dress, or wardrobe, the time so spent shall be work time.

C. When makeup or hair dress other than ordinary street makeup or hair dress is required by Producer, a professional hairdresser and makeup artist shall be provided for the purpose of applying and maintaining such makeup and hair dress. If a Producer requires a Performer to furnish any special hair dress necessitating an expenditure, Producer shall provide an advance covering the expenditure at facilities designated by Producer.

D. Adequate facilities shall be provided for removing makeup and hair dress which may be the same facilities used for applying makeup and hair dress. Time spent in removal of complicated or Extra Performer ordinary makeup or hair dress shall be work time, but not removal of ordinary makeup and hair dress.

E. On-camera Performers who supply specified personal wardrobe worn during rehearsals or production shall receive a maintenance fee for each complete wardrobe change at the following rates:

1. Non-evening wear: $15.00 per costume change.

2. Evening wear: $25.00 per costume change for each two (2) days or part thereof.

F. "Wardrobe Change": A single wardrobe change shall consist of at least one (1) additional clothing item worn above the waist (such as a blouse or shirt) and at least one (1) additional clothing item worn below the waist (such as slacks or skirt) unless only one (1) such area is visible to the camera. If so, one (1) additional item in the visible area shall be considered a wardrobe change. Items such as dresses, gown, overcoats, etc. shall be considered a change by themselves unless always worn as part of a single outfit. Further, each item of clothing shall be counted only once in determining the total number of changes even though the item may be used in more than one (1) outfit. No additional fees shall be charged for mixing and matching wardrobe items. For example, if outfit #1 is a blue blazer and tan slacks and outfit #2 is a gray suit, use of the blazer and suit pants to create a

EXHIBIT 5-1 Screen Actors' Guild Producer Incentive Media Agreement (continued)

third outfit shall not require an additional fee. Accessories such as scarves, ties, and jewelry shall not be counted as items of clothing for this purpose.

G. Wardrobe supplied by the on-camera Performer which is damaged or lost in the course of employment shall be repaired or replaced at the expense of Producer provided that notice of such damage or loss is given Producer within a reasonable time after such damage.

H. Stunt doubles shall be provided with duplicated, properly fitting wardrobe which shall be appropriately cleaned after prior use by another Performer.

12. REST PERIOD; LIQUIDATED DAMAGES FOR VIOLATION

A. A Performer shall be entitled to a rest period of twelve (12) consecutive hours from the time he/she is finally dismissed for the day until his/her first call thereafter, whether for makeup, wardrobe, hair dress or any other purpose.

B. The above provisions regarding the rest period shall be subject to the following exceptions:

1. Where the Producer is shooting on a nearby location, only if exterior photography is required on the day before and on the day after such reduced rest period, the twelve (12) hour rest period may be reduced to ten (10) hours, but such reduction may not again be allowed unless three (3) days without such reduction intervenes. The reduction to ten (10) hours in the circumstances described applies only if both of the days between which the rest period intervenes are spent at a nearby location.

2. Where a Performer arrives at his/her place of lodging on an overnight location after 9:00 p.m. and does not work that night, the rest period with respect to the first call following such arrival may be ten (10) hours instead of twelve (12) hours, but the first call must be at the place of lodging.

3. The Performer shall be entitled to a rest period of fifty-eight (58) consecutive hours (thirty-six (36) consecutive hours if on overnight location) once each week.

C. The Performer may waive the rest period without the Guild's consent, but if he/she does so, he/she shall be entitled to Liquidated Damages of a day's pay or nine hundred fifty dollars ($950.00), whichever is the lesser sum. The Performer may be required to waive the rest period if the violation is not over one and one half (1-1/2) hours. The above Liquidated Damages of a day's pay or nine hundred fifty dollars ($950.00), whichever is the lesser sum, shall be automatically incurred

EXHIBIT 5-1 Screen Actors' Guild Producer Incentive Media Agreement (*continued*)

in any case in which the Performer waives the rest period. The Liquidated Damages may not be waived without the consent of the Guild.

13. MEAL PERIODS; ALLOWANCES; LIQUIDATED DAMAGES

A. Allowable meal periods shall not be counted as work time for any purpose. The Performer's first meal period shall commence within six (6) hours following the time of his/her first call for the day. Succeeding meal periods of the same Performer shall commence within six (6) hours after the end of the preceding meal period. A meal period shall not be less than one-half (1/2) hour nor more than one (1) hour in length. If, upon the expiration of such six (6) hour period, the camera is in the actual course of photography, it shall not be a violation to complete such photography. If, on location or while traveling to or from location, the delay is not due to any fault or negligence of the Producer, its agents, or persons contracted by it to render the catering service, or if delay is caused by common carriers such as railroads, there shall be no damages due for violation of the above provisions. If the caterer is chosen carefully and is delayed in reaching the location beyond the required time for commencing a meal period, there shall be no damages due for the violation; but if such delay shall continue beyond one-half (1/2) hour, work shall cease and the time intervening between such cessation of work and the meal period shall be work time.

If by reason of a long makeup, wardrobe or hair dress period of a Performer, application of the above stated rule would require calling a meal period for such Performer at a time earlier than that required for the rest of the set, Producer shall not be required to call such meal period if food, such as coffee and sandwiches, is made available to such Performer before the time for his/her established call, it being understood that no deduction shall be made from work time for such period. It is further understood however, that such Performer shall be given a meal period within six (6) hours from the time such food is made available to the Performer.

B. The Liquidated Damages for meal period violations shall be:
$25 to each Performer for the first one-half hour of violation or fraction thereof;
$35 to each Performer for the 2nd one-half hour or fraction thereof;
$50 to each Performer for the 3rd and each additional one-half hour or fraction thereof.

C. Meals must be provided on all locations. All Performers shall be entitled to a basic $48.40 per diem meal allowance on overnight locations. The Producer shall have the right to deduct from the per diem meal allowance the following amounts for each meal furnished, as follows: breakfast: $9.30; lunch: $14.00; dinner: $25.10.

EXHIBIT 5-1 Screen Actors' Guild Producer Incentive Media Agreement (*continued*)

D. Whenever Producer supplies meals or other food or beverages to the cast or crew, or provides money in lieu thereof, the same shall be furnished to all Performers. Regarding beverages, this provisions is applicable only in those situations where the Producer supplies beverages to the cast and crew and is not applicable where isolated groups may supply their own beverages (e.g., prop truck with cooler for beverages). When meals are served to Performers, tables and seats shall be made available for them. No time shall be deducted from work time for any meal supplied by the Producer until the Performers are given the opportunity to get in line for the actual feeding of Performers.

"Meal" means an adequate, well-balanced serving of a variety of wholesome, nutritious foods. The furnishing of snacks, such as hot dogs or hamburgers, to Performers by Producer shall not constitute a meal period. Meals supplied by the Producer shall not be deducted from the Performer's wages but may be deducted from the per diem allowances specified herein.

14. STORY, SONG, AND PRODUCTION CONFERENCES

Story, song, and production conferences on any day on which the Performer is not otherwise working shall not be counted as work time for any purpose. This provision shall not be construed to interrupt the consecutive employment of a Performer.

15. STUDY OF LINES OR SCRIPTS

Study of lines or scripts shall not be counted as work time for any purpose except during the period between reporting and dismissal.

16. PUBLICITY INTERVIEWS AND STILLS

A. Publicity Interviews: Time spent by the Performer in publicity interviews whether on a day the Performer works or otherwise, shall not be counted as work time for any purpose, but the Performer shall be under no obligation to report for such interviews on days other than work days.

B. Publicity Stills: If the Producer desires the services of the Performer on a day when the Performer is not otherwise engaged hereunder to make publicity stills, and if the Performer agrees to render such services, Performer shall receive fifty percent (50%) of the Day Performer rate for up to four (4) hours of services. Any time in excess of four (4) hours for any day spent solely in taking publicity stills shall require payment of the Day Performer minimum. Use of such stills is strictly limited to publicity of the Interactive Program itself and not for general client brochures, magazine ads, etc., which are unrelated to the Interactive Program produced in which the Performer appears.

EXHIBIT 5-1 Screen Actors' Guild Producer Incentive Media Agreement (*continued*)

17. REHEARSAL TIME

A. The reading of lines, acting, singing or dancing in preparation for the Performer's performance, in the presence and under the supervision of a representative of Producer, constitutes "rehearsal" time. Rehearsals shall be counted as work time.

B. Auditions, tests, makeup, and wardrobe tests do not constitute rehearsals.

C. The Guild agrees to grant waivers freely for the training of a Performer in a particular skill such as horseback riding, fencing, etc.. Compensation, if any, shall be agreed to between the Performer and the Producer, subject to the approval of the Guild in the event of a dispute.

D. Neither tests, auditions, fittings, publicity stills, pre-production stills, pre-recording of Material prior to Principal Photography, nor training specified in Subsection C, above, after engagement but before the starting date of the Performer's employment, shall start the employment period of such Performer. Compensation, if any, for such services shall be as otherwise provided herein.

18. START DATES

A. The phrase "on or about" as used in a Weekly or Three-Day Performer's contract, shall allow a latitude of twenty-four (24) hours (exclusive of Saturdays, Sundays, and holidays) either prior to or after the date specified in the contract for the commencement of a Performer's services.

B. The "on or about clause" may be used for Three-Day or Weekly Performers but only if a contract is delivered to the Performer at least seven (7) days before the starting date of services. If a contract is delivered to a Performer less than seven (7) days before the specified starting date, a definite starting date must be specified and the "on or about" clause shall not be used.

C. If a Performer is engaged and a firm start date has not yet been provided to the Performer by the Producer, Performer may terminate such engagement to accept bona fide employment as a professional actor from a third party which conflicts with the date of services of Producer's contract, subject however, to the Performer first giving Producer the following minimum periods during which Producer may specify a start date which then becomes binding: (i) if the Performer informs Producer before noon of a business day, and Producer informs Performer of a start date by the end of the same day; or (ii) if Performer informs Producer at any other time, if Producer informs Performer of a start date by noon of the next business day.

EXHIBIT 5-1 Screen Actors' Guild Producer Incentive Media Agreement (*continued*)

19. DELIVERY OF CONTRACTS; COMPLETION OF FORMS

A. Producer shall give Performer a copy of a contract for services hereunder not later than the first day of Performer's employment. The present rule that a Performer may not be required to sign contacts on the set shall continue. Delivery to a Performer's agent constitutes delivery to the Performer.

B. Where Producer chooses to deliver a copy of a contract directly to the Performer on the set, an Extra Performer copy for retention by the Performer shall be provided.

C. Any and all forms required by any governmental authority to complete employment and payment (such as I-9 forms to confirm eligibility to work in the United States and W-4 forms required by the Internal Revenue Service) shall be presented to Performer no later than the first day of employment. Such forms shall be available on every set and it shall be the Performer's responsibility to return completed forms to Producer in a timely manner. A Producer shall not be required to make retroactive adjustments to withholdings when a Performer fails to return such forms in a timely fashion.

20. SATURDAY AND SUNDAY WORK; NIGHT WORK; HOLIDAYS

A. All on-camera Performers shall receive double time for the sixth and seventh day of work in a work week (except with respect to overnight locations, as specified in Subsection D., below). Voice-Over Performers shall receive double time for Saturday and Sunday work, regardless of the length of the work week.

B. Any Performer required to work at night in New York City and not dismissed by 9:30 p.m. will be provided transportation by Producer to Grand Central Station, Penn Station, or the Port Authority Bus Terminal, unless the place of dismissal is within a zone bordered by 34th Street on the south, 59th Street on the north, and Third and Eighth Avenues on the east and west, respectively.

C. Performers shall receive Overtime for work on any of the following holidays: New Year's Day; Dr. Martin Luther King, Jr.'s Birthday; Washington's Birthday (President's Day); Memorial Day; July 4th; Labor Day; Thanksgiving Day; or Christmas. A Performer shall be paid for a holiday which is not worked only if a Performer is required to spend any such holiday on an overnight location. The amount of Overtime paid on such holidays shall be the same rate as for the first eight (8) hours of work times two (2) (double-time of regular workday pay). There shall be no compounding of the premium pay provided herein.

D. A work week rendered on "overnight location", as defined herein, shall be deemed to be a

EXHIBIT 5-1 Screen Actors' Guild Producer Incentive Media Agreement (*continued*)

workweek consisting of six (6) overnight location days or six (6) days of any combination of studio and overnight location days, which combination includes a sixth day overnight location day. An "overnight location" day shall be deemed to mean any day on which a Performer is being paid by Producer which is spent or worked by Performer on an overnight location on the day of departure or return to and/or from such location (provided the Performer does not actually work otherwise for Producer at its studio).

On an overnight location, the on-camera Performer rate is based on a six (6) day, forty-four (44) hour workweek at not less than $2064.00, instead of a five (5) day, forty (40) hour week at not less than $1,876.00. Daily Overtime is paid after eight (8) hours at rates not less than the following:

From 1/1/00 until 12/31/00
9th & 10th hour $1,876.00 / 40 × 1.5 = $70.35 / hour
11th hour on $1,876.00 / 40 × 2 = $93.80 / hour
Total work time over the forty-four (44) hour workweek is to be paid at not less than $70.53/hour ($1,876.00/40 × 1.5).

E. The salary ceilings specified in Subsection 6.B. of this Article II, above shall be applicable to the provisions of this Section 20.

21. WEATHER PERMITTING CALLS/DAY PERFORMERS ONLY

Weather permitting calls are allowable for Day Performers subject to the following limitations and conditions.

A. Weather permitting calls shall not be issued for stages in studios.

B. A Day Performer receiving two (2) times Scale per day or less shall be paid a half-day's compensation upon the cancellation of any weather permitting call. This sum shall entitle the Producer to hold the Day Performer for a time period not exceeding four (4) hours. The Day Performer shall receive a half-day's compensation for each additional four (4) hours, or portion thereof, during which he/she is held by the Producer. During this waiting period the Producer has the privilege of putting Day Performers into costumes, rehearsing, or making other use of their services. If, however, any recording or photography is done by Producer, whether still pictures or otherwise, the Day Performer shall be paid the agreed daily wage.

C. A Day Performer may only be issued a weather-permitting call once per production.

EXHIBIT 5-1 Screen Actors' Guild Producer Incentive Media Agreement (*continued*)

D. At the time of acceptance by a Day Performer of a weather permitting call, the Day Performer shall advise Producer of any possible conflict for immediate subsequent days.

22. SCRIPT LINES; UPGRADE OF EXTRA PERFORMERS (NON-SCRIPTED LINES ONLY)

A. The Producer agrees that all scripted parts shall be played by Performers hired directly as such, and not by Extra Performers adjusted on the set, except where a Performer has been hired to play the part and for any reason is unavailable or unable to portray the part properly. Except as provided in the foregoing sentence, no Extra Performer hired as such may be employed for script lines on location; and no Extra Performer hired as such may be employed for script lines for work at the studio on the same day as the day on which he/she was hired as an Extra Performer. "Non-scripted" lines are defined as lines which are not pre-planned or preconceived and which are not deliberately omitted for the purpose of evading these provisions.

B. An Extra Performer hired as such may speak non-scripted lines. In such cases the Extra Performer shall be signed off as an Extra Performer and employed as a Day Performer and shall receive payment as a Day Performer from the beginning of such day. The Performer so adjusted may be signed off as a Day Performer and be re-employed in the same Program to perform Extra Performer work but not in the same part for which he/she was adjusted. If such person is again adjusted to perform Day Performer services in the different role in the same Interactive Program, he/she shall not be entitled to consecutive days of employment between the time when he/she is first signed off as a Day Performer and the time when he/she is again adjusted. If an Extra Performer has been adjusted to perform Day Performer work, the Producer may retake the scene with a different Day Performer, without any penalty for failure to recall such Extra Performer. An Extra Performer adjusted for non-script lines shall not be entitled to the Day Performer pay for any day or days before he/she was adjusted.

The day's compensation due a Performer hired as an Extra Performer, whether by the day or by the week, and adjusted for Day Performer work, including services as an Extra Performer and as a Day Performer, shall be computed as if the Extra Performer were employed from the beginning of the day as a Day Performer.

23. STUNT ADJUSTMENT
Unless otherwise bargained for at the time of the engagement, a Performer not engaged as a stunt Performer shall receive an adjustment of not less than one (1) additional day's pay at Day Performer Scale for any day on which such Performer performs a stunt. In no event shall the Performer ever receive less than Day Performer minimum for any day on which such Performer performs a stunt which was not bargained for at the time of original engagement. Overtime compensation on such day shall be based on the Performer's aggregate compensation for such day.

EXHIBIT 5-1 Screen Actors' Guild Producer Incentive Media Agreement (*continued*)

24. PRE-RECORDINGS; PRE-PRODUCTION STILLS

A. Pre-recordings, including rehearsals therefore, after confirmation of engagement but before the starting date of such engagement, shall not start the consecutive days of employment of a Performer. Such Performer shall be paid for the day or days on which he/she renders services in connection with pre-recordings at not less than Day Performer minimum, pro-rated for hours actually worked.

B. Pre-production stills, including rehearsals and preparations therefore, after confirmation of engagement but before the starting date of such engagement, shall not start the consecutive days of employment of Performer. Such Performer shall be paid for day or days on which he/she renders services in connection with pre-production stills at not less than Day Performer minimum, pro-rated for hours actually worked.

25. TOURS AND PERSONAL APPEARANCES

Tours and personal appearances made in connection with employment hereunder shall be in accordance with the following:

A. Nearby locations: A Performer shall be paid one-half day's pay pro-rata for up to four (4) hours' time. If over four (4) hours of the Performer's time is required, the Performer shall be paid a pro-rated day's pay.

B. Overnight locations: A Performer shall be paid a pro-rated day's pay.

C. When the Performer is required to travel for tours and personal appearances, he/she shall be provided transportation and reasonable expenses.

D. Producer shall cooperate to see that the Performers receive adequate meal periods and rest periods when on tours and personal appearances.

26. DRESSING ROOMS; MISCELLANEOUS AMENITIES

A. Producer shall provide clean and accessible dressing rooms and toilet facilities in studios and on locations. Such dressing rooms shall be provided with adequate locks or Producer shall provide facilities for checking normal personal belongings.

B. Chairs shall be available for all Performers in the dressing rooms, on the stage and on location.

C. Dressing rooms shall be clean and in good repair and Producer shall designate a person responsible to implement the foregoing. Adequate space and reasonable privacy shall be provided

EXHIBIT 5-1 Screen Actors' Guild Producer Incentive Media Agreement (*continued*)

for wardrobe changes for each Performer. Heaters or fans shall be provided as needed in all dressing rooms. In the event compliance with the foregoing is not feasible because of space, physical or legal limitations or location practicalities, the matter shall be discussed with the Guild. Waivers shall be not unreasonably withheld under such circumstances.

27. FLIGHT INSURANCE

When a Performer is requested by Producer to travel by airplane, Producer shall reimburse the Performer up to an additional fee of ten dollars ($10.00) for flight insurance, if purchased by Performer. When a Producer requests a Performer to fly by non-commercial or non-scheduled carrier, Producer shall obtain a short-term insurance policy for the Performer providing insurance equal to the amount available for ten dollars ($10.00) on a commercial carrier. Notwithstanding anything to the contrary, the maximum insurance required under this Section 27 shall be the maximum amount reasonably available in the ordinary course of business from an insurance company.

28. EXPENSES

When a Performer is specifically required by the Producer to spend money in connection with services under this Agreement, Producer shall provide an advance for such expenditures. Upon completion of all work and prior to any additional reimbursements, Performer shall submit to Producer an itemized report of expenses incurred at Producer's direction in connection with travel to and from locations, such as cab fares or mileage to and from air terminals and parking. All pertinent receipts and bills shall be attached to the report as substantiation of such expenditures.

Producer shall reimburse Performer for such expenses within two (2) weeks from the date that the Performer presents such substantiation of such expenditures. Producer shall not be obligated to reimburse a Performer for sums beyond the minimum per diem and/or allowances for travel specified in the Agreement without written verification (receipts) in a form accepted pursuant to standard accounting practices.

29. PROTECTION OF PERFORMERS; SPECIAL CONDITIONS

A. General: Producer shall make all attempts to secure the safety of all Performers engaged hereunder while said Performers are working under the direction and control of Producer, and shall use good faith attempts to comply with any reasonable standards established within the entertainment industry in connection therewith. Producer shall obtain copies of all safety guidelines issued by the Entertainment Labor/Management Safety Committee. Producer shall comply with all Federal, State and local laws with respect to the use of hazardous substances, and all appropriate local fire and safety codes for interviewing, casting, fittings or recording of all Materials where the services of Performers are used.

EXHIBIT 5-1 Screen Actors' Guild Producer Incentive Media Agreement (*continued*)

B. Medical Aid: When hazardous work or stunt work is contemplated, Producer shall have available medical and/or first aid assistance at the studio and on location. First-aid kits shall always be available on studio sets and locations.

C. Safety Measures: The following precautions shall be taken by Producer ensure the safety of the Performer:

1. *STUNTS*

a. General: A Performer's consent shall be required prior to performing stunts or stunt-related activity, and shall be limited to the stunt or stunt-related activity for which the consent was given. Where scripted or unscripted stunts or other hazardous activity are required of Performers, an individual qualified by training and/or experience in the planning, setting up and performing the type of stunt involved shall be engaged and present on the set. No Performer shall be requested to perform a stunt without the opportunity for prior consultation with such individual. The foregoing provision shall not apply to a Stunt Performer who is qualified to plan and perform the stunt in question, when both the planning and performance of the stunt do not involve other Performers.

b. Explosives: No Performer shall be rigged with any type of explosive charge of any nature whatsoever without the use of a qualified special effects person who is a professional and is duly licensed under any applicable State and Federal laws to handle hazardous Materials, if any.

c. Driving: When an on-camera Principal Performer is doubled because the level of driving skill requires a professional driver, the driver double shall qualify as a stunt Performer. This would also apply to doubling passengers for the safety of the on-camera Principal Performer. Dust or smoke where a windshield is obscured shall be consider a hazardous driving condition. Driving close to explosives and/or pyrotechnics shall be considered stunt driving.

2. *ANIMALS*
No Performer shall be requested to work with an animal which a reasonable person would regard as dangerous under the circumstances unless an animal handler or trainer qualified by training and/or experience is present.

3. *SMOKE/DUST*
All Performers shall be notified prior to the date of hiring if work in artificially or mechanically created smoke is involved. A Performer may refuse to perform in smoke and will be paid one

EXHIBIT 5-1 Screen Actors' Guild Producer Incentive Media Agreement (*continued*)

(1) day's compensation or the Day Performer rate, whichever is greater, if a Performer is not so notified. Producer shall comply with all Federal and State laws and regulations applicable to the use of substances utilized in the creation of smoke. Performers shall be given a fifteen (15) minute break away from the area of smoke or dust during each hour in which he/she is required to work in smoke or dust.

4. *SWIMMING*
Swimmers shall not be required to go into the water within thirty (30) minutes following a regular meal period.

5. *PHYSICAL ELEMENTS*
It shall be the responsibility of the Producer to provide Performers the opportunity to utilize physical protection from sunburn, frostbite, and extremes of temperature during work hours usual and customary in the industry.

6. *PROPS*
Producer shall exercise care, including prior testing of equipment (breakaway props, etc.) during rehearsals to avoid injury to the Performer.

7. *DANCERS*

a. Standard Floors: Floors for Choreographed Dancers must be resilient, flexible and level in accordance with industry standards. Industry standards generally provide for 1" of airspace beneath wood flooring or 3" or 4" of padding under battleship linoleum laid over a concrete or wood-on-concrete floor. Floor surfaces must be clean and free of splinters, wax, nails, etc. Floors should be swept and mopped at least daily with a germ-killing solution. If Producer requires dancing on surfaces which do not meet the foregoing general standards, such work shall be deemed to be "hazardous work" and shall be subject to all the hazardous work provisions of the Agreement.

b. Hazardous Work: If Producer requires dancing in inclement weather, out-of-season clothing, or costuming which by virtue of its fit or nature may subject the dancer to physical injury or health hazard, or if Producer requires "wire flying", it shall be deemed to be hazardous work and shall be subject to the "dancer's premium payment" additional pay of sixty-five dollars ($65.00) per day.

c. Warm-up Spaces: Adequate space must be provided to permit all dancers to warm-up (perform limbering exercises) thirty (30) minutes prior to dancing.

EXHIBIT 5-1 Screen Actors' Guild Producer Incentive Media Agreement (*continued*)

d. Breaks: Dancers will have at least ten (10) minutes rest during each hour of actual rehearsal or shooting unless rehearsal or shooting is of a continuous nature. If so, at the choreographer's discretion, dancers may continue until a total of ninety (90) minutes has elapsed after which time a twenty (20) minute break must be called.

e. Temperature: Stage or rehearsal area temperature for Choreographed Dancers must not fall below seventy five (75) degrees Fahrenheit. Air ventilation (circulation) shall be provided at all times but air conditioning is not acceptable unless strictly regulated to prevent drafts.

f. Meal Periods: Dancers cannot be required to dance or skate within thirty (30) minutes following a regular meal period. If Producer does not provide meal service and dancers must leave the premises or location to eat, an additional fifteen (15) minutes must be allowed both before and after meal break to permit the dancer to change clothes. Such fifteen (15) minute period may be included in the thirty (30) minute waiting period following a meal.

g. Emergency Treatment: Producer will use best efforts to have a doctor qualified to treat dancers on call in case of an emergency and will notify the deputy elected by the dancers of the doctor's name and phone number.

h. Footwear: Footwear provided by the Producer shall be appropriate to the work and shall be clean, properly fitted, braced and rubberized. Any dancer who is directed to and reports with his or her own footwear shall be paid an allowance of ten dollars ($10.00) per day for each pair of shoes utilized in the performance.

8. *SINGERS*
Singers shall be given a five (5) minute rest period in each hour of recording.

9. *NUDITY*
The Producer's representative will notify the Performer (or his/her representative) of any nudity or sex acts expected in the role prior to the first interview or audition (if known at the time). During any production involving nudity or sex scenes, the set shall be closed to all persons having no business in connection with the production. No still photography of nudity or sex acts will be authorized by the Producer to be made without the consent of the Performer. The appearance of a Performer in a nude or sex scene or doubling of a Performer in such a scene shall be conditioned upon his or her prior written consent. If a Performer has agreed to appear in such scenes and then withdraws his/her consent, Producer shall have the right to double, but consent may not be withdrawn as to the film already photographed.

EXHIBIT 5-1 Screen Actors' Guild Producer Incentive Media Agreement (*continued*)

30. TRAVEL

A. Definitions

1. "Studio zone(s)" are:

a. *Los Angeles:* Thirty (30) mile radius from the intersection of Beverly Boulevard and La Cienega Boulevard.

b. *New York City:* Eight (8) mile radius from Columbus Circle. However, if a Performer is asked to report to a pick up spot, such spot must be within the area between 23rd Street and 59th Street, bounded by the East River and the Hudson River.

c. *San Francisco:* Fifty (50) mile radius mile from the intersection of Powell and Market Streets.

d. *Phoenix and Tucson:* Twenty-five (25) miles from the center of the city.

e. In all other areas where the Guild has established local offices, the studio zone shall be that zone defined by the contract between the local offices and the Producer therein located. If such zone is not defined, the studio zone shall be subject to negotiation and, upon failure to reach agreement, arbitration.

f. The Guild shall promptly notify all local offices and appropriate Producer organizations of any locally agreed-upon studio zones.

2. A "nearby location" is a location beyond the studio zone to which the Performer travels and returns in the same day,

3. An "overnight location" is a location beyond the studio zone to which the Performer travels but is required to stay overnight.

4. "Travel time" is time spent traveling between the place at which a Performer is required to report for services and the actual location at which such services will be rendered and, if applicable, the time between an overnight location and overnight location housing. Travel time, as defined herein, is work time.

EXHIBIT 5-1 Screen Actors' Guild Producer Incentive Media Agreement (*continued*)

a. When Producer provides transportation:

(i) all time between call time at the pick-up point and arrival at the shooting site shall be travel time;

(ii) all time between the commencement of return travel and arrival at the original pick-up point shall be travel time; and

(iii) any time spent waiting for commencement of travel at the end of the work day is travel time.

b. When the Performer provides transportation:

(i) all time spent in actual travel shall be travel time;

(ii) any time intervening between the Performer's arrival and the time of his/her call is not travel time; and

(iii) at the end of the work day, return travel time begins when the Performer is dismissed.

B. A Performer may be asked to report to any site or to Producer's studio within a studio zone without the Producer providing transportation or reimbursement for travel time thereto. When a Performer is asked to report to a site other than within the studio zone, work time shall begin as though the Performer has reported to the Producer's studio or offices within the studio zone and end as though the Performer had returned to the same, and the driver only shall be paid thirty cents ($.30) per mile.

C. Travel time for Performers shall be computed at straight time in hourly units, with no compounding of payment for travel and work, based on hourly rates of:

(i) 1/4 of the Voice-Over rate for off-camera Performers;

(ii) 1/8 of the Day Performer rate;

(iii) 1/24 of the Three-Day Performer rate, or

(iv) 1/40 of the Weekly Performer rate, as appropriate, not to exceed eight (8) hours in any one (1) day.

EXHIBIT 5-1 Screen Actors' Guild Producer Incentive Media Agreement (*continued*)

D. A Producer may choose not to provide overnight lodging at overnight locations if it is reasonably feasible for Performers to travel to such overnight location within the work day and Producer does not provide overnight lodging to other cast, crew, or personnel in connection with the Program. In such instance, Producer shall provide transportation (or reimbursement mileage) to Performers to such overnight location. If Producer provides air transportation to overnight locations, such transportation may be coach, provided no other cast, crew or production personnel fly any other class, and bus and railroad transportation is acceptable if no other means is available or feasible under the circumstances. If a Performer is required to drive his/her own car to a nearby or overnight location, he/she shall receive thirty cents ($.30) per mile. Should a Performer elect to use any form of transportation other than that provided by the Producer, he/she shall be reimbursed at an amount equivalent to what the Producer would have paid for hours spent if the Performer had used the Producer's transportation.

E. A Performer shall be dismissed at the place at which he/she reported to work, not at a subsequent location.

F. Nothing in this Section shall be deemed to break the consecutive employment of the Performer.

G. Reasonable meal periods shall be given during traveling and allowable meal periods of not less than one-half (1/2) hour nor more than one (1) hour each shall be deducted from travel time.

31. MINORS

A. Recognizing the special situation that arises when minor children are employed, the parties hereto have formulated the following guidelines to ensure that the work environment is a proper one for the minor: that the conditions of employment are not detrimental to the health, education and morals of the minor, "morals" being defined as set forth in the penal code of the applicable state of employment; and that the best interest of the minor be the primary consideration of the parent and the adults in charge of the production, with due regard to the age of the minor.

B. A "minor" is: any Performer under the age of eighteen (18) years or legal age of majority in the state in which services are performed, except that it shall not include any such Performer if the Performer is legally emancipated, legally married, or a member of the United States armed forces.

C. A "parent" is a parent or other adult who has the legal right to act as guardian of the child. A guardian, who shall be not less than the age of majority in the state in which the services are rendered, may be appointed by the parent to fulfill the supervisory functions of the parent required by this Agreement, provided that: (i) Producer is provided with written certification of such

EXHIBIT 5-1 Screen Actors' Guild Producer Incentive Media Agreement (*continued*)

appointment by the parent; and (ii) such appointment confers legal authority of the parent to such guardian. In such instance where a parent has appointed a guardian to supervise the child's services hereunder, the term "parent" shall be deemed to include such guardian.

D. Interviews, Tests and Fittings: Calls for interviews, tests and fittings for minors shall not take place at any time during which the minor would otherwise be attending school, and shall be completed prior to 7:00 p.m. Two (2) adults shall be present at all times during any such sessions, and the minor shall not be removed from the reasonable, immediate proximity of the parent. Casting directors or other representatives of the Producer shall make reasonable efforts to safeguard the minor's health, well-being and dignity during these sessions and shall not engage in any behavior which will embarrass, discredit, disconcert, or otherwise compromise the dignity and mental attitude of the minor.

E. Engagement:

1. Producer shall advise the parent of the minor of the terms and conditions of the employment (studio location, estimated hours, hazardous work, special abilities required, etc.) to the extent that they are known at the time of hiring.

2. Prior to the first date of engagement, the parent shall obtain, complete and submit to the Producer or its representative the appropriate documents required by State and local law related to the employment of a minor.

3. Upon employment of any minor in any areas outside of California, Producer shall notify the Guild local office by telephone where such employment will take place. The Union will acknowledge receipt of this information to Producer in writing.

F. Meals: Whenever Producer supplies meals or other food or beverages to the cast or crew, the same shall be furnished to all minors. Regarding beverages, this provision is applicable only in those situations where Producer supplies beverages to the cast and crew and is not applicable where isolated groups may supply their own beverages (e.g., prop trucks with cooler for beverages). When meals are served to minors, tables and seats shall be made available for them. No time shall be deducted from work time for any meal supplied by producer until the minors are given the opportunity to get in the line for the actual feeding. "Meal" means an adequate, well-balanced serving of a variety of wholesome, nutritious foods. The furnishing of snacks, such as hot dogs or hamburgers, to minors by Producer shall not constitute a meal period. Meals supplied by the Producer shall not be deducted from the minors' wage but may be deducted from the per diem.

EXHIBIT 5-1 Screen Actors' Guild Producer Incentive Media Agreement (*continued*)

G. Supervision:

1. A parent must be present at all times while a minor is working, and shall have the right, subject to the production requirements, to be within sight and sound of the minor. The parent shall not interfere with the production or bring other minors not engaged by Producer to the studio or location.

2. A parent will accompany a minor to wardrobe, makeup, hairdressing, and dressing room facilities. No dressing room shall be occupied simultaneously by a minor and an adult Performer or by minors of the opposite sex.

3. No minor shall be required to work in a situation which places the child in clear and present danger to life or limb. If a minor believes he or she to be in such a dangerous situation after having discussed the matter with the stunt coordinator and parent, then the minor shall not be required to perform in such situation regardless of the validity of his or her belief.

4. When a Producer engages a minor, Producer must designate one individual on each set to coordinate all matters relating to the welfare of the minor and shall notify the minor's parent of the name of such individual.

5. When a minor is required to travel to and from location, the Producer shall provide minor's parent with the same transportation, lodging, meals, mealtimes, and per diem allowance provided to the minor.

6. Whenever Federal, State or local laws so require, a qualified child care person (e.g., LPN, RN or Social Worker) shall be present on the set during the work day.

H. Play Area: Producer will provide a safe and secure place for minors to rest and play.

I. Working Hours: When a minor is at location, the minor must leave location as soon as reasonably possible following the end of his or her working day. Minors' maximum hours of work shall be as outlined below (does not include meal time):

Maximum Hours
Age of Minor Of Work End of Day

0–5 years 6 hours 7:00 p.m.
6–11 years 8 hours 8:00 p.m./school days
10:00 p.m./non-school days

EXHIBIT 5-1 Screen Actors' Guild Producer Incentive Media Agreement (*continued*)

12–17 8 hours 10:00 p.m./school days
12:30 a.m./non-school days

1. Work Hours and Rest Time:

a. The work day for minors shall begin no earlier than 7:00 a.m. for studio productions (6:00 a.m. for location productions) and shall end no later than the time specified above.

b. The maximum work time for a minor shall not exceed that provided by the laws of the state governing his/her employment, but in no event shall work time exceed the maximum hours of work stated above. Work time shall not include meal time, but shall include a mandatory five (5) minute break for each hour of work.

2. Producer shall make every effort to adjust a minor's call time so that a minor need not spend unnecessary hours waiting on the set.

J. Unusual Physical, Athletic or Acrobatic Ability

1. A minor may be asked to perform unusual physical, athletic and/or acrobatic activity or stunts, provided that the minor and parent represent that the minor is fully capable of performing such activity and the parent grants prior written consent thereto.

2. If the nature of the activity so requires, a person qualified by training and/or experience with respect to the activity involved will be present at the time of production.

3. Producer will supply any equipment needed and/or requested for safety reasons.

K. Child Labor Laws

1. Producer agrees to determine and comply with all applicable child labor laws governing the employment of minors, and, if one is readily available, shall keep a summary of said laws in the production office.

2. Any provisions of this Section 31 which are inconsistent and less restrictive than any other child labor law or regulation in the applicable state or other applicable jurisdiction, shall be deemed modified to comply with such law or regulation.

3. Inconsistent terms: The provisions of this Section 31 shall prevail over any inconsistent and less restrictive terms contained in any other Sections of this Agreement which would otherwise

EXHIBIT 5-1 Screen Actors' Guild Producer Incentive Media Agreement (*continued*)

be applicable to the employment of the minor, but such terms shall be ineffective only to the extent of such inconsistency without invalidating the remainder of such provision.

L. Medical Care

1. Prior to a minor's first call, Producer shall be provided with the written consent of the minor's parent for medical care in the case of an emergency. However, if the parent refuses to provide such consent because of religious convictions, Producer shall have the right to require written consent for external emergency aid for the child should such need arise.

32. INDEMNIFICATION

A. Producer shall indemnify and hold the Performer harmless from and against any liability, loss, damages, and costs, including reasonable counsel's fees, by reason of any injury or damages incurred by a third party, including any other member of the cast, production staff, crew or any other person, firm, or corporation, which injury or damages are caused by another Performer's performance (including stunts) which occurs under the direction and control of Producer within the scope of the Performer's employment by Producer. Performer shall immediately notify Producer of any such pending or threatened legal action and the Producer shall, at its own cost and expense and without undue delay, provide the defense thereof. Performer shall cooperate with Producer as requested by Producer in the defense of any such action. No settlement shall be effected with respect to any such action by Performer without the express consent of Producer.

B. A stunt coordinator engaged pursuant to this Agreement who is acting within the scope of employment shall be entitled to indemnification in the same manner and to the same extent as specified in Subsection 32.A above, if said stunt coordinator was directly employed by Producer.

C. Nothing contained herein shall be deemed to confer greater liability on Producer than that which may be conferred by law, regulation, or statute.

33. CAST CREDITS
Producer shall accord all Principal Performers with a screen credit on the Interactive Program for which he/she renders services, which credit shall be in a color, size and style which is readily readable consistent with industry standards.

34. MISCELLANEOUS

A. An on-camera Performer who gives an off-camera narration other than as the character portrayed on-camera, shall be paid full additional off-camera wages for such narration.

EXHIBIT 5-1 Screen Actors' Guild Producer Incentive Media Agreement (*continued*)

B. All employment of Performers in Interactive Programs shall be under one of the forms of hiring specified herein, except to the extent specified in Article I, Section 38.

C. If any Program includes a union label, the Guild shall have the right to have its label incorporated into the Program.

D. Producer shall maintain a telephone within a reasonable distance on all locations where practical.

E. The Producer believes that it has a highly commendable record of protecting animals and of preventing their abuse during production of Interactive Programs, and hereby confirms the commitment to the principle that animals should be humanely treated during the production of Interactive Programs. The following constitutes acceptable standards of animal treatment: (i) Producer shall make known throughout its organization its own insistence on the humane treatment of animals; (ii) Producer shall cooperate with the American Humane Association on Programs involving the use of animals when appropriate; and (iii) Producer shall require its production staff to observe adequate safeguards against the cruelty or killing of animals on or off-camera.

ARTICLE III

WORKING CONDITIONS

EXTRA PERFORMERS

1. APPLICATION

A. This Article III contains provisions applicable to the working conditions of Extra Performers. In addition, the following provisions of Article II shall be also deemed incorporated herein:

1. Section 5, "Work Time - Definitions & Exceptions";
2. Section 6, "Overtime";
3. Section 10, "Fittings, Wardrobe Tests and Makeup Tests";
4. Section 11, "Makeup, Hair dress, Wardrobe Allowance";
5. Section 12, "Rest Period; Liquidated Damages for Violation";
6. Section 13, "Meal Periods; Allowances; Liquidated Damages";
7. Section 17, "Rehearsal Time";
8. Section 20, "Saturday and Sunday Work; Night Work; Holidays";

EXHIBIT 5-1 Screen Actors' Guild Producer Incentive Media Agreement (*continued*)

9. Section 19, "Delivery of Contracts; Completion of Forms";

10. Section 22, "Script Lines, Upgrade of Extra Performers (Non-Scripted Lines Only)";

11. Section 26, "Dressing Rooms; Miscellaneous Amenities";

11. Section 29, "Protection of Performers; Special Conditions";

12. Section 30, "Travel";

13. Section 31, "Minors".

B. In the event of a conflict between the provisions of Article II applicable to Extra Performers by this reference and the provisions of this Article III, the provisions of Article III shall govern.

2. INSERTS

A. Extra Performers notified in advance may do inserts for a single Interactive Program for the same day's pay. Extra Performers notified in advance and specifically called to do inserts in two (2) or more Programs in the same day, may do up to and including five (5) such inserts for the same day's pay, but shall be paid an additional day's pay for each five (5) additional inserts thereafter (or fraction thereof). For example, if he/she does a total of seven (7) such inserts in one day, he/she would be entitled to two (2) days' pay. If he/she does a total of fifteen (15) such inserts in one day, he/she would be entitled to three (3) days' pay.

B. Extra Performers notified in advance may do wardrobe tests for more than one Program for the same day's pay.

C. No Extra Performer shall be permitted to perform any work for more than one Program for the same day's pay, including Overtime, except for: inserts; wardrobe tests; work for different Platforms of the same Program.

3. WAIVERS

A. If a Producer requests a waiver affecting Extra Performers, the Guild will issue the waiver without the imposition of any conditions if it believes that the Producer is entitled thereto. In the absence of misstatement or concealment of the facts the waiver will be final. If the Guild believes that the Producer is not entitled to such final waiver, it shall issue a reviewable waiver (which is equivalent to a refusal of a waiver), or it may issue a conditional waiver wherein it will designate the conditions upon which it is willing to have the Producer proceed. Producer may either accept such conditions or refuse to accept the same.

EXHIBIT 5-1 Screen Actors' Guild Producer Incentive Media Agreement (*continued*)

B. If a conditional waiver is issued and the Producer rejects the conditions thereof, or if the Guild issues a reviewable waiver, the Producer may nevertheless proceed as though a final waiver had been issued. If the Producer proceeds without first obtaining a final waiver or without complying with the conditional waiver, it shall notify the Guild in writing to that effect within a reasonable time thereafter.

C. Either party shall have the right to invoke the arbitration procedure as provided in Article I, Section 37, to resolve any dispute regarding waivers.

D. All waivers shall be requested as far in advance as reasonably possible and shall be acted upon promptly by the Guild. If the Guild fails to do so, the Producer may proceed as though the Guild had issued a reviewable waiver, by so notifying the Guild in writing.

E. The application for a waiver by any Producer shall not be deemed an admission that the Producer cannot proceed without obtaining such waiver, nor shall the issuance by the Guild of a waiver be an admission that the Producer is entitled to such a waiver.

4. HAZARDOUS WORK

A. When Extra Performers are required to do night work, "wet" work, or work of a rough or dangerous character, the Producer shall notify the Extra Performers at the time of the call. When an Extra Performer is not so notified, he/she shall be given the option of refusing to perform the work. If he/she refuses, he/she must be paid for all time elapsed from the time he/she is called until he/she is dismissed or one half (1/2) day's pay, whatever is greater. Such refusal shall not result in discrimination against such Extra Performer.

B. Extra Performers who are hired at Scale, and who thereafter accept hazardous work, shall be entitled to additional compensation. The amount of additional compensation shall be agreed to between the Extra Performer and the Producer, or the Producer's representative, prior to the performance of such work.

C. The Producer will not deliberately hire anyone but Qualified Professional Extra Performers to perform hazardous Extra Performer work in accordance with this agreement. No stunt person hired as such may be employed for Extra Performer work on location except for bona fide emergencies not within the contemplation of the Producer. No stunt person hired as such may be employed for Extra Performer work at the studio on the day he/she was employed as a stunt person on the same production. Upon a written request from the Guild, the Producer will submit a report to the Guild indicating whether any stunt persons have been employed on a particular Program. Upon the

EXHIBIT 5-1 Screen Actors' Guild Producer Incentive Media Agreement (*continued*)

written request of the Guild, the Producer will also furnish a copy of the script involved and make a tape available to the Guild for viewing.

D. For violation of this Section 4, the following Liquidated Damages shall apply per person per day: $215.00 for the first violation; $350.00 for the second and each succeeding violation.

These Liquidated Damages shall not apply if there is a bona fide dispute as to whether the work is "Extra Performer work" or "Stunt work."

5. WET, SNOW AND SMOKE WORK

An Extra Performer required to get wet, or to work in snow or in smoke shall receive additional compensation of $14.00 per day. An Extra Performer not notified at the time of booking that wet, snow or smoke work was required may refuse to perform in wet, snow or smoke and, if so, shall receive one half day's pay or the actual hours worked, whichever is greater.

6. BODY MAKEUP, SKULL CAP, HAIR GOODS

An Extra Performer who is directed to and does have body makeup or oil applied to more than fifty percent (50%) of his/her body and/or who is required to and does wear a rubber skull cap, and/or who is required to and does wear hair goods affixed with spirit gum (specified as full beards, mutton chops or a combination of goatee and mustache) and/or who, at the time of his/her employment, is required to and does wear his/her own natural full-grown beard as a condition of employment, shall be entitled to additional compensation of eighteen dollars ($18.00) per day.

It is also understood and agreed that any female Extra Performer required to have body makeup applied to her arms, shoulders and chest while wearing a self-furnished low-cut gown, and any Extra Performer, male or female, required to have body makeup applied to his or her full arms and legs shall be entitled to such additional compensation therefor.

7. INTERVIEWS

A. Extra Performers reporting for an interview shall receive an allowance for the first two (2) hours of the interview in the amount of five dollars ($5.00). For additional time of the interview, Extra Performers shall be paid in units of two (2) hours at the specified regular hourly rate for the call being filled. If, within any period of interview time, any recording or photography, still or otherwise, is done for use in any production, Extra Performers shall be paid the agreed daily wage; except that still pictures to be used exclusively for identification of the Extra Performer or wardrobe may be taken by Producer without making such payment.

EXHIBIT 5-1 **Screen Actors' Guild Producer Incentive Media Agreement** (*continued*)

B. Upon completion of the interview the Extra Performer shall be notified whether or not he/she has been selected, and he/she shall be advised as to the daily or weekly rate of compensation to be paid. If the Extra Performer is not used in the production for which he/she was selected, he/she shall be paid the agreed wage (one (1) day or one (1) week) unless the Extra Performer is not available when called, in which event he/she shall not be entitled to any payment.

C. The Producer agrees to give the Guild written notification within forty-eight (48) hours after the interview, as to persons so selected on interview.

D. An Extra Performer required to report for a second interview for the same job shall be paid not less than two (2) hours pay at the established daily rate.

E. Extra Performers who are required to and do report for an interview in dress clothes shall be paid an additional six dollars ($6.00) over and above the regular interview allowance.

8. SIXTEEN-HOUR RULE

A. Extra Performers shall not be employed in excess of a total of sixteen (16) hours, including meal periods, travel time and actual time required to turn in wardrobe or property, in any one day of twenty-four (24) hours.

B. The Liquidated Damages for violation of the foregoing sixteen (16) hour rule shall be one (1) day's pay (at the Extra Performer's daily rate including any additional compensation) for each hour, or fraction thereof, of such violation. Such damages shall be paid at straight time, unless the violation occurs on a day for which double-time is provided under Article II, Section 20.A. above.

C. This provision shall not apply in any case where such violation occurred as a result of circumstances or conditions, other than production considerations or conditions, beyond the control of the Producer with respect to or affecting the return of such Extra Performers from location. Where the Liquidated Damage payment is excused the Extra Performer shall receive all applicable Overtime. The Guild will not claim any breach of contract resulting from the violation of the sixteen (16) hour rule unless the damages specified above are incurred and not paid.

9. CALL BACKS

A. A "call back," as the phrase is used herein, means instruction by the Producer to the Extra Performer given prior to the dismissal of such Extra Performer to return to work on the same Interactive Program.

EXHIBIT 5-1 Screen Actors' Guild Producer Incentive Media Agreement (continued)

B. Producer agrees that call backs for Extra Performers shall be made as early as possible on the day prior to that specified in such call back. When given a definite call back, an Extra Performer may not be canceled with respect thereto after 4:30 p.m. of that day, except in accordance with the provisions of Sections 10 and 11 of this Article III. Unless the Extra Performer has been given a definite "call back" to return the following day by 5:00 p.m. of a particular day of which shooting commences prior to 2:00 p.m., he/she shall be free to seek and accept other employment commitments.

C. Notwithstanding the foregoing, if the Extra Performer is established so that he/she cannot be replaced and the Producer requires his/her services on the following work day by giving him/her a definite call back, the Extra Performer shall report pursuant to such call back. An Extra Performer, who is given a call back after accepting another employment commitment and who must report pursuant to such call back because he/she has been established and cannot be replaced, will receive the assistance of the Producer giving the call back or its designated casting agency in arranging for him/her to be relieved of such other employment commitment.

10. CANCELLATION OF CALLS

A. The Producer shall have the right to cancel any call for any of the following reasons beyond his/her control: (1) illness in principal cast; (2) fire, flood or other similar catastrophe or event of force majeure; or (3) governmental regulations or order issued due to a national emergency. In the event of any such cancellation, the Extra Performer so canceled shall receive a one-half (1/2) day's pay, except as provided in Subsections D. and G. below.

B. The Producer shall be entitled to hold and use such Extra Performers for four (4) hours only to the extent herein provided. For each additional two (2) hours or fraction thereof, the Extra Performer shall receive a one-quarter (1/4) day's pay.

C. During the time which the Extra Performer is so held, the Producer has the privilege of putting the Extra Performer into costume, rehearsing, or making other use of his/her services. If, however, any recordation or photography is done, whether still pictures or otherwise, Extra Performer Performers shall be paid the agreed daily wage.

D. If any Extra Performer is notified of such cancellation before 6:00 p.m. of the work day previous to the work date specified in such call, or is otherwise employed on the same work date by the same production Producer at a rate equal to or higher than the rate applicable to such Extra Performer as specified in such canceled call, he/she shall not be entitled to such one-half (1/2) day's pay.

EXHIBIT 5-1 **Screen Actors' Guild Producer Incentive Media Agreement** (continued)

E. If the Extra Performer's second work assignment is for a time to commence less than four (4) hours after the time of his/her canceled call, the Extra Performer shall receive in lieu of the one-half (1/2) day's pay an allowance for the cancellation of the call on a straight time hourly basis, computed in thirty (30) minute units from the time of the first call to the time of his/her second call. Overtime, if any, on the second work assignment is computed without reference to the first call. If the second work assignment is for a time to commence more than four (4) hours after the time of his/her canceled call, the Extra Performer shall receive the one-half (1/2) day's pay. Overtime, if any, shall be computed without reference to the first call.

F. If an Extra Performer has not been notified as contemplated by Subsection D. above, then notice must be posted at the hour designated for the call, stating that the set will not work.

G. Nothing herein contained shall enlarge the Producer's right to cancel calls.

11. WEATHER PERMITTING CALLS

A. When scheduled photography is canceled by Producer because of weather conditions, Extra Performers reporting pursuant to a "weather permitting" call shall be paid one-half (1/2) day's pay, which shall entitle the Producer to hold the Extra Performer for not more than four (4) hours; the Extra Performer shall receive a one-quarter (1/4) day's pay for each additional two (2) hours or fraction thereof, during which he/she is thereafter held.

B. During this time the Producer may costume, rehearse or otherwise use the Extra Performer on the specified photoplay, except for recording or photography still or otherwise, of such Extra Performer.

C. If the Extra Performer is used for such recording or photographing, he/she shall receive a day's pay.

D. The Extra Performer may cancel a weather permitting call previously accepted by notifying the agency which issued the call prior to 7:30 p.m. or the closing time of such agency, whichever is earlier, unless he/she has been established in the picture.

E. Weather permitting calls shall not be issued for stages in studios, nor shall a weather permitting call back be issued to any Extra Performer after he/she has been established.

F. When a weather permitting call is given, the Producer must specify that the Extra Performer is to work: (1) if it is raining; (2) if it is cloudy; or (3) if the sun is shining; provided that if any other

EXHIBIT 5-1 Screen Actors' Guild Producer Incentive Media Agreement (*continued*)

special type of weather is a condition precedent to the Extra Performer working, the same may be specified, but must be described sufficiently so as to be capable of understanding by an Extra Performer.

G. Producer agrees that it will not request the Extra Performers to call in the early morning hours of the following day for a possible weather permitting call.

12. UNDIRECTED SCENES

Upon request of Producer, the Guild will grant an automatic and unconditional waiver whereby the Producer may photograph long shots of the normal activities of crowds at public events or crowd scenes. The events must be open to the general public and publicized as such. The crowd so photographed shall appear only as atmospheric background except that Extra Performers or photographic doubles may be used if the Producer stages one or more tie-in shots using Qualified Professional Performers and/or Extra Performers in connection with such tie-in scenes.

13. OMNIES

Any Extra Performer who speaks atmospheric words, commonly known in the industry as "omnies," shall be entitled to the basic wage for the particular call.

14. HIRING PRACTICES

A. No Extra Performer shall be employed on account of personal favoritism.

B. Rotation of work shall be established to such reasonable degree as may be possible and practicable.

C. No person having authority from the Producer to hire, employ or direct the services of Extra Performers shall demand or accept any fee, gift, or other remuneration in consideration of hiring or employing any person to perform work or services as an Extra Performer, or permitting such person to continue in said employment.

End

EXHIBIT 5-1 Screen Actors' Guild Producer Incentive Media Agreement (*continued*)

CHAPTER

6

LIVE STAGE PERFORMANCES

CHAPTER OVERVIEW

As in other areas of entertainment, theater is one that is not wholly independent of general concepts of law. To mount a production for the stage, one must create a business entity, clear copyrights, and work within the parameters of unions and their regulations. It is also necessary to hire artists (singers, dancers, actors) and people to control the production (directors and producers).

Live stage performances are governed by an organization called Actors' Equity. Actors' Equity, or Equity, was created in 1913 to protect the rights of theatrical entertainers, and today stands as the premier union and governing body of the American theater. This chapter provides a discussion of material specific to the area of dramatic theatrical productions as influenced by Equity and general American law. The specifics of other forms of live entertainment are discussed in the chapters dealing with the type of performance being presented.

ACTORS' EQUITY AND EQUITY CONTRACTS

In chapter 3, the concept of boilerplate contractual language was introduced. As well as the need to be conversant with the specific terminology of a given industry, for live stage performances one must also be aware of the clauses and forms, which for the most past are determined by various unions. This section of the chapter introduces those clauses mandated by the Actors' union.

The Union

Actors' Equity
The actors' and stage managers' union that negotiates and administers national and regional agreements with theatrical employers.

Actors' Equity (Equity) is the actor's and stage manager's union that negotiates and administers national and regional agreements with theatrical employers. In terms of labor-law terminology, Equity operates as a clearinghouse for actors so that they may be hired for professional productions at the local, regional, and national level. As with other entertainment unions, Equity mandates certain minimum hours, wages, and associated health and pension employee benefits for its member professionals. Further, Equity's endorsed contracts guarantee safe and sanitary working conditions and job security, rights that have not always been afforded actors in the past.

Historically, in order to be able to audition and consequently be hired for most professional live stage productions, an actor or stage manger had to belong to Equity. However, because of a settlement resulting from a lawsuit filed against it, in 1988 Equity agreed that nonunion members would be entitled to audition for Equity-sanctioned productions. To become a member of Equity, an actor or stage manager must meet one of the following criteria:

1. The person must be working in a current Equity production
2. The person must be a member of a "sister" union, such as the Screen Actors' Guild (SAG), for at least one year and have worked on productions sanctioned by that union during that period of time.

An actor or stage manager who has been hired for an Equity production prior to becoming a member must join the union within thirty days of being hired for that production. The initial fee for joining Equity is $800, with yearly dues.

— *Example*

A young actress is hired for her first professional job in an Equity production of a Shakespeare play in which she will carry a spear. This employment will entitle her to become a member of Equity, but she must join within thirty days of the start of her contract.

Because of the settlement mentioned above and the high cost of the annual dues, many actors, the majority of whom cannot support themselves exclusively

temporary withdrawal
Equity classification in which a person may still audition for Equity productions without full membership.

suspended payment
Equity classification in which a person may still audition for Equity productions without full membership.

on their acting salaries, have opted to suspend their memberships, changing their status from active to **temporary withdrawal** or **suspended payment** classification. These classifications enable them to audition for Equity productions and, if hired, then renew their full membership, similar to the procedures discussed with respect to Screen Actors' Guild members in the preceding chapter.

— *Example*

A young actor was able to join Equity when he had a small part in a regional Equity production two years ago, but he has not had an acting job since that time. To reduce his expenses, he temporarily withdraws from full Equity membership, planning to keep auditioning and renew as a full member as soon as he lands another acting job.

The Union Contract

Equity contracts are designed for three types of stage professionals:

1. Principal performers
2. Members of the chorus
3. Stage managers.

Equity provides standard contracts for each of these professionals that are based on the nature of the intended production, such as cabaret, off-Broadway, regional theater, and so forth. The rules governing Equity contracts can be viewed at the Equity Web site, http://www.actorsequity.org. For the purposes of live stage performances, only those provisions that are not addressed in other chapters and which have direct bearing on theatrical productions will be scrutinized.

Agents

Equity requires that any agent who negotiates on behalf of an actor for an Equity production be franchised by the union. If any actor uses the services of a nonfranchised agent, the actor is liable to suspension or other disciplinary action by the union. If a producer contacts an actor directly, the actor need not use the services of a franchised agent and is not responsible for any agent's commission.

— *Example*

A young actor is represented by an agent who is not franchised by Equity, because he could not find a franchised agent to represent him. If this agent negotiates a contract for him, the actor may be subject to Equity disciplinary sanctions, even though no Equity agent would handle him.

Alien Performers

Nonresident aliens may only be hired for Equity productions if such employment is first approved by the union. The purpose of this provision is to protect American performers, but it has caused problems when foreign productions want to come to the United States with their original cast members.

Auditions

open auditions
Tryouts at which anyone can audition.

Equity requires that before any performer is hired for a production, the producer must hold **open auditions**, tryouts for which no appointment is needed. This rule is designed to provide job opportunities for as-yet unknown actors. Also, Equity provides strict guidelines with respect to the locations and timings of such auditions.

Billing

The names of all actors in a production must appear on the show's billboards, placed outside the theater or prominently displayed on posters in the theater lobby if no billboard is available. Further, each production must provide the audience with a free playbill or program in which each actor is listed, and the actor's name and biography must appear on any souvenir programs published by the producer.

— *Example*

A young actress is appearing in her first professional production in a city far away from her hometown. Her family is unable to attend, so she sends them a copy of the playbill in which her name and the part she plays appears, as well as a souvenir program in which her biography is given.

Blacklisting

blacklisting
Placing a performer on a list to ensure that he or she will not be hired.

Blacklisting refers to the submission by a producer of a list of persons who the producer does not wish to see employed. This practice is deemed violative of Equity standards.

— *Example*

An actress develops a reputation for being disruptive. Several producers get together and decide to see that she is never hired again. This is an example of a blacklist.

Clothes and Makeup

These items are the responsibility of the producer to provide to all actors, and all costumes are required to be cleaned periodically at the producer's expense.

Cuts in Salary

Any reduction in a performer's salary must be approved by Equity, regardless of the reason for the cut.

— Example

Because of a poor economy, a Broadway show is not generating sufficient ticket sales to continue. The producers suggest a cut in salary for the performers so that the show can continue. Any such salary reduction, even one to keep the actors employed, must be approved by Equity.

Equity Representative

Every Equity-authorized production must permit an Equity representative free access to the stage and the actors at all times to ascertain if Equity standards are being maintained.

Nudity

Sex acts are not permitted under Equity contracts, and any nude scenes required by the production must first be approved by Equity before the actor is required to disrobe.

Performances

Performances are limited to eight per week, and cannot be performed on more than six out of seven consecutive days. Actors are entitled to a full weekly salary, even if fewer performances are given in any consecutive seven-day period, unless the lack of performances was due to fire, accident, strike, riot, an Act of God, or a public enemy that could not have been foreseen.

— Example

When the World Trade Center was attacked and Broadway performances were cancelled, such cancellations, because they were caused by an enemy attack, could have relieved producers from paying the actors their full salaries.

Rehearsals

Rehearsal schedules and salaries are specifically delineated in the standard Equity contract.

Transportation

Whenever a production is scheduled for out-of-town performances, either in pre-Broadway tryouts or as a part of a road tour, the Equity contract indicates specific obligations of the producer with respect to baggage handling, transportation, hotels, and meals.

CAST MEMBERS

The term *cast members*, as used in this section, refers to those entertainment professionals involved in the live stage production, such as the producer and juvenile actors.

The Producer

The first important decision one must make before production of a play can begin is the selection of a producer. A theatrical producer manages the production of the play and the running of the theater. The producer is an integral participant in the production of a live stage performance because he or she has many duties that are essential to the success of the play:

1. A producer initiates and controls the creative, financial, technical, and administrative aspects of a production and must be careful to adhere to the regulations set forth by each cast member's respective union.
2. A producer runs everything and is involved from the beginning to the end of the production.
3. A producer finances the production either by putting up the money himself or by finding people to invest in his play.
4. A producer is in charge of the budget for the production.
5. A producer is responsible for selecting and supervising other staff members; this includes a variety of technical personnel such as stage hands, lighting people, and so forth, as well as the cast.
6. A producer deals with any and all production problems the staff or cast might encounter.

In addition to all of the above, the producer is also responsible for promoting and publicizing the production. In other words, the producer has the primary responsibility for the success or failure of a production.

Juvenile Actors

There is probably no other area of entertainment where children are so in demand as in theater. Children have had parts in dramatic works, musicals, and operas, to name a few, and Equity productions mandate that certain conditions and standards be met in order to address the special needs of minors.

Children under the age of sixteen who appear in performances for which admission is charged need permits to work. This is similar to the working papers needed by sixteen-year-olds who wish to have summer jobs. These work permits can be obtained from local authorities; they must be signed by the child's parent or guardian. The procurement of a license allows for regulations that prescribe different hours of work, rest periods, and meals, depending on the age of the child. The application must specify the number of performance days and the period that such employment will cover. There are some exceptions to the requirement of a license for a child to perform. These exceptions include nonpaid performances and school performances. If the child is under fourteen, a license will not be granted unless the role the child has been hired to fill cannot be performed except by a child of about the same age.

Equity requires that separate dressing rooms be maintained for all juvenile performers, and that child actors must be supervised by a competent adult. Rehearsals and performances must be designed so as not to interfere with the child's schooling, either by scheduling the juvenile's participation after normal school hours or providing for special tutoring at the theater.

There are statutory provisions relating to record keeping and children in general. Generally, contracts for minors must go through the courts. Failure to have a court sign off on a contract involving a child usually makes the contract void or voidable. The courts will regulate the times a child may work and the length of the work day. Courts will also regulate schooling and safety issues for a child.

FILMING AND TAPING

As a general statement, it would be accurate to say that filming or taping of live stage productions is not permitted unless approval had been obtained from Actors' Equity. Further, unless special circumstances are demonstrated, Equity generally will not withhold such approval; if no approval is given, the prohibition against filming and taping stays in effect until nineteen weeks after the production has closed. If a cast album is contemplated, such album must meet the standards of AFTRA contracts for recordings (detailed in chapter 7).

experimental contract
Contract for low-budget or advertising production not subject to strict Equity guidelines.

For many theatrical productions, in order to garner an audience the producers will want to film excerpts from the production to use as advertisements on network television, cable, and more recently, the Internet. Such limited filming for advertising purposes is permitted under what Equity calls an **experimental contract**, which is used both for small-budget productions and for advertising slots with reduced Equity-mandated costs. If complete recording of the production is being sought for commercial release (usually by means of television, Internet, or video rental), the producers must negotiate such use with the professionals involved according to Equity specifications, which include additional payments to the individual holding the rights to the production.

bootlegging
Making an unauthorized tape of a theatrical performance.

reproduction
Photocopying, transcribing, or recording.

One aspect of filming live performances that has received considerable media attention is bootlegging. **Bootlegging** is the taping of a live performance without the authorization of the participants. Such taping may be either for private home use or for financial gain. At one time, such bootlegged films were readily discernable because of the relatively poor quality of the **reproduction**. However, currently, with vastly improved technology, such films may appear to have a professional quality indistinguishable from one that has been authorized and professionally produced. These bootlegged tapes may result in copyright infringement actions against the bootlegger, if not specifically under the Copyright Act of 1976, then under the Berne Convention.

— *Example* —

A tourist from the Midwest comes to New York for the first time and attends a Broadway show. As a souvenir, and to entertain the folks back home, the tourist surreptitiously tapes the show without consent. The tourist may have violated copyright laws, even though the taping was for a private, noncommercial use.

COPYRIGHT CONSIDERATIONS

adaptation
An alteration of an original work to create a new copyrightable work.

dramatic work
The story.

musical work
The score and lyrics.

Theatrical ventures are usually based on an original concept, an **adaptation** of a story, or even music. Copyright protects all three of these sources. It protects **dramatic works** such as a play, as in the instance of "Hamlet." It protects **musical works**, both written as a basis for a theatrical production such as "Mama Mia!", as well as songs written for a production such as "Oklahoma!". It protects written material such as novels, as in the production of "The Scarlet Letter." In addition, copyright law plays a role in the production of sound recordings, which usually take the form of cast albums and films, as in the taping of "Death of a Salesman."

Copyright permission will be required for the performance, reproduction, or adaptation of a copyrighted work. Unlike the request to cover, or perform, a song, there are no compulsory licenses when it comes to putting on a concert, play, or musical. A copyright owner may refuse permission to use his or her material. Use of material that has not been cleared may result in copyright infringement.

— *Example* —

A book that has gotten the attention of a popular talk-show host and made her reading club list has also caught the interest of a local theater company. The theater company believes it would be quite easy to adapt as a play. They rewrite the novel, rehearse, and advertise the play. The author of the original book hears about this new play and contacts the theater company to tell them to stop production. If the theater does not get permission from the author of the book, it will result in copyright infringement.

One exception to copyright requirement is if the copyright has expired. If the copyright has expired, no permission from the original author of the work is required. Refer to chapter 2 on copyright law to determine when a copyright term has expired.

Public Performance

public performance
A performance that is done outside a domestic setting.

script
Written words performed by the actors.

A performance is a **public performance** regardless of whether or not a profit is made unless it is in a domestic setting. Musicals contain dramatic works, the story, and the musical score and lyrics. Usually only the script needs to be cleared before the production of a play. A **script** consists of the written words performed by the actors. Permission should not only be obtained for music, lyrics, and plays, but also for performances of poems and prerecorded music and sound recordings.

— *Example*

Maggie gives a performance of "The Lion King" in her living room for the neighborhood children. Even if she sells tickets to the performance, she will not be in violation of copyright protection because her living room, unless it is an unusually large theater, constitutes a domestic setting.

Reproduction

Reproduction of materials includes photocopying, transcribing, or recording. If a theatrical production has background music, permission should be obtained for the use of the music from both the record company and the music publisher, especially if any of the music will be used in the production of a cast album. Permission should also be obtained before scores, sheet music, or the play itself is photocopied.

— *Example*

The script for an upcoming play is photocopied and handed out to individual cast members. Permission should be obtained from the owner of the copyrighted work prior to such reproduction, or a violation of copyright may occur.

Adaptation

Not only is one required to get permission to use a copyrighted work, but it is also necessary to get permission to adapt, or alter, the work. As in the above situation, if the term of the copyright has expired, then no permission is necessary. However, if the piece has been previously arranged, permission will be needed to rearrange the arrangement.

Also, since the owner of copyright in a literary work holds that right exclusively, even if one is translating a literary work, he or she must get permission from the owner.

Other Issues

Other issues that require copyright permission include recording concerts, plays, and musicals. Contacting the appropriate entities, such as the publishers of a book or a song, is required.

Permission is necessary if one prints summaries of a play that someone else has written in the program or if part of a song or part of the script is included in the program. Also, if someone else's artwork is used on the cover, permission must be obtained.

Consider also the use of the reproduction of an artwork in the setting of the play. Much like the use of footage in a film, permission must be obtained if an original piece of art is used as part of the set or as a prop.

— *Example*

In an attempt to help the audience understand the play they are about to see, the stage manager includes an excerpt from a well-known summary source. If the stage manager does not get permission to use the excerpt, it is a violation of copyright law.

amateur performance
A performance where there are no professionals or paid actors.

stock performance
A theatrical company formed to perform a repertoire of plays, usually at one theater.

Royalties

As in the case of a music-publishing royalty, royalties are paid for the use of a copyrighted play. These royalties are determined by the publishing house that holds the right to the work. Contributing factors include whether the performance is an amateur production or a professional or stock performance. An **amateur performance** is one where there are no professionals or paid actors. A **stock performance** is one performed at a summer repertoire company.

CHAPTER REVIEW

While much of what must be considered in the production of a theatrical production is similar to concepts discussed in other chapters, some concepts are unique to the field.

Arguably more than in any other area of entertainment law, the actors' union, Equity, plays a significant role. Equity is responsible for the protection of actors and stage managers, ensuring that their members receive just compensation and work under safe conditions. The provisions of the Equity rules governing employment form the basis of all theatrical contracts for union productions; consequently, a working knowledge of these rules is of paramount importance for the entertainment-law professional.

There are unique concepts in copyright law that must be addressed. Plays must clear the dramatic work prior to performance. For musical productions, both the musical and dramatic work must be cleared.

Additionally, the use of any copyrighted works in the production (setting, props, music) must be cleared. Royalties must be paid to the owner of the original copyright.

JUDICIAL DECISION

This case discusses problems associated with receiving royalties.

April Productions, Inc. v. G. Schirmer, Inc.

284 AD 639 (1st Dept 1954)

Plaintiff recovered judgment for accumulated royalties under a letter agreement, dated September 14, 1917. Defendant appeals.

The nub of the case turns on the duration of the 1917 agreement. It contained no expressed term, but provided that defendant was entitled to publish an English adaptation of a German musical play, "Maytime," and for this right defendant was to pay a royalty on each published copy of the play or selections from the play.

When the agreement was made Sam S. & Lee Shubert, Inc., apparently an affiliate of plaintiff's predecessor, held an annually renewable agreement from the German owner to reproduce an English adaption of the play, together with the right to interpolate new musical numbers. At the expiration of the agreement or on default by the Shuberts, all rights would revert to the German owner. The musical play was a "hit" in 1917, when the agreement in suit was executed.

Defendant was and is a well-known musical publisher. It faithfully paid the royalties due under the agreement until the copyrights entered in defendant's name expired in 1945. In 1946, defendant made an agreement with the author of the interpolated music, Sigmund Romberg, and renewal copyrights were taken out by Mr. Romberg, and assigned to defendant. Since the expiration of the earlier copyrights in 1945, defendant has declined to pay the royalties.

It is significant in evaluating the background for these arrangements that Mr. Romberg was retained by the Shuberts to perform his services. He was expressly hired on a salary basis for the purpose of composing the incidental music and songs, which have become the subject of this litigation. It is these songs and selections which have retained their popularity through the years. They were consequently the product of an employment arranged for and paid for by the Shuberts.

There can be no question that the Shuberts and the publisher could have agreed on any term for the payment of royalties. The period could have been less than the term of the copyright, for the term of the copyright, or for a period extending beyond the term of the copyright. Indeed, the parties could have agreed upon a lump sum payment, or installments, or for royalties of indefinite duration, in each case as consideration for the right to publish the musical selections, which right the Shuberts at the time had the power to extend (*Ehrlich v. Jack Mills, Inc.*, 215 AppDiv 116, affd. 248 NY 598).

The publishers insist that the term for the royalties is limited to the term of the original copyright. There is no such provision in the agreement. Plaintiff insists that the term for the royalties is indefinite, so long as defendant publishes the musical selections. Plaintiff relies on the failure of the agreement to specify a terminal date.

There is nothing in the agreement or in the status of the parties at the time of the agreement to indicate that the royalties to be paid were dependent upon the statutory copyright to be later obtained. The word royalty is not so limited in definition (*Matter of Elsner*, 210 AppDiv 575, 578; *Bouvier's Law Dictionary* (Rawle's 3d Revision) "Royalty," p. 2975; 37A *Words & Phrases* [Perm. ed], "Royalty," p. 597). Authorities which determine that royalties are no longer due, because of a failure of consideration in supplying an exclusive license as required by the agreement for royalties, are not applicable (E.g., *Bottlers Seal Co. v. Rainey*, 225 NY 369, and *Pomeroy v. New York Hippodrome Corp.*, 197 AppDiv 114).

Consequently, to fix a term for the royalties in the 1917 agreement is to write into the agreement a term which the parties did not provide. That we may not do unless it is required as a matter of necessary implication. But we may not imply such a term; for it was as reasonable for the parties to intend and contract for indefinite royalties as it was for them to provide royalties limited to a period. The basic play was a "hit." The burden of royalties would always be related to the success of publication. The fewer the copies sold, the lighter the burden. The converse would be equally true, and for this the parties would very much wish.

The renewal of the copyrights by agreement with Sigmund Romberg, the composer of the interpolated selections, does not change the picture. His cooperation was required as a matter of Federal statute. That necessity, in the event of renewal of the copyrights, was always foreseeable, and is not the question in this case. The issue here is whether the publishers agreed to pay a royalty of indefinite duration for the privilege of publication of selections from a musical hit. That latter consideration the publishers received in 1917, and three decades later, as a consequence in part at least, they were still the publishers. What incidental arrangements they have been obliged to effect to continue their publication is immaterial, so long as it is not due to any default or failure on the part of the Shuberts, who extended to them their initial opportunity to publish the music from the play "Maytime."

On parallel reasoning, the later termination of the agreement between the Shuberts and the German owner in 1942, by court decision, does not affect the bargain made in 1917. The learned Special Term found and we agree, that bargain was for royalties for an indefinite duration, in consideration of the initial right to publish the play and selections therefrom. Moreover, the publishers assumed as much, because they continued to pay royalties after the 1942 termination of the agreement between the Shuberts and the German owner, and until the copyrights expired in 1945.

There is a procedural issue in the case. The action was brought in equity, but the cause of action made out was one at law, for breach of contract entitling plaintiff to money damages. Under some circumstances this would merit reversal of the judgment and dismissal of the complaint (*International Photo Recording machs. v. Microstat Corp.*, 269 AppDiv 485; *Ehrlich v. Jack Mills, Inc.*, supra). Candor requires that we confess some discordance in the precedents whether the complaint should be dismissed, whether it should not, and whether the case should be sent to the law side for trial (See 3 Carmody on New York Practice (2d ed, 1931), § 898, and the cases cited; 30 CJS, Equity, § 67, especially pp. 420, 421; 19 AmJur, Equity, §§ 125, 129, 135). However, there was no prejudice to defendant in the instant case. The right to a jury trial is hardly significant, since the case turns on the interpretation of the written agreement, an issue properly determinable by the court alone. True, if treated as an action at law, damages could be computed only to the date of the beginning of the action, rather than to the date of trial, as was done here. But this is not a right derived from a principle of justice. It derives rather from the forms of procedure. And forms of procedure should not serve to frustrate a result just and clear on the face of the matters proven. That we consider to be the spirit and effect of § 111 of the Civil Practice Act. This becomes particularly the correct result when defendant has stipulated, as it has here, the amount of the accrued royalties to the date of trial. This is not an instance where a party has slept on his rights and the Statute of Limitations has run on a part of his claim. But if the complaint were dismissed the effect would be the same. Plaintiff may have mistaken its remedy, but that is all. Equity should not effect an inequity by dismissing the complaint for merely technical reasons, although the right to a remedy is clear. Moreover, equity should have, and has, the power to render the appropriate judgment, regardless of technical labels, so long as its jurisdiction was properly couched in the first instance and it is retained.

We do not consider that the holding in the *International* case (*supra*) requires a different result. In that case plaintiff sought reformation of the contract, and such moneys as would be due under the contract as reformed. "It did not plead a cause of action for damages at law under the contract as it was written" (p 490). In the instant case plaintiff alleged and relied upon the terms of the 1917 agreement, and sought (in addition to certain equitable relief to which it was not entitled) an accounting for the royalties due. Thus, while in the *International* case a recovery of judgment upon the original unreformed contract was arguable outside the scope of the pleadings, the complaint here clearly tendered issues relating to construction of the pleaded agreement, and to liability for royalties accrued thereunder.

In the *International* case (*supra*) it was argued that there were possible defenses or counterclaims available to defendant in an action at law which were not presented by the pleadings or litigated at the trial. Such a contention cannot be made here, as the issues of fact and law tendered under the equity complaint are identical with those resolved under the breach of contract theory upon which this case was decided. Also, as indicated, there is no issue as to the amount of damages. It is difficult to conceive how the defendant, fairly apprised of the plaintiff's claim by the complaint in equity, would be surprised, confused or prejudiced. Moreover, the potential for confusion in the *International* case was compounded by the fact that the plaintiff discontinued an action at law in the City Court in order to bring the action in equity.

Finally, we are not limited by a jurisdiction of courts. The distinction between courts of equity and of law was long ago abolished insofar as the jurisdiction of courts is concerned (Civ. Prac. Act, § 8). We continue to be limited in a proper case by those forms of procedure that bear a rational relationship to the justice they are intended to effect. But where, as here, the form serves no useful purpose, and indeed would work unnecessary and unjust injury, we are permitted to and should disregard it (see *Westergren v. Everett*, 218 AppDiv 172, 177, and *Thomas v. Schumacher*, 17 AppDiv 441 aff'd. 163 NY 554).

The judgment appealed from should be affirmed, without costs.

JUDICIAL DECISION

This case concerns various practices of Actors' Equity.

H. A. Artists & Associates, Inc. v. Actors Equity Association and Donald Grody

622 F2d 647 (2d Cir 1980)

Appellants, theatrical agents who act as intermediaries between actors and producers, appeal from a judgment of the District Court for the Southern District of New York, 478 FSupp 496 (1979), holding certain practices of defendant union Actors Equity ("Equity") immune from challenge under the antitrust laws because protected by the "statutory labor exemption." We affirm.

At issue in this case is Equity's system of "franchising" theatrical agents. Agents pay a fee and agree to abide by certain restrictions in return for certification as "franchised" agents. Equity encourages agents to become franchised by forbidding its members to deal with unfranchised agents. Equity members who negotiate contracts using the services of unfranchised agents are subject to union discipline, including fines.

The most important of the restrictions placed upon franchised agents is the requirement that they renounce any right to take commissions on contracts under which an actor receives scale wages. Scale wages are set by a collective bargaining agreement between Equity and theatrical producers, to which the agents are not parties. To the extent that a contract includes provisions under which an actor will sometimes receive scale pay (as for rehearsal periods and "chorus" employment) and sometimes more, the franchise regulations deny the agent any commission on the scale portions of the contract. Franchised agents are also precluded from taking commissions on certain expense money paid to union members; commissions are limited on wages within 10% of scale pay; and agents must allow actors to terminate a representation contract if the agent is unsuccessful in procuring employment for the actor within a specified period of time.

Some theatrical agents find this system acceptable, and this group which has formed a trade association called TARA is not a party in this litigation.

The district court did not reach the question of whether or not the franchise system is an unreasonable restraint of trade, or constitutes per se illegal price-fixing, because it found that the union's actions in creating and maintaining the franchise system were fully protected by the "statutory" labor exemption from the antitrust laws, which removes from antitrust scrutiny unilateral action by a labor union pursuing the interests of its members. The "statutory" exemption has its source in judicial readings of §§ 6 and 20 of the Clayton Act, 15 USC § 17, 29 USC § 52 and of the Norris-LaGuardia Act, 29 USC §§ 105–115. Under the leading "statutory" labor exemption case of *United States v. Hutcheson*, 312 US 219, 61 S Ct 463, 85 LEd 788 (1941), the threshold issue is whether or not Equity's franchising of agents has involved any combination between Equity and any "non-labor groups" or persons who are not "parties to a labor dispute" (*Id.* at 232, 61 S Ct at 466). If it has, the protection of the exemption does not apply.

Most employers qualify as a "non-labor group," and the court below considered whether or not there was any agreement, either explicit or tacit, between Equity and the producers to establish or police the franchise system. We do not believe the district court was clearly erroneous in finding that the collective bargaining agreement does not reveal any combination between Equity and the producers with respect to agents, (FedRCivP 52(a), *Meat Cutters v. Jewel Tea Co.*, 381 US 676, 694, 85 S Ct 1596, 1604, 14 LEd2d 640 (1965)).

Appellants argue that the provision in the collective bargaining agreement that standard employment contracts include a space for the actor's agent's name, and another provision of the agreement that requires this line to be filled in, is evidence that the producers agree with Equity to help the union police its franchise system. We disagree. As the district court found, there was evidence that contracts were often executed leaving blank the line left for the agent's name, and that, even so, Equity honored such contracts and did not take any action against members who worked under such contracts. The provision requiring that every line be filled in far antedated the appearance of the line for "name of agent." The district court was not clearly erroneous in concluding that Equity did not in fact require that this line be filled in.

The collective bargaining agreement aside, appellants argue that various statements made by Equity officials to union members and to producers are evidence of a combination between Equity and the producers with regard to agent franchising. We have examined each of the statements in the record adduced to support this point and we conclude that the district court's finding that they do not demonstrate any such combination cannot be labeled clearly erroneous. Unilateral pronouncements by Equity such as that "only franchised agents may negotiate employment deals for Equity performers" are not proof of an agreement because they may mean no more than that Equity members are forbidden from dealing with unfranchised agents. Such a prohibition, of course, since it serves the union's self-interest in a matter of proper union concern and does not involve a non-labor group, is safe from antitrust scrutiny under the statutory exemption (*United States v. Hutcheson, supra*).

There is some evidence in the record that Equity sought the producers' cooperation in enforcing the franchise system during the 1975 negotiations between Equity, TARA and the producers. And Equity officials did tell their membership that producers had an "obligation" to avoid using unfranchised agents. But such unilateral expressions, in the absence of any indication from the producers that they had agreed to cooperate or that they had accepted Equity's view of their "obligations," is not evidence from which the court was required to find that a "combination" had been formed. Our conclusion is also based on the fact that there was no evidence at trial that any producer had considered himself bound by the union's statements; nor did any producer testify that he had been pressured not to deal with unfranchised agents, or that he had reported unfranchised agents to the union.

But on the record in this case we discern a combination between the union and individuals who appear as if they might be members of a "non-labor" group. These individuals are those agents who have agreed

with the union to become franchised, and these agreements must be scrutinized to determine if they are agreements that would divest Equity's franchise system of the protection of the "statutory" exemption. In our view, they do not because the agents involved are a "labor group."

In *American Federation of Musicians v. Carroll*, 391 US 99, 88 S Ct 1562, 20 LEd2d 460 (1967), the Supreme Court identified the test for distinguishing a labor group from a non-labor group as "... the presence of job or wage competition or some other economic inter-relationship affecting legitimate union interests between the union members and the independent contractors. If such a relationship existed, the independent contractors were a 'labor group' ..." (391 US at 106, 88 S Ct at 1567, quoting 241 FSupp at 887). The above language is taken from the *Carroll* court's discussion of whether or not bandleaders in the "club date" field could be subjected to certain forms of union restrictions. Since the central holding in the case was that the fact that bandleaders sometimes performed as musicians meant that such restrictions were valid, most of the opinion deals with the "job or wage competition" branch of the disjunctive test quoted above. But the *Carroll* court also approved the musicians' union's restrictions on booking agents' commissions, which were enforced through a "licensing" system analogous to the "franchising" system at issue in the case at bar (391 US at 116–17, 88 S Ct at 1572–73).

Unlike the bandleaders, the agents in *Carroll* were not in any kind of "job or wage competition" with union members. The court's sub silentio application of the statutory exemption therefore supports the view that the musicians and the booking agents were in a sufficient "economic interrelationship" to justify union regulation. Because of the vagueness of this term, however, we believe the matter calls for further explanation.

Most unions are in an "economic interrelationship" with the employers of their membership. When the union gains a wage increase, the employers give up corresponding amounts of money (though not necessarily corresponding profits, because labor costs can often be passed along to consumers). But such an "economic interrelationship" does not suffice to make an employer a "labor group", or even a "party to a labor dispute"; otherwise there would be no need for the "non-statutory" exemption, which was developed largely to provide an exemption for union agreements with employers (*Connell Construction Co. v. Plumbers Local 100*, 421 US 616, 622, 95 S Ct 1830, 1835, 44 LEd2d 418 (1975)). To choose a different example, there is an "economic interrelationship" between a labor union and the buyers of goods produced by the union members' employer. If, for example, steelworkers were to win a wage raise of enormous size, various users of steel products, such as automobile manufacturers, would be adversely affected. Yet a combination between the steelworkers and an automobile manufacturer would not be entitled to the benefit of the statutory exemption because of this "economic interrelationship."

For purposes of this case, it is enough to note that the "economic interrelationship" test has never been used to immunize from antitrust challenge anything more than a union's effort to regulate parties, who, because of industry structure, stand athwart the current of wages paid by employers to union members; and that these efforts have been associated with attempts to defend the integrity of minimum wages (see, e.g., *Adams, Ray & Rosenberg v. William Morris Agency*, 411 FSupp 403 (CDCal1976)). In industries where it is necessary or customary for union members to secure employment through agents, and agents' fees are calculated as a percentage of wages set by a collective bargaining agreement, such agents must be considered a "labor group" because the union cannot eliminate wage competition among its members without regulation of the fees of the agents.

Once it is determined that the union's actions have involved no combination with a non-labor group, it remains, under *United States v. Hutcheson, supra,* only to decide if the goal being pursued is within the area of the union's legitimate self-interest. In the case at bar, Equity, through its franchising system, seeks primarily to protect from encroachment a minimum wage in an industry where the maintenance of a minimum wage poses problems of particular intractability. The possibility that job-hungry actors will work through agents who take excessive commissions is a matter of legitimate union concern. The goal of the agent restrictions is the elimination of wage competition, traditionally one of the most sacrosanct goals of national labor policy.

To this point, we have been concerned with the core of Equity's franchising system the securing by the union of an agreement from the agents not to charge commissions on certain types of work obtained. A second aspect of the franchising system, under which the union charges a fee to agents who become franchised, is more troublesome. These fees ($200 for the initial franchise; $60 per year thereafter for each agent, and $40 for any sub-agent working in the office of another), are not segregated from other union funds. While the union argues that they are necessary to pay the union's expenses in administering the franchise system, no evidence was presented at trial to show that the union's costs justified the franchise fees.

Clearly the union could not, legally, exact more from the agents than it needs to offset the costs of the franchising system. Such exactions would be unconnected with any of the goals of national labor policy which justify the antitrust exemption for labor. Nevertheless, this case in its present posture can best be disposed of by approving the fees as they stand today. There was testimony that at least one full-time Equity employee was engaged in updating lists of franchised agents and correlating contracts with these lists. There was also testimony that approximately 200 theatrical agents or agencies are affected by the union practices under challenge. Assuming an average yearly charge of $60, Equity's franchising revenues would amount to approximately $12,000. Such a sum, plus initial franchise fees collected during the year, cannot be incommensurate with Equity's expenses in maintaining a full-time employee to administer the system. In such circumstances, a remand to the district court would not serve any useful purpose.

AFFIRMED.

KEY TERMS

Actors' Equity

adaptation

amateur performance

blacklisting

bootlegging

dramatic work

experimental contract

musical work

open auditions

public performance

reproduction

script

stock performance

suspended payment

temporary withdrawal

EXERCISES

1. Obtain from your local authorities a permit application to work as a minor.

2. Go on-line and look at an Actors' Equity contract for a stage manager.

3. Locate a play and determine if it is still protected by copyright or if the copyright term has expired.

4. Contact a publishing company and determine who holds the publishing rights to a certain play.

5. Do you feel that Actors' Equity has a stranglehold on live stage productions? Explain.

6. Access the Actors' Equity Web site and download its Equity/League Production Contract and analyze its provisions. What other types of contracts are available from this Web site?

7. What additional legal problems might be encountered in a live stage production of a musical? Explain and discuss.

8. Using the Equity Web site, indicate the benefits that accrue to members.

9. What types of legal liabilities might attach to the owners of a theater during a live production? Discuss.

10. Does your state have any specific statutes designed to encourage live theater? If so, what are they? Do you believe they are effective?

CHAPTER

7

RECORDING AND MUSIC PUBLISHING

CHAPTER OVERVIEW

There are many aspects of entertainment law that impact the musician. Entertainment law professionals are a part of all aspects of the musician's career from the artistic to the business segments.

Musicians enter into a variety of contracts with a wide array of individuals. A musician may have a manager, business manager, agent, accountant, and attorney, just to name a few. Each of these individuals oversees a segment of the musician's career. Each of these individuals greatly impacts the artist's career. Consequently, each contract that the musician enters into must be negotiated and executed by a trained professional.

Additionally, musicians must pay special attention to certain aspects of copyright law. A musician often takes segments of songs (samples) or whole songs written by other artists and performs them as his or her own. Special licenses must be obtained from the original owner or owners before the artist uses the song or song segment.

THE PLAYERS

The entertainment law professional plays an important role in a musician's life. The entertainment professional can help a musician find a manager or agent, negotiate a recording agreement, shop his or her music to labels and publishers, and get Artist and Recording people to listen to the music. In fact, if such a person is an attorney, he or she is responsible for negotiating all agreements from merchandising agreements to band agreements. And, should the need arise (and it usually does at one point or another in a musician's career), an attorney can help get musicians out of inopportune deals.

An attorney should be contacted before any agreements are entered into. One of the biggest mistakes a musician can make is to arrange a contract that has not been negotiated by an experienced attorney. Usually, the first agreement a musician will consider entering into is a management agreement. Other people that are important early in a musician's career are agents and accountants.

Management Agreements

manager
The person who acts as a liaison between the musician and the record company, booking agent, and business manager.

scope
A specified range in a contract.

term
The length of a contract.

gross income
The total amount that an artist earns before deductions for expenses and taxes.

post-term commission
Commission or payment that a manager is entitled to after the artist/management agreement has been terminated.

A **manager** oversees a musician's entire career. The manager acts as a liaison between the musician and the record company, booking agent, and business manager. Management agreements are generally standard, albeit complicated.

The standard **scope** of a management agreement states that the manager is to be the "sole and exclusive personal manager, representative and advisor, throughout the world, in all of the Artist's affairs in the entertainment industry." If a musician is also an actor, then it may be in the artist's best interest to define the term *entertainment industry*. The **term** of the agreement is generally for a period of three to five years, and the manager is usually entitled to ten to twenty percent of the **gross income**, depending on the manager's experience. It is important to define what is considered gross income so that it is clear exactly from what income the percentage is to be determined. Recording costs, touring costs, fees, and recoupable income should all be considered when determining what is considered gross income. It is also important to define how long after the musician/manager relationship ends that the manager will be entitled to such compensation, or what **post-term commission** the manager is entitled to.

— *Example* —

"Term: Manager is hereby engaged as the exclusive personal manager and advisor to Artist p/k/a "Superstar." This agreement ("Agreement") shall be for one (1) year (hereinafter the "initial term") from the effective date of this Agreement and shall be renewed for five (5) one (1) year periods automatically unless either party shall give written notice of termination to the other not later than thirty (30) days prior to the expiration of the initial term or the then current renewal period, as applicable, subject to the terms and conditions in this Agreement."

Here, the manager would have the right to represent the musician for a minimum of one year to a maximum of six years. Since this particular clause entitles either party to terminate the contract after one year and at the end of each additional year thereafter, it protects an artist from being bound to a manager who does nothing for the artist.

Example

"*Post Term Commission:* The Manager shall be entitled to commission on income arising from works recorded or commercially 1st released during the Term and in addition to income arising from such works recorded or 1st released during the Term for a period of one calendar year following the termination of this agreement."

Since a manager can secure work for an artist that continues to be profitable after the term of the artist/management relationship terminates, the manager is usually entitled to compensation for a period of time after the termination.

Example

"*Compensation:* In compensation for Manager's services Artist agrees to pay to Manager, as and when received by Artist, and during and throughout the term hereof, a sum equal to ten (10) percent (not to exceed twenty-five (25) percent) of any and all gross monies or other considerations, sums and other things of value which Artist may receive as a result of Artist's activities in and throughout the music, recording, publishing, amusement, multimedia, Internet and entertainment industries, including any and all sums resulting from the use of Artist's artistic talents and the results and proceeds thereof and, without in any manner limiting the foregoing, the matters upon which Manager's compensation shall be computed shall include any and all of Artist's activities in connection with matters as follows: records, and all forms of recordings used as entertainment including, without limitation, compact discs or any other type of discs of any size or speed, cassette tapes or any other types of magnetic recording tape or any other medium for reproduction of artistic performances primarily for entertainment now known or which may hereafter become known, whether embodying sound alone or sound synchronized with or accompanied by visual images, e.g. "sight and sound" devices, publications, music, radio, television, motion pictures, multimedia, Internet, literary and theatrical engagements, personal appearances, public appearances, in places of amusement and entertainment, and the use of Artist's name, likeness and talents for purposes of advertising, merchandising and trade. The term "gross monies or other considerations" shall include, without limitation, salaries, earnings, fees, royalties, gifts, bonuses, shares of profits, shares of stock, partnership interests, percentages and the total amount paid for a package television, radio, or Internet program (live or recorded), motion picture, multimedia, or other entertainment packages, income from any and all of Artist's professional interests earned or received directly or indirectly by Artist or Artist's heirs, executors, administrators or assigns or by any other person, firm or corporation on Artist's behalf."

This clause specifies what is considered gross monies. It is important to specify from where the manager is entitled to draw his percentage. It is also important to specify how *entertainment industry* is defined.

performance plateau
This clause will allow the musician to terminate the management agreement in the event that the musician's gross income does not equal or surpass a negotiated amount.

To protect the musician, a **performance plateau** can be negotiated. This clause will allow the musician to terminate the management agreement in the event that the musician's gross income for a period does not equal or surpass a negotiated amount.

— *Example* —

"Manager will have the option to extend the Term for the First Option Period only in the event that the Artist's Gross Income for the Initial Period is equal to or greater than Fifty Thousand Dollars ($50,000)."

This allows recourse for the artist who is not competently represented by management. If the manager does not secure employment for the artist, then the artist has the right to terminate the contract.

power of attorney clause
A contract provision that allows the manager to enter into legal agreements and to act on issues on the musician's behalf.

Another standard management clause is the **power of attorney clause**. A power of attorney clause legally allows the manager to enter into legal agreements and act on issues on the musician's behalf. Again, a sub-clause can be inserted in the power of attorney clause to restrict the authority the manager.

— *Example* —

"Artist hereby irrevocably appoints Manager for the term of this Agreement and any extensions hereof as his true and lawful attorney-in-fact to sign, make, execute, accept, endorse, collect and deliver any and all bills of exchange, checks, and notes as his said attorney; to demand, sue for, collect, recover, and receive all goods, claims, money, interest and other items that may be due him or belong to him; and to make, execute, and deliver receipts, releases, or other discharges therefore under sale or otherwise and to defend, settle, adjust, compound, submit to arbitration and compromise all actions, suits, accounts, reckonings, claims, and demands whatsoever that are or shall be pending in such manner and in all respects as in any way limiting the foregoing; generally to do, execute and perform any other act, deed, or thing whatsoever deemed reasonable that ought to be done, executed, and performed of any and every nature and kind as fully effectively as Artist could do if personally present; and Artist hereby ratifies and affirms all acts performed by Manager by virtue of this power of attorney."

While it is a somewhat uneasy feeling to allow someone else to enter into contracts on your behalf, it is sometimes necessary. The artist can specify that they must ratify the contract or that the manager must first confer with the artist before entering into any major deals.

Agents

booking agent
Person who only negotiates live appearances for the musician.

A **booking agent** *only* negotiates live appearances for the musician. This is different from the sports or motion picture agents who seek out and negotiate deals for their clients. Agent agreements, like management agreements, are usually standard. An agent is entitled only to ten percent of the musician's gross income, or whatever other percentage has been negotiated, without any deductions.

The key terms in a live performance contract are:

1. How and when the musician will get paid
2. When the performance is to start and finish
3. When the musician can set up for the show and do sound checks

rider
A clause that states what the musician is entitled to backstage.

4. The wording of the **rider**, a clause that states what the musician is entitled to with respect to meals, accommodations, lighting, and other backstage arrangements.

American Federation of Musicians (AFM)
100,000-member union uniting musicians across the United States and Canada.

These contracts are typically standard because they are regulated by the **American Federation of Musicians (AFM)** and the **American Federation of Television and Radio Artists (AFTRA)** unions.

AFM is a 100,000-member union that unites musicians across the United States and Canada. The union provides member services such as health benefits, pensions, credit unions, assistance programs, payroll service, rehearsal-space rental, and instrument insurance.

American Federation of Television and Radio Artists (AFTRA)
National labor union for the entertainment industry.

AFTRA is a national labor union affiliated with the AFL-CIO. AFTRA represents its members in four major areas: (1) news and broadcasting, (2) entertainment programming, (3) the recording business, and (4) commercials and nonbroadcast, industrial educational media.

AFTRA's 80,000 members are seen or heard on television, radio, and sound recordings and include actors, announcers, news broadcasters, singers (including royalty artists and background singers), dancers, sportscasters, disc jockeys, talk show hosts, and others.

Accountants and Business Managers

accountant
A licensed professional who maintains and creates financial books and records.

An **accountant** is usually certified as a professional in the state in which he or she works. A **business manager** is sometimes an accountant, but need not be, who provides more than just accounting services. The most important function the accountant/business manager provides is to take control of the money coming in and the taxes being paid. Too many musicians are ruined by their failure to pay taxes. Business managers are also responsible for the musician's daily business expenses. He or she may also review **royalty statements**, discussed later in the chapter.

business manager
A person responsible for the musician's daily business expenses.

royalty statements
Statements issued as an accounting of royalties due an artist.

Music Publisher

music publisher
Entity that secures
commercially released
recordings of the songs
it controls.

**music publishing
agreement**
An agreement between
the writer of a song and
a music publisher that
transfers ownership of
copyright in exchange
for an advance against
royalties.

A **music publisher** arranges for the commercial release of recordings of the songs it controls. An artist can contract with a publisher by entering into a **music publishing agreement**. After a song has initially been recorded and released, the publisher will try to secure commitments from other recording artists or producers to include the composition on future albums or singles.

Another necessary and important service provided by the publisher is that of proper administration of musical compositions: registering copyrights, filing necessary information to mechanical and performing rights organizations, auditing record companies and other licensees, bookkeeping, negotiating licenses, checking the correctness of incoming royalty statements, and collecting monies due.

Some basic music publishing contracts include:

1. Single song agreement
2. Exclusive songwriter agreement
3. Copublishing agreement
4. Administration agreement.

Single Song Agreement

The most basic of these music publishing contracts is the single song agreement which grants rights to the music publisher for an agreed-upon price.

When dealing with music publishing, it is important to distinguish between what the publisher will receive and what the writer will receive. Generally, it is a 50/50 split, but this is negotiable and can change depending on the type of agreement. One of the easiest ways to explain it is that the publisher is entitled to 50 percent of the mechanical, performance, or other royalties because he or she is the owner of the copyright; the writer is entitled to 50 percent of the mechanical, performance, or other royalties because he or she wrote the song.

A standard publishing agreement is similar to a recording contract. What it does is transfer copyright ownership to a publisher who, in turn, gives the songwriter an advance royalty.

The specific publishing agreements vary in term and scope. The single song agreement transfers 100 percent of the copyright to a specified number of songs to the publisher. The songwriter has no further obligations to the publisher under this agreement and may even enter into other publishing deals for other songs with other publishers.

Exclusive Songwriter Agreement

An exclusive songwriter publishing agreement transfers 100 percent of the copyright in any songs written by the songwriter during a specific term (i.e., one year). Similar to the recording contract, the term is negotiable and can have option periods. See the discussion of term and options later in the chapter.

Copublishing Agreement

Because many people create their own publishing company but later sign with a publisher (who can help secure a recording contract and take care of royalty administration), they enter into copublishing agreements. A copublishing agreement is between the writer, the writer's publishing company, and another publisher. The writer still keeps his or her 50 percent share and the two publishers get a negotiated percentage each.

Administrative Agreement

The only type of publishing agreement that allows the writer to retain his or her copyright interest is an administrative agreement. Here the publisher is not entitled to ownership rights. The publisher is only entitled to a percentage fee. Since it is only administrative and ownership is not at stake, the term of this contract is generally short.

Some things the artist can do is try to limit the term or scope of the contract. An artist can also request that the copyright ownership in songs that are not commercially produced revert back to the songwriter.

SPECIFIC COPYRIGHT APPLICATIONS FOR MUSICIANS

In addition to the copyright discussion in the chapter on copyrights, there are specific copyright applications that apply to the musician. An owner of copyright can reproduce a copyrighted work, prepare derivative works, distribute copies of copyrighted works, and perform the copyrighted work publicly.

The owner of a copyright has exclusive rights in that work. These rights, however, are separable. In other words, the owner of a copyright may grant a subsequent owner the exclusive right to distribute a record in Europe and another subsequent owner the exclusive right to distribute a record in the United States.

--- *Example* ---

"Assignment of exclusive rights: Upon the timely occurrence and performance of all material events and obligations required to produce the Recording, Artist shall assign to the Company all of his/her rights, title, and interest in and to the following property, for distribution and commercial exploitation in the United States and Canada:

1. The Songs
2. Artist's performance of the Songs contained in the Recording
3. The title of the Recording."

First Sale Doctrine
An owner of an exclusive right exercises control over that right only until the copyrighted work is sold or otherwise given away. Once the copyrighted work has been sold, the owner has the right to do what he wants with it.

An owner of an exclusive right exercises control over that right only until the copyrighted work is sold or otherwise given away. Once the copyrighted work has been sold, the owner has the right to do what he wants with it. This is referred to as the **First Sale Doctrine.**

— *Example*

Pony Records owns the exclusive right to distribute and exploit the sound recording "Song." Once that record is purchased by an individual, it becomes the property of that individual and no longer the property of the record label.

In order to reproduce a copyrighted work, a musician must acquire a mechanical license. A **mechanical license** is granted by the owner of the copyright or the publisher. The following requirements must be met to obtain a **compulsory mechanical license**:

1. The song must be a "non-dramatic musical work"
2. The song must have been "distributed to the public in phonorecords"
3. The use of the song must be limited to phonorecords.

Although at times it may be necessary to apply for a compulsory mechanical license, it is much more convenient, and economical, to apply for a mechanical license from the publisher. When obtaining a mechanical license from the publisher, terms, such as accounting and the number of copies of the song one must pay royalties on, are negotiable. If, however, the publisher doesn't grant the mechanical license, it will become necessary to apply for a compulsory one.

Another copyright issue impacting on the recording industry is the work for hire contract. A work for hire is a musical composition that is created and/or performed by the artist, but is owned by the artists' employer. In other words, an employer may hire an artist to create or perform a sound recording.

A work for hire contract is a general contract—the artist agrees, for a fee, to perform a song for the purpose of recording a record. The employer pays the artist a set fee. The artist is only entitled to compensation for the act, and is not entitled to ownership of the work or its copyright. While the work for hire can become more complicated for artist's who have more clout, a basic discussion is sufficient for the new, unknown artist.

— *Example*

A singer is hired to sing a song created by DJ Jay. She is contracted to record the song and is paid $500.00 for her performance. She is not entitled to future compensation, or royalties.

As defined in chapter 2, which discussed copyright, a work for hire must be either

A work prepared by an employee within the scope of his or her employment

or

A work specifically ordered or commissioned for use as

- a contribution to a collective work
- a part of a motion picture or other audio-visual work
- a translation

mechanical license
Similar to the compulsory mechanical license, only it is granted by the publisher.

compulsory mechanical license
A compulsory grant of the right to a song by the copyright office.

- a supplementary work
- a compilation
- an instructional text
- an atlas.

Unfortunately, an artist who contracts as a work for hire generally has no subsequent authority over the work. In other words, if the owner of that work wishes to recreate (remix, rerecord, and so forth) the work, the artist cannot stop her from doing so.

—— *Example* ——————————————————————————

While listening to the radio, the singer from the example above hears a remix of the song she performed for DJ Jay. She absolutely hates the new mix and is furious that DJ Jay has changed the song she recorded. If Sandy tries to sue DJ Jay for remixing the song, she will be unsuccessful because she is not the owner of the copyright.

Oftentimes, an attorney will have to deal with what is known as a **joint work**. A joint work is simply a copyrightable work prepared by two or more people who have the intent to produce a merged or coproduced work. Joint works are generally subject to a **collaboration agreement**. A collaboration agreement defines each party's interest in the work.

joint work
A copyrightable work prepared by two or more people who have the intent to produce a merged or coproduced work.

collaboration agreement
A contract that defines each party's interest in a work.

—— *Example* ——————————————————————————

With the intent to later merge words and a melody, the singer from the previous two examples writes the lyrics for a song. She then meets DJ Jay, who has written a melody he hopes to find lyrics for at a later date. To their surprise, the words and the lyrics make a pretty good song, and they decide to collaborate. When the song is completed, they will have created a joint work.

Owners of a joint work, no matter how many, own an equal share in the work produced, regardless of their individual contributions, unless a collaboration agreement specifies otherwise. Since it is highly unlikely that each contributor contributes an equal share to the work, a collaboration agreement can specify exactly what percentage each individual is entitled to according to each collaborator's contribution to the project.

—— *Example* ——————————————————————————

With the intent to later merge words and a melody, Sandy and DJ Jay decide to collaborate and write a hit song. To make it clear how much Sandy and DJ Jay each contributed to the creation of the song, they have a collaboration agreement drafted. For example, if Sandy contributed 75 percent of the song and DJ Jay contributed 25 percent, then each could stipulate in the collaboration agreement their respective contribution and each would be entitled to their respective share of the profits.

sampling
The use of a piece of a song that is not owned by the user.

covering
Recording of a song by an artist who does not own the song.

derivative work
A new song created from the original song.

Sampling is yet another unique copyright concern for the entertainment attorney. Unlike obtaining a mechanical license for the reproduction or **covering** of a song, one is not entitled to a compulsory license for a sample. A sample is what it sounds like; an artist takes a tiny piece of a song and includes it in his or her new song. Samples are basically by-products of a previously copyrighted song. This new song created from the original is what is called a **derivative work**. The right to prepare derivative works based on the copyrighted work belongs to the copyright owner. The copyright owner *must* grant permission (a mechanical license) before the copyrighted song can be used.

Even if a single phrase is sampled without permission, it constitutes copyright infringement. Under United States copyright law, the true test for such infringement is not the number of notes sampled, but whether the sample is "substantially similar" to the original work. The other main question is whether it should qualify as "fair use." See chapter 2 for further information.

clearing house
A company who specializes in clearing samples for use in derivative works.

It is of utmost importance that any and all samples are cleared. Therefore, either an attorney or a **clearing house**, a company that specializes in clearing samples for use in derivative works, should clear a work.

To get permission, it is first recommended that the artist contact one of the performance rights organizations such as The American Society of Composers, Authors, and Performers (ASCAP); Broadcast Music, Inc. (BMI); or The Society of European Stage Authors and Composers (SESAC) to determine who owns the song of which the sample is a derivative.

ASCAP, BMI, and SESAC are membership associations of composers, songwriters, and publishers of every kind of music. They protect the rights of their members by licensing and distributing royalties for the non-dramatic public performances of their members' copyrighted works. In order to comply with the United States copyright law, any establishment that plays copyrighted music is legally required to secure permission to use it, whether in a live performance or by mechanical means.

THE RECORDING CONTRACT

record deal
The contract between the artist and the record label that promises that the artist will record for the label and the label will produce the record.

exclusivity clause
A contract provision that limits a party from entering into contracts with others.

A recording deal, or a **record deal**, is what every artist strives to achieve. This section will focus on the most confusing, and potentially damaging, clauses. Like the management contract, the term of the record deal is very important.

Exclusivity

Because a label can potentially spend a lot of money on an artist, contracts have an **exclusivity clause**. This is logical. No one wants to make a huge investment only to have their artist (insert investment here) go someplace else after their money made the artist a household name. The term of exclusivity ends when the contract terminates.

Term

The term of the contract depends on the number of albums the artist is required to produce, the number of option periods the record label can exercise, and the scheduled date of delivery for each album promised.

The **initial term** of the contract lasts from the date the contract is entered into until a specified time after the delivery of the number of albums promised. In other words, if the artist is signed to a contract that requires that two records be produced in the initial term (**firm records**) and states that the initial term ends six months after the delivery of the album, then if the second record is delivered on the first of the year, the initial period would end July first.

An **option** is a right exercisable by the record label only. Usually, the label will request about five option periods. The artist cannot terminate the contract after the initial term, but the label can exercise their option. The option period, like the initial term, specifies how many records must be produced per each option term.

— *Example*

A singer has agreed to sign with Endorfun Records© for an initial term that requires her to produce two records. At the end of the initial period, which is nine months after the delivery of the second record, Endorfun Records© exercises its option to have the singer produce another record. The singer is unhappy with the label, but has no choice but to comply with the label's request for another album. If the contract has seven option periods, then Sandy could be committed to produce seven more records for Endorfun Records©.

It is in an artist's best interest to allow the label to exercise as few options as possible and to have the label commit to as many records as possible in the initial term. If the label does not fulfill its commitment to the firm records, it must pay the artist for breaking the terms of the contract. A pay-or-play clause addresses the penalty for the label not fulfilling the commitment. Generally, the penalty is the difference between the amount allocated for recording costs and the amount it actually cost to record the first record.

— *Example*

If Endorfun Records© does not want the singer from the previous example to produce the second firm record in the initial term, then they would be required to pay a penalty for not fulfilling their commitment. Assuming the contract has a standard pay-or-play clause, and the singer was given $100,000 to record the first record and the actual cost to record the first record was $75,000, the singer would be entitled to $25,000.

initial term
Term in a contract that lasts from the date the contract is entered into until a specified time after the delivery of the specified number of albums promised.

firm records
Albums that a record company promises to produce in a recording contract.

option
The right to extend the term of a contract for another specified period of time.

Recoupable Advances

An **advance** for an artist usually comes in the form of money to produce the record. Most recording contracts have a maximum and minimum amount they will pay to have an artist make a record. When it comes to subsequent albums, the label will pay two-thirds of the amount of royalties collected in the United States during a specified period of time. The label does not generally include royalties derived from outside the United States.

The tricky part to advances is determining what is recoupable. **Recoupment** is taking money received in the form of royalties and applying it to the amount advanced or paid to the artist to make the record. Unfortunately, most costs are recoupable. Here is where the entertainment professional can negotiate what is and is not considered recoupable. A talented artist may even be able to negotiate a **signing bonus**. A signing bonus is a cash incentive for an artist to sign with a particular label. These, if specified, are non-recoupable.

ROYALTIES

Royalties represent an artist's paycheck. Unlike mechanical royalties, which are paid to the songwriter and the publisher, record royalties are payments on records performed. These royalties are determined using several factors: the royalty base rate, the royalty rate, and the number of records sold.

The **royalty base rate** is the suggested retail price of a record. From this, the cost of packaging is deducted. There are three types of records. The first record, the **top-of-the-line record**, is the most expensive type. To determine the current top-line price, look at the trade magazines and see what they are listed as. The other ranked records are the **mid-line record** and the **budget record**. As the suggested retail price of the record is lowered, so are the royalties received.

The **royalty rate** is the percentage of the price the artist will receive on each album sold. If the deal specifies that the artist will receive an all-in base royalty rate on the record, the artist is responsible for paying royalties to all the people (musicians, and so forth) who are entitled to a piece of the profits. If a record label is unwilling to negotiate the base royalty rate, it is sometimes possible to negotiate incremental increases based on the number of records sold or the number of albums released.

— *Example* —

The singer from the previous example contracts with Endorfun Records©. The contract specifies that her record will be a top-of-the-line record and her base royalty rate will be 15 percent. If the record is selling at $20.00, she will receive 15 percent of the suggested retail price less the packaging costs. If the packaging deduction is a set 25 percent, she will receive $2.25 per record ($20.00 × 25% = $15.00; $15.00 × 15% = $2.25).

compilation
An album that features several artists who contribute a song or songs.

For the up-and-coming artist, it is important to discuss **compilations**, or multi-artist albums. Because an artist may only contribute one song to a compiled album, the artist is only entitled to a percentage of the negotiated royalty based on the number of songs on the album and the number of songs the artist contributed.

— *Example*

The singer from the previous example contributes a song to a compilation. There are 20 songs on the record. The royalty rate is 15 percent. The base royalty rate is $20.00. The base royalty rate, less the packaging costs, is $15.00. To determine what royalty percentage she will receive, divide the number of songs she has by the number of songs on the record and multiply the result by the royalty rate. In other words, $(1/20) \times 15\% = 0.0075$, or three-quarters of one percent.

There are several other factors that will alter the royalty rate. The format of the record, or whether the record is a cassette, compact disc, or vinyl, can lower the rate. Also, if the record is released outside of the United States, the rate is often deducted for those foreign territories. Sometimes separate deals can be made for foreign territories.

The final factor considered when trying to determine what will actually be made per record is the number of records sold. Generally, a label will only pay on a percentage of the records actually sold, for example 90 percent of the record sales. This is based on the concept that vinyl records break easily and that not all of the records made will actually make it to the shelf. Additional deductions will also be incurred for the free records (promotional records) and specials given to record stores to have the album heard, displayed, or promoted.

Accounting

An important clause in the recording contract is the accounting clause. It is important because it gives the artist the right to inspect the record label's books. However, this right is not an absolute right. First notice must be given to the label that the artist wishes to have the books audited. There should be a designated place and time established for such viewing. Further, the person auditing the books usually is required to be an attorney or a certified public accountant.

Also important is the time frame an artist has to act on what he or she thinks may be an improper figuring of royalties. This is a kind of built-in **statute of limitations**, or time period the artist has to institute an action against the label for not paying him or her their royalties.

Statute of Limitations
Time period the artist has to sue the label.

Since accounting can be quite complicated (i.e., cross-collateralization and other creative ways record labels have of configuring royalty payments), a knowledgeable professional should be contacted.

CHAPTER REVIEW

Many different people play a role in a musician's career. Managers manage both the artistic and business aspects of a musician's career. The relationship between the manager and the musician is controlled (time, payment, and so forth) by a management agreement.

Agents are responsible for negotiating terms of live performances. Live performances are bound by unions, and as a result are limited in the demands they can make upon performers.

To determine what percentage of ownership each contributing musician may have, a publishing deal may be drafted. Publishing deals can be drawn up between individuals, publishing companies, or both.

When dealing with copyrights, several specifics apply to musicians. Licenses must be obtained when using a piece of a song or an entire song written or performed by someone other than the original artist. Oftentimes musicians are hired to perform a song, but they have no rights in the song. This is called a work for hire.

Accountants are especially important when determining what royalties the artist is entitled to and the taxes that must be paid on them.

JUDICIAL DECISION

The following case provides a detailed discussion of various problems associated with the recording industry, including the impact of technological advances.

A & M Records, Inc. v. NAPSTER, Inc. et al.
284 F3d 1091 (9th Cir 2002)

Plaintiffs are engaged in the commercial recording, distribution and sale of copyrighted musical compositions and sound recordings. The complaint alleges that Napster, Inc. ("Napster") is a contributory and vicarious copyright infringer. On July 26, 2000, the district court granted plaintiffs' motion for a preliminary injunction. The injunction was slightly modified by written opinion on August 10, 2000 (*A&M Records, Inc. v. Napster, Inc.*, 114 FSupp2d 896 (NDCal 2000)). The district court preliminarily enjoined Napster "from engaging in, or facilitating others in copying, downloading, uploading, transmitting, or distributing plaintiffs' copyrighted musical compositions and sound recordings, protected by either federal or state law, without express permission of the rights owner" (*Id* at 927). *Federal Rule of Civil Procedure* 65(c) requires

successful plaintiffs to post a bond for damages incurred by the enjoined party in the event that the injunction was wrongfully issued. The district court set bond in this case at $5 million.

We entered a temporary stay of the preliminary injunction pending resolution of this appeal. We have jurisdiction pursuant to 28 USC § 1292(a)(1). We affirm in part, reverse in part and remand.

I

We have examined the papers submitted in support of and in response to the injunction application and it appears that Napster has designed and operates a system which permits the transmission and retention of sound recordings employing digital technology.

In 1987, the Moving Picture Experts Group set a standard file format for the storage of audio recordings in a digital format called MPEG-3, abbreviated as

"MP3." Digital MP3 files are created through a process colloquially called "ripping." Ripping software allows a computer owner to copy an audio compact disk ("audio CD") directly onto a computer's hard drive by compressing the audio information on the CD into the MP3 format. The MP3's compressed format allows for rapid transmission of digital audio files from one computer to another by electronic mail or any other file transfer protocol.

Napster facilitates the transmission of MP3 files between and among its users. Through a process commonly called "peer-to-peer" file sharing, Napster allows its users to: (1) make MP3 music files stored on individual computer hard drives available for copying by other Napster users; (2) search for MP3 music files stored on other users' computers; and (3) transfer exact copies of the contents of other users' MP3 files from one computer to another via the Internet. These functions are made possible by Napster's MusicShare software, available free of charge from Napster's Internet site, and Napster's network servers and server-side software. Napster provides technical support for the indexing and searching of MP3 files, as well as for its other functions, including a "chat room," where users can meet to discuss music, and a directory where participating artists can provide information about their music.

A. Accessing the System

In order to copy MP3 files through the Napster system, a user must first access Napster's Internet site and download the MusicShare software to his individual computer. See http://www.Napster.com. Once the software is installed, the user can access the Napster system. A first-time user is required to register with the Napster system by creating a "user name" and password.

B. Listing Available Files

If a registered user wants to list available files stored in his computer's hard drive on Napster for others to access, he must first create a "user library" directory on his computer's hard drive. The user then saves his MP3 files in the library directory, using self-designated file names. He next must log into the Napster system using his user name and password. His MusicShare software then searches his user library and verifies that the available files are properly formatted. If in the

correct MP3 format, the names of the MP3 files will be uploaded from the user's computer to the Napster servers. The content of the MP3 files remains stored in the user's computer. Once uploaded to the Napster servers, the user's MP3 file names are stored in a server-side "library" under the user's name and become part of a "collective directory" of file available for transfer during the time the user is logged onto the Napster system. The collective directory is fluid; it tracks users who are connected in real time, displaying only file names that are immediately accessible.

C. Searching For Available Files

Napster allows a user to locate other users' MP3 files in two ways: through Napster's search function and through its "hotlist" function.

Software located on the Napster servers maintains a "search index" of Napster's collective directory. To search the files available from Napster users currently connected to the network servers, the individual user accesses a form in the MusicShare software stored in his computer and enters either the name of a song or an artist as the object of the search. The form is then transmitted to a Napster server and automatically compared to the MP3 file names listed in the server's search index. Napster's server compiles a list of all MP3 file names pulled from the search index which include the same search terms entered on the search form and transmits the list to the searching user. The Napster server does not search the contents of any MP3 file; rather, the search is limited to "a text search of the file names indexed in a particular cluster. Those file names may contain typographical errors or otherwise inaccurate descriptions of the content of the files since they are designated by other users" (*Napster*, 114 FSupp2d at 906).

To use the "hotlist" function, the Napster user creates a list of other users' names from whom he has obtained MP3 files in the past. When logged onto Napster's servers, the system alerts the user if any user on his list (a "hotlisted user") is also logged onto the system. If so, the user can access an index of all MP3 file names in a particular hotlisted user's library and request a file in the library by selecting the file name. The contents of the hotlisted user's MP3 file are not stored on the Napster system.

D. Transferring Copies of an MP3 file

To transfer a copy of the contents of a requested MP3 file, the Napster server software obtains the Internet address of the requesting user and the Internet address of the "host user" (the user with the available files) (See generally *Brookfield Communications, Inc. v. West Coast Entm't Corp.*, 174 F3d 1036, 1044 (9th Cir 1999) (describing, in detail, the structure of the Internet)). The Napster servers then communicate the host user's Internet address to the requesting user. The requesting user's computer uses this information to establish a connection with the host user and downloads a copy of the contents of the MP3 file from one computer to the other over the Internet, "peer-to-peer." A downloaded MP3 file can be played directly from the user's hard drive using Napster's Music-Share program or other software. The file may also be transferred back onto an audio CD if the user has access to equipment designed for that purpose. In both cases, the quality of the original sound recording is slightly diminished by transfer to the MP3 format.

This architecture is described in some detail to promote an understanding of transmission mechanics as opposed to the content of the transmissions. The content is the subject of our copyright infringement analysis.

II

We review a grant or denial of a preliminary injunction for abuse of discretion (*Gorbach v. Reno*, 219 F3d 1087, 1091 (9th Cir 2000) (*en banc*)). Application of erroneous legal principles represents an abuse of discretion by the district court (*Rucker v. Davis*, F3d ____, 2001 WL 55724, at 4 (9th Cir Jan 24, 2001) (*en banc*)). If the district court is claimed to have relied on an erroneous legal premise in reaching its decision to grant or deny a preliminary injunction, we will review the underlying issue of law de novo (*Id* at 4 (citing *Does 1-5 v. Chandler*, 83 F3d 1150, 1152 (9th Cir 1996))).

On review, we are required to determine, "whether the court employed the appropriate legal standards governing the issuance of a preliminary injunction and whether the district court correctly apprehended the law with respect to the under-lying issues in the case." (*Id*). "As long as the district court got the law right, 'it will not be reversed simply because the appellate court would have arrived at a different result if it had

applied the law to the facts of the case'" (*Gregorio T. v. Wilson*, 59 F3d 1002, 1004 (9th Cir 1995) (quoting *Sports Form, Inc. v. United Press, Int'l*, 686 F2d 750, 752 (9th Cir 1982))).

Preliminary injunctive relief is available to a party who demonstrates either: (1) a combination of probable success on the merits and the possibility of irreparable harm; or (2) that serious questions are raised and the balance of hardships tips in its favor (*Prudential Real Estate Affiliates, Inc. v. PPR Realty, Inc.*, 204 F3d 867, 874 (9th Cir 2000)). "These two formulations represent two points on a sliding scale in which the required degree of irreparable harm increases as the probability of success decreases" (*Id*).

III

Plaintiffs claim Napster users are engaged in the wholesale reproduction and distribution of copyrighted works, all constituting direct infringement. The district court agreed. We note that the district court's conclusion that plaintiffs have presented a prima facie case of direct infringement by Napster users is not presently appealed by Napster.

A. Infringement

Plaintiffs must satisfy two requirements to present a prima facie case of direct infringement: (1) they must show ownership of the allegedly infringed material and (2) they must demonstrate that the alleged infringers violate at least one exclusive right granted to copyright holders under 17 USC § 106 (see 17 USC § 501(a) (infringement occurs when alleged infringer engages in activity listed in § 106); see also *Baxter v. MCA, Inc.*, 812 F2d 421, 423 (9th Cir 1987); see, e.g., *S.O.S., Inc. v. Payday, Inc.*, 886 F2d 1081, 1085 n3 (9th Cir 1989) ("The word 'copying' is shorthand for the infringing of any of the copyright owner's five exclusive rights. ...")). Plaintiffs have sufficiently demonstrated ownership. The record supports the district court's determination that "as much as eighty-seven percent of the files available on Napster may be copyrighted and more than seventy percent may be owned or administered by plaintiffs" (*Napster*, 114 FSupp2d at 911).

The district court further determined that plaintiffs' exclusive rights under § 106 were violated: "here the evidence establishes that a majority of Napster users use the service to download and upload copyrighted music. ... And by doing that, it constitutes—the uses constitute direct infringement of plaintiffs' musical compositions, recordings" (*A&M Records, Inc. v. Napster, Inc.*, Nos 99-5183, 00-0074, 2000 WL 1009483, at (NDCal July 26, 2000) (transcript of proceedings)). The district court also noted that "it is pretty much acknowledged ... by Napster that this is infringement" (*Id*) We agree that plaintiffs have shown that Napster users infringe at least two of the copyright holders' exclusive rights: the rights of reproduction, § 106(1); and distribution, § 106(3). Napster users who upload file names to the search index for others to copy violate plaintiffs' distribution rights. Napster users who download files containing copyrighted music violate plaintiffs' reproduction rights.

Napster asserts an affirmative defense to the charge that its users directly infringe plaintiffs' copyrighted musical compositions and sound recordings.

B. Fair Use

Napster contends that its users do not directly infringe plaintiffs' copyrights because the users are engaged in fair use of the material (see 17 USC § 107 ("[T]he fair use of a copyrighted work ... is not an infringement of copyright.")). Napster identifies three specific alleged fair uses: sampling, where users make temporary copies of a work before purchasing; space-shifting, where users access a sound recording through the Napster system that they already own in audio CD format; and permissive distribution of recordings by both new and established artists.

The district court considered factors listed in 17 USC § 107, which guide a court's fair use determination. These factors are: (1) the purpose and character of the use; (2) the nature of the copyrighted work; (3) the "amount and substantiality of the portion used" in relation to the work as a whole; and (4) the effect of the use upon the potential market for the work or the value of the work (see 17 USC § 107. The district court first conducted a general analysis of Napster system uses under § 107, and then applied its reasoning to the alleged fair uses identified by Napster. The district court concluded that Napster users are not fair users. We agree. We first address the court's overall fair use analysis.

1. Purpose and Character of the Use

This factor focuses on whether the new work merely replaces the object of the original creation or instead adds a further purpose or different character. In other words, this factor asks "whether and to what extent the new work is 'transformative'" (see *Campbell v. Acuff-Rose Music, Inc.*, 510 US 569, 579 (1994)).

The district court first concluded that downloading MP3 files does not transform the copyrighted work (*Napster*, 114 FSupp2d at 912). This conclusion is supportable. Courts have been reluctant to find fair use when an original work is merely retransmitted in a different medium (see, e.g., *Infinity Broadcast Corp. v. Kirkwood*, 150 F3d 104, 108 (2d Cir 1994) (concluding that retransmission of radio broadcast over telephone lines is not transformative); *UMG Recordings, Inc. v. MP3.com, Inc.*, 92 FSupp2d 349, 351 (SDNY) (finding that reproduction of audio CD into MP3 format does not "transform" the work), certification denied, 2000 WL 710056 (SDNY June 1, 2000) ("Defendant's copyright infringement was clear, and the mere fact that it was clothed in the exotic webbing of the Internet does not disguise its illegality.")).

This "purpose and character" element also requires the district court to determine whether the allegedly infringing use is commercial or noncommercial (see *Campbell*, 510 US at 584–85. A commercial use weighs against a finding of fair use but is not conclusive on the issue (*Id*). The district court determined that Napster users engage in commercial use of the copyrighted materials largely because (1) "a host user sending a file cannot be said to engage in a personal use when distributing that file to an anonymous requester" and (2) "Napster users get for free something they would ordinarily have to buy" (*Napster*, 114 FSupp2d at 912). The district court's findings are not clearly erroneous.

Direct economic benefit is not required to demonstrate a commercial use. Rather, repeated and exploitative copying of copyrighted works, even if the copies are not offered for sale, may constitute a commercial use (see *Worldwide Church of God v. Philadelphia Church of God*, 227 F3d 1110, 1118 (9th Cir 2000) (stating that church that copied religious text for its members "unquestionably profit[ed]" from the unauthorized "distribution and use of [the text] without having to account to the copyright holder"); *American Geophysical Union v. Texaco, Inc.*, 60 F3d 913, 922 (2d Cir 1994) (finding that researchers at for-profit laboratory gained indirect economic advantage by photocopying copyrighted scholarly articles)). In the record before us, commercial use is demonstrated by a showing that repeated and exploitative unauthorized copies of copyrighted works were made to save the expense of purchasing authorized copies (see *Worldwide Church*, 227 F3d at 1117–18; *Sega Enters. Ltd. v. MAPHIA*, 857 FSupp 679, 687 (NDCal 1994) (finding commercial use when individuals downloaded copies of video games "to avoid having to buy video game cartridges"); see also *American Geophysical*, 60 F3d at 922). Plaintiffs made such a showing before the district court.

We also note that the definition of a financially motivated transaction for the purposes of criminal copyright actions includes trading infringing copies of a work for other items, "including the receipt of other copyrighted works" (see No Electronic Theft Act ("NET Act"), PubL No 105–147, 18 USC § 101 (defining "Financial Gain")).

2. The Nature of the Use

Works that are creative in nature are "closer to the core of intended copyright protection" than are more fact-based works (see *Campbell*, 510 US at 586). The district court determined that plaintiffs' "copyrighted musical compositions and sound recordings are creative in nature ... which cuts against a finding of fair use under the second factor" (*Napster*, 114 FSupp2d at 913). We find no error in the district court's conclusion.

3. The Portion Used

"While 'wholesale copying does not preclude fair use per se,' copying an entire work 'militates against a finding of fair use.'" (*Worldwide Church*, 227 F3d at 1118 (quoting *Hustler Magazine, Inc. v. Moral Majority, Inc.*, 796 F2d 1148, 1155 (9th Cir 1986))). The district court determined that Napster users engage in "wholesale copying" of copyrighted work because file transfer necessarily "involves copying the entirety of the copyrighted work" (*Napster*, 114 FSupp2d at 913). We agree. We note, however, that under certain circumstances, a court will conclude that a use is fair even when the protected work is copied in its entirety (see, e.g., *Sony Corp. v. Universal City Studios, Inc.*, 464 US 417, 449–50 (1984) (acknowledging that fair use of time-shifting necessarily involved making a full copy of a protected work)).

4. Effect of Use on Market

"Fair use, when properly applied, is limited to copying by others which does not materially impair the marketability of the work which is copied" (*Harper & Row Publishers, Inc. v. Nation Enters.*, 471 US 539, 566–67 (1985)). "[T]he importance of this [fourth] factor will vary, not only with the amount of harm, but also with the relative strength of the showing on the other factors" (*Campbell*, 510 US at 591 n21). The proof required to demonstrate present or future market harm varies with the purpose and character of the use:

> A challenge to a noncommercial use of a copyrighted work requires proof either that the particular use is harmful, or that if it should become widespread, it would adversely affect the potential market for the copyrighted work. ... If the intended use is for commercial gain, that likelihood [of market harm] may be presumed. But if it is for a noncommercial purpose, the likelihood must be demonstrated (*Sony*, 464 US at 451).

Addressing this factor, the district court concluded that Napster harms the market in "at least" two ways: it reduces audio CD sales among college students and it "raises barriers to plaintiffs' entry into the market for the digital downloading of music" (*Napster*, 114 FSupp2d at 913). The district court relied on evidence plaintiffs submitted to show that Napster use harms the market for their copyrighted musical compositions and sound recordings. In a separate memorandum and order regarding the parties' objections to the expert reports, the district court examined each report, finding some more appropriate and probative than others (*A&M Records, Inc. v. Napster, Inc.*, Nos 99-5183 & 00-0074, 2000 WL 1170106 (NDCal August 10, 2000)). Notably, plaintiffs' expert, Dr. E. Deborah Jay, conducted a survey (the "Jay Report") using a random sample of college and university students to track their reasons for using Napster and the impact Napster had on their music purchases (*Id* at 2). The court recognized that the Jay Report focused on just one segment of the Napster user population and found "evidence of lost sales attributable to college use to be probative of irreparable harm for purposes of the preliminary injunction motion" (*Id* at 3).

Plaintiffs also offered a study conducted by Michael Fine, Chief Executive Officer of Soundscan, (the "Fine Report") to determine the effect of online sharing of MP3 files in order to show irreparable harm. Fine found that online file sharing had resulted in a loss of "album" sales within college markets. After reviewing defendant's objections to the Fine Report and expressing some concerns regarding the methodology and findings, the district court refused to exclude the Fine Report insofar as plaintiffs offered it to show irreparable harm (*Id* at 6).

Plaintiffs' expert Dr. David J. Teece studied several issues ("Teece Report"), including whether plaintiffs had suffered or were likely to suffer harm in their existing and planned businesses due to Napster use (*Id*). Napster objected that the report had not undergone peer review. The district court noted that such reports generally are not subject to such scrutiny and overruled defendant's objections (*Id*).

As for defendant's experts, plaintiffs objected to the report of Dr. Peter S. Fader, in which the expert concluded that Napster is beneficial to the music industry because MP3 music file-sharing stimulates more audio CD sales than it displaces (*Id* at 7). The district court found problems in Dr. Fader's minimal role in overseeing the administration of the survey and the lack of objective data in his report. The court decided the generality of the report rendered it "of dubious reliability and value." The court did not exclude the report, however, but chose "not to rely on Fader's findings in determining the issues of fair use and irreparable harm" (*Id* at 8).

The district court cited both the Jay and Fine Reports in support of its finding that Napster use harms the market for plaintiffs' copyrighted musical compositions and sound recordings by reducing CD sales among college students. The district court cited the Teece Report to show the harm Napster use caused in raising barriers to plaintiffs' entry into the market for digital downloading of music (*Napster*, 114 FSupp2d at 910). The district court's careful consideration of defendant's objections to these reports and decision to rely on the reports for specific issues demonstrates a proper exercise of discretion in addition to a correct application of the fair use doctrine.

Defendant has failed to show any basis for disturbing the district court's findings.

We, therefore, conclude that the district court made sound findings related to Napster's deleterious effect on the present and future digital download market. Moreover, lack of harm to an established market cannot deprive the copyright holder of the right to develop alternative markets for the works (see *L.A. Times v. Free Republic*, 54 USPQ2d 1453, 1469–71 (CDCal 2000) (stating that online market for plaintiff newspapers' articles was harmed because plaintiffs demonstrated that "[defendants] are attempting to exploit the market for viewing their articles online"); see also *UMG Recordings*, 92 FSupp2d at 352 ("Any allegedly positive impact of defendant's activities on plaintiffs' prior market in no way frees defendant to usurp a further market that directly derives from reproduction of the plaintiffs' copyrighted works.")). Here, similar to *L.A. Times* and *UMG Recordings*, the record supports the district court's finding that the "record company plaintiffs have already expended considerable funds and effort to commence Internet sales and licensing for digital downloads" (114 FSupp2d at 915). Having digital downloads available for free on the Napster system necessarily harms the copyright holders' attempts to charge for the same downloads.

Judge Patel did not abuse her discretion in reaching the above fair use conclusions, nor were the findings of fact with respect to fair use considerations clearly erroneous. We next address Napster's identified uses of sampling and spaceshifting.

5. Identified Uses

Napster maintains that its identified uses of sampling and space-shifting were wrongly excluded as fair uses by the district court.

a. Sampling

Napster contends that its users download MP3 files to "sample" the music in order to decide whether to purchase the recording. Napster argues that the district court: (1) erred in concluding that sampling is a commercial use because it conflated a noncommercial use with a personal use; (2) erred in determining that sampling adversely affects the market for plaintiffs' copyrighted music, a requirement if the use is non-commercial; and

(3) erroneously concluded that sampling is not a fair use because it determined that samplers may also engage in other infringing activity.

The district court determined that sampling remains a commercial use even if some users eventually purchase the music. We find no error in the district court's determination.

Plaintiffs have established that they are likely to succeed in proving that even authorized temporary downloading of individual songs for sampling purposes is commercial in nature (see *Napster*, 114 FSupp2d at 913). The record supports a finding that free promotional downloads are highly regulated by the record company plaintiffs and that the companies collect royalties for song samples available on retail Internet sites (*Id*). Evidence relied on by the district court demonstrates that the free downloads provided by the record companies consist of thirty-to-sixty second samples or are full songs programmed to "time out," that is, exist only for a short time on the downloader's computer (*Id* at 913–14). In comparison, Napster users download a full, free and permanent copy of the recording (*Id* at 914–15). The determination by the district court as to the commercial purpose and character of sampling is not clearly erroneous.

The district court further found that both the market for audio CDs and market for online distribution are adversely affected by Napster's service. As stated in our discussion of the district court's general fair use analysis: the court did not abuse its discretion when it found that, overall, Napster has an adverse impact on the audio CD and digital download markets. Contrary to Napster's assertion that the district court failed to specifically address the market impact of sampling, the district court determined that "[e]ven if the type of sampling supposedly done on Napster were a non-commercial use, plaintiffs have demonstrated a substantial likelihood that it would adversely affect the potential market for their copyrighted works if it became widespread" (*Napster*, 114 FSupp2d at 914). The record supports the district court's preliminary determinations that: (1) the more music that sampling users download, the less likely they are to eventually purchase the recordings on audio CD; and (2) even if the audio CD market is not harmed, Napster has adverse effects on the developing digital download market.

Napster further argues that the district court erred in rejecting its evidence that the users' downloading of "samples" increases or tends to increase audio CD sales. The district court, however, correctly noted that "any potential enhancement of plaintiffs' sales ... would not tip the fair use analysis conclusively in favor of defendant" (*Id* at 914). We agree that increased sales of copyrighted material attributable to unauthorized use should not deprive the copyright holder of the right to license the material. (See *Campbell*, 510 US at 591 n21 ("Even favorable evidence, without more, is no guarantee of fairness. Judge Leval gives the example of the film producer's appropriation of a composer's previously unknown song that turns the song into a commercial success; the boon to the song does not make the film's simple copying fair."); see also *L.A. Times*, 54 USPQ2d at 1471–72). Nor does positive impact in one market, here the audio CD market, deprive the copyright holder of the right to develop identified alternative markets, here the digital download market (see *Id* at 1469–71).

We find no error in the district court's factual findings or abuse of discretion in the court's conclusion that plaintiffs will likely prevail in establishing that sampling does not constitute a fair use.

b. Space-Shifting

Napster also maintains that space-shifting is a fair use. Space-shifting occurs when a Napster user downloads MP3 music files in order to listen to music he already owns on audio CD (see *Id* at 915–16). Napster asserts that we have already held that space-shifting of musical compositions and sound recordings is a fair use. (See *Recording Indus. Ass'n of Am. v. Diamond Multimedia Sys., Inc.*, 180 F3d 1072, 1079 (9th Cir 1999) ("Rio [a portable MP3 player] merely makes copies in order to render portable, or 'space-shift,' those files that already reside on a user's hard drive. ... Such copying is a paradigmatic noncommercial personal use."). See also generally *Sony*, 464 US at 423 (holding that "time-shifting," where a video tape recorder owner records a television show for later viewing, is a fair use)).

We conclude that the district court did not err when it refused to apply the "shifting" analyses of *Sony* and *Diamond*. Both *Diamond* and *Sony* are inapposite because the methods of shifting in these cases did not also simultaneously involve distribution of the copyrighted material to the general public; the time or space-shifting of copyrighted material exposed the material only to the original user. In *Diamond*, for example, the copyrighted music was transferred from the user's computer hard drive to the user's portable MP3 player. So too *Sony*, where "the majority of VCR purchasers ... did not distribute taped television broadcasts, but merely enjoyed them at home" (*Napster*, 114 FSupp2d at 913). Conversely, it is obvious that once a user lists a copy of music he already owns on the Napster system in order to access the music from another location, the song becomes "available to millions of other individuals," not just the original CD owner. (See *UMG Recordings*, 92 FSupp2d at 351–52 (finding space-shifting of MP3 files not a fair use even when previous ownership is demonstrated before a download is allowed); *cf. Religious Tech. Ctr. v. Lerma*, No 95-1107A, 1996 WL 633131, at 6 (EDVa Oct 4, 1996) (suggesting that storing copyrighted material on computer disk for later review is not a fair use)).

c. Other Uses

Permissive reproduction by either independent or established artists is the final fair use claim made by Napster. The district court noted that plaintiffs did not seek to enjoin this and any other noninfringing use of the Napster system, including: chat rooms, message boards and Napster's New Artist Program (*Napster*, 114 FSupp2d at 917). Plaintiffs do not challenge these uses on appeal.

We find no error in the district court's determination that plaintiffs will likely succeed in establishing that Napster users do not have a fair use defense. Accordingly, we next address whether Napster is secondarily liable for the direct infringement under two doctrines of copyright law: contributory copyright infringement and vicarious copyright infringement.

IV

We first address plaintiffs' claim that Napster is liable for contributory copyright infringement. Traditionally, "one who, with knowledge of the infringing activity, induces, causes or materially contributes to the infringing conduct of another, may be held liable as a

'contributory' infringer" (*Gershwin Publ'g Corp. v. Columbia Artists Mgmt., Inc.*, 443 F2d 1159, 1162 (2d Cir 1971); see also *Fonovisa, Inc. v. Cherry Auction, Inc.*, 76 F3d 259, 264 (9th Cir 1996)). Put differently, liability exists if the defendant engages in "personal conduct that encourages or assists the infringement" (*Matthew Bender & Co. v. Delmar Publ'g Co.*, 158 F3d 693, 706 (2d Cir 1998)).

The district court determined that plaintiffs in all likelihood would establish Napster's liability as a contributory infringer. The district court did not err; Napster, by its conduct, knowingly encourages and assists the infringement of plaintiffs' copyrights.

A. Knowledge

Contributory liability requires that the secondary infringer "know or have reason to know" of direct infringement (*Cable/Home Communication Corp. Network Prods., Inc.*, 902 F2d 829, 845 & 846 n29 (11th Cir 1990); *Religious Tech. Ctr. v. Netcom On-Line Communication Servs., Inc.*, 907 FSupp 1361, 1373–74 (NDCal 1995) (framing issue as "whether Netcom knew or should have known of" the infringing activities)). The district court found that Napster had both actual and constructive knowledge that its users exchanged copyrighted music. The district court also concluded that the law does not require knowledge of "specific acts of infringement" and rejected Napster's contention that because the company cannot distinguish infringing from non-infringing files, it does not "know" of the direct infringement (114 FSupp2d at 917).

It is apparent from the record that Napster has knowledge, both actual and constructive, of direct infringement. Napster claims that it is nevertheless protected from contributory liability by the teaching of *Sony Corp. v. Universal City Studios, Inc.*, 464 US 417 (1984). We disagree. We observe that Napster's actual, specific knowledge of direct infringement renders *Sony's* holding of limited assistance to Napster. We are compelled to make a clear distinction between the architecture of the Napster system and Napster's conduct in relation to the operational capacity of the system.

The *Sony* Court refused to hold the manufacturer and retailers of video tape recorders liable for contributory infringement despite evidence that such machines could be and were used to infringe plaintiffs' copyrighted television shows. *Sony* stated that if liability "is to be imposed on petitioners in this case, it must rest on the fact that they have sold equipment *with constructive knowledge of the fact* that their customers may use that equipment to make unauthorized copies of copyrighted material" (*Id* at 439 (emphasis added)). The *Sony* Court declined to impute the requisite level of knowledge where the defendants made and sold equipment capable of both infringing and "substantial noninfringing uses" (*Id* at 442 (adopting a modified "staple article of commerce" doctrine from patent law). See also *Universal City Studios, Inc. v. Sony Corp.*, 480 F. Supp. 429, 459 (CDCal 1979) ("This court agrees with defendants that their knowledge was insufficient to make them contributory infringers."), rev'd, 659 F2d 963 (9th Cir 1981), rev'd, 464 US 417 (1984); Alfred C. Yen, Internet Service Provider Liability for Subscriber Copyright Infringement, Enterprise Liability, and the First Amendment, 88 GeoLJ 1833, 1874 & 1893 n210 (2000) (suggesting that, after *Sony*, most Internet service providers lack "the requisite level of knowledge" for the imposition of contributory liability)).

We are bound to follow *Sony*, and will not impute the requisite level of knowledge to Napster merely because peer-to-peer file sharing technology may be used to infringe plaintiffs' copyrights (see 464 US at 436 (rejecting argument that merely supplying the "'means' to accomplish an infringing activity" leads to imposition of liability)). We depart from the reasoning of the district court that Napster failed to demonstrate that its system is capable of commercially significant noninfringing uses (see *Napster*, 114 FSupp2d at 916, 917–18). The district court improperly confined the use analysis to current uses, ignoring the system's capabilities (see generally *Sony*, 464 US at 442–43 (framing inquiry as whether the video tape recorder is "capable of commercially significant noninfringing uses") (emphasis added)). Consequently, the district court placed undue weight on the proportion of current infringing use as compared to current and future noninfringing use (see generally *Vault Corp. v. Quaid Software Ltd.*, 847 F2d 255, 264–67 (5th Cir 1997) (single noninfringing use implicated Sony)). Nonetheless, whether we might arrive at a different result is not the issue here (see *Sports Form, Inc. v. United Press Int'l, Inc.*, 686 F2d 750, 752 (9th Cir 1982)). The instant appeal occurs at an early point

in the proceedings and "the fully developed factual record may be materially different from that initially before the district court. ..." (*Id* at 753). Regardless of the number of Napster's infringing versus noninfringing uses, the evidentiary record here supported the district court's finding that plaintiffs would likely prevail in establishing that Napster knew or had reason to know of its users' infringement of plaintiffs' copyrights.

This analysis is similar to that of *Religious Technology Center v. Netcom On-Line Communication Services, Inc.*, which suggests that in an online context, evidence of actual knowledge of specific acts of infringement is required to hold a computer system operator liable for contributory copyright infringement (907 FSupp at 1371). Netcom considered the potential contributory copyright liability of a computer bulletin board operator whose system supported the posting of infringing material (*Id* at 1374). The court, in denying Netcom's motion for summary judgment of noninfringement and plaintiff's motion for judgment on the pleadings, found that a disputed issue of fact existed as to whether the operator had sufficient knowledge of infringing activity (*Id* at 1374–75).

The court determined that for the operator to have sufficient knowledge, the copyright holder must "provide the necessary documentation to show there is likely infringement" (907 FSupp at 1374; cf. *Cubby, Inc. v. Compuserve, Inc.*, 776 FSupp 135, 141 (SDNY 1991) (recognizing that online service provider does not and cannot examine every hyperlink for potentially defamatory material)). If such documentation was provided, the court reasoned that Netcom would be liable for contributory infringement because its failure to remove the material "and thereby stop an infringing copy from being distributed worldwide constitutes substantial participation" in distribution of copyrighted material (*Id*).

We agree that if a computer system operator learns of specific infringing material available on his system and fails to purge such material from the system, the operator knows of and contributes to direct infringement (see *Netcom*, 907 FSupp at 1374). Conversely, absent any specific information which identifies infringing activity, a computer system operator cannot be liable for contributory infringement merely because the structure of the system allows for the exchange of copyrighted material (see *Sony*, 464 US at 436,

442–43). To enjoin simply because a computer network allows for infringing use would, in our opinion, violate Sony and potentially restrict activity unrelated to infringing use.

We nevertheless conclude that sufficient knowledge exists to impose contributory liability when linked to demonstrated infringing use of the Napster system (see *Napster*, 114 FSupp2d at 919 ("Religious Technology Center would not mandate a determination that Napster, Inc. lacks the knowledge requisite to contributory infringement.")). The record supports the district court's finding that Napster has actual knowledge that specific infringing material is available using its system, that it could block access to the system by suppliers of the infringing material, and that it failed to remove the material (see *Napster*, 114 FSupp2d at 918, 920–21).

B. Material Contribution

Under the facts as found by the district court, Napster materially contributes to the infringing activity. Relying on *Fonovisa*, the district court concluded that "[w]ithout the support services defendant provides, Napster users could not find and download the music they want with the ease of which defendant boasts" (*Napster*, 114 FSupp2d at 919–20 ("Napster is an integrated service designed to enable users to locate and download MP3 music files.")). We agree that Napster provides "the site and facilities" for direct infringement (see (*Fonovisa*, 76 F3d at 264; *cf. Netcom*, 907 FSupp at 1372 ("Netcom will be liable for contributory infringement since its failure to cancel [a user's] infringing message and thereby stop an infringing copy from being distributed worldwide constitutes substantial participation.")). The district court correctly applied the reasoning in *Fonovisa*, and properly found that Napster materially contributes to direct infringement.

We affirm the district court's conclusion that plaintiffs have demonstrated a likelihood of success on the merits of the contributory copyright infringement claim. We will address the scope of the injunction in part VIII of this opinion.

V

We turn to the question whether Napster engages in vicarious copyright infringement. Vicarious copyright liability is an "outgrowth" of respondeat superior (*Fonovisa*, 76 F3d at 262). In the context of copyright law, vicarious liability extends beyond an employer/employee relationship to cases in which a defendant "has the right and ability to supervise the infringing activity and also has a direct financial interest in such activities" (*Id* (quoting *Gershwin*, 443 F2d at 1162); see also *Polygram Int'l Publ'g, Inc. v. Nevada/TIG, Inc.*, 855 FSupp 1314, 1325-26 (DMass 1994) (describing vicarious liability as a form of risk allocation)).

Before moving into this discussion, we note that *Sony*'s "staple article of commerce" analysis has no application to Napster's potential liability for vicarious copyright infringement. (see *Sony*, 464 US at 434–435; see generally Melville B. Nimmer & David Nimmer, Nimmer On Copyright 12.04[A][2] & [A][2][b] (2000) (confining Sony to contributory infringement analysis: "Contributory infringement itself is of two types—personal conduct that forms part of or furthers the infringement and contribution of machinery or goods that provide the means to infringe"); 617 PLI/Pat 455, 528 (Sept. 2, 2000) (indicating that the "staple article of commerce" doctrine "provides a defense only to contributory infringement, not to vicarious infringement")). The issues of Sony's liability under the "doctrines of 'direct infringement' and 'vicarious liability'" were not before the Supreme Court, although the Court recognized that the "lines between direct infringement, contributory infringement, and vicarious liability are not clearly drawn" (*Id* at 435 n17). Consequently, when the Sony Court used the term "vicarious liability," it did so broadly and outside of a technical analysis of the doctrine of vicarious copyright infringement (*Id* at 435 ("[V]icarious liability is imposed in virtually all areas of the law, and the concept of contributory infringement is merely a species of the broader problem of identifying the circumstances in which it is just to hold one individual accountable for the actions of another."); see also *Black's Law Dictionary* 927 (7th ed 1999) (defining "vicarious liability" in a manner similar to the definition used in Sony)).

A. Financial Benefit

The district court determined that plaintiffs had demonstrated they would likely succeed in establishing that Napster has a direct financial interest in the infringing activity (*Napster*, 114 FSupp2d at 921–22). We agree. Financial benefit exists where the availability of infringing material "acts as a 'draw' for customers" (*Fonovisa*, 76 F3d at 263–64 (stating that financial benefit may be shown "where infringing performances enhance the attractiveness of a venue")). Ample evidence supports the district court's finding that Napster's future revenue is directly dependent upon "increases in userbase." More users register with the Napster system as the "quality and quantity of available music increases" (114 FSupp2d at 902). We conclude that the district court did not err in determining that Napster financially benefits from the availability of protected works on its system.

B. Supervision

The district court determined that Napster has the right and ability to supervise its users' conduct (*Napster*, 114 FSupp2d at 920–21 (finding that Napster's representations to the court regarding "its improved methods of blocking users about whom rights holders complain ... is tantamount to an admission that defendant can, and sometimes does, police its service")). We agree in part.

The ability to block infringers' access to a particular environment for any reason whatsoever is evidence of the right and ability to supervise (see *Fonovisa*, 76 F3d at 262 ("Cherry Auction had the right to terminate vendors for any reason whatsoever and through that right had the ability to control the activities of vendors on the premises."); cf. *Netcom*, 907 FSupp at 1375–76 (indicating that plaintiff raised a genuine issue of fact regarding ability to supervise by presenting evidence that an electronic bulletin board service can suspend subscriber's accounts)). Here, plaintiffs have demonstrated that Napster retains the right to control access to its system. Napster has an express reservation of rights policy, stating on its website that it expressly reserves the "right to refuse service and terminate accounts in [its] discretion, including, but not limited to, if Napster believes that user conduct violates applicable law ... or for any reason in Napster's sole discretion, with or without cause."

To escape imposition of vicarious liability, the reserved right to police must be exercised to its fullest extent. Turning a blind eye to detectable acts of infringement for the sake of profit gives rise to liability (see, e.g., *Fonovisa*, 76 F3d at 261 ("There is no dispute for the purposes of this appeal that Cherry Auction and its operators were aware that vendors in

their swap meets were selling counterfeit recordings."); see also *Gershwin*, 443 F2d at 1161–62 (citing *Shapiro, Bernstein & Co. v. H.L. Greene Co.*, 316 F2d 304 (2d Cir 1963), for the proposition that "failure to police the conduct of the primary infringer" leads to imposition of vicarious liability for copyright infringement)).

The district court correctly determined that Napster had the right and ability to police its system and failed to exercise that right to prevent the exchange of copyrighted material. The district court, however, failed to recognize that the boundaries of the premises that Napster "controls and patrols" are limited (see, e.g., *Fonovisa*, 76 F2d at 262–63 (in addition to having the right to exclude vendors, defendant "controlled and patrolled" the premises); see also *Polygram*, 855 FSupp at 1328–29 (in addition to having the contractual right to remove exhibitors, trade show operator reserved the right to police during the show and had its "employees walk the aisles to ensure 'rules compliance'")). Put differently, Napster's reserved "right and ability" to police is cabined by the system's current architecture. As shown by the record, the Napster system does not "read" the content of indexed files, other than to check that they are in the proper MP3 format.

Napster, however, has the ability to locate infringing material listed on its search indices, and the right to terminate users' access to the system. The file name indices, therefore, are within the "premises" that Napster has the ability to police. We recognize that the files are user-named and may not match copyrighted material exactly (for example, the artist or song could be spelled wrong). For Napster to function effectively, however, file names must reasonably or roughly correspond to the material contained in the files, otherwise no user could ever locate any desired music. As a practical matter, Napster, its users and the record company plaintiffs have equal access to infringing material by employing Napster's "search function."

Our review of the record requires us to accept the district court's conclusion that plaintiffs have demonstrated a likelihood of success on the merits of the vicarious copyright infringement claim. Napster's failure to police the system's "premises," combined with a showing that Napster financially benefits from the continuing availability of infringing files on its system, leads to the imposition of vicarious liability. We address the scope of the injunction in part VIII of this opinion.

VI

We next address whether Napster has asserted defenses which would preclude the entry of a preliminary injunction. Napster alleges that two statutes insulate it from liability. First, Napster asserts that its users engage in actions protected by § 1008 of the Audio Home Recording Act of 1992, 17 USC § 1008. Second, Napster argues that its liability for contributory and vicarious infringement is limited by the Digital Millennium Copyright Act, 17 USC § 512. We address the application of each statute in turn.

A. Audio Home Recording Act

The statute states in part:

> No action may be brought under this title alleging infringement of copyright based on the manufacture, importation, or distribution of a digital audio recording device, a digital audio recording medium, an analog recording device, or an analog recording medium, or based on the noncommercial use by a consumer of such a device or medium for making digital musical recordings or analog musical recordings (17 USC § 1008).

Napster contends that MP3 file exchange is the type of "noncommercial use" protected from infringement actions by the statute. Napster asserts it cannot be secondarily liable for users' nonactionable exchange of copyrighted musical recordings.

The district court rejected Napster's argument, stating that the Audio Home Recording Act is "irrelevant" to the action because: (1) plaintiffs did not bring claims under the Audio Home Recording Act; and (2) the Audio Home Recording Act does not cover the downloading of MP3 files (*Napster*, 114 FSupp2d at 916 n19).

We agree with the district court that the Audio Home Recording Act does not cover the downloading of MP3 files to computer hard drives. First, "[u]nder the plain meaning of the Act's definition of digital audio recording devices, computers (and their hard drives) are not digital audio recording devices because their 'primary purpose' is not to make digital audio copied recordings" (*Recording Indus. Ass'n of Am. v. Diamond Multimedia Sys., Inc.*, 180 F3d 1072, 1078 (9th Cir 1999)). Second, notwithstanding Napster's

claim that computers are "digital audio recording devices," computers do not make "digital music recordings" as defined by the Audio Home Recording Act (*Id* at 1077 (citing SRep 102–294)

("There are simply no grounds in either the plain language of the definition or in the legislative history for interpreting the term `digital musical recording' to include songs fixed on computer hard drives.")).

B. Digital Millennium Copyright Act

Napster also interposes a statutory limitation on liability by asserting the protections of the "safe harbor " from copyright infringement suits for "Internet service providers" contained in the Digital Millennium Copyright Act, 17 USC § 512 (see *Napster*, 114 FSupp2d at 919 n24). The district court did not give this statutory limitation any weight favoring a denial of temporary injunctive relief. The court concluded that Napster "has failed to persuade this court that subsection 512(d) shelters contributory infringers" (*Id*).

We need not accept a blanket conclusion that § 512 of the Digital Millennium Copyright Act will never protect secondary infringers (see SRep 105–190, at 40 (1998) ("The limitations in subsections (a) through (d) protect qualifying service providers from liability for all monetary relief for direct, vicarious, and contributory infringement."), reprinted in Melville B. Nimmer & David Nimmer, Nimmer on Copyright: Congressional Committee Reports on the Digital Millennium Copyright Act and Concurrent Amendments (2000); see also Charles S. Wright, Actual Versus Legal Control: Reading Vicarious Liability for Copyright Infringement Into the Digital Millennium Copyright Act of 1998, 75 WashLRev 1005, 1028-31 (July 2000) ("[T]he committee reports leave no doubt that Congress intended to provide some relief from vicarious liability")).

We do not agree that Napster's potential liability for contributory and vicarious infringement renders the Digital Millennium Copyright Act inapplicable per se. We instead recognize that this issue will be more fully developed at trial. At this stage of the litigation, plaintiffs raise serious questions regarding Napster's ability to obtain shelter under § 512, and plaintiffs also demonstrate that the balance of hardships tips in their favor (see *Prudential Real Estate*, 204 F3d at 874; see also *Micro Star v. Formgen, Inc.* 154 F3d 1107, 1109 (9th Cir 1998) ("A party seeking a preliminary injunction must show ... 'that serious questions going to the merits were raised and the balance of hardships tips sharply in its favor.'")).

Plaintiffs have raised and continue to raise significant questions under this statute, including: (1) whether Napster is an Internet service provider as defined by 17 USC § 512(d); (2) whether copyright owners must give a service provider "official" notice of infringing activity in order for it to have knowledge or awareness of infringing activity on its system; and (3) whether Napster complies with § 512(i), which requires a service provider to timely establish a detailed copyright compliance policy (see *A&M Records, Inc. v. Napster, Inc.*, No. 99-05183, 2000 WL 573136 (NDCal May 12, 2000) (denying summary judgment to Napster under a different subsection of the Digital Millennium Copyright Act, § 512(a))).

The district court considered ample evidence to support its determination that the balance of hardships tips in plaintiffs' favor:

> Any destruction of Napster, Inc. by a preliminary injunction is speculative compared to the statistical evidence of massive, unauthorized downloading and uploading of plaintiffs' copyrighted works—as many as 10,000 files per second by defendant's own admission (see *Kessler* DecP 29). The court has every reason to believe that, without a preliminary injunction, these numbers will mushroom as Napster users, and newcomers attracted by the publicity, scramble to obtain as much free music as possible before trial (114 FSupp2d at 926).

VII

Napster contends that even if the district court's preliminary determinations that it is liable for facilitating copyright infringement are correct, the district court improperly rejected valid affirmative defenses of waiver, implied license and copyright misuse. We address the defenses in turn.

A. Waiver

"Waiver is the intentional relinquishment of a known right with knowledge of its existence and the intent to relinquish it" (*United States v. King Features Entm't, Inc.*, 843 F2d 394, 399 (9th Cir 1988)). In copyright, waiver or abandonment of copyright "occurs only if there is an intent by the copyright proprietor to surrender rights in his work" (Melville B. Nimmer & David Nimmer, Nimmer On Copyright P 13.06 (2000); see also *Micro Star v. Formgen, Inc.*, 154 F3d 1107, 1114 (9th Cir 1998) (discussing abandonment)).

Napster argues that the district court erred in not finding that plaintiffs knowingly provided consumers with technology designed to copy and distribute MP3 files over the Internet and, thus, waived any legal authority to exercise exclusive control over creation and distribution of MP3 files. The district court, however, was not convinced "that the record companies created the monster that is now devouring their intellectual property rights" (*Napster*, 114 FSupp2d at 924). We find no error in the district court's finding that "in hastening the proliferation of MP3 files, plaintiffs did[nothing] more than seek partners for their commercial downloading ventures and develop music players for files they planned to sell over the Internet" (*Id*).

B. Implied License

Napster also argues that plaintiffs granted the company an implied license by encouraging MP3 file exchange over the Internet. Courts have found implied licenses only in "narrow" circumstances where one party "created a work at [the other's] request and handed it over, intending that [the other] copy and distribute it" (*SmithKline Beecham Consumer Healthcare, L.P. v. Watson Pharms., Inc.*, 211 F3d 21, 25 (2d Cir 2000) (quoting *Effects Assocs., Inc. v. Cohen*, 908 F2d 555, 558 (9th Cir 1990)), cert. denied, 121 SCt 173 (2000)). The district court observed that no evidence exists to support this defense: "indeed, the RIAA gave defendant express notice that it objected to the availability of its members' copyrighted music on Napster" (*Napster*, 114 FSupp2d at 924–25). The record supports this conclusion.

C. Misuse

The defense of copyright misuse forbids a copyright holder from "secur[ing] an exclusive right or limited monopoly not granted by the Copyright Office" (*Lasercomb Am., Inc. v. Reynolds*, 911 F2d 970, 977–79 (4th Cir 1990), quoted in *Practice Mgmt. Info. Corp. v. American Med. Ass'n*, 121 F3d 516, 520 (9th Cir.), amended by 133 F3d 1140 (9th Cir 1997)). Napster alleges that online distribution is not within the copyright monopoly. According to Napster, plaintiffs have colluded to "use their copyrights to extend their control to online distributions."

We find no error in the district court's preliminary rejection of this affirmative defense. The misuse defense prevents copyright holders from leveraging their limited monopoly to allow them control of areas outside the monopoly (see *Lasercomb*, 911 F2d at 976–77; see also *Religious Tech. Ctr. v. Lerma*, No. 95-1107A, 1996 WL 633131, at *11 (EDVa Oct 4, 1996) (listing circumstances which indicate improper leverage)). There is no evidence here that plaintiffs seek to control areas outside of their grant of monopoly. Rather, plaintiffs seek to control reproduction and distribution of their copyrighted works, exclusive rights of copyright holders (17 USC § 106; see also, e.g., *UMG Recordings*, 92 FSupp2d at 351 ("A [copyright holder's] 'exclusive' rights, derived from the Constitution and the Copyright Act, include the right, within broad limits, to curb the development of such a derivative market by refusing to license a copyrighted work or by doing so only on terms the copyright owner finds acceptable.")). That the copyrighted works are transmitted in another medium—MP3 format rather than audio CD—has no bearing on our analysis. (see *Id* at 351 (finding that reproduction of audio CD into MP3 format does not "transform" the work)).

VIII

The district court correctly recognized that a preliminary injunction against Napster's participation in copyright infringement is not only warranted but required. We believe, however, that the scope of the injunction needs modification in light of our opinion. Specifically, we reiterate that contributory liability may potentially be imposed only to the extent that Napster: (1) receives reasonable knowledge of specific infringing files with copyrighted musical compositions and sound recordings; (2) knows or should know that such files are available on the Napster system; and (3) fails to act to prevent viral distribution of the works (see *Netcom*, 907 FSupp at 1374–75. The mere existence of the Napster system, absent actual notice and Napster's demonstrated failure to remove the offending material, is insufficient to impose contributory liability (see *Sony*, 464 US at 442–43).

Conversely, Napster may be vicariously liable when it fails to affirmatively use its ability to patrol its system and preclude access to potentially infringing files listed in its search index. Napster has both the ability to use its search function to identify infringing musical recordings and the right to bar participation of users who engage in the transmission of infringing files.

The preliminary injunction which we stayed is overbroad because it places on Napster the entire burden of ensuring that no "copying, downloading, uploading, transmitting, or distributing" of plaintiffs' works occur on the system. As stated, we place the burden on plaintiffs to provide notice to Napster of copyrighted works and files containing such works available on the Napster system before Napster has the duty to disable access to the offending content. Napster, however, also bears the burden of policing the system within the limits of the system. Here, we recognize that this is not an exact science in that the files are user named. In crafting the injunction on remand, the district court should recognize that Napster's system does not currently appear to allow Napster access to users' MP3 files.

Based on our decision to remand, Napster's additional arguments on appeal going to the scope of the injunction need not be addressed. We, however, briefly address Napster's First Amendment argument so that it is not reasserted on remand. Napster contends that the present injunction violates the First Amendment because it is broader than necessary. The company asserts two distinct free speech rights: (1) its right to publish a "directory" (here, the search index) and (2) its users' right to exchange information. We note that First Amendment concerns in copyright are allayed by the presence of the fair use doctrine (see 17 USC § 107; see generally *Nihon Keizai Shimbun v. Comline Business Data, Inc.*, 166 F3d 65, 74 (2d Cir 1999); *Netcom*, 923 FSupp at 1258 (stating that the Copyright Act balances First Amendment concerns with the rights of copyright holders)). There was a preliminary determination here that Napster users are not fair users. Uses of copyrighted material that are not fair uses are rightfully enjoined (see *Dr. Seuss Enters. v. Penguin Books USA, Inc.*, 109 F3d 1394, 1403 (9th Cir 1997) (rejecting defendants' claim that injunction would constitute a prior restraint in violation of the First Amendment)).

IX

We address Napster's remaining arguments: (1) that the court erred in setting a $5 million bond, and (2) that the district court should have imposed a constructive royalty payment structure in lieu of an injunction.

A. Bond

Napster argues that the $5 million bond is insufficient because the company's value is between $1.5 and $2 billion. We review objections to the amount of a bond for abuse of discretion (*Walczak v. EPL Prolong, Inc.*, 198 F3d 725 (9th Cir 1999)).

We are reluctant to dramatically raise bond amounts on appeal (see *GoTo.com, Inc. v. The Walt Disney Co.*, 202 F3d 1199, 1211 (9th Cir 2000); see also FedRCivP 65(c)). The district court considered competing evidence of Napster's value and the deleterious effect that any injunction would have upon the Napster system. We cannot say that Judge Patel abused her discretion when she fixed the penal sum required for the bond.

B. Royalties

Napster contends that the district court should have imposed a monetary penalty by way of a compulsory royalty in place of an injunction. We are asked to do what the district court refused.

Napster tells us that "where great public injury would be worked by an injunction, the courts might ... award damages or a continuing royalty instead of an injunction in such special circumstances" (*Abend v. MCA, Inc.*, 863 F2d 1465, 1479 (9th Cir 1988) (quoting 3 Melville B. Nimmer & David Nimmer, Nimmer On Copyright § 14.06[B] (1988)), aff'd, 495 US 207 (1990)). We are at a total loss to find any "special circumstances" simply because this case requires us to apply well-established doctrines of copyright law to a new technology. Neither do we agree with Napster that an injunction would cause "great public injury." Further, we narrowly construe any suggestion that compulsory royalties are appropriate in this context because Congress has arguably limited the application of compulsory royalties to specific circumstances, none of which are present here (see 17 USC § 115).

The Copyright Act provides for various sanctions for infringers (see, e.g., 17 USC §§ 502 (injunctions); 504 (damages); and 506 (criminal penalties); see also 18 USC § 2319A (criminal penalties for the unauthorized fixation of and trafficking in sound recordings and music videos of live musical performances)). These statutory sanctions represent a more than adequate legislative solution to the problem created by copyright infringement.

Imposing a compulsory royalty payment schedule would give Napster an "easy out" of this case. If such royalties were imposed, Napster would avoid penalties for any future violation of an injunction, statutory copyright damages and any possible criminal penalties for continuing infringement. The royalty structure would also grant Napster the luxury of either choosing to continue and pay royalties or shut down. On the other hand, the wronged parties would be forced to do business with a company that profits from the wrongful use of intellectual properties. Plaintiffs would lose the power to control their intellectual property: they could not make a business decision not to license their property to Napster, and, in the event they planned to do business with Napster, compulsory royalties would take away the copyright holders' ability to negotiate the terms of any contractual arrangement.

X

We affirm in part, reverse in part and remand.

We direct that the preliminary injunction fashioned by the district court prior to this appeal shall remain stayed until it is modified by the district court to conform to the requirements of this opinion. We order a partial remand of this case on the date of the filing of this opinion for the limited purpose of permitting the district court to proceed with the settlement and entry of the modified preliminary injunction.

Even though the preliminary injunction requires modification, appellees have substantially and primarily prevailed on appeal. Appellees shall recover their statutory costs on appeal (see FedRAppP 39(a)(4) ("[i]f a judgment is affirmed in part, reversed in part, modified, or vacated, costs are taxed only as the court orders.")).

AFFIRMED IN PART, REVERSED IN PART AND REMANDED.

KEY TERMS

accountant

advance

American Federation of Musicians (AFM)

American Federation of Television and Radio Artists (AFTRA)

booking agent

budget record

business manager

clearing house

collaboration agreement

compilations

compulsory mechanical license

covering

derivative work

exclusivity clause

firm records

First Sale Doctrine

gross income

initial term

joint work

manager

mechanical license

mid-line record

music publisher

music publishing agreement

option

performance plateau

post-term commission

power of attorney clause

record deal

recoupment

rider

royalty base rate

royalty rate

royalty statements

sampling

scope

signing bonus

Statute of Limitations

term

top-of-the-line record

EXERCISES

1. Find two artist/management agreements, one that favors the artist and one that favors the manger. Discuss the different clauses that affect the favorability of each contract.

2. Locate Web sites of the three performance rights organizations: BMI, ASCAP, and SESAC. Compare them, including how to join them and the advantages and disadvantages of joining one over the other.

3. Find a case that deals with the illegal use of a sample. How did the courts determine the use was illegal? What was the court's remedy?

4. Calculate the royalties that a performer would receive if the following were true (include the cost of the production deduction):

   A. The base royalty rate is $17.99

   B. The royalty rate is 15 percent

   C. The record company pays royalties only on 90 percent of the records sold.

5. Calculate the royalties the performer in question 4 would receive if the record is a compilation and the performer only contributed one song of twenty to the album.

6. Read *Dolman v. Agee*, 157 F3d 708. What does the court say about copyright infringements in motion-picture soundtracks? How do these facts relate to works for hire?

7. Using the Internet, access an Artist Management Agreement and analyze its provisions.

8. Access the American Federation of Musicians on the Internet and download one of its Booking Agent Agreements. Analyze its provisions.

9. Research and draft a collaboration agreement between a composer and a lyricist.

10. Discuss the impact of MP3 and DVDs on the music publishing industry.

CHAPTER

PUBLISHING

CHAPTER OVERVIEW

The written word is one of the oldest means of creating entertainment. All of the various forms of entertainment and laws that have been discussed in the previous chapters have their bases in writing. As a consequence, legal professionals must be familiar and comfortable with the law surrounding the dissemination of the written word—publishing.

As an industry, publishing encompasses not only the exploitation of material specifically designed to be read, but also hardcopy formats of film, stage, art, music, and photography that are intended for inclusion in written and published materials. Further, in developing the published end-product, various entertainment and artistic professionals in addition to writers generally become involved, from copyeditors and design coordinators who are responsible for the look and readability of the finished product to the photographers and plastic artists whose nonverbal materials are included as part of the original design of the publication. All of the rights and responsibilities of these individuals form the basis of the legal aspects of the publishing field.

In dissecting the law of publishing into its component parts, the primary areas of legal concern have already been analyzed: the federal laws governing constitutional rights of privacy and copyright protection and the basic contractual-law principles. All publishing law can be viewed as emanating from the contractual arrangement between and among the persons involved in producing the published work and the persons involved in creating the published work. Therefore, this chapter will concentrate on those contractual provisions that apply to creating and defining the legal relationship among the people involved in producing a publication. The chapter will also address the practical concerns of literary authors, playwrights, and other creative artists involved in the publishing industry, as well as the impact of new computer technology on the legal rights and obligations of authors and publishers.

LITERARY AUTHORS

For the general publishing industry, the majority of its product involves what can be categorized as literary works. The term *literary work* encompasses all forms of publication that are specifically created to be read in a traditional book format, from fiction to nonfiction to technical materials. The publishing industry divides these works into three broad categories.

technical book
Book designed for a specific and limited market, like a textbook.

1. *Technical books.* **Technical books** are texts that are designed for a specific market or industry and not meant for general circulation. This textbook is an example of a technical book.

trade book
Mass market book.

2. *Trade books.* **Trade books** are works defined as all nontechnical works, and therefore include all forms of books that are intended for dissemination to the general public. Examples would be "best-selling" novels and classical works of literature, as well as books of verse and so forth. In many instances, these books may be derived from other sources, such as films or television, or may themselves generate works in other media.

film rights
The right to create a screenplay from another medium.

— *Example* —

A man writes a book about young people growing up in rural Alabama. The novel is a tremendous success and a film company approaches the writer to acquire the book's **film rights**, the legal permission to use the novel as the basis of a screenplay. The writer agrees, and an award-winning film results. Based on the novel and the film, a Broadway producer decides that she would like to adapt the work for the stage. This is an example of a trade book being the source of various adaptations into different media.

vanity press
Private publication of a work that has no readily ascertainable market.

3. *Vanity press.* **Vanity press** is a term, sometimes considered derogatory, that is applied to works that do not fall into the above categories and for which a commercial publisher cannot be found. In this instance, the author has the work published at his or her own expense; the resulting publication is usually given to the author's friends and family, with little or no distribution to the general public.

— *Example*

A wealthy dowager decides to write a history of her family but cannot find a publisher for her manuscript because no one feels that the general public would be interested in the material. The woman has 500 copies printed at her own expense and distributes them as birthday and holiday gifts to her friends. This work has been published to satisfy the author's own vanity to see her name in print.

literary agent
Artist's representative who negotiates publishing contracts.

commission
Fee paid to an agent.

In most instances, the publishing agreement that eventually materializes, regardless of the nature of the work, begins with the author acquiring a literary agent. A **literary agent** is a person who, for a commission, will negotiate the sale of the author's work to a publisher. Many jurisdictions require that such agents be licensed to protect the authors who turn over their works to these agents and in whom they place their trust. As compensation for his or her work, the agent receives a fee called a **commission**. The commission earned by the agent is a set percentage of the royalties, or fees (see chapter 2) that the author receives for the work. The typical commission currently charged by literary agents is 15 percent for domestic sales of the work and 20 percent for foreign sales. The higher percentage for foreign sales is attributable to the fact that the American agent usually must employ the services of a foreign sub-agent to consummate the transaction. These commissions cover all income produced by the original work as well as any adaptations of that work that may follow, such as film, television, and stage performances.

The typical agent's contract states that the agent will receive commissions for all exploitations of the work, even if the author eventually employs the services of a new agent. Most literary agent contracts are entered into for a one- or two-year renewable term.

— *Example*

An author acquires a literary agent to handle her unpublished work. The parties agree that the agent will receive a 15 percent commission on all income earned by the author on that work. The material is published and the work enjoys a modest success. After two years, the author decides to find a new agent. The new agent negotiates a film deal for the work that nets the author hundreds of thousands of dollars. The original agent may be entitled to 15 percent of this income, depending upon the specific wording of the initial contract.

Most writers are happy to pay the agent his or her commission because the agent provides several valuable services, including

1. Assisting the writer in revising the manuscript to a "publishable form"; for example, in a form that will make it attractive to publishers

2. Marketing the work to potential publishers to which the writer may not have access

3. Negotiating the publishing contract to provide the author with a greater percentage of royalties than the author may be able to negotiate him or herself

4. Continuing to market the work to secure agreements to exploit the work in different media

5. Encouraging and assisting the author in creating new works.

Publishing contracts fall into two broad categories: (1) general contracts for new works for which the author receives a royalty and (2) works for hire for which the author is hired to create a specific work for a set fee with all of the rights to the work belonging to the publisher, as discussed in chapter 2. For the author, the difference lies in obtaining money upfront, in consideration of foregoing all other rights to the work, or having to wait for a percentage of the work's sales, which could prove to be financially unfavorable if the work sells poorly. Many lawsuits have emanated out of publishing contracts because the parties were not specific in their terms (or had no written agreement), and the courts had to be called upon to determine whether or not the work was a "work for hire." In making its assessment, the court looks at several factors:

1. Who has control over the material

2. Who owns the copyright

3. Who initiated the idea.

The greater the degree of control by the publisher, the more likely it is that the work will be considered a work for hire. Under this circumstance, the rights of the author are limited to those agreed upon and once the work is published he or she has no further rights or obligations with respect to the work.

All other agreements are arrangements in which the author and the publisher negotiate the extent of each side's rights and obligations, and the author's royalties are based on the sales of the work. In the typical publishing contract, regardless of whether it is a technical book or a trade book, the following clauses appear:

1. *Description and name of the work.* This clause, although apparently straightforward, is crucial to avoid potential litigation. In many instances, even though a contract has been signed, one or both of the parties may decide to terminate the relationship and may then attempt to renegotiate a contract for an identical work. By detailing the nature of the work, even if the title changes (which usually does happen by the time of actual publication), the parties' rights may be protected. Ideas

for fiction are legally considered to be the property of the person who came up with the concept.

— *Example* —

In the opening clause of a publishing contract, a novel tentatively entitled *Jerome* is described as telling the story of an elderly man's affair with a fifteen-year-old girl he meets while on vacation in Nice. The author and the publisher have a falling out, and the contract is discarded. Three months later, a novel is published entitled *Jerald*, the story of an elderly man's affair with a fifteen-year-old girl he meets while on vacation in Aruba. Because of the extreme similarity of the storyline, one or both of the parties may have a cause of action for the usurpation of the original work.

2. *Grant of rights*. This clause indicates who has the copyright and what use the other party may make of the copyrighted work. It is the general licensing provision, as discussed in chapter 2. The clause may also indicate the form the published work will take, either hard or softbound, and will specify that if the initial work is published in a hardbound format, all subsequent printings may be softbound. In this context, it is important for the parties to specify whether such subsequent softbound versions will be either a trade or mass market paperback. A **trade paperback** is one that mimics the format of the hardbound version but is produced on less-expensive paper and is bound in paper. A **mass market paperback** is a version that may be edited for softbound dissemination, and the cover may be redesigned to entice a greater audience.

3. *Advances*. An advance is a payment made to the author prior to publication, which the author typically retains even if the work does not sell. If the work does sell, the advance is set off by the royalties so that the first royalties the author receives are those above the amount of the advance. There has been considerable litigation with regard to advances. Depending on how the clause is written, the author may or may not be required to return the advance if the work is not completed within a specified time or is not delivered in a "publishable form." What is, and who determines "publishable form" has also been the subject of extensive litigation.

trade paperback
Softbound version of a hardbound book that is published faithfully to the original but in a less-expensive form.

mass market paperback
Softbound book that may be substantially edited from its hardbound version to attract a greater audience.

— *Example* —

A famous actress decides to write a romance novel and her agent negotiates a publishing contract with a major publishing house. Because of the actress' name recognition, the publisher gives her a multimillion-dollar advance, half payable upon signing the contract and the other half payable when the completed work is delivered in publishable form. When the actress sends in the final version, the publisher declares it "unpublishable" and refuses to pay the remaining advance. The actress sues. Depending on how "publishable form" is defined by the contract and the court, either the actress or the publisher will prevail.

4. *Royalties*. Royalties represent the set percentage of the sales price the author is entitled to receive as compensation. The percentage will vary depending upon whether the work is a trade or technical work and the estimated potential market for the work. Technical works usually provide for a greater royalty percentage because sales are more limited and in many instances the selling price is greater. In the context of negotiating this royalty clause, accounting practices may be specified so that the total net sales on which the royalty is based can be ascertained to both sides' satisfaction. For a more detailed discussion, see chapter 7.

subsidiary rights
Rights to exploit the work in different media.

5. **Subsidiary rights.** These rights include marketing the work in different formats and media, such as developing a screenplay from the original work or producing T-shirts with the work's title printed on the front. The income derived from these rights may be greater than those derived from the sales of the work itself.

—— *Example* ——

A published work is fairly successful and provides the author with a decent income. However, a phrase from the work has become extremely well-known, and the author, who holds the subsidiary rights, has a T-shirt printed with the phrase on the shirt's back. Sales of the T-shirt far exceed sales of the book and produce a greater income than do the royalties.

6. *Pass through clause*. This provision may allocate subsidiary rights so that the publisher and the author share such income until a certain amount is realized, at which point the right reverts to the author.

7. *Audit rights*. This clause permits the author to audit the financial sales records of the publisher to substantiate that the publisher has paid the author the appropriate royalty.

8. *Delivery*. All publishing contracts indicate a date on which the final manuscript must be delivered to the publisher. Further, the contract may specify times for drafts to be delivered for review and revision. As a practical matter, few authors actually meet these deadlines, but it is rare for a publisher to use the excuse of a late delivery to avoid a contract. However, in certain circumstances, time may be of the essence, in which case the author's failure to deliver the work on the due date may be treated as a contractual breach.

—— *Example* ——

A politician is involved in a sex scandal and lawsuit. A former aid to the politician contracts to write a "tell-all" book about the politician. Because of the notoriety of the scandal, the publisher demands that the book be completed within three months to take advantage of the publicity surrounding the lawsuit, time being of the essence. If the aid fails to meet this deadline, she may be held to be in breach of contract.

9. *Warranties and permissions*. Publishing contracts require that the author guarantee that the work produced is an original work or one for which the author has the necessary rights to reproduce or exploit another's work. If a work contains material taken from another source, the author must so indicate and provide releases from the holders of the copyrights for such uses.

—— *Example* ——

The author of a legal casebook wishes to include sample legal forms as part of the text. The forms he wants to use are copyrighted by a legal printer. In order to include these forms in the casebook, the author must obtain releases from the printer for such inclusion.

10. *Rejection*. All publishing contracts reserve the right for the publisher to reject a work deemed "unpublishable." As indicated above, this clause has generated much litigation. However, the clause should also specify that if a work is rejected, the publisher releases all rights it may have under the contract to the author, who is then free to market the work to a different publisher.

—— *Example* ——

The actress from the example on page 283 loses her lawsuit against the publisher and cannot receive the reminder of her advance. However, pursuant to the contract, the publisher releases to her all rights it had under the agreement. The actress then finds a new publisher who agrees to publish the work that, because of the publicity surrounding the lawsuit with the first publisher, generates millions of dollars in sales. The first publisher has no rights to this income.

11. *Editing*. Editing involves not only grammar and spelling, but also deletions, rearrangements, and additions to the submitted work. Most contracts specify that all editing will be in the control of the publisher, and the author agrees to assist in the editorial process. However, in many instances, unless the author has a tremendous amount of clout, the final decisions on editorial changes rest with the publisher.

12. *Non-competition*. Publishing contracts, like most other forms of contracts for personal services, demand that the author and the publisher not produce works that are in direct competition with the subject publication. This clause benefits both parties, but the determination of what may be "in competition" with the publication may engender legal action.

—— *Example* ——

A writer publishes a book about basic computer programming with a publisher. The contract for the book includes a non-competition clause. One year later, the writer publishes a book with a different publisher on basic computer technology that includes a chapter on computer programming. This may or may not be considered to be in competition with the first work, but such determination is a factual one that may have to be resolved by a court.

These twelve items represent the major provisions that specifically relate to publishing that appear in a standard publishing contract. The other common clauses are those that appear in most contracts, as discussed in chapter 3. An example of a typical publishing contract appears as Exhibit 8-1 at the end of this chapter on pages 300–307.

MUSIC PUBLISHING

The specifics of the law surrounding the music industry have been discussed previously in chapter 7. However, in order to protect oneself, the musician must be familiar with the typical provisions of a music publishing contract.

Most musical works are produced when the composer transfers his or her rights to a music publisher who, in fact, "publishes" nothing. Music publishers obtain the copyrights to original music and then license some of these rights to other entities who produce CDs (and records in former times) for retail and per-forming-rights societies. The performing-rights societies act as clearing houses to broadcasters and retailers who obtain performing licenses directly from these performing rights societies. The three main performing-rights societies in the United States are the **American Society of Composers, Authors, and Performers (ASCAP)**, the **Society of European Stage Authors and Composers (SESAC)**, and **Broadcast Music, Inc. (BMI)**.

In consideration for their services, music publishers receive a commission that generally greatly exceeds the commissions permitted to literary agents. To be entitled to these fees, a music publisher performs the following functions:

1. Introduces the composer to producers
2. Finds an artist to perform the work
3. Manages the business of promoting the music
4. Oversees the composer's work
5. Helps market the music
6. Advances money to the composer (though not always)
7. Provides the composer with work.

Unlike general publishing contracts in which the artist may retain some rights, in the typical music publishing contract the composer transfers all of his or her copyrights to the publisher. Such rights include the right to the work's title, words, and music; these rights are usually deemed valid as against

American Society of Composers, Authors, and Performers (ASCAP)
Organization that protects the rights of composers, performers and writers.

Society of European Stage Authors and Composers (SESAC)
Performing-rights society.

Broadcast Music, Inc (BMI)
Performing-rights society.

the entire world. In other words, the songwriter basically gives up worldwide control of his or her work to the publisher. Some of the most significant of these rights are

1. *Public performance rights.* **Public performance rights** enable the holder (the publisher) to license the right to permit a performance of the work on radio, television, or any other medium. This license is effectuated by the performance society granting a license to broadcast the music as it wishes; the performance society then monitors the licensee to determine the amount of performance royalties it is entitled to collect on behalf of the publisher and the artist.

public performance rights
The legal ability to determine when and how a work will be performed.

— *Example*

BMI licenses a radio station to broadcast a song that has been registered with it. BMI then listens to the station for the period of the license to determine how often the song is played, and then computes the royalties it is owed. These royalties are in turn allocated among all the persons and entities entitled to receive a percentage of performance fees.

creative rights
The legal right to make changes to a copyrighted work.

2. *Creative rights.* **Creative rights** enable the publisher to make any changes to the work that it deems warranted. In some instances, the composer may be able to retain some control by requiring notification from the publisher prior to effectuating any change to the work. If such a clause is included, the contract may state that the composer may not unreasonably withhold approval of the change. However, determination of what may or may not be considered "reasonable" may necessitate judicial intervention.

mechanical rights
The legal ability to reproduce a work mechanically, such as on a CD.

3. *Mechanical and synchronization rights.* **Mechanical rights** refer to the legal ability to permit the work to be reproduced in a mechanical format such as a CD. The publisher is entitled to a mechanical royalty for each mechanical reproduction of the work. **Synchronization rights** refer to the legal ability to permit the work to be reproduced on a soundtrack in synchronization to the visual action. The **National Music Publishers Association** represents thousands of music publishers in negotiating and collecting mechanical and synchronization royalties.

synchronization right
The legal ability to permit a composition to be used on a soundtrack.

National Music Publishers Association
Organization that represents music publishers in negotiating and collecting royalties.

4. *Print publication rights.* **Print publication rights** permit the publisher to authorize reproduction of the music as sheet music, orchestrations, and in other printed formats.

print publication rights
Rights that permit the publisher to authorize reproduction of music in various printed formats.

Although it may at first appear that these contracts are unduly weighted in favor of the publishers, for most composers this is the only way that they can have their works produced. However, as the composer becomes more well-known, he or she may be able to negotiate a single song agreement, whereby the contract only covers the publication of a single composition, rather than all of the composer's output for the period of the arrangement. Also, many composers have opted to form their own music publishing company to retain greater artistic and financial control of the results of their creativity.

PHOTOGRAPHERS AND VISUAL ARTISTS

Publishing involves more than the printing of the written word. Many published works involve the compilation of photographs or artistic works, all of which may form the basis of the entire work. In producing the end-product, the publisher will employ the services of such artistic professionals as photographers and artists to produce a visually attractive publication.

For the most part, the general laws involved with taking photographs and creating graphic works of art have been fully discussed in earlier chapters dealing with constitutional law and copyrights (chapter 1) and federal regulations (chapter 2). For the purpose of focusing on the publishing aspects of disseminating graphic and photographic art, a few specific contractual provisions should be highlighted.

First, if the work involves the taking of photographs, the photographer must be sure to obtain appropriate releases from the subjects so photographed, unless the object of the photograph is in a public forum with no expectation of privacy. The typical publishing contract will include a provision in which the artist guarantees such permissions, and the artist may be held legally responsible if a subject who has not granted permission to use his or her likeness sues to enjoin publication of the work.

— *Example*

A photographer is working on a collection of photographs of bald men. To create this portfolio, the photographer stands on a busy street taking pictures of all the bald men who pass by, but only after obtaining permission from them. When he takes the pictures, members of the general public appear in the background. If the photographer eventually uses these pictures for publication, he must be sure that he has the written permission of all of the bald subjects; the people in the background who just happened to be on the street do not need to give a release, as they had no expectation of privacy when they were walking on a public street.

For all original creative works, the artist must be prepared to provide the publisher with proof of his or her copyright. In many instances, the publisher may permit or allow the artist to retain the copyright in the original photograph.

To avoid problems, the contract should specify who bears the risk of loss of the original artwork if it is lost or damaged during the production process. This may require that the publisher or the artist obtain insurance to cover any potential damage to the work.

The artist usually will retain a right to have the property returned to him or her after a specified period of time if the publisher has not published the work. This protects the artist so that he or she may seek another publisher for the work and provides an incentive to the publisher to see that the work is produced and marketed within a reasonable period of time.

If the artistic work is not the main focus of the publication, but rather is intended as a cover or an illustration within the written work, such use must be detailed in the contract. Should the publisher decide to make any nonspecified use of the work, the artist may have a cause of action against the publisher. These use-limitation clauses protect the integrity of a work.

— Example

A contract calls for an artist to create a front cover for a novel, which she does. During production, the publisher decides that the work would be more effective as the back cover. If the contract does not grant the publisher such editorial rights, the publisher may be in breach of contract.

Possibly one of the most important considerations included in a publishing contract concerns the nature of the credit that will be allocated among all of the artists who contribute to the finished work. These credits are referred to as **labels**, and are the method of indicating the degree of contribution each artist has made to the publication. The most common types of labeling in current use are

labels
Method of allocating credits among contributors to a finished work.

co-authors
Label indicating that two or more persons share equal credit as authors.

1. **Co-authors**, by which the publication indicates that each person contributed equally to the end-product. Note that this label only refers to the credits, not necessarily to the division of rights and royalties.

— Example

A writer submits a work that needs substantial revisions. To assist the writer, the publisher hires another writer. Pursuant to their agreement, the new writer is indicated as a co-author, but he is only entitled to 25 percent of the original writer's royalties.

based upon
Label indicating that the work is not an original idea.

adapted from
Label generally indicating the original author also wrote the subsidiary work.

2. **Based upon**, by which the publisher indicates that the publication was not an original idea, but rather was derived from another source. In such circumstances, the appropriate releases must be obtained from the copyright holder of the based-upon work.
3. **Adapted from**, which is an original work created from a preexisting work. In many instances, this label is used when an artist has created the current work from one of his or her own works that first appeared in a different medium.

— *Example*

A woman wrote an award-winning short story and her publisher would like her to write a full-length novel. If she writes a novel using the characters and plot appearing in the short story, she may decide to use the label indicating that she adapted the novel from her short story.

Labeling is crucial for works that are produced by multiple collaborators. Many lawsuits have resulted when an artist feels shortchanged by the credit he or she has been given with respect to the work. All publishing contracts should specify the nature of the label to be given for each contributor.

ELECTRONIC PUBLISHING

As with many other areas of law and life, computer technology has had a tremendous impact on the field of publishing. With the proliferation of personal computers, many people prefer to read material from a computer screen rather than from hardcopy and, in the past few years, many publishers have addressed this new form of publication. Some of the most significant impacts of electronic publishing (e-publishing) have been

ISBN
International standard book number.

1. Easy access to vanity presses. Certain companies have emerged that provide access for writers to have their works published on line. Such companies will perform editorial services for the writer, arrange an **international standard book number (ISBN)** for the work, format the material, and sell it over the Internet. These services are paid for by the author rather than a publisher, as opposed to the more traditional arrangements.

2. Greater profits for the author. All publishers require the author to provide both a hardcopy and a disk when the work is submitted. If an author decides to market the work by means of the Internet, the same disk is provided, but he or she can bypass the publisher and contact the audience directly without having to share the royalties with the publisher. Further, because the material is accessed on line, many production costs can be reduced or eliminated altogether. A few years ago, Stephen King self-published a novel on line and made more sales and greater profits than he had using a traditional publishing format.

Digital Rights Management (DRM)
Computer encryption program.

3. Copyright protection. Because of downloading capabilities of computer technology, there exists the problem of protecting the copyright of the work for the author. To alleviate the problem of copyright infringement, a program entitled **Digital Rights Management (DRM)** has been developed. This program encrypts the work so that it can only be accessed and downloaded if a fee has been paid. However, encryption programs are not foolproof, and copyright concerns still exist.

E-publishing has not changed basic law, but has added its own interpretation to existing legal principles. Some of the most popular of the e-publishing Web sites are

http://www.ipublish.com

http://www.mightywords.com

http://www.ylibris.com

CHAPTER REVIEW

As with many areas of entertainment law, the law involved in publishing is simply a specific facet of general contract and constitutional law. For the legal professional, an understanding of the contractual clauses that directly relate to publishing is crucial so as to provide adequate representation of a client.

Most publishing agreements begin with an author acquiring a literary agent. This agent, for a fee, negotiates the sale of the author's work to a publisher, arranging the most favorable deal for the author as possible. Most literary agent agreements last for one to two years.

Once a publisher is found, the author and the publisher enter into a contractual relationship in which the author agrees to provide the publisher with a manuscript in "publishable form" in exchange for a fee, called a royalty, that represents a percentage of the eventual sales of the work. In certain circumstances, the publisher may "hire" a work to be written. Here the author only receives a one-time payment for the work. This arrangement is called a work for hire, and all rights to the material belong to the publisher.

One of the most important rights associated with a publishing contract concerns control of subsidiary rights, the legal right to exploit a work in other media. In many instances, these rights may prove to be more financially rewarding than the income derived from the written work itself.

With any publishing venture, many creative people are involved in producing the end-product. Photographers, illustrators, graphic artists, editors, and so forth all contribute to the final publication, and each of these individuals contracts for his or her own financial arrangements and rights with respect to the work each produces.

Recently, computer technology has impacted the publishing world, and many authors have published their works directly on the Internet through the online publishing companies that have emerged. Even traditional publishing houses have started creating Web sites to attract the modern reader who would prefer to read from a computer screen than from a piece of paper. These online publishers can provide authors with greater financial rewards than is possible in standard publishing because of reduced production costs and immediate access to a global market.

JUDICIAL DECISION

The following case discusses copyrght problems involved with electronic publishing.

Tasini et al. v. The New York Times Company, Inc.; Newsday, Inc.; The Time Incorporated Magazine Company; Mead Data Central Corp.; and University Microfilms International
206 F3d 161 (SDNY 1999)

Six freelance writers appeal from a grant of summary judgment dismissing their complaint. The complaint alleged that appellees had infringed appellants' various copyrights by putting individual articles previously published in periodicals on electronic databases available to the public. On cross motions for summary judgment, the United States District Court for the Southern District of New York held that appellees' use of the articles was protected by the "privilege" afforded to publishers of "collective works" under § 201(c) of the Copyright Act of 1976 ("Act" or "1976 Act"), (17 USC § 201(c)). We reverse and remand with instructions to enter judgment for appellants.

Background

Appellants are freelance writers (individually, "Author" and collectively, "Authors") who write articles for publication in periodicals. Their complaint alleged that certain articles were original works written for first publication by one of the appellee publishers between 1990 and 1993. None of the articles was written at a time when its Author was employed by the particular periodical; nor was any such article written pursuant to a work-for-hire contract. The Authors registered a copyright in each of the articles.

The appellee newspaper and magazine publishers (collectively, "Publishers") are periodical publishers who regularly create "collective works" (see 17 USC § 101) that contain articles by free lance authors as well as works created for-hire or by employees. With respect to the free lance articles pertinent to this appeal, the Publishers' general practice was to negotiate due-dates, word counts, subject matter and price; no express transfer of rights under the Author's copyright was sought. As to one article alleged in the complaint, however, authored by appellant David S. Whitford for *Sports Illustrated*, a publication of appellee The Time

Incorporated Magazine Company ("Time"), a written contract expressly addressed republication rights. We address Whitford's claim separately below.

Appellee Mead Data Central Corp. owns and operates the NEXIS electronic database. NEXIS is a massive database that includes the full texts of articles appearing in literally hundreds of newspapers and periodicals spanning many years. Mead has entered into licensing agreements with each of the Publishers. Pursuant to these agreements, the Publishers provide Mead with much of the content of their periodicals, in digital form, for inclusion in NEXIS. Subscribers to NEXIS are able to access an almost infinite combination of articles from one or more publishers by using the database's advanced search engine. The articles may be retrieved individually or, for example, together with others on like topics. Such retrieval makes the article available without any material from the rest of the periodical in which it first appeared.

We briefly describe the process by which an issue of a periodical is made available to Mead for inclusion in NEXIS. First, an individual issue of the paper is stripped, electronically, into separate files representing individual articles. In the process, a substantial portion of what appears in that particular issue of the periodical is not made part of a file transmitted to Mead, including, among other things, formatting decisions, pictures, maps and tables, and obituaries. Moreover, although the individual articles are "tagged" with data indicating the section and page on which the article initially appeared, certain information relating to the initial page layout is lost, such as placement above or below the fold in the case of The New York Times. After Mead further codes the individual files, the pieces are incorporated into the NEXIS database.

Appellee University Microfilms International ("UMI") markets, inter alia, CD-ROM database products. Pursuant to an agreement with *The New York Times* and Mead, UMI produces and markets the "NY Times OnDisc" ("NYTO") CD-ROM, which contains the full texts of articles from *The New York Times*. It also produces and markets a "General Periodicals OnDisc"

("GPO") CD-ROM, which contains selected *New York Times* articles and thousands of other articles. Pursuant to its agreement with Mead and *The New York Times*, UMI incorporates the files containing *Times* articles into its NYTO database. UMI uses a somewhat different methodology to incorporate articles from the *NY Times* Sunday book-review and magazine sections onto its GPO CD-ROM. As to these pieces, UMI scans them directly onto "image-based" files. The image-based files are also abstracted and included on the text-based CD-ROM; the abstracts facilitate access to the image-based disk.

The gist of the Authors' claim is that the copyright each owns in his or her individual articles was infringed when the Publishers provided them to the electronic databases. Appellees do not dispute that the Authors own the copyright in their individual works. Rather, they argue that the Publishers own the copyright in the "collective works" that they produce and are afforded the privilege, under § 201(c) of the Act, of "reproducing and distributing" the individual works in "any revision of that collective work" (17 USC § 201(c)). The crux of the dispute is, therefore, whether one or more of the pertinent electronic databases may be considered a "revision" of the individual periodical issues from which the articles were taken. The district court held that making the articles available on the databases constitutes a revision of the individual periodicals and that appellees' licensing arrangements were protected under § 201(c) (see *Tasini v. New York Times Co.*, 972 FSupp 804 (SDNY 1997) ["Tasini I"]). It therefore granted appellees' motion for summary judgment. After a motion for reconsideration was denied (see *Tasini v. New York Times Co.*, 981 FSupp 841 (SDNY 1997) ["Tasini II"]), appellants brought this appeal.

Discussion

We review de novo the grant or denial of summary judgment and view the evidence in the light most favorable to the non-moving party (see *Turner v. General Motors Acceptance Corp.*, 180 F3d 451, 453–54 (2nd Cir 1999)). Summary judgment is appropriate only if the pleadings and evidentiary submissions demonstrate the absence of any genuine issue of material fact and that the moving party is entitled to judgment as a matter of law (see *Id* at 453).

The unauthorized reproduction and distribution of a copyrighted work generally infringes the copyright unless such use is specifically protected by the Act. To reiterate, each Author owns the copyright in an individual work and, save for Whitford, see *infra*, has neither licensed nor otherwise transferred any rights under it to a Publisher or electronic database. These works were published with the Authors' consent, however, in particular editions of the periodicals owned by the Publishers. The Publishers then licensed much of the content of these periodicals, including the Authors' works, to one or more of the electronic database providers. As a result, the Authors' works are now available to the public on one or more electronic databases and may be retrieved individually or in combination with other pieces originally published in different editions of the periodical or in different periodicals.

In support of their claim, the Authors advance two principal arguments: first, § 201(c) protects only the Publishers' initial inclusion of individually copyrighted works in their collective works does not permit the inclusion of individually copyrighted works in one or more of the electronic databases; and, second, any privilege the Publishers have under § 201(c) is not a transferrable "right" within the meaning of § 201(d) and hence may not be invoked by the electronic database providers. The district court rejected both arguments, reasoning that the "privilege" under § 201(c) is a "subdivision" of a right that is transferrable under § 201(d)(2), 972 FSupp at 815, and that the scope of the "privilege" was broad enough to permit the inclusion of the Authors' pieces in the various databases (see *Id* at 824–25). We hold that § 201(c) does not permit the Publishers to license individually copyrighted works for inclusion in the electronic databases. We need not, and do not, reach the question whether this privilege is transferrable under § 201(d).

a) The § 201(c) Presumption (or, simply, "§ 201(c)")

Section 201 of the Act provides, inter alia, that as to contributions to collective works, the "copyright in each separate contribution ... is distinct from copyright in the collective work as a whole, and vests initially in the author of the contribution" (17 USC § 201(c)). Correspondingly, § 103, which governs copyright in compilations and derivative works, provides in pertinent part that:

The copyright in a compilation or derivative work extends only to the material contributed by the author of such work, as distinguished from the preexisting material employed in the work, and does not imply any exclusive right in the preexisting material (17 USC § 103(b)).

Section 101 states that "the term 'compilation' includes collective works" (17 USC § 101). It further defines "collective work" as "a work, such as a periodical issue, anthology, or encyclopedia, in which a number of contributions, constituting separate and independent works in themselves, are assembled into a collective whole" (Id).

Publishers of collective works are not permitted to include individually copyrighted articles without receiving a license or other express transfer of rights from the author. However, § 201(c) creates a presumptive privilege to authors of collective works. § 201(c) creates a presumption that when the author of an article gives the publisher the author's permission to include the article in a collective work, as here, the author also gives a non-assignable, non-exclusive privilege to use the article as identified in the statute. It provides in pertinent part that:

In the absence of an express transfer of the copyright or of any rights under it, the owner of copyright in the collective work is presumed to have acquired only the privilege of reproducing and distributing the contribution as part of that particular collective work, any revision of that collective work, and any later collective work in the same series (17 USC § 201(c)).

Under this statutory framework, the author of an individual contribution to a collective work owns the copyright to that contribution, absent an express agreement setting other terms (see Id). The rights of the author of a collective work are limited to "the material contributed by the [collective-work] author" and do not include "any exclusive right in the preexisting material" (17 USC § 103(b)). Moreover, the presumptive privilege granted to a collective-work author to use individually copyrighted contributions is limited to the reproduction and distribution of the individual contribution as part of: (i) "that particular [i.e., the original] collective work"; (ii) "any revision of that collective work"; or (iii) "any later collective work in the same series" (17 USC § 201(c)). Because it is undisputed that the electronic databases are neither the original collective work—the particular edition of the periodical—in which the Authors' articles were

published nor a later collective work in the same series, appellees rely entirely on the argument that each database constitutes a "revision" of the particular collective work in which each Author's individual contribution first appeared. We reject that argument.

We begin, as we must, with the language of the statute (see Lewis v. United States, 445 US 55, 60, 63 LEd2d 198, 100 SCt 915 (1980)). The parameters of § 201(c) are set forth in the three clauses just noted. Under ordinary principles of statutory construction, the second clause must be read in the context of the first and third clauses (see General Elec. Co. v. Occupational Safety & Health Review Comm'n, 583 F2d 61, 64-65 (2d Cir 1978) ("the meaning of one term may be determined by reference to the terms it is associated with" (citing 2A Sutherland, Statutory Construction §§ 47.16 (Noscitur a sociis), 47.17 (Ejusdem generis) (4th ed 1973)); see also Securities & Exch. Comm'n v. National Sec., Inc., 393 US 453, 466, 89 SCt 564, 21 LEd2d 668 (1969) ("The meaning of particular phrases must be determined in context.") (citation omitted)). The first clause sets the floor, so to speak, of the presumptive privilege: the collective-work author is permitted to reproduce and distribute individual contributions as part of "that particular collective work." In this context, "that particular collective work" means a specific edition or issue of a periodical. (see 17 USC § 201(c)). The second clause expands on this, to permit the reproduction and distribution of the individual contribution as part of a "revision" of "that collective work," i.e., a revision of a particular edition of a specific periodical. Finally, the third clause sets the outer limit or ceiling on what the Publisher may do; it permits the reproduction and distribution of the individual contribution as part of a "later collective work in the same series," such as a new edition of a dictionary or encyclopedia.

The most natural reading of the "revision" of "that collective work" clause is that § 201(c) protects only later editions of a particular issue of a periodical, such as the final edition of a newspaper. Because later editions are not identical to earlier editions, use of the individual contributions in the later editions might not be protected under the preceding clause. Given the context provided by the surrounding clauses, this interpretation makes perfect sense. It protects the use of an individual contribution in a collective work that is somewhat altered from the original in which the copyrighted article was first published, but that is not in any ordinary sense of language a "later" work in the "same series."

In this regard, we note that the statutory definition of "collective work" lists as examples "a periodical issue, anthology, or encyclopedia" (17 USC § 101). The use of these particular kinds of collective works as examples supports our reading of the revision clause. Issues of periodicals, as noted, are often updated by revised editions, while anthologies and encyclopedias are altered every so often through the release of a new version, a "later collective work in the same series." Perhaps because the "same series" clause might be construed broadly, the House Report on the Act noted that the "revision" clause in § 201(c) was not intended to permit the inclusion of previously published freelance contributions "in a new anthology or an entirely different magazine or other collective work," i.e., in later collective works not in the same series (HRRep No 94-1476, at 122–23 (1976), reprinted in 1976 USCAAN 5659, 5738).

Moreover, Publishers' contention that the electronic databases are revised, digital copies of collective works cannot be squared with basic canons of statutory construction. First, if the contents of an electronic database are merely a "revision" of a particular "collective work," e.g., the August 16, 1999 edition of *The New York Times*, then the third clause of § 201(c)—permitting the reproduction and distribution of an individually copyrighted work as part of "a later collective work in the same series"—would be superfluous (see *Regions Hosp. v. Shalala*, 522 US 448, 118 SCt 909, 920, 139 LEd2d 895 (1998) (Scalia, J., dissenting) ("It is a cardinal rule of statutory construction that significance and effect shall, if possible, be accorded to every word. As early as in *Bacon's Abridgment*,§ 2, it was said that 'a statute ought, upon the whole, to be so construed that, if it can be prevented, no clause, sentence, or word shall be superfluous, void, or insignificant.'") (quoting *Market Co. v. Hoffman*, 101 US 112, 115–16, 25 LEd 782 (1879))). An electronic database can contain hundreds or thousands of editions of hundreds or thousands of periodicals, including newspapers, magazines, anthologies, and encyclopedias. To view the contents of databases as revisions would eliminate any need for a privilege for "a later collective work in the same series."

Second, the permitted uses set forth in § 201(c) are an exception to the general rule that copyright vests initially in the author of the individual contribution. Reading "revision of that collective work" as broadly as appellees suggest would cause the exception to swallow the rule (see *Commissioner v. Clark*, 489 US 726, 739, 103 LEd2d 753, 109 SCt 1455 (1989) (when a statute sets forth exceptions to a general rule, we generally construe the exceptions "narrowly in order to preserve the primary operation of the [provision]")). Under Publishers' theory of § 201(c), the question of whether an electronic database infringes upon an individual author's article would essentially turn upon whether the rest of the articles from the particular edition in which the individual article was published could also be retrieved individually. However, § 201(c) would not permit a Publisher to sell a hard copy of an Author's article directly to the public even if the Publisher also offered for individual sale all of the other articles from the particular edition. We see nothing in the revision provision that would allow the Publishers to achieve the same goal indirectly through NEXIS.

Appellees' reading is also in considerable tension with the overall statutory framework. Section 201(c) was a key innovation of the Copyright Act of 1976. Because the Copyright Act of 1909 contemplated a single copyright, authors risked losing their rights by allowing an article to be used in a collective work (see 3 Melville Nimmer & David Nimmer, Nimmer on Copyright § 10.01[A] (1996 ed) (discussing doctrine of indivisibility)). To address this concern, the 1976 Act expressly permitted the transfer of less than the entire copyright (see 17 USC § 201(d)), in effect replacing the notion of a single "copyright" with that of "exclusive rights" under a copyright (Id §§ 106, 103(b)). Section 201(d), which governs the transfer of copyright ownership, provides:

(1) The ownership of a copyright may be transferred in whole or in part … .

(2) Any of the exclusive rights comprised in a copyright, including any subdivision of any of the rights specified by § 106, may be transferred as provided by clause (1) and owned separately. The owner of any particular exclusive right is entitled, to the extent of that right, to all of the protection and remedies accorded to the copyright owner by this title (Id § 201(d) (emphasis added); see also Id § 204 (executions of transfers of copyright ownership)).

Similarly, § 501, which sets forth the remedies for infringement of copyright, provides in pertinent part that "anyone who violates any of the exclusive rights of the copyright owner ... is an infringer" (Id § 501(a)). Were the permissible uses under § 201(c) as broad and as transferrable as appellees contend, it is not clear that the rights retained by the Authors could be considered "exclusive" in any meaningful sense.

In light of this discussion, there is no feature peculiar to the databases at issue in this appeal that would cause us to view them as "revisions." NEXIS is a database comprising thousands or millions of individually retrievable articles taken from hundreds or thousands of periodicals. It can hardly be deemed a "revision" of each edition of every periodical that it contains.

Moreover, NEXIS does almost nothing to preserve the copyrightable aspects of the Publishers' collective works, "as distinguished from the preexisting material employed in the work" (17 USC § 103(b)). The aspects of a collective work that make it "an original work of authorship" are the selection, coordination, and arrangement of the preexisting materials (Id § 101; see also *Feist Publications, Inc. v. Rural Tel. Serv. Co.*, 499 US 340, 349, 113 LEd2d 358, 111 SCt 1282 (1991) (discussing factual compilations)). However, as described above, in placing an edition of a periodical such as the August 16, 1999 *New York Times*, in NEXIS, some of the paper's content, and perhaps most of its arrangement are lost. Even if a NEXIS user so desired, he or she would have a hard time recapturing much of "the material contributed by the author of such [collective] work" (17 USC § 103(b)). In this context, it is significant that neither the Publishers nor NEXIS evince any intent to compel, or even to permit, an end user to retrieve an individual work only in connection with other works from the edition in which it ran. Quite the contrary, *The New York Times* actually forbids NEXIS from producing "facsimile reproductions" of particular editions (see *Tasini I*, 972 FSupp at 826 n17). What the end user can easily access, of course, are the preexisting materials that belong to the individual author under §§ 201(c) and 103(b).

The UMI databases involved in this appeal present a slightly more difficult issue than does NEXIS. One, NYTO, is distinguishable from NEXIS in that it contains articles from only one publisher; the other, GPO, is distinguishable because it includes some image-based, rather than text-based, files. Nevertheless, we also conclude that the Publishers' licensing of Authors' works to UMI for inclusion in these databases is not within the § 201(c) revision provision.

The NYTO database operates very much like NEXIS; it contains many articles that may be retrieved according to criteria unrelated to the particular edition in which the articles first appeared. Moreover, because the files it contains are provided by Mead pursuant to an agreement between UMI, Mead, and *The New York Times*, no more of the *Times'* original selection and arrangement is evident or retained in NYTO than is retained in NEXIS. In every respect save its being limited to *The New York Times*, then, NYTO is essentially the same as NEXIS. That limitation, however, is not material for present purposes. The relevant inquiry under § 201(c), is, as discussed above, whether the republication or redistribution of the copyrighted piece is as part of a collective work that constitutes a "revision" of the previous collective work, or even a "later collective work in the same series." If the republication is a "new anthology" or a different collective work, it is not within § 201(c) (HRRep No 94-1476, at 122–23 (1976), reprinted in 1976 USCAAN 5659, 5738). Because NYTO is for present purposes at best a new anthology of innumerable editions of the Times, and at worst a new anthology of innumerable articles from these editions, it cannot be said to be a "revision" of any (or all) particular editions or to be a "later collective work in the same series."

For the same reason, GPO is not protected by § 201(c). Although this database contains scanned photo-images of editions of *The New York Times* Sunday book review and magazine, it also contains articles from numerous other periodicals. In this respect, then, it is also substantially similar to NEXIS, and it, too, is at best a new anthology.

We emphasize that the only issue we address is whether, in the absence of a transfer of copyright or any rights thereunder, collective-work authors may re-license individual works in which they own no rights. Because there has by definition been no express transfer of rights in such cases, our decision turns entirely on the default allocation and presumption of rights provided by the Act. Publishers and authors are free to contract around the statutory framework. Indeed, both the Publishers and Mead were aware of the fact that § 201(c) might not protect their licensing agreements, and at least one of the Publishers has already instituted a policy of expressly contracting for electronic re-licensing rights.

b) Whitford

As noted, Whitford entered into an express licensing agreement with *Time*. That agreement granted, in pertinent part, to *Time*:

(a) the exclusive right first to publish the Story in the Magazine;

(b) the non-exclusive right to license the republication of the Story ... provided that the Magazine shall pay to [him] fifty percent [] of all net proceeds it receives for such republication; and

(c) the right to republish the Story or any portions thereof in or in connection with the Magazine or in other publications published by [Time], provided that [he] shall be paid the then prevailing rates of the publication in which the Story is republished.

Time subsequently licensed Whitford's article to Mead without notifying, obtaining authorization from, or compensating, him.

In response to Whitford's infringement action, *Time* contended that its "first publication" rights under clause (a) permitted it to license Whitford's article to Mead. The district court rejected this argument (see *Tasini I*, 972 FSupp at 811–12). Nevertheless, it granted summary judgment in favor of *Time* on this claim. Upon appellants' motion for reconsideration, the district court explained that because Whitford's contract appeared to grant republication rights broad enough to cover *Time*'s agreement with Mead, his remedy under the circumstances was a breach of contract claim against *Time* (see *Tasini II*, 981 FSupp at 845). Such a contract claim would be based on the fact that *Time* had licensed Whitford's piece to Mead without compensating Whitford pursuant to their agreement. Whitford's failure to raise such a claim, in the court's view, undermined his infringement claim (see *Id*). The court also explained that the privilege afforded collective-works authors under § 201(c) operates as a "'presumed' baseline" (see *Id*, 981 FSupp at 846). Because Whitford's agreement failed to limit *Time*'s rights to less than those otherwise afforded under § 201(c), *Time* was presumed to have rights to Whitford's piece to the full extent of § 201(c) (see *Id*). Having already determined that § 201(c) protected

the defendant newspapers' license agreements with Mead, the district court held that *Time*, too, was protected.

However, the fact that a party has licensed certain rights to its copyright to another party does not prohibit the licensor from bringing an infringement action where it believes the license is exceeded or the agreement breached (see *Schoenberg v. Shapolsky Publishers, Inc.*, 971 F2d 926, 932 (2nd Cir 1992) ("If a breach of a condition is alleged, then the district court has subject matter jurisdiction.")). Rather, where an author brings an infringement action against a purported licensee, the license may be raised as a defense (see *Bourne v. Walt Disney Co.*, 68 F3d 621, 631 (2nd Cir 1995)). Where the dispute turns on whether there is a license at all, the burden is on the alleged infringer to prove the existence of the license (see *Id*). Where the dispute is only over the scope of the license, by contrast, "the copyright owner bears the burden of proving that the defendant's copying was unauthorized" (*Id*). In either case, however, an infringement claim may be brought to remedy unauthorized uses of copyrighted material (see *Id*). Whitford did not, therefore, have the burden of pleading a contract claim against *Time*.

With respect to express transfers of rights under § 201(c), that provision provides in pertinent part that "in the absence of an express transfer of the copyright or of any rights under it, the owner of copyright in the collective work is presumed to have acquired only the privilege of reproducing and distributing the contribution [in limited circumstances]" (17 USC § 201(c)). Whitford contends that this provision, by its plain terms, does not apply where there is "an express transfer of copyright or of any rights under it," and that his license agreement with *Time constitutes* just such an express transfer. Therefore, he contends, the court erred in applying the privilege at all.

As noted, the district court rejected this argument, observing that "Section 201(c) does not provide that the specified privileges apply 'only' in the absence of an express transfer of rights," but rather that "in the absence of an express transfer of rights, publishers are presumed to acquire 'only' the delineated privileges" (*Tasini II*, 981 FSupp at 845). The district court went on to hold that "the specified privileges represent a floor—i.e., a minimum level of protection which, if unenhanced by express agreement, publishers are generally presumed to possess. In other words, ... in the absence of an express transfer of 'more,' a publisher is presumed to acquire, at a minimum [], the delineated privileges" (*Id* at 845–46).

Under the district court's reasoning, therefore, unless *Time*'s agreement with Whitford explicitly narrowed its "privilege" under § 201(c), the privilege accorded by that § would continue to exist concurrently with any other rights obtained under the agreement. Given the district court's previously expressed broad view of the § 201(c) privilege, *Time* prevailed, not because the agreement authorized the licensing of Whitford's article to Mead but because the agreement did not forbid it.

The district court is mistaken. As discussed above, § 201(c) creates only a presumption by the parties as to what an author means to convey by giving consent to inclusion of an article in a collective work. Section 201(c) does not permit a collective-work author in

Time's shoes to license to Mead an individually-copyrighted work such as Whitford's article. *Time*'s rights to license the article to Mead must, therefore, be derived from its agreement with Whitford. However, we agree with the district court that paragraph (a) of that agreement does not authorize such a license, and the record is clear that *Time* cannot invoke the conditional license provided in paragraphs (b) and (c). There being no other basis for *Time* to license Whitford's article to Mead, summary judgment should have been granted in favor of Whitford on his claim.

Conclusion

We therefore reverse and remand with instructions to enter judgment for appellants.

KEY TERMS

adapted from

American Society of Composers, Authors, and Performers (ASCAP)

based upon

Broadcast Music, Inc (BMI)

co-author

commission

creative rights

Digital Rights Management (DRM)

ISBN

film rights

labels

literary agent

mass market paperback

mechanical rights

National Music Publishers Association

print publication rights

public performance rights

Society of European Stage Authors and Composers (SESAC)

subsidiary rights

synchronization right

technical book

trade book

trade paperback

vanity press

Writers' Guild of America

EXERCISES

1. Research whether your jurisdiction requires literary agents to be licensed.

2. Explain why auditing rights are important considerations in a publishing contract.

3. Indicate how an artist could guarantee control over his or her work.

4. Obtain form releases that could be used to acquire rights to copyrighted works.

5. Analyze the provisions of the publishing contract appearing as Exhibit 8-1 on page 300.

6. Read *In re Stein and Day, Inc.*, 80 BR 297. What does the court say about royalties to be paid once the author dies? Do you agree with the court's decision?

7. Draft a form publishing agreement using forms you acquire from the library and the Internet.

8. Contact the publisher of the last novel you read to find out how you could acquire rights to use sections of the work in a book of your own.

9. Explain how music publishing differs from literary publishing.

10. Access a publishing Web site to determine what you would have to agree to in order for the site to publish an original work of yours.

EXHIBIT

A sample publishing agreement follows as Exhibit 8-1.

Publishing Agreement

AGREEMENT made this ___day of _____, 2002 between _____ ("Author"), whose mailing address is _____ and Dandelion Books, LLC, an Arizona Limited Liability Company located at 5250 South Hardy Drive, Number 3067, Tempe, Arizona 85283 ("*PUBLISHER*").

Recitals

1. *PUBLISHER* publishes books that it sells and distributes through all available distribution channels including but not limited to the World Wide Web (the "Web"), at the universal resource locator ("URL") http://www.Dandelionbooks.net.

2. *PUBLISHER* is currently engaged in a joint venture to publish original works of selected authors into books for online promotion, sale and distribution, with PMC4, LLC, a Florida Limited Liability Company located at 20500 W. Country Club Dr., Suite 814, Aventura, Florida 33180 ("PMC4"), pursuant to a separate Publishing and Promotion Agreement.

3. AUTHOR is an individual who desires to have his/her original written work published, promoted and sold by *PUBLISHER*, under the auspices of the aforementioned Publishing and Promotion Agreement, pursuant to the terms and conditions set forth herein.

Agreement

For and in consideration of the mutual terms and conditions set forth herein, and other good and valuable consideration, the sufficiency of which is hereby acknowledged, AUTHOR, *PUBLISHER*, and PMC4 agree to the following, concerning the written work by AUTHOR, provisionally entitled _____ ("*WORK*")

1) **Delivery**. AUTHOR agrees to deliver to PUBLISHER within sixty (60) days of the countersigning of this Agreement, the manuscript of his/her *WORK* in its entirety, in a form, length and content acceptable to the *PUBLISHER*, and to help in securing whatever *PUBLISHER* may request to render the WORK ready for printing, together with any other permissions, releases, material and/or illustrations that *PUBLISHER* may request.

2) **Licenses**. In consideration of the payments later specified in Clause 12 below, *AUTHOR* hereby grants to *PUBLISHER* the sole right and exclusive license to produce, publish and license the WORK or any abridgement or substantial part thereof, in all languages, for the legal term of copyright, throughout the world.

3) **AUTHOR Warranties**. *AUTHOR* warrants that the *WORK* is original; that *AUTHOR* owns the copyright to the *WORK* and is free to grant all rights in this Agreement. *AUTHOR* further warrants that the *WORK* contains nothing libelous or obscene; that all statements presented as fact (and not as opinions) are true and verifiable; and, that any recipes, formulas and instructions contained therein cannot mislead or injure the user. *AUTHOR* will

EXHIBIT 8-1 *Sample Publishing Agreement*

indemnify *PUBLISHER* and PMC4 against any legal costs that *PUBLISHER* and/or PMC4 may suffer through any breach of these warranties. If any such loss or claim is being pursued, *PUBLISHER* and/or PMC4, as the case may be, will notify *AUTHOR* thirty (30) days in advance, by email or written notice. However, to forestall and avoid any such losses or claims, *AUTHOR* shall alter the text of the *WORK* as requested by *PUBLISHER's* and/or PMC4's legal advisors to eliminate any breach of the warranties that may occur.

4)   **Responsibility for Loss**. *PUBLISHER* will take reasonable care of any materials supplied by *AUTHOR*, but will not be responsible for any loss or damage while these materials are in transit, in *PUBLISHER's* possession, or during production of the *WORK*.

5)   **Permission to Reprint**. Unless otherwise agreed to in writing, *AUTHOR* shall obtain written permission to reprint any material, including illustrations, to which a third party owns the existing copyright. (Under currently accepted publishing standards of fair use, however, *PUBLISHER* allows the *AUTHOR* to quote up to 250 words of copyrighted prose, without obtaining permission.) Where permissions are required, *AUTHOR* shall obtain them for all English editions of the *WORK* published for the Territory, and agrees to bear all expenses for the fees of such material. For purposes of this Agreement, the Territory shall include North America, the United Kingdom and Europe.

6)   **Galley Proofs**. *PUBLISHER* will send the *AUTHOR* galley proofs of the *WORK* before publication. The *AUTHOR* will correct and return the proofs to the *PUBLISHER* within thirty (30) working days.

7)   **Pre-Sale Duties of Publisher**. Before the *WORK* goes on sale, *PUBLISHER* agrees to provide editing, book design, cover design, proofing after the design is complete, and proofing of the galleys or blue lines. *PUBLISHER* further agrees to perform the following duties, at its own effort and expense: obtain the *WORK's* ISBN number; to register the *WORK* with the Library of Congress; and, to copyright it in the name of _____. If he/she wishes, *AUTHOR* may provide original artwork for the cover and cover design, which shall be subject to *PUBLISHER's* approval.

8)   **Establishing Retail Price**. *PUBLISHER* shall set the retail price of the *WORK*.

9)   **AUTHOR's Copies**. *PUBLISHER* will ship two (2) copies of the *WORK*, free of charge, including shipping costs, to *AUTHOR's* home address and one (1) copy of each Title of the *WORK*, free of charge, including shipping costs, to the office address of *AUTHOR's* agent.

10)   **AUTHOR's Discounts**. Within the first thirty (30) days of publication, *AUTHOR* shall have the one-time right to purchase one hundred (100) copies of each of the Titles included in the *WORK* at a forty percent (40%) discount off list price. Such purchase must be pre-paid and comprise a single transaction shipped to a single address. Thereafter, *AUTHOR* shall have the right to purchase more copies of each of the Titles included in the *WORK* at a discount: for single orders up to twenty (20) of each of the Titles in the *WORK*, a discount of twenty percent (20%) off list price. For single orders of twenty-one (21) to ninety-nine (99) copies, a discount of thirty percent (30%) off list price. For single orders of one hundred (100) or more copies, a discount of thirty-five percent (35%) off list price. *AUTHOR* shall pre-pay in full for any such purchases. Neither *PUBLISHER* nor PMC4 shall pay royalties on any copies of the *WORK* purchased by the *AUTHOR*.

EXHIBIT 8-1 *Sample Publishing Agreement* (*continued*)

11) **Subsidiary Rights**. *AUTHOR* grants to *PUBLISHER* and PMC4 the exclusive right to sell in print, electronic, and all other existing or future mediums, and to exercise all other publishing rights to the *WORK* in the English language in the Territory. Such rights include but are not limited to the following:

   a) the right to publish all or part of the text in a newspaper, magazine or other periodical;
   b) the right to license syndication rights;
   c) the right to re-publish the *WORK* in book club, Trade paperback and mass-market paperback editions;
   d) the right to license audio recordings of the *WORK*;
   e) the right to publish the *WORK* in Braille, large-type, and other formats for the handicapped; and,
   f) the right to any methods of text distribution yet to be invented.

PUBLISHER and/or PMC4 may make the *WORK* available for online viewing in electronic formats to allow individual readers to browse the material. However, *PUBLISHER* and PMC4 shall exercise their best reasonable efforts to avoid the downloading and reproduction of the *WORK* by unauthorized persons. *PUBLISHER* and/or PMC4 shall negotiate the royalties for subsidiary rights not covered by Paragraph 11 with the *AUTHOR* and royalties for Foreign Rights in separate Agreements, not later than thirty (30) days after any such offers or inquires are received by the *PUBLISHER* and/or PMC4.

12) **Royalties**.

   a) Printed Copies. AUTHOR will receive One Dollar and 25/100 ($1.25) per book for every printed version of the *WORK* sold and not returned. Printed copies include, but are not limited to, versions distributed to the purchaser in the form of traditionally printed, print-on-demand and bound editions, and other ink-on-paper editions of the *WORK*.

   b) Electronic Copies. AUTHOR will receive One Dollar and 00/100 ($1.00) per book for every electronic version sold of the *WORK*. Electronic versions of the *WORK* include, but are not limited to: CD-ROMs, DVDs, and other magnetic or optical storage media; multimedia in all forms; electronic databases; online distribution; satellite distribution; ebooks; and, any other device for electronic reproduction, distribution, or transmission. If *PUBLISHER* charges for the service to make the *WORK* available for online viewing in electronic formats, *AUTHOR* will receive a royalty set by the *PUBLISHER* after consultation with PMC4.

   c) Term of Payments. *PUBLISHER* will compute all payments, royalties and others due the *AUTHOR* twice annually (January 1 to June 30 and July 1 to December 31). Within sixty (60) days of the end of each accounting period, PUBLISHER shall provide *AUTHOR's* Agent with a full accounting together with full payment, payable to
   _____.

EXHIBIT 8-1 Sample Publishing Agreement *(continued)*

d) <u>Publisher's Non-Compliance, Termination</u>. In the event *PUBLISHER* fails to compute, and to account, and to pay all royalties and all other payments due to the AUTHOR according to Paragraph 12(c), and *AUTHOR* shall have notified *PUBLISHER* in writing of such failure, and *PUBLISHER* shall not have cured such failure within thirty (30) days after receiving *AUTHOR*'s written notification, *AUTHOR* at his/her option, and notwithstanding all of his/her other rights and remedies at law or otherwise and, in addition hereto, may terminate this Agreement without notice upon giving notification in writing to *PUBLISHER*.

13)   **Copyright**. Barring specific written notice from the *AUTHOR*, the *WORK's* copyright shall remain the property of the *AUTHOR's* designates, named above. The copyright notice appearing in every copy of the *WORK* shall remain in their names.

14)   **Publication Details**. *PUBLISHER* and PMC4 shall make the *WORK* available for distribution after the *WORK* has been edited and *PUBLISHER* deems it ready. *PUBLISHER* and PMC4 shall exercise their best reasonable efforts to affect the availability of the WORK for distribution one hundred and twenty (120) days after it has been edited and prepared for production. Such time shall be extended for delays caused by circumstances beyond the *PUBLISHER's* and/or *PMC4's* control. If either *PUBLISHER* or PMC4 does not make the *WORK* available within such time, *AUTHOR's* sole remedy shall be to give *PUBLISHER* and/or PMC4 a written or e-mail request that *PUBLISHER* and/or PMC4 place the *WORK* on sale within the next thirty (30) days. If either *PUBLISHER* or PMC4 fails to comply, this Agreement shall terminate on the day thereafter, i.e. the 31st day after receiving *AUTHOR's* request, with any and all rights to the *WORK* granted under this Agreement automatically reverting to the *AUTHOR*.

15)   **Publicity**. *AUTHOR* hereby grants to *PUBLISHER* and PMC4 the nonexclusive right to use, publish and distribute in the English language in the Territory whatever materials the *AUTHOR* has submitted to the *PUBLISHER*, including the names, likenesses, and biographical information of the *AUTHOR* and any other persons appearing or mentioned in the *WORK*. Also, *AUTHOR* agrees to assist *PUBLISHER* and PMC4 in the promotion of his/her *WORK*, including but not limited to the dedication of reasonable placement of banner ads, pop-up windows, or other marketing related advertisements promoting the GoOff.com website or other related websites on the *AUTHOR's* own website(s), as determined by *PMC4* in consultation with *PUBLISHER*. *AUTHOR* agrees to notify *PUBLISHER* and PMC4 before posting any parts of the *WORK* on his/her or any other website. *AUTHOR* agrees to establish standards of consistency and quality in publicizing the *WORK* and *PUBLISHER* and PMC4 each reserves the right to edit *AUTHOR's* publicity materials as it sees fit.

16)   **Right of First Refusal**. *PUBLISHER* reserves a first-refusal option to publish all subsequent [list genre(s)] titles by *AUTHOR*, either written solely by the *AUTHOR* or in collaboration with other authors, for a period of five (5) years from the publication date of the *WORK*. Such option shall include the right to license subsidiary rights as defined and enumerated in this Agreement. Barring unforeseen circumstances, *PUBLISHER* agrees to notify *AUTHOR* of acceptance or refusal of any subsequent submission, within six (6) weeks after receiving either a completed draft of the manuscript, or a full book proposal with a full chapter outline that includes: definition of the target readership; analysis of why this new

EXHIBIT 8-1 *Sample Publishing Agreement* (*continued*)

WORK should sell well, even against existing or future competition; and, at least the first two chapters in complete and final form.

17) **Miscellaneous**.

a) Amendment and Integration Clause. This Agreement represents the entire agreement of the parties with respect to the subject matter hereof and, except for the aforementioned Publishing and Promotion Agreement, all agreements entered into prior hereto are revoked and superseded by this Agreement, and no representations, warranties, inducements or oral agreements have been made by any of the parties except as expressly set forth herein or in other contemporaneous written agreements. This Agreement may not be changed, modified or rescinded except in writing signed by all parties hereto, and any attempt at oral modification of this Agreement shall be void and of no effect.

b) Notices. Any notice, election or communication to be given to any party under the terms of this Agreement shall be in writing and delivered in person or deposited, certified or registered, in the United States mail, postage prepaid, addressed as set forth below or to such address as either party may hereafter designate by written notice hereunder. Such notices shall be effective on the earlier of (i) the date when received by such party if delivered via hand delivery or via facsimile transmission if received prior to 5:00 p.m., Mountain Standard Time ("MST"); or, (ii) the next day if delivered via facsimile transmission and received after 5:00 p.m. MST; or, (iii) 48 hours after the date if sent by registered or certified mail, return receipt requested, postage and fees prepaid and addressed as follows:

If to AUTHOR: (ADDRESS)

   with a copy to:

If to PUBLISHER: Carol Adler, President
                    Dandelion Books, LLC
                    5250 South Hardy Drive, #3067
                    Tempe, Arizona 85283

   with a copy to:

If to PMC4:   Rico Sogocio, General Counsel
               PMC4, LLC
               20500 W. Country Club Dr., Suite 814
               Aventura, Florida 33180

c) Severability. In case any one or more of the provisions contained in this Agreement shall for any reason be held to be invalid, illegal or unenforceable in any respect, such invalidity, illegality or unenforceability shall not affect any other provisions hereof and this Agreement shall be construed as if such invalid, illegal or unenforceable provision had never been contained herein.

EXHIBIT 8-1 Sample Publishing Agreement (*continued*)

d) <u>Additional Acts and Documents</u>. Each party agrees to do all such things, take all such actions and to make, execute and deliver such other documents and instruments, as shall be reasonably requested to carry out the provisions, intent and purposes of this Agreement.

e) <u>Assignments</u>. *PUBLISHER* may assign this Agreement to any entity, the majority (more than 50%) of which is owned by Carol Adler or a trust for her benefit. Likewise, this Agreement may be assigned by PMC4 to any entity to which PMC4 is the majority shareholder.

f) <u>Counterparts</u>. This Agreement may be executed in any number of counterparts; all such counterparts (or a facsimile thereof) shall be deemed to constitute one and the same instrument; and, each of said counterparts shall be deemed an original hereof.

g) <u>Time</u>. Time is of the essence for purposes of this Agreement and each and every provision hereof. Any extension of time granted for the performance of any duty under this Agreement shall not be considered an extension of time for the performance of any other duty under this Agreement.

h) <u>Time Periods</u>. In the event the time for performance of any obligation hereunder, or any time period hereunder, expires on a Saturday, Sunday or legal holiday, the time for performance shall be extended to the next day that is not a Saturday, Sunday or legal holiday. In computing any period of time provided for in this Agreement, or provided for by any applicable statute, the day of the act, event or default from which the designated period begins to run shall not be included. The last day of the period of time shall be included, unless it is a Saturday, Sunday or a legal holiday, in which event the time period runs until the end of the next day which is not a Saturday, Sunday or a legal holiday.

i) <u>Captions</u>. Captions and paragraph headings used herein are for convenience only and are not a part of this Agreement and shall not be deemed to limit or alter any provision hereof and shall not have any legally binding effect in the meaning, construction or interpretation of this Agreement.

j) <u>Governing Law</u>. This Agreement shall be deemed to be made under, and shall be construed in accordance with and governed by, the laws of the State of Arizona, and suit to enforce any provision of this Agreement or to obtain any remedy with respect hereto shall be brought in Superior Court, Maricopa County, Arizona, and for this purpose each party hereby expressly and irrevocably consent to the jurisdiction of said court.

k) <u>Interpretation</u>. To the extent permitted by the context in which used, (a) words in the singular number shall include the plural, words in the masculine gender shall include the feminine and neuter, and vice versa, and (b) references to "persons" or "parties" in this Agreement shall be deemed to refer to natural persons, corporations, general partnerships, limited partnerships, trusts and all other entities.

EXHIBIT 8-1 *Sample Publishing Agreement* (*continued*)

l) <u>Indemnity</u>. Each party to this Agreement agrees to indemnify each other party and hold it harmless, from and against all claims, damages, costs and expenses (including reasonable attorneys' fees) attributable, directly or indirectly, to the breach by such indemnifying party of any obligation hereunder or the inaccuracy of any representation or warranty made by such indemnifying party herein or in any instrument delivered pursuant hereto or in connection with the transactions contemplated hereby. In the event either party hereto receives notice of a claim against which it is entitled to indemnification pursuant to this section, such party shall promptly give notice thereof to the other party to this Agreement. The party obligated to indemnify shall immediately take such measures as may be reasonably required to properly and effectively defend such claim, and may defend with counsel of its own choosing approved by the other party (which approval shall not be unreasonably withheld or delayed); provided, however, if the party being indemnified determines that counsel chosen by the indemnifying party has a conflict of interest, then the indemnified party shall be entitled to select and appoint such defense counsel, at the sole cost and expense of the indemnifying party. In the event the party obligated to indemnify fails to properly and effectively defend such claim, then the party entitled to indemnification may defend such claim with counsel of its own choosing at the expense of the party obligated to indemnify.

m) <u>Expenses</u>. Except as expressly provided herein, each party to this Agreement shall pay his or its own costs and expenses related to the transaction contemplated, including, but not limited to, all attorneys' fees.

n) <u>Waiver of Conditions</u>. Any of the parties hereto may in writing waive any provision of this Agreement intended for its benefit; provided, however, such waiver shall in no way excuse the other parties from the performance of any of its other obligations under this Agreement unless otherwise provided herein or in such written waiver. Failure of any party to exercise any right or option arising out of a breach of this Agreement shall not be deemed a waiver of any right or option with respect to any subsequent or different breach of the same or any other covenant or condition of this Agreement.

o) <u>Construction</u>. The parties agree that each party and its counsel have reviewed and revised this Agreement and that any rule of construction to the effect that ambiguities are to be resolved against the drafting party shall not apply to the interpretation of this Agreement or any amendments or exhibits hereto.

p) <u>Binding</u>. This Agreement shall be binding on the heirs, executors, administrators and assigns or successors in business of the respective parties.

IN WITNESS WHEREOF, the Parties have caused their duly authorized representatives to execute this Agreement on the date indicated below:

EXHIBIT 8-1 Sample Publishing Agreement (*continued*)

AUTHOR:

By:　　　　　　＿＿＿＿＿＿＿＿＿＿＿＿＿＿＿＿

Printed Name:　＿＿＿＿＿＿＿＿＿＿＿＿＿＿＿＿

Date:　　　　　＿＿＿＿＿＿＿＿＿＿＿＿

DANDELION BOOKS, LLC:

By:　　　　　　＿＿＿＿＿＿＿＿＿＿＿＿＿＿＿＿

Printed Name:　＿＿＿＿＿＿＿＿＿＿＿＿＿＿＿＿

Date:　　　　　＿＿＿＿＿＿＿＿＿＿＿＿

PMC4, LLC:

By:　　　　　　＿＿＿＿＿＿＿＿＿＿＿＿＿＿＿＿

Printed Name:　＿＿＿＿＿＿＿＿＿＿＿＿＿＿＿＿

Date:　　　　　＿＿＿＿＿＿＿＿＿＿＿＿

EXHIBIT 8-1 Sample Publishing Agreement (*continued*)

CHAPTER

9

SPORTS LAW

CHAPTER OVERVIEW

For many people, the areas of sports and entertainment do not automatically coexist. However, under a broad concept of entertainment in which *entertainment* is defined as any pastime activity, sports would be included and well represented. Furthermore, in terms of the legal implications of a sports activity, sports law can be viewed as a subset of general entertainment law.

As indicated in previous chapters, most of entertainment law is merely specific combinations of contract, tort, and business law designed for the problems associated with a given activity and is a subset of the general legal field. In this context, sports law is no different than any of the other subsets already discussed in this text. Sports law is, therefore, nothing more than the law of contracts, torts, and employment as they apply to the athletic arena.

This chapter will focus on the two broad categories of activities that exist under the heading of sports: professional and amateur athletics. Professional sports are a business, no different than any other entrepreneurial activity, with certain aspects designed for the problems affecting both participants and spectators. Amateur sports, while also a business in many instances, involve unique situations for which the law has seen fit to prescribe certain regulations to protect the participants. Each of these aspects will be individually reviewed.

In addition to the distinctions between professional and amateur athletic activities, two areas of law overlap. Antitrust law, which is designed to foster competition and hinder monopolies, directly impacts the way that both professional and amateur sports are regulated. Endorsements, a particular kind of contract in which a person lends his or her name and reputation to a product, also affect the players in both professional and amateur sports. Each of these legal concepts will be examined in turn.

It should always be borne in mind, however, that sports law is nothing more than a legal interpretation of general American law as it applies to athletics.

PROFESSIONAL SPORTS

professional sports
Athletic endeavors in which participants receive compensation.

Professional sports can be defined as any athletic endeavor in which the player participants are expected to receive compensation for their performances. All athletic activities in which this is a primary goal of the participant fall under this category, regardless of the exact nature of the sport involved.

It should be noted that there are several types of endeavors that may be viewed as falling between sports and artistry, such as figure skating and bodybuilding, but these distinctions, although important on an entertainment level for the viewer, are basically irrelevant with respect to the law that regulates these activities. The distinction is only important in the specific terminology associated with the particular endeavor involved, not in the basic law.

To understand the legal concepts involved in professional sports, the topic must be divided into three areas: the law covering the contracts with the participants, the effect of general law on these activities, and the potential tort liability for the spectators who attend these athletic events.

The Participants

There are two broad categories of persons who are typically included in professional athletic endeavors: the athletes and the agents. The legal rights and obligations of these persons are generally defined and determined by the terms of the contracts that they enter into with each other and the owners of the teams that engage their services. The general law of contracts has already been discussed in chapter 3. This chapter will focus on the specific provisions and clauses that directly relate to sports contracts.

The Athletes

The contracts that athletes enter into are primarily employment contracts in which the athletes agree, for a specified consideration, to provide their athletic skills for the benefit of the respective teams that have engaged them. In this context it is generally no different than an agreement to employ a writer or an opera singer. However, because the pool of potential employers for athletes is considerably smaller than for many other activities, many courts have viewed these contracts as having the potential of being a contract of adhesion. A **contract of adhesion** is a legal agreement in which one contracting party has an unfair bargaining position with respect to the other party to the agreement. In other words, under certain circumstances, it may be viewed as though the party with the stronger bargaining position can force the other side to adhere to the agreement because that party lacks the ability to negotiate.

contract of adhesion
Agreement in which one side has an unfair bargaining position.

— ***Example*** —————————————————————

A young woman has always dreamed of being a professional hockey player. However, there is only one professional women's hockey league and it only has a limited number of teams. If one of those teams offers her a position at what she considers to be a very low salary, she has little choice but to accept if she wants to play hockey professionally. It may be viewed as a contract of adhesion because there is almost no other choice for the woman but to accept this team's offer; there is no competition.

The greater the athlete's clout, or bargaining power, the less likely it is that the agreement will be viewed as an unfair employment contract.

— ***Example*** —————————————————————

A basketball player was the captain and lead scorer of his college team and was captain of the United States Olympic team that won a gold medal. He has received a tremendous amount of notoriety based on his athletic performance. Under these circumstances, the athlete may possess sufficient clout to bargain for a favorable contract with a professional basketball team.

As with all employment contracts for personal services, the athlete cannot be forced to perform against his or her will, and performance may be curtailed because of injuries the athlete suffers. Because sports are based on an athlete's physical performance, the contract may call for periodic physical examinations for the athlete. The team's obligation to continue to compensate an injured athlete will be determined by the terms of the agreement.

— ***Example*** —————————————————————

A football player's contract contains a clause that the contract will be terminated and the obligation of the team to continue payment to the athlete will end if the athlete becomes so injured that he can no longer participate in the sport. During a pre-season game, a linebacker's leg is broken in several places, and the team doctor determines that he will no longer be able to participate fully as a team player. The obligation of the team is now one that may have to be determined by a court or by workers' compensation.

The following is a list of certain clauses that are peculiar to the sports industry:

League Rights In many professional sports the individual teams are regulated by a league headed by a commissioner. Many sports contracts require that a copy of the contract be filed with the league within so many days of its signing and typically provide that the player may be fined by the league for any violation of the league rules. This imposes a contractual burden on the player for infractions of league rules and regulations. By including this clause, these rules and regulations are **incorporated by reference** into the contract and thereby become a part of the total agreement.

incorporation by reference
Making a separate agreement part of a contract by mentioning it.

— Example

A league regulation states that it is an infraction for a player to be seen intoxicated in public. After a particularly difficult win, a player celebrates with his friends at a local tavern, and gets into a fight with another patron. This drunken brawl is reported in the media. Under the provisions of the contract, the player may be fined by his league.

option
Ability to exercise a contract right.

Options An **option** is a contractual clause that gives one party to the contract the right to renew the contract at a specified term if he or she so decides. In many sports contracts, the agreement has a clause in which the team has the option to renew the contract for a year, or a term of years, at a set amount of consideration. Although this clause may seem favorable for a rookie because it indicates the possibility of a continuing employment relationship, the amount of the compensation may seem insignificant several years later when his or her performance has been so outstanding that the athlete could demand a much higher salary. Also, there is no guarantee that the option will be exercised, so the athlete may be unemployed at the end of the initial agreement.

— Example

A baseball scout finds a young man who he thinks has potential as a pitcher. The pitcher signs a two-year contract with the scout's team for an initial salary of $45,000 per year, with an option to renew the contract for an additional year at a salary of $55,000. The young man starts playing and is a genuine find, pitching three no-hitters in each of his first two years and having the highest strike-out record in the league. At the end of the two years the team wants to exercise the option, but the pitcher thinks he should be able to make more than $55,000 per year.

reserve clause
Agreement providing for a perpetual option; now obsolete.

It should be noted that historically baseball contracts included a **reserve clause** that provided the team with a perpetual option, meaning that if the player did not agree to the renewal she either had to leave the sport or get traded to another team. These reserve clauses were abolished in 1975.

No-Cut Clause A no-cut clause means that an athlete cannot be removed from the team during the period of the contract. However, because sports are totally dependent upon physical ability and health, such clauses are not always included in athletes' contracts. Generally, there are three types of no-cut clauses used in standard athletic contracts:

1. *No cut based on lack of skill.* Because skill is a subjective standard, this type of clause only allows the player to be cut because of a physical or mental defect that renders him or her unable to participate in the sport and is not based on the players presumed "skill."

2. *The National Football League provision.* This no-cut clause states that the player will not be cut provided that he maintains superior physical condition. The question then becomes What would constitute a "superior physical condition"?

3. *The "Hudson Model".* This no-cut clause resulted from a federal court decision (*Minnesota Huskies v. Hudson*) in which the team agreed to continue to pay a player even though the player could no longer participate in the sport.

Realize that even if an athlete cannot be cut, a spot on the team is not automatically guaranteed if he or she does not have the physical ability to continue to play.

Collective Bargaining Most professional sports are influenced and regulated by general labor law doctrines, including the concept of collective bargaining. This means the player's contract may be modified by any collective bargaining agreement entered into by the team or the league with any players' association involved in the sport.

Termination As previously stated, sports are dependent on a high degree of physical ability; therefore, sports contracts typically include termination provisions that provide for the cancellation of a contract if an athlete is no longer in shape, becomes too impaired to continue to participate in the sport, or for the general termination grounds discussed in chapter 3. Note that the athlete's compensation may be protected, however, if the athlete's contract contains one of the no-cut provisions previously discussed.

Assignments As discussed in chapter 3, an assignment is a transfer of contractual rights. In relation to sports law and players' contracts, this is interpreted as the right of a team to **trade** a player to a different team. Most players' contracts contain such clauses granting the team the ability to trade the player at will unless the player has been able to insert a no-transfer clause.

trade
Transferring a player to another team.

— Example

A baseball player signs a contract with a New York team because he is from the Northeast and wants to stay in that area. The contract contains an assignment clause. Three months after starting with the team the player is traded to a team on the West Coast. The player is upset, but has no choice in the matter.

Remedies Because a player's contract is one for personal services, there are certain types of remedies that the court will not permit. For example, a team cannot seek specific performance for a breach directing the player to perform according to the agreement because that would resemble involuntary servitude. However, the court will permit the team to acquire an injunction to prevent the player from playing for another team during the period of the contract. Of course, if the injury caused by the breach of contract can be remedied by a monetary award, the court will permit the injured party to seek damages.

— Example

A football player is dissatisfied with his team manager and refuses to play for the team. He signs with a different team in contravention of his contract. The first team seeks to enjoin him from playing for its competitor, which the court will probably allow because, as a professional athlete, his abilities are considered to be unique. However, the player cannot be forced to play for the original team. Also, because the team may have to hire a replacement player who may cost more money, the team may be able to seek damages from the player to compensate for its increased costs.

The specifics of any given player's contract are governed by two factors: (1) the player's ability, which gives him or her the necessary clout to bargain and (2) the negotiating skills of the athlete or the athlete's agent. Further, because many athletic endeavors have been unionized, the collective bargaining process has provided athletes with more favorable contracts than had previously been available to them, thus compensating for the limited number of professional athletic teams and the large numbers of would-be players, which factors give the teams the greater bargaining power.

The Agent

In order to negotiate more favorable contracts, many athletes employ the services of an agent. An agent is a fiduciary hired to represent the athlete in entering into contracts on the athlete's behalf. Many states require any person who holds out to be a sports (or theatrical) agent to be registered with the state. Generally, there are two types of regulatory statutes dealing with athletic agents:

1. *The Florida rule*. The states that follow this rule require all agents who represent athletes within the state to register with the state. Criminal penalties, which qualify as a felony, are imposed for violations of this registration law.

2. *The California rule*. This type of state statute mandates that any agent who represents an athlete must register with the state and post a bond to ensure the faithful performance of his or her duties. These statutes generally exempt licensed attorneys and persons who do not directly negotiate contracts. Violation of these statutes is considered to be a misdemeanor.

The specifics of each state's law with respect to the registration of agents must be analyzed prior to negotiating any contract on behalf of an athlete. Also, a new uniform law has been proposed, the Uniform Athletic Agents Act, to provide consistency among the jurisdictions.

Many of the sports players' associations, in order to protect their members, also require agents who wish to represent union members to be registered with the union as well as with the state. All of the major sports unions now include some form of agent registration.

Some of the unions, such as the National Football League Players Association, require participating agents to pay a fee to the union and to provide background information regarding their education, employment, and any criminal history. Once registered, the agent agrees to abide by all union rules and percentage compensation guidelines established by the union. If the agent violates any of these policies, the agent may be fined or have his or her registration revoked.

All of the registration regulations have been enacted to provide athletes with protection from unscrupulous persons.

The primary obligation of a sports agent is to exercise due care in negotiating contracts on behalf of the athlete and in managing the athlete's money. The agent is required to use his or her best abilities in negotiating the contract and to act in good faith on behalf of the athlete client. The agent will not be held liable simply because he or she failed to obtain the "best" contract, provided that the agent has met these fiduciary standards.

— *Example* —

A registered agent signs an agreement with an athlete to negotiate a contract for her with a professional team. Using his best skills, the agent negotiates a contract with a salary of $300,000 a year. After the contract is signed, an official for the team says the team would have gone as high as $325,000 a year. The agent is not liable to the athlete for this $25,000-a-year difference because he exercised his best skills on her behalf in good faith.

An agent usually does not receive a set salary for his or her services, but he or she is entitled to a contractually agreed-upon commission, a percentage of the consideration of the contract the agent has negotiated. In addition to contract negotiation, an agent may also provide other services to the athlete, including but not limited to the following, depending on the agent's career field:

1. Financial and estate planning
2. Endorsement contracts
3. Career development
4. Training
5. Legal counseling
6. Tax planning and preparation
7. General business and investment advice.

conflict of interest
Representing opposing interests.

As a fiduciary, a person held to be in a position of trust, the agent must avoid any **conflict of interest,** meaning that he or she is precluded from representing players whose interests may be in opposition to each other. The same person may not represent both the team and the athlete in negotiating the same contract. An agent is expected to disclose any actual or potential conflict of interest to the prospective athlete client, who may then decide to seek the services of a different agent. If the agent believes that a conflict may exist, the agent should document such potential conflict in a letter to the client.

— *Example*

An agent represents a major league first baseman, and has done so for several years. A young athlete who also plays first base wants the agent to represent him. Because there may be a conflict of interest in representing two first basemen, even though at the current time they play for different teams, this potential conflict must be disclosed. If either or both of the athletes sees a potential conflict, the agent is precluded from representing both. However, if the disclosure is made and the athletes do not mind, and if the agent believes no actual conflict will arise, he may then represent both players because he has made a full disclosure and such representation is agreed to by both athletes.

The agent plays a crucial part in the financial well-being of the professional athlete. A sophisticated agent can protect an athlete from adverse financial consequences of injuries or trades and may help develop an overall financial plan for the athlete to provide income to the player after his or her athletic career is over.

Labor Law

Historically, the professional athletic organization was exempt from the provisions of the early labor relation statutes. However, over the years and by means of judicial interpretations, the athletes and other employees involved in professional sports have been deemed to be covered by the provisions of the National Labor Relations Act.

The **National Labor Relations Act (NLRA)**, 29 USC § 151–166, also known as the **Wagner Act**, was enacted in 1935 and forms the basis of modern American labor relations law. There are three main provisions of this statute:

1. It created the **National Labor Relations Board (NLRB)** to administer its provisions
2. It defined unfair labor activities
3. It established collective bargaining standards.

The NLRB is an administrative agency that hears disputes in a manner similar to a judicial trial presided over by an **administrative law judge (ALJ)**. The ALJ renders decisions based on disputes arising under the NLRA, and the Board has jurisdiction over all businesses that do at least $50,000 a year in interstate commerce. Because most professional sports are played or viewed by means of television in more than one state, and the earnings generally exceed $50,000 for such multi-jurisdictional activities, they are usually deemed to come within the purview of the NLRA.

According to the provisions of the NLRA, the parties to a dispute may only seek judicial relief after all of the remedies provided by the Wagner Act have been exhausted.

Disputes arising under the provisions of the NLRA commence when a party, referred to as the **charging party**, claims that he or she has been subject to an unfair labor practice. The NLRA defines an **unfair labor practice** as being any one of the following:

On the part of the employer:

1. To interfere with, restrain, or coerce employees in the exercise of their right to unionize
2. To dominate or interfere with the formation or administration of any labor organization, or contribute financial or other support to a labor organization
3. To discriminate with regard to hiring or firing, or any other form of activity used to encourage or discourage union membership
4. To discharge or discriminate against any employee who has filed a complaint under the NLRA
5. To refuse collective bargaining.

—— *Example* ——

A group of professional wrestlers feel that they are being treated unfairly by the management and decide to form a union to better their bargaining position. Management tells them that if they attempt to form a union, they will be barred from the sport. This act on the part of the wrestling management would constitute an unfair labor practice.

National Labor Relations Act (NLRA)
Federal statute governing labor organizations.

National Labor Relations Board (NLRB)
Agency that administers the NLRA.

administrative law judge
Person who presides at administrative hearings.

charging party
Person who files a dispute under the NLRA.

unfair labor practice
Certain activities deemed illegal under the NLRA.

On the part of the union:

1. To restrain or coerce employees in their right to organize
2. To restrain or coerce employees in the selection of a representative
3. To encourage an employer to discharge an employee, except for the employee's failure to tender his or her union dues
4. To refuse to bargain in good faith
5. To engage in strikes, **boycotts**, and other specified activities used to compel an employee to join a labor organization
6. To charge its members excessive dues or fees
7. Featherbedding, or payment for work that is not actually performed.

boycott
Unfair labor practice.

— *Example*

A famous, world-class basketball player has just been signed by a professional basketball team. A representative from the players' union approaches the athlete asking him to join the union, but he refuses. The union representative feels that if all the players do not belong to the union, the less well-known players will be severely injured. She approaches the team's owner demanding that the team refuse to hire the athlete or she will call for a boycott of the team. This type of attempted coercion would constitute an unfair labor practice, as defined in the NLRA.

collective bargaining
Labor law concept requiring good faith negotiation of employment contracts.

Arguably, the provision of the NLRA that has the most far-reaching impact is the provision concerning collective bargaining. The concept of **collective bargaining** requires that an employer and a union negotiate the terms of employment with one another, and the failure to do so is considered an unfair labor practice.

Negotiation alone is insufficient under the Act; the parties must bargain with each other in good faith, which is defined by the NLRA as negotiating with an open mind and with the sincere purpose of reaching an agreement. To determine this element, the NLRB will look at the entire negotiation process, and not just an isolated incident.

The requirement of bargaining in good faith arises in three situations:

1. When a union is first organized
2. When a representative is certified to the NLRB
3. When a union contract is being negotiated or renegotiated.

To settle a collective bargaining dispute, the NLRB must first determine the appropriate bargaining unit, in other words, the actual employer. For professional sports, the NLRB usually views the sport as a whole, such as the National Hockey League, to be the bargaining unit, not just a particular team. However, the NLRB is not limited to this application and, where appropriate, may consider an individual team or group of teams to be the correct bargaining unit.

— *Example* ————————————————

In an American League baseball dispute, the NLRB may decide to exercise its jurisdiction only on the teams situated in the United States and eliminate the Canadian team from its deliberation, even though it forms a part of the entire league and employment relationship. This decision as to the appropriate bargaining unit is left up to the Board or the court if judicial review is sought.

Pursuant to the NLRA, the categories of issues that are subject to collective bargaining are

1. Wages, hours, and conditions of employment
2. Notice regarding the sale of the business
3. Items that must be included in the final collective bargaining agreement, such as the certification of the union.

If either side refuses to bargain on any one of these issues, it is considered an unfair labor practice.

— *Example* ————————————————

The union representative for the womens' ice hockey league refuses to negotiate regarding percentage of bonuses and pension plans, which he states is "non-negotiable." This is considered to be an unfair labor practice.

The objective of the collective bargaining provision is the creation of a **collective bargaining agreement**, which is the contract between the employer and the union. This agreement is similar to all other employment contracts previously discussed, but it includes certain provisions particular to labor organizations. These provisions are

collective bargaining agreement
Contract resulting from the collective bargaining process.

successor in interest
Person who takes over a contract right and obligation.

union shop
Business in which all employees must belong to the union.

strike
Employees' refusal to work.

lockout
Employer refusing to let union workers into the workplace.

1. Recognition of the union
2. The obligation of all successors in interest to adhere to the provisions of the agreement (a **successor in interest** is anyone who takes over from the employer or the union)
3. The requirement that all employees must be union members, which is referred to as a **union shop**
4. Grievance procedures, which determine the precise procedures to be followed should there be a breach of the agreement
5. A provision forbidding strikes or lockouts.

A **strike** is an employee's refusal to work. In recent years, many sports fans have been subject to disappointment when a players' union has called a strike against the owners of a particular sport. A **lockout** arises when an employer refuses to let the union members enter the workplace. This rarely happens in the sports industry with respect to athletes, whereas it may occur for nonathletic union workers, such as groundskeepers or other workers who belong to a union.

In order to minimize the negative aspect of a breakdown in the collective bargaining process, most collective bargaining agreements provide for arbitration and/or mediation procedures. An **arbitrator** is a neutral third person who performs a function similar to that of a judge. The parties agree to submit a dispute to the arbitrator who hears evidence submitted by both sides and eventually renders a decision that will be enforced by a court of law.

Conversely, a **mediator** is a neutral third person who does not decide the matter for the parties but who attempts to work with the parties to assist them in reaching their own resolution of the problem.

The ability of professional athletes to form and join unions provides *all* professional players, not just the most famous ones, a degree of clout with respect to negotiating an employment contract greater than each might have individually. Also, regardless of the individual terms of a particular player's contract, if the sport is unionized, that contract is also subject to the provisions of the collective bargaining agreement.

arbitrator
An individual who oversees a nonjudicial method of resolving disputes.

mediator
A third person who helps parties with a dispute reach a mutual resolution.

Tort Liability

A tort can be defined simply as a civil wrong, any wrong that cannot be compensated by reference to a specific area of law such as contracts or property. In the professional sports industry, the potential liability for injuries resulting from athletic activities can have a far-reaching impact. Generally, the kinds of torts that are associated with athletic endeavors fall into the following categories:

1. Injuries to the participants
2. Injuries to the spectators
3. Injuries resulting from defective equipment
4. Defamation.

Each of these potential types of injuries will be discussed in turn.

Injuries to the Participants

In this instance, the participant is considered to be the athlete participating in the sport. Because this person has voluntarily and knowingly consented to participate in the athletic activity, general injuries that result from the playing of the sport will not render the person who caused the injury liable to the athlete. However, this general statement of non-liability is not true under the following circumstances:

1. *Violation of a safety rule.* By definition, safety rules are enacted in order to prevent certain injuries from resulting from specified conduct. If the athlete fails to follow these rules and is injured, the resultant injury will not engender liability for anyone else. The athlete, by failing to follow these rules, may be considered to have caused his or her own injury.

— *Example* —

Safety rules require all baseball players to wear a hard hat with ear protectors when they are at bat. If a player refuses to wear such protection and is hit in the head by a fastball, the injury is caused by his or her own actions and no one else will be deemed to be legally responsible.

However, if the injury results from the injurer, not the victim, failing to follow safety regulations, the injurer may be held responsible.

— *Example* —

For safety reasons, promoters of triathlons must provide boats to protect the athletes during the swimming portion of the event if the swim takes place in open water. To save money, a promoter neglects to have boats available and a swimmer cramps and drowns during the swim. The promoter may be held liable if it can be shown that the athlete would have been saved if a boat had been available as required.

The athlete who is injured by another person's failure to follow safety precautions may sue either the person directly or, if the person was employed to provide such services by someone such as the owner of the team, the athlete can sue the employer under a doctrine of liability called **respondeat superior**. This doctrine holds an employer legally responsible for the negligent act of his or her employee that injures a third person, if such negligent act was committed while furthering the employer's interests. Note, however, that an employer will not be responsible if one of its employees negligently injures another of its employees (players on the same team), or if the act was not caused by negligence but was intentionally committed.

respondeat superior
Holding an employer liable for the tortious acts of his employee.

2. *Unsportsmanlike conduct.* If an athlete engages in unsportsmanlike conduct that results in an injury to another player, he or she will be liable for any injuries resulting from such action. This would be an example of a voluntary act causing the injury.

— *Example* —

During an ice hockey game, a player on one team intentionally skates over the hand of a player from the opposing team when that player has fallen on the ice. This act causes the fallen player to lose three fingers. The athlete who engaged in this unsportsmanlike conduct may be held legally responsible for the injuries.

assumption of the risk
Person voluntarily engaging in hazardous acts is assumed to know of the hazard involved.

3. *Contact sports.* In any sport that involves physical contact between the athletes, the possibility that an injury might occur is assumed, and an athlete cannot recover for such assumed potential injury. Under the law, the athlete is considered to have taken **assumption of the risk** of such

injuries. However, if any injury results from an act that is not reasonably foreseeable, the injured athlete may recover from the perpetrator.

— Example

Professional boxers assume the risk of certain injuries when they enter the ring. However, one of these foreseeable injuries does not include having an opponent bite off the ear of the other participant during the match. If this occurs, the injured pugilist would have a cause of action because the risk of that type of injury was not assumed.

Always associated with, but rarely thought of as a participant, is the referee who is hired to maintain order at athletic events. The referee may be held liable if he or she fails in one of the following duties:

1. Enforcing the prescribed rules of the sport
2. Protecting the participants form unsportsmanlike conduct
3. Warning the athletes of potential danger
4. Anticipating and nullifying potential dangers.

In several jurisdictions, by statute or judicial interpretation, referees can be held legally liable for injuries resulting from a breach of these duties if such breach is considered to be grossly negligent. Simple negligence, failing to fulfill a legal duty, will not suffice to render the referee liable in these jurisdictions. Each state's approach to this matter must be individually scrutinized.

Injuries to the Spectators

Historically, spectators at sporting events were deemed to have assumed the risk of injury from the sport that they had gone to observe. Under the present law, the athlete and the promoters are under no legal duty to protect patrons from such injuries.

— Example

A woman goes to a baseball game and is hit in the head when a foul ball flies into the stands. The woman cannot recover for this injury because she assumed the risk of such occurrence when she decided to attend the game.

However, the owner of the sports facility will be liable for injuries to spectators that result from its failure to provide an adequately safe facility or to maintain the facility in good repair.

— Example

The owner of a racetrack fails to make sure that the stands are adequately cleaned. One day a spectator slips on the steps to her seat because food wrappers were not removed and the stairs were over-waxed. Because the owner of the racetrack has not properly maintained the facility, the owner may be legally responsible for the patron's injuries.

Injuries Resulting from Defective Equipment

product liability
Area of tort law concerned with defectively manufactured goods.

absolute (strict) liability
Being held legally responsible for injuries regardless of degree of care.

Under general tort law, this type of injury is referred to as **product liability**—the manufacturer or retailer of a defective good is held liable for any injuries resulting form the use of that defective product. This liability is **absolute (strict) liability**, meaning that the manufacturer/seller will be held responsible regardless of how careful it was in making the product, provided that the injured party used the product in the prescribed manner. Misuse of the product in question may preclude recovery.

In the case of sports law, this type of liability may attach to any of the equipment used by the players that causes injury to the player or a spectator because of its defect. The injured party may sue both the retailer and the manufacturer, and the court will allocate their respective liability.

— *Example*

A football player uses a helmet manufactured by Acme Sporting Goods that was sold directly to his team. During the game the protective face guard detaches and the player is injured. Under normal use as a football helmet, the face guard is not supposed to detach. The player may have a cause of action against Acme based on product liability.

Example

During a polo match, the head of a mallet becomes loose and flies into the stands, injuring a spectator. The mallet is brand new and such detachment is not considered usual. The spectator may be able to maintain a cause of action against the manufacturer/seller of the mallet based on product liability.

Defamation

Because professional athletes may be considered public figures whose reputation is important to their professional standing, they may be subject to being defamed. Defamation is also considered to be a form of tort, and has been previously discussed in chapter 1.

AMATEUR SPORTS

amateur sports
Sports in which the participants do not receive compensation.

Although the athletic endeavors are the same, there is a major difference between professional and **amateur sports**. Professional athletes are expected to receive compensation for their athletic ability, whereas the amateur athlete is expected to perform exclusively for the joy of the sport with no remuneration. However, as amateur sports rules have relaxed their definition of *amateur*, these athletes are permitted to receive certain forms of compensation, such as athletic scholarships, sponsorships, or endorsements. However, any money made from sponsorships or endorsements must be placed into a trust account until the athlete relinquishes his or her amateur status.

Amateur sports are divided into two broad groups: **restricted competitions** that occur at the high school and college level that require the athlete to be an enrolled student to participate and **unrestricted competitions**, which are open to athletes who maintain an amateur status. To determine whether or not an athlete is considered to be an amateur or a professional, the athlete must look to the rules of the organization governing the particular sport.

The organizations that govern amateur sports are considered to be voluntary associations of members, and as such, their published rules and regulations are considered to be controlling over their members; courts rarely overturn decisions of the organization that are based on these rules. This approach applies to restricted as well as unrestricted competitions, except that if the school is state supported, its rules must meet certain federal and state laws with respect to eligibility and enforcement.

The threshold question for any athlete who wishes to participate in an amateur sport is whether or not he or she is deemed eligible pursuant to the appropriate governing rules. For unrestricted competitions, the published rules generally will prevail. However, for restricted competitions, in which some form of state action is involved, a primary concern of the court is the determination of whether participation is a right or a privilege.

If participation is deemed to be a right, the state cannot restrict such right in any way that violates the provisions of the United States (or State) Constitution. This means that the athlete must be afforded **equal protection** with respect to participation; specific categories of persons may not be arbitrarily excluded unless a legitimate reason exists for such exclusion. Further, if an athlete is excluded he or she is entitled to **due process**, meaning that he or she must be afforded a fair and impartial hearing to determine eligibility.

restricted competition
Brand of amateur sports in which participation is limited to select persons.

unrestricted competition
Branch of amateur sports open to all amateur athletes.

equal protection
Constitutional guarantee that all persons are to be treated the same.

due process
Constitutional guarantee of a fair hearing.

— *Example*

A state college rule states that only nonmarried students may participate in college sports. This rule singles out a specific class of person—married students—and denies them access to college sports. Marriage is considered to be a fundamental right, and there is no rational basis for the college singling out this class. In this instance, the rule would be considered unconstitutional, as it denys equal protection to married students. Also, if a student who is alleged to be married wished to challenge that assertion, but the rule stated that the school's determination was final, the student would be denied due process by not being able to assert his actual marital status.

Regulation of Amateur Athletics

In order to determine participation in restricted competition sports, schools have developed various rules with respect to student eligibility. The most common of these rules include:

- *Red shirting*. These rules deny a student eligibility for a specified sport if it is determined that the student has been kept back so that he or she can develop physically and have an advantage over other students in the same academic year because of an advanced age and physical maturity.

- *No-transfer rules*. These rules preclude students from transferring schools simply to be able to participate in the new school's team.

- *No-agent rules*. These rules were adopted by the National College Athletic Association (NCAA) to prevent amateurs from becoming professionals. Therefore, if an amateur athlete acquires an agent, he or she may lose amateur status because it is assumed that acquiring an agent may be the first step in turning professional (read the rule to determine whether it applies in a given situation).

- *Academic standing*. Many schools mandate that a student maintain a minimum grade-point average to be eligible to participate is school sports in order to ensure that the student's education is not neglected. Further, certain organizations, such as the NCAA, require that students who receive athletic scholarships be awarded such on the basis of grades as well as athletic performance in order to maintain the amateur status of the student athlete.

Tort Liability

Similar to professional sports, the organizers of an amateur athletic event may be held liable under a tort claim for injuries to participants and spectators. In order to determine whether liability exists, the threshold question is whether the school or the organizer has a duty to protect the player or the patron. The liability for injuries to spectators remains the same regardless of whether the event is professional or amateur. However, because of the special relationship that may exist between the organizer, usually a school, and the participant, typically a student, a heightened duty may be deemed to exist.

The potential tort liability for the school or organizer may arise in one of the following ways:

Vicarious Liability

As discussed in relation to professional sports, **vicarious liability** would arise if a person engaged by the school is negligent in performing his or her duties and that negligence results in an injury to a player or spectator. The employer is held liable for the actions of its employee.

Example

A school team is going to an out-of-town meet on the school bus. The driver, a school employee, negligently causes the bus to run off the road, injuring the passengers. In this instance, the students may be able to sue the school as the employer under the theory of vicarious liability.

Negligent Hiring

negligent hiring
Failure to exercise due care in employing an unqualified person who injures a third party.

In a case of **negligent hiring,** the employer would be held directly liable because of its own actions in engaging the services of someone who is unqualified for the job. The theory is based on the employer's duty to determine the qualifications of its employees.

Example

A school hires a coach who has been convicted of sexual abuse. The school has failed to check his background. A few months later, when the coach sexually assaults a student, the student may be able to sue the school under a theory of negligent hiring.

Negligent Supervision

This theory is based on a school's duty to make sure that all school activities are properly monitored. Failure to supervise these activities is a breach of a duty that may give rise to tort liability.

Example

A school leaves the door to its swimming pool unlocked even when there is no lifeguard on duty. One day a student goes for a swim when there is no lifeguard, gets a cramp, and drowns. The school may be liable to the student's estate for negligent supervision.

Failure to Warn

If the school or its agents fail to warn a student about the potential dangers of an activity or to instruct the student in the proper use of the athletic equipment, and such failure causes injury, the school may be held liable.

Example

A school maintains a small skeet-shooting program. The coach fails to instruct the students in the proper use of the skeet gun, and a student, not knowing how the gun operates, accidentally injures a fellow student. The school may be held responsible for the injuries resulting from this failure to instruct.

Failure to Maintain the Facilities and Equipment

Similar to product liability, once equipment is purchased the buyer has an obligation to maintain the product in good repair if the buyer knows that other persons will regularly use these products. If the school fails to maintain such items and someone is injured, the school may be held responsible.

— Example —

A school, to save money, has reduced its maintenance crew. The result is that the stadium is only cleaned once a month or after each game. During the winter, because of the reduced staff, the school fails to clear ice from the stadium parking lot. A spectator arriving at the game slips on the ice and breaks her arm. The school may be held liable for failing to maintain the stadium in good repair, knowing that it will be used by members of the public.

As can be seen, many of the same legal theories apply to both professional and amateur sports.

DISCRIMINATION

In terms of amateur athletics, the athlete may be the subject of discriminatory treatment on one of two fronts: physical disability or gender. Both of these categories of prohibited discrimination are subject to federal and state statutes prohibiting such treatment; however, because of the peculiarities of the sports arena, in which physical attributes form the core of the activity, such laws may not afford satisfaction to a given athlete.

Physical Disability

Rehabilitation Act
Federal statute used to permit handicapped persons to participate in amateur sports.

Americans with Disabilities Act (ADA)
Federal statute providing for equal access for persons with mental or physical impairments.

handicap
Impairment under the Rehabilitation Act.

Discriminatory treatment based on a person's physical abilities are prohibited by two specific federal statutes, the **Rehabilitation Act**, 29 USC § 794, and the **Americans with Disabilities Act (ADA)**, 42 USC § 12101. According to the provisions of the Rehabilitation Act, no qualified handicapped person may be excluded from participation in any program receiving federal funds simply because of the handicap. Most amateur sports, because of school or association governance, are the recipients of some federal funding; therefore, this statute may be used as the basis for providing access to sports participation for the handicapped individual. A **handicap** is defined as a "physical or mental impairment which substantially limits one or more of a person's major life functions."

— Example —

A high school student slips in her bathroom and breaks her leg. Even though this injury limits her activity, it is not a permanent disability and therefore would not be considered a handicap under the Rehabilitation Act.

Example

A high school student is injured in a car accident and has to have one of her legs amputated. This permanent loss of a limb would constitute a handicap.

However, in order to be afforded protection against discrimination under the Rehabilitation Act, the athlete must be able to demonstrate that the particular handicap will not interfere with his or her participation in the sport. Most sports define eligibility, on a physical basis, by reference to guidelines established by medical associations that recommend that certain types of disabilities should be automatic disqualifications for certain sports activities because of the potential for exacerbation of the physical problem. However, just as the sporting organization cannot automatically exclude a person because of a handicap under the assumption that the person would be physically unable to participate in the sport, the athlete must also be able to demonstrate that the disability does not hinder his or her performance.

— *Example*

A college student has lost the use of his left hand. He wants to participate in a student soccer league. Because soccer does not require the use of a player's hands, in these circumstances it would appear that this disability does not disqualify the student form such participation.

Under § 504 of the Rehabilitation Act, a school must analyze the particular problems of an individual handicapped student and devise an appropriate program that will enable that student to participate within the limitations of his or her handicap. In this context, the Rehabilitation Act is similar to the requirement of "reasonable accommodation" under the ADA.

The ADA covers professional as well as amateur sports, as it concerns employers, which would include the professional athletic teams and leagues. This statute extends protection to disabled athletes so that they may participate in professional sports. In one fairly recent case, a professional golfer with a physical disability that limited his ability to walk was permitted, by court order, to use a golf cart on the course of a professional match, even though the Professional Golfers' Association had a rule prohibiting the use of carts during such competitions. The ADA requires that employers make **reasonable accommodation** to allow for the special needs of the disabled individual.

reasonable accommodation
An employer/business owner's duty to allow for the special needs of the disabled.

However, just as with the Rehabilitation Act, the athlete must be able to demonstrate that he or she is otherwise qualified to participate in the sport. This burden of proof may be more difficult for the professional athlete than the amateur athlete.

The ADA prohibits discrimination against disabled persons in public accommodation, which would apply to the stadiums and other facilities in which professional and amateur sports are played. The owners of such facilities must provide access to disabled people both as participants and spectators.

—— *Example* ——————————————

In order to accommodate disabled spectators, a public sports arena has installed elevators and ramps to provide access to its facilities.

It must also be noted that both of these statutes apply to mental impairments that may affect a person's participation in an athletic endeavor, but most of the cases in this area concern physical disabilities.

Gender

Title IX
Civil rights act dealing with education.

Pursuant to the provisions of **Title IX** of the Civil Rights Act, a person cannot be discriminated against in education based on race, color, national origin, gender, or religion. This title corresponds to Title VII that affords such protection in the workplace. Title IX does distinguish between contact and noncontact sports in that women are permitted to participate on men's teams in noncontact sports, but may be precluded from such participation in contact sports. The sports that are considered to be contact sports are

- Boxing
- Wrestling
- Rugby
- Ice hockey
- Basketball
- Baseball and soccer (sometimes).

In such circumstances, the school must provide for equal teams so that both genders have an equal opportunity to participate in such sports.

—— *Example* ——————————————

A state university has a large and well-funded boxing program. In the past several years, many of the female students have expressed an interest in boxing, and so the school has established a separate women's boxing program, separating the genders, because boxing is a contact sport. Such a program is permitted and mandated by the provisions of Title IX.

In order to come within the provisions of Title IX, the institution must receive some form of federal funding. Further, these provisions apply to providing athletic scholarships to both genders as well as providing participation in the sports.

ANTITRUST IMPLICATIONS

American antitrust laws came into existence at the end of the nineteenth century in an attempt to foster commerce by prohibiting monopolies as noncompetitive conduct. The first antitrust statute was the Sherman Act, 15 USC § 1. This statute made it illegal to engage in any conduct that restricted competition in interstate commerce. This prohibition has been applied to both professional and amateur sports, affecting the way they are organized and the way they are presented to the public.

Professional Sports

Professional sports, by their nature, are run by a small group of individuals in leagues that maintain the rules and regulations of a given athletic endeavor. Under ordinary antitrust concepts, having only two baseball leagues and one baseball governing body for the entire country would be considered a combination designed to restrict trade. However, pursuant to cases and laws enacted over the years, certain exemptions from these laws have been carved out. For the purposes of this text, the most important of these exceptions are

1. *Professional baseball*, as the result of an early United States Supreme Court decision (*Federal Base Ball Club of Baltimore, Inc. v. National League of Professional Base Ball Clubs*)
2. *Organized labor*, exempted under the provisions of the labor law statutes previously discussed
3. *The National Football League*, with respect to blackouts of home games and selling of video packages
4. *The National Basketball Association*, permitted to establish a salary cap

Rozelle Rule
Acquiring team must compensate player's previous team.

5. **The Rozelle Rule**, which requires that a club that acquires a player compensate the player's previous team; however, this exemption is determined on a case-by-case basis.

However, not all activities by teams and players are exempt from antitrust scrutiny. Over the years several specific situations have been interpreted according to United States antitrust laws:

franchising
Letting a team operate in a given geographic area.

rule of reason
Antitrust concept looking at actual factors to determine whether there is an antitrust violation.

1. *Franchising.* **Franchising** involves a league permitting a team to operate in a specific geographic location. The antitrust question involved concerns a league deciding to permit a franchise that grants exclusive geographic rights to one team, thereby denying the public access to different teams. In analyzing whether such activity restrains trade, the court has generally applied a **rule of reason** to the agreement, looking at all of the factors involved in the decision to determine whether trade and/or commerce is actually being negatively affected.

2. *Athletic restraints.* Historically, the use of a draft system by professional teams to acquire collegiate athletes acted as a restraint on trade because teams were only permitted to contract with athletes on a predetermined rota system. However, over the past several decades this practice has been modified pursuant to collective bargaining agreements, and so currently does not act as an anticompetition action.

3. *Marketing.* Most professional sports teams (as well as the amateur ones) make money by marketing the broadcasts of their games to the regular television networks as well as to the cable channels. In most of these instances, the teams only permit one channel to broadcast the games, meaning that the other channels cannot broadcast the event. Recently, many professional sports teams have contracted the broadcast rights to their games to cable channels that do not provide free access to viewers, but require viewers to pay additional fees. To date, in the professional arena, such agreements have not been challenged as violating the antitrust law, but have been litigated in the amateur sports realm.

Amateur Sports

Many of the antitrust implications of sports do not apply to amateur sports because of the lack of compensation to the athlete and the general lack of profit motive among the organizers. However, in recent years there has been significant litigation with respect to the marketing of amateur sports events to network and cable television channels.

The primary case in this area involved the NCAA limiting the transmission of its sporting events to specific cable channels. This licensing was found to violate the antitrust law because it restricted the total number of games that an NCAA member could transmit and precluded member schools from licensing the broadcast of these events independent of the NCAA. In this fashion, the NCAA was controlling all amateur sports that were within its system and thereby restricting trade.

ENDORSEMENTS

endorsement
Contract in which a person lends his name and reputation to a product for consideration.

An **endorsement** is a contract in which a person lends his or her name and reputation to a particular product for compensation. The purpose of an endorsement is to convince a potential consumer of the value of the product based on the endorser's statement regarding its benefits. For athletes, endorsements can represent a major portion of their yearly income.

The unique feature of an endorsement contract is the consideration given by the endorser—the endorser's name and reputation. In many instances the athlete agrees to license the use of his or her likeness as well as his or her statements, and agrees that the contracting company may use the likeness and statement for advertising in print, film, and radio. These types of contracts have existed for over 150 years and are interpreted according to general contract law. However, to be legal, the endorser must actually use the product being endorsed.

— *Example* ——————————————————————

Winnie Wimbleton, the world-famous tennis champion, agrees to lend her name to Ekin Tennis Shoes. Pursuant to this agreement, in consideration of Ekin giving Winnie $3,000,000, Winnie agrees to be photographed for ads that say that she only wears Ekins. Winnie wants this contract to increase her earnings, and Ekin wants the contract to increase its sales to tennis players who want to be just like Winnie. Note that with this endorsement Winnie must actually wear Ekins to avoid a charge of false advertising.

---

licenses
When an individual athlete allows his or her name to be used by another, such as on a T-shirt.

tie-in
Illegal agreements under the antitrust laws.

As a subset of endorsement contracts and as a corollary to antitrust law, in certain circumstances an athlete or a team may grant its name or its logo to be used on a T-shirt or other such item as an official insignia. These agreements, when made by an individual athlete, are called **licenses**. These contracts, in which the use of a name or logo is permitted by someone other than the owner, are perfectly legal. However, if team or league agrees to lend its name or insignia to a product for a large sum provided that the team uses another product manufactured by the other contracting party, such an agreement may be considered an illegal tie-in. A **tie-in** is a contract in which two separate, but interrelated, contracts are made dependent upon each other. An example would be a professional team agreeing to lend its logo to a clothing manufacturer for a huge sum of money provided that the team purchases all of its uniforms from that manufacturer. If the result of such a contract is to restrain or limit competition, the entire agreement would be deemed illegal; if it is merely an additional consideration that does not hinder competition, it would be valid. This determination is made on a case-by-case basis.

CHAPTER REVIEW

Sports law falls into two broad categories: professional and amateur. Professional sports involve persons who are compensated for their athletic performance, whereas amateur sports involve persons who participate without compensation.

In professional sports, contract law governs the relationship between the team and the player and the player and his or her agent. The greater the bargaining power of the player, the more favorable his or her contract will be. At present, most professional athletes belong to players' associations and their individual contracts are modified by collective bargaining agreements.

Professional sports teams and players may be subject to liability for injuries resulting from tortious conduct. Although athletes and spectators are deemed to have assumed the risk of certain types of injuries associated with the event, they still may recover for injuries resulting from acts that are not foreseeable with respect to the athletic endeavor. Also, injuries may result from defective products used or maintained by the team and the manufacturer/seller of such a product may be held liable for resulting injuries regardless of the degree of care used in the manufacture.

Amateur sports are divided into restricted and nonrestricted competitions in which eligibility is limited to a specific group or open to all amateurs. Amateur sports are governed by rules and regulations enacted by each particular sport's governing body.

In addition to tort liability, which corresponds to the tort liability for professional sports, amateur sports may be subject to federal and state anti-discrimination laws. These laws permit athletes with physical and/or mental impairments to participate in sports events that receive federal funding and to prevent gender discrimination with respect to sports participation.

Both professional and amateur sports are subject to federal antitrust laws to prevent monopolies and to foster competition, but the legality of each action is usually decided on a case-by-case basis.

JUDICIAL DECISION

The following case discusses the antitrust implications of the NBA draft system.

Bridgeman et al. v. National Basketball Association et al.
675 FSupp 960 (DNJ 1987)

Plaintiffs, a group of current and former players and first round draft choices in the NBA ("the players"), brought this action pursuant to §§ 4 and 16 of the Clayton Act, 15 USC §§ 15 and 26, and the Sherman Antitrust Act, 15 USC § 1 et seq. Their complaint alleges that the enforcement by the National Basketball Association and its 23 member teams (collectively referred to as "the NBA") of the college player draft, the salary cap, and the right of first refusal constitutes an antitrust violation.

I. PROCEDURAL HISTORY

Before instituting this action, plaintiffs and the National Basketball Players Association ("the Players Association") filed a class action complaint with this court on October 1, 1987 (*Bridgeman I*), alleging on behalf of themselves and all class members the same antitrust violations against the same defendants that are included in the instant complaint (87 Civ 4001).

Because the plaintiffs in *Bridgeman I* sought speedy resolution of the labor exemption issue and the NBA defendants had raised objections to the class action allegations contained in that complaint, I suggested that a second complaint be filed eliminating the class allegations so as to put the case in a procedural posture that would permit an early resolution of the labor exemption issue. Plaintiffs filed the complaint in the present action (*Bridgeman II*) on October 16, 1987.

The matter is now before the court on the players' motion for partial summary judgment and a declaratory judgment declaring any labor exemption to the antitrust laws inapplicable to the practices at issue in this case. The NBA has cross-moved for an order directing plaintiffs to join the National Basketball Players Association ("the Players Association") as a party, and for summary judgment dismissing the complaint.

II. FACTS

The following facts are undisputed. As noted above, the practices at issue are the college player draft, the salary cap, and the right of first refusal. Under the college player draft, the NBA defendants allocate the exclusive rights to negotiate with and sign rookie players. The salary cap is a system whereby the NBA defendants agree to set maximum limits on the aggregate amount teams can spend to compensate their players. Under the right of first refusal, an NBA team has the right to retain a veteran free agent's services indefinitely by matching offers received by that player from other NBA teams. As described below, the players agreed to these practices for a limited period of time in a settlement agreement that arose out of an antitrust class action lawsuit.

The Robertson Litigation and Settlement Agreement

In 1970, the NBA players commenced a class action suit against the NBA in the federal district court for the Southern District of New York, challenging on antitrust grounds certain player restrictions imposed by the NBA team owners, including the NBA college player draft and the reserve system. The NBA defendants moved for summary judgment, arguing, among other things, that the practices were shielded from the anti-trust laws by a labor exemption. The district court denied the NBA's motion (*Robertson v. National Basketball Association*, 389 FSupp 867, 884–89 (SDNY 1975)).

In 1976, the parties in the *Robertson* litigation entered and the district court approved a settlement agreement. This agreement effected a number of changes in the operation of the NBA, including modification of the college player draft and institution of the right of first refusal. The settlement agreement provided that it would expire at the end of the 1986–1987 NBA season, and further provided that

> Neither the settlement of the Class Action, nor entry into this Stipulation and Settlement Agreement or any collective bargaining agreement or any Player Contract, nor the effectuation thereof, nor any practice or course of dealing thereunder shall be deemed to be a waiver or estoppel by any NBA player or players or the Players Association of their right to challenge in a court of competent jurisdiction any future unilateral imposition by the NBA or any NBA member of any rule, regulation, policy, practice or agreement, or to contend (subject to the right of the NBA to contend otherwise) that the same is not a mandatory subject of collective bargaining or a subject over which they are otherwise required to collectively bargain, nor

do they concede that the same is a mandatory subject of collective bargaining or a subject over which they are otherwise required to collectively bargain.

Collective Bargaining in the NBA

When the Robertson settlement agreement was adopted in 1976, the Players Association and the NBA also entered into a multi-year collective bargaining agreement that incorporated the substantive terms of the settlement agreement. The 1976 collective bargaining agreement expired on June 1, 1979, and on October 10, 1980, the parties again entered into a multi-year collective-bargaining agreement that expressly incorporated the terms of the *Robertson* settlement agreement.

The 1980 agreement expired on June 1, 1982. In 1983, the NBA defendants sought for the first time to introduce the salary cap, contending that such a restriction was necessary because the majority of NBA teams were losing money, in part because of rising player salaries and benefits. The players responded by filing a lawsuit challenging the legality of the proposed practice (*Lanier v. National Basketball Association*, 82 Civ 4935 (SDNY)). A Special Master appointed to hear disputes under the *Robertson* settlement agreement determined that the salary cap would violate the terms of the settlement agreement, and therefore could not be imposed absent a modification of that agreement.

The Players Association and the NBA entered into a Memorandum of Understanding that modified the expired 1980 collective bargaining agreement to include, among other things, a salary cap, and continued the agreement in force through the end of the 1986–87 season. On June 13, 1983, the district court approved a modification of the *Robertson* settlement agreement to incorporate the terms of the Memorandum of Understanding.

Negotiations for a New Collective Bargaining Agreement

Since February 11, 1987, the parties have held meetings seeking to reach agreement on a new collective bargaining agreement. There has been considerable disagreement on the three player restrictions at issue in this case, with the players demanding elimination of at least the college player draft and the right of first refusal.

On June 8, 1987, the NBA and the Players Association executed a "moratorium agreement," agreeing to postpone any lawsuit and player signings, while continuing to engage in good faith negotiations in an effort to reach a new collective bargaining agreement. No agreement, however, has been reached, and the moratorium agreement expired on October 1, 1987.

The players have informed the NBA that they no longer consent to any player restraints. By letter dated October 14, 1987, the Players Association stated that it would not engage in any further collective bargaining negotiations until this lawsuit had been resolved. On November 3, 1987, the NBA filed an unfair labor practice charge with the National Labor Relations Board seeking a directive that the Players Association return to the bargaining table. The NBA has continued to operate under the terms of the most recent collective bargaining agreement, including the practices at issue in this case.

III. DISCUSSION

The NBA's Motion for Joinder

FedRCivP 19(a) provides that

A person who is subject to service of process and whose joinder will not deprive the court of jurisdiction ... shall be joined as a party in the action if ... [the person] claims an interest relating to the subject of the action and is so situated that the disposition of the action in the person's absence may (i) as a practical matter impair or impede the person's ability to protect that interest or (ii) leave any of the persons already parties subject to a substantial risk of incurring double, multiple or otherwise inconsistent obligations by reason of the claimed interest. If the person has not been so joined, the court shall order that the person be made a party.

In support of its motion to require joinder of the Players Association, the NBA contends that the Players Association has an interest in the outcome of this litigation, and that disposition of the case in its absence could lead to inconsistent decisions by different courts on the identical issue. However, the risk of inconsistent determinations on the issues in this suit will remain whether or not the Players Association is joined. A judgment against the union in this case would have preclusive effect only against the union; players not named as plaintiffs would not be barred from bringing the same claims in separate suits

whether or not the union has been joined as a plaintiff (see *O'Hare v. General Marine Transport Corp.*, 740 F2d 160, 167 (2nd Cir 1984)). Preclusive effect against all of the NBA players would be possible only in the *Bridgeman I* action if the plaintiff class is certified and that action moves forward.

Moreover, a judgment in this case may have preclusive effect against the union whether or not it is joined here as a party, since attorneys for the players do not dispute that the union has an interest in, and has sponsored and financed this litigation from the beginning (see, e.g., *Gill and Duffus Services, Inc. v. A. M. Nural Islam*, 218 US App DC 385, 675 F2d 404, 406 (DC Cir 1982) (*per curiam*)). Thus, although there is a possibility of inconsistent determinations on the issues in this case, that risk would not be alleviated by a joinder of the Players Association. The NBA's motion to require joinder is denied.

The Cross-Motions for Summary Judgment

The concept of a labor exemption finds its source in §§ 6 and 20 of the Clayton Act, 15 USC § 17 and 29 USC § 52, and the Norris-LaGuardia Act, 29 USC §§ 104, 105 and 113. Those provisions declare that labor unions are not combinations or conspiracies in restraint of trade, and specifically exempt certain union activities such as secondary picketing and group boycotts from the coverage of antitrust laws (see *Connell Co. v. Plumbers and Steamfitters*, 421 US 616, 621–22, 95 SCt 1830, 44 LEd2d 418 (1975)). This statutory exemption insulates inherently anticompetitive collective activities by employees because they are favored by federal labor policy (see *Apex Hosiery Co. v. Leader*, 310 US 469, 60 SCt 982, 84 LEd 1311 (1940)).

The statutory exemption extends to legitimate labor activities unilaterally undertaken by a union in furtherance of its own interests (see *United States v. Hutcheson*, 312 US 219, 61 SCt 463, 85 LEd 788 (1941)). It does not extend to concerted action or agreements between unions and non-labor groups. This is where the nonstatutory exemption comes into play. The Supreme Court has held that in order to properly accommodate the congressional policy favoring free competition in business markets with the congressional policy favoring collective bargaining under the National Labor Relations Act, 29 US.C § 151 et seq ("NLRA"), certain union-employer agreements must be accorded a limited nonstatutory exemption from antitrust sanctions (see *Connell Co., supra*).

In a 1976 case involving player restraints in the National Football League, the Eighth Circuit summarized the scope of the nonstatutory labor exemption:

First, the labor policy favoring collective bargaining may potentially be given preeminence over the antitrust laws where the restraint on trade primarily affects only the parties to the collective bargaining relationship. Second, federal labor policy is implicated sufficiently to prevail only where the agreement sought to be exempted concerns a mandatory subject of collective bargaining. Finally, the policy favoring collective bargaining is furthered to the degree necessary to override the antitrust laws only where the agreement sought to be exempted is the product of bone fide arm's-length bargaining.

The practices challenged by plaintiffs—the player draft, the right of first refusal, and the salary cap—we included in the most recent collective bargaining agreement between the players and the NBA. The players do not dispute that the restrictions at issue were covered by the labor exemption when the collective bargaining agreement was still in effect. However, the players, noting that courts have generally refused to find antitrust immunity in the absence of a collective bargaining agreement, argue that the practices are not protected by the nonstatutory exemption because they are not the subject of any currently effective collective bargaining agreement, and because the players have not otherwise consented to them. The NBA vigorously disputes this reading of the exemption, proposing instead that antitrust immunity should continue after expiration of the agreement as long as the league continues to apply without modification the player restrictions that were included in the agreement.

As the players observe, courts have generally applied the nonstatutory exemption only where the challenged practices are authorized by a collective bargaining agreement, rejecting broad arguments that labor principles should automatically override antitrust principles as long as an exclusive bargaining representative is in place, or that the antitrust laws do not reach labor market restraints at all.

However, none of the cases cited by the parties address the issue presented in this case, where the challenged provisions were included in a collective bargaining agreement that is no longer in effect. Thus, although I accept the test enunciated in *Mackey* as the correct starting point, resolution of this case requires moving one step beyond *Mackey*. Doing so requires examination of the policies underlying the labor exemption.

The nonstatutory exemption represents an effort to balance the concerns of the federal antitrust and labor laws. The availability of the exemption turns upon whether the federal labor interest in collective bargaining is deserving of preeminence over the federal antitrust interest in free competition under the circumstances of the particular case (see *Connell Co., supra; Jewel Tea, supra; United Mine Workers v. Pennington*, 381 US 657, 85 SCt 1585, 14 LEd2d 626 (1965); *Mackey*, 543 F2d at 613). By protecting only those practices that were included in a collective bargaining agreement after being subject to arm's-length bargaining, the exemption encourages substantive, good faith bargaining on important issues and guards against unilateral imposition of terms as to which there is no agreement.

Applying these considerations, I find no merit in the players' contention that restrictions included in a collective bargaining agreement should lose their antitrust immunity the moment the agreement expires. At the outset, such a rule is unrealistic in light of the requirement that employers must bargain fully and in good faith before altering a term or condition of employment subject to mandatory bargaining even after the collective bargaining agreement expires (see, e.g., *Industrial Union of Marine and Shipbldg. Workers v. NLRB*, 320 F2d 615, 620 (3d Cir 1963), cert. denied sub nom; *Bethlehem Steel Co. v. NLRB*, 375 US 984, 11 LEd2d 472, 84 SCt 516 (1964); *NLRB v. Katz*, 369 US 736, 747–48, 82 SCt 1107, 8 LEd2d 230 (1962)). If an employer unilaterally alters such a term or condition of employment before negotiations reach an "impasse," it may be guilty of committing an unfair labor practice under 29 USC § 158(a)(5). This obligation to maintain the status quo until impasse means that, in a practical sense, terms and conditions of employment that are subjects of mandatory bargaining survive expiration of the collective bargaining agreement.

In fact, the history of collective bargaining in the NBA is punctuated by interim periods between agreements during which the league maintained the status quo and continued to negotiate with the players. This suggests that there is at least a possibility that some of the provisions in the most recent expired agreement will be reenacted in the same form in a future agreement. It would be anomalous for such restraints to enjoy antitrust immunity during the period of the previous agreement, to lose that immunity automatically upon expiration of the agreement—regardless of the status of negotiations for a new agreement—and then to regard immunity upon entry of the new agreement.

Stripping player restraints of their antitrust immunity the instant a collective bargaining agreement expires would also inhibit the collective bargaining process, a result that is contrary to the purpose of the nonstatutory exemption. Because agreements often expire without immediate replacement, employers operating under such a rule would in many cases be reluctant to agree to potentially anticompetitive restraints, even where desired by their employees, for fear that such practices would expose them to antitrust suits during any period between agreements.

The federal labor policy of encouraging collective bargaining also requires rejection of the NBA's position that the exemption should continue indefinitely after an agreement expires so long as the employer maintains the status quo by not imposing any new restraints. This facile manner of evading the antitrust laws would discourage unions from entering collective bargaining agreements, since doing so might forever bar them from challenging those restraints in court. Although, as noted above, the rules embodied in a collective bargaining agreement are not automatically disregarded the instant the clock runs out on the agreement, the game cannot last forever.

Thus, a time will come after expiration of the agreement when the practices that were included in the agreement can no longer be said to exist as an extension of the agreement. At such time, those practices are no longer protected by the labor exemption. The relevant question is when that moment occurs.

The players argue that the exemption cannot extend beyond an "impasse" in the negotiations because at that moment, there is no longer mutual consent to the restraints. Impasse is certainly a plausible point at which to end the labor exemption, for by its very definition it implies a deadlock in negotiations, which could in some cases imply that the employees' consent to the restraints of the prior agreement has

ended. The moment of impasse in negotiations is significant, for an employer may, after bargaining with the union to an impasse, make "unilateral changes that are reasonably comprehended within his preimpasse proposals" (*Taft Broadcasting* Co., 163 NLRB at 476). After impasse, either party is free to decline to negotiate further (*Cheney California Lumber Co. v. NLRB*, 319 F2d 375, 380 (9th Cir 1963)).

However, an impasse is not equivalent to the end of negotiations, or the loss of hope that any of the practices subject to negotiation will be incorporated in a new agreement. "As a recurring feature in the bargaining process, impasse is only a temporary deadlock or hiatus in negotiations 'which in almost all cases is eventually broken, through either a change of mind or the application of economic force'" (*Charles D. Bonanno Linen Service v. NLRB*, 454 US 404, 412, 102 SCt 720, 70 LEd2d 656 (1982) (quoting *Charles D. Bonanno Linen Service*, 243 NLRB 1093, 1093–1094 (1979))). An impasse may be brought about intentionally by one or both parties as a device to further, rather than halt, the bargaining process. "Suspension of the process as a result of an impasse may provide time for reflection and a cooling of tempers; it may be used to demonstrate the depth of a party's commitment to a position taken in the bargaining; or it may increase economic pressure on one or both sides, and thus increase the desire for agreement" (*Charles Bonanno Linen Service*, 243 NLRB 1093, 1094 (1979), enf'd, 630 F2d 25 (1st Cir 1980), aff'd, 454 US 404, 102 SCt 720, 70 LEd2d 656 (1982)).

Because an impasse occurs only when the entire negotiating process has come to a standstill, the prospects for incorporating a particular practice into a collective bargaining agreement may also disappear before a full impasse in the negotiations is actually reached. It is at least theoretically possible for the parties, without ever reaching impasse, to enter a collective bargaining agreement that omits one or more of the practices that were included in the previous agreement.

Thus, impasse is a concept developed to deal with the problems of labor law, not with the unique intersection of labor law and antitrust law at issue in this case. I cannot choose the criteria for determining the endpoint of the labor exemption without reference to its purpose—encouraging collective bargaining.

An extension of the *Mackey* formulation produces a rational criterion for declaring when the labor extension expires after termination of the collective bargaining agreement. I find that the exemption for a particular practice survives only as long as the employer continues to impose that restriction unchanged, and reasonably believes that the practice or a close variant of it will be incorporated in the next collective bargaining agreement. When the employer no longer has such a reasonable belief, it is then unilaterally imposing the restriction on its employees, and the restraint can no longer be deemed the product of arm's-length negotiation between the union and the employer.

This formulation is meant to determine the point at which agreement ends on the practices at issue, instead of tying the fate of the exemption to progress in the negotiations as a whole. In any particular case, the exemption may expire before, during or after impasse, and the facts bearing on the impasse question may also bear on the determination of the expiration of the labor exemption. However, they are different questions.

This result is not hampered in this case by the provision in the *Robertson* settlement agreement reserving the players' "right to challenge in a court of competent jurisdiction any future unilateral imposition [of any practice] by the NBA. ..." This provision, which appears to be a mutual reservation of rights by the Players Association and the NBA, simply applies where the league unilaterally imposes restrictions. As long as the NBA has a reasonable belief that a practice may be included in the agreement being negotiated, it is not imposing the practice unilaterally; rather, the restriction is deemed a product of arm's-length negotiations.

Quite obviously, application of this rule in the present case involves issues of material fact that cannot be decided on a motion for summary judgment on the present state of the record. Indeed, resolution of this factual matter may not be possible until after the parties have resolved their differences and entered a new collective bargaining agreement. Therefore, I have denied both the players' and the NBA's motions for summary judgment.

IV. CONCLUSION

The NBA's motion to require joinder of the Players Association is denied, and the players' and the NBA's motions for summary judgment are denied.

KEY TERMS

absolute (strict) liability

administrative law judge

amateur sports

Americans with Disabilities Act (ADA)

arbitrator

assumption of the risk

boycott

charging party

collective bargaining

collective bargaining agreement

conflict of interest

contract of adhesion

due process

endorsement

equal protection

franchise

handicap

incorporation by reference

licenses

lockout

mediator

National Labor Relations Act
(NLRA)

National Labor Relations Board
(NLRB)

negligent hiring

option

product liability

professional sports

reasonable accomodation

red shirt

Rehabilitation Act

reserve clause

respondeat superior

restricted competition

Rozelle Rule

rule of reason

strike

successor in interest

tie-in

Title IX

trade

unfair labor practice

union shop

unrestricted competition

vicarious liability

EXERCISES

1. Research your state's law to determine how it regulates sports agents.

2. Find three examples of endorsements by an athlete.

3. What procedures should a school enact in order to avoid a charge of failing to instruct?

4. Obtain a copy of the rules and regulations of an amateur sport in which you participate.

5. What is your opinion of athletes who receive scholarships, endorsements, and sponsors being able to maintain their status as amateurs?

6. Read *United States v. Walter & Bloom*, 711 FSupp 1435, regarding agents and criminal activities. What is your opinion of amateur sports being the object of racketeering? Discuss.

7. Research the Internet to obtain a copy of the Uniform Player's Contract for the National League of Professional Baseball Clubs and analyze its provisions in light of the material discussed in this chapter.

8. Download an example of the rules of conduct for an amateur athletic association and compare its provisions with a professional sports contract.

9. How would you protect an athlete client from having her name exploited? Would her contracting for endorsements affect her ability to protect herself?

10. What provisions would you want included in an endorsement contract? Explain.

CHAPTER
10

ENTERTAINMENT LAW AND CYBERSPACE

CHAPTER OVERVIEW

The entertainment industry, like all fields, has been greatly affected by the overwhelming growth of modern technology. However, unlike other industries in which the application of the Internet has only expanded markets, in the entertainment field such access has generated a host of problems with respect to protecting the rights of the artists and other entertainment professionals whose works may now appear on household computers all over the world. In order to protect the rights of these entertainment professionals, a new area of law has developed to deal exclusively with cyberspace.

At this point in time, the problems associated with entertainment law and the new technology are ones dealing with the application of existing legal principles to the Internet rather than the creation of a whole new body of law that bears little relationship to existing legal doctrines. The most frequently encountered problem in this area concerns the constitutionally guaranteed right of free speech coupled with the statutory right of artists to protect their works pursuant to domestic and international copyright laws. Of special concern are the rights of parents and other interested adults in preventing children from being able to access pornography by means of the Internet.

One of the major legal problems in this area is the determination of the appropriate forum to both regulate and adjudicate rights associated with the new technology. Because the Internet and cyberspace are international in scope with no definite and identifiable physical location, an individual's rights may be infringed upon by someone who is not easily capable of being located. Also, because this infringement may occur in many countries simultaneously, the question arises as to who has the legal authority and jurisdiction to create law to regulate such use. These problems have forced governments and individuals to seek international regulation of cyberspace and the creation of international forums in which such cyberspace issues can be resolved.

This chapter will explore and examine two distinct areas of entertainment law and the new technology: (1) the problems associated with cyberspace, such as the regulation of obscenity, protection against Internet defamation, and copyright and trademark protection and (2) international protections that have developed—such as the World Intellectual Property Organization Copyright Treaty—to address the legitimate concerns of the entertainment industry.

CYBERSPACE

cyberspace
Technology associated with the Internet.

cyberlaw
Legal doctrines that apply to cyberspace.

Cyberspace is the term used to refer to computer technology and the Internet. **Cyberlaw** refers to the legal implications and principles associated with cyberspace technology. For the entertainment law practitioner, cyberspace and cyberlaw have become increasingly important both as a method of disseminating the entertainment product and as a method by which certain legal rights with respect to those products may be infringed. For this reason, all entertainment law professionals must be conversant with the benefits and detriments of operating an entertainment entity in the new technological environment.

This section will explore four distinct areas of operation that relate to the entertainment industry: obscenity, defamation, encryption, and copyright and trademark.

Obscenity

As discussed in chapter 1, freedom of speech is the bulwark of all artistic endeavors. Without the ability to express oneself freely, art would stagnate. However, as also discussed, not all speech is afforded constitutional protections.

Material that is considered to be obscene, that which panders to prurient interests, may be circumscribed by the government with respect to its production and its dissemination. For the purposes of this section of the text, only dissemination by means of the Internet will be addressed.

Generally, an adult is permitted to access material that would be considered pornographic. However, the dissemination of such matter, even if not found to be obscene, is restricted to adults, those persons over the age of 18. It is universally considered to be a crime if pornographic material is distributed to minors.

Communications Decency Act (CDA)
Federal statute designed to prevent obscene material from being transmitted over the Internet; found unconstitutional.

Telecommunications Act of 1996
Federal statute that governs various areas of telecommunications.

vague
Constitutional mandate that statutes be precise in their wording.

Child Online Protection Act (COPA)
Federal statute designed to prevent children from accessing obscene material on the Internet; found unconstitutional.

overbreadth
Constitutional proscription against having statutes overly inclusive.

filtering software
Computer program that can screen out specifically designated material.

In order to limit access to pornographic material over the Internet by minors, in 1996 Congress enacted the **Communications Decency Act (CDA)** as part of the general **Telecommunications Act of 1996.** Pursuant to this statute, the "knowing transmission" of pornographic material to persons under the age of 18 over the Internet was deemed a crime. However, the immediate question arose as to how a provider of such material would be able to ascertain the age of the person accessing such matter. Even though access was limited to persons with a credit card, a child could be using a parent's credit card to view the material. Consequently, the provisions of the statute were challenged as being unconstitutionally vague. In order to meet constitutional standards, a statute must be precise in its wording so as to leave no doubt as to its interpretation. If such a standard could not be determined from the wording of the act, the statute is considered to be **vague.**

In 1997, the United States Supreme Court declared that the CDA was unconstitutionally vague. Even though the government has a legitimate interest in protecting children from pornography, the statute was written in such a fashion that it could not be properly administered.

Following this decision, Congress enacted another statute to address this problem. The new statute, entitled the **Child Online Protection Act (COPA),** makes it a crime to make "any communication for commercial purposes that is accessible to any minor and that includes any material that is harmful to minors." This act was also determined to be unconstitutional for **overbreadth,** meaning that its wording was too inclusive. Therefore, to date, no law has been able to pass a constitutional challenge so as to limit access to obscene material by minors over the Internet.

The most common method currently used to limit such access is **filtering software,** a computer program that can be purchased by parents that screens out specifically identified material. Although proper when used privately, certain problems arise when these programs are used by public libraries (i.e., government) because they can limit access to material that is constitutionally protected as well.

For the entertainment law professional and entrepreneur, the ability to disseminate artistic material is crucial and, whereas the state may legally limit access to pornographic matter, it cannot use any method that would limit such access to adults. Further, the government cannot restrain the free flow of artistic and creative material; to do so would hinder the creative process.

Defamation

bulletin-board site
A Web site that provides information on general or specific topics.

The concept of defamation has been defined and discussed in chapters 1 and 9. With respect to cyberspace, the principles of defamation arise with respect to the use of bulletin-board sites to make defamatory statements. A **bulletin-board site** is a site that provides information on various topics, both specific and general, for its subscribers. The legal question, aside from the basic concept of defamation as previously analyzed, is the responsibility of the provider for the content of the material that appears on these sites.

The courts have been presented with various problems associated with the responsibility of the provider for defamatory and obscene matters that appear on the sites; basically, the courts will or will not hold the provider liable depending upon the degree of control the provider exercises over the material that is posted on the board. The greater the control, the more likely that the provider will be liable for its content.

— *Example*

A bulletin-board provider hires people to review any objectionable material that appears on its site and to delete such matter. Because of the control exercised by the provider, the provider may be treated in the same manner as a publisher and be held legally responsible for the material that appears on the site.

Example

A bulletin-board provider maintains no control over the material appearing on its site. Because it does not review the material appearing on the bulletin board, the provider may not be held liable for defamatory material appearing on the board. In this instance, the provider is acting in a manner similar to a telephone directory, and it is not responsible for the site's content.

If it is deemed to be acting like a publisher, a bulletin-board site provider is subject to the same legal rights and obligations of all publishers, as discussed in chapter 8. Therefore, such providers may be subject to liability for the material that they publish on the site.

Encryption

encryption
Method of encoding material for security.

Encryption refers to the use of a code or codes to secure material transmitted by means of the Internet. Two specific problems are associated with encryption: (1) whether the software that creates these codes is copyrightable as intellectual property and (2) whether the sale of such software could involve security risks for the government.

Originally, encryption was not considered to be copyright eligible because such programs were viewed as functional rather than as a means of intellectual expression. After numerous court challenges, it was eventually determined that encryption is an outgrowth of speech and the intellectual process, and so currently encryption software may be copyrighted and licensed, just like all other forms of intellectual property. This is important, not only for the creator of the encryption program, but also for any owner of intellectual property who wishes to use such a program to safeguard the fruits of his or her intellectual process when transmitting such property by means of the Internet.

— *Example* —

A publisher wishes to market its titles over the Internet by using a Web site, but she is concerned by the potential unauthorized use of the material without payment of a royalty. For this reason, the publisher develops a specific encryption program that can only be accessed by a customer who purchases the titles from the publisher. Further, the program can also secure the customer's credit and other personal information.

During the 1990s, encryption programs were specifically categorized for export under the Department of Commerce's Bureau of Export Administration. This meant that this software could be freely exported, with two exceptions:

1. The software could not be exported to countries deemed to present a security risk to the United States, including Cuba, Iran, Iraq, Libya, North Korea, Sudan, and Syria

2. Any individual selling encryption software to a government must first obtain a license from the United States' government.

Prior to this change in the government's attitude, such programs were not permitted to be exported. With this change in policy, concerns over possible security risks were reduced while still permitting the software to be freely traded.

Copyrights and Trademarks

A significant area in which entertainment and cyberlaw overlap is in the area of copyrights and trademarks. As discussed in chapter 2, one of the primary protections afforded creators is the ability to limit the use of the results of the creative process by means of registering copyrights and trademarks. The increased use of the Internet as a means of disseminating information has resulted in a correspondingly increased ability of people to make unauthorized use of protected material. This section will examine this important aspect of cyberlaw in three distinct areas:

1. MP3
2. Deep-linking
3. Domain names.

MP3

MP3
Digital program to
condense music.

MP3 is a digital format that can be used to store vast amounts of music in a limited space with almost no loss in the quality of the recording. With this format, the music can be transmitted over computer networks all around the world. Unfortunately, this format has been used to record and disseminate songs that are copyrighted without obtaining permission or paying royalties to the copyright holder.

In order to protect the copyright of the holder, the Recording Industry Association of America has attempted to enjoin the production of MP3 programs and has sued for copyright infringement. However, to date these strategies have had limited success, arguably because the copyright infringer is difficult to locate and obtain jurisdiction over because of the global aspect of the Internet.

— *Example*

A songwriter created a song that she copyrighted and produced. The song is very popular, and it is bringing in a great deal of income to the creator by means of royalties. One day, while surfing the net, the songwriter accesses a Web site that allows users to download her song. She never granted permission and receives no royalties for this use. However, it appears that the infringer is located in the Middle East with no contact with the United States other than the Web site. Under this circumstance, it is extremely difficult for the songwriter to protect her rights.

**Digital Millennium
Copyright Act (DMCA)**
Federal statute designed to
extend copyright protection
to new technology.

In order to remedy this situation, in 1998 Congress passed the **Digital Millennium Copyright Act (DMCA)** to implement the World Intellectual Property Organization (WIPO) Copyright Treaty and the WIPO Performance and Phonograms Treaty, both of which will be discussed in the next section of this chapter. The DMCA makes it illegal to use any technology that circumvents copyright protections. For example, it has been used to enjoin production of systems that could permit persons to make unauthorized copies of DVDs.

— *Example*

A Web site has converted several popular television programs to a digital format and is showing them on its site. Using the provisions of the DMCA, the television network that holds the copyright may be able to enjoin such unauthorized use.

Deep-Linking

deep-linking
One Web site providing
access to another site by
bypassing the second
site's home page.

Deep-linking is a method that permits the use of one Web site to link onto, or access, another Web site without first having to access the second site's homepage. If the homepage requires a fee to access the remainder of the Web site, this method of deep-linking could infringe upon the second Web site's property rights.

framing
Having one Web site appear in a window on another Web site.

domain name
Unique name to identify a Web site.

Internet Corporation for Assigned Names and Numbers
Agency that licenses organizations to assign domain names.

Network Solutions, Inc.
Organization licensed to assign domain names.

Verisign
Took over from Network Solutions, Inc. in 2001.

Uniform Domain Name Dispute Resolution Policy (UDRP)
Act that mandates arbitration of domain name disputes.

Anticybersquatting Consumer Protection Act (ACPA)
Federal law designed to prevent cyberpiracy.

cyberpiracy
Registering a well-known name as a domain name to prevent the trademark holder from using the mark as a domain name.

Related to deep-linking is **framing**, whereby one Web site appears in a window on another Web site. In this fashion, the rights of the framed Web site may be infringed. Both of these practices are currently the subject of lawsuits to enjoin such use, but to date no judicial determination has been made regarding these practices.

Domain Names

A **domain name** is a unique name that identifies a particular Web site in the same manner that a corporate name identifies a specific corporation. Such name can be, and usually is, trademarked; consequently, any person using that name, or a name so similar as to cause potential confusion with the public, is considered to have infringed on a trademark right.

At this point in time, assignment of domain names comes under the auspices of the **Internet Corporation for Assigned Names and Numbers**, which licenses organizations to assign unique domain names. Prior to 1999, such assignment of domain names was made under the exclusive control of **Network Solutions, Inc**. In 2001, Network Solutions became **Verisign**, and is but one of the organizations licensed to assign domain names.

— ***Example*** —

A chain store retailer wants to use its trademarked name as a domain name for a Web site to sell its merchandise. The retailer registers its mark with Verisign and can now be assured that no one else will be able to use its mark as a domain name.

In 1999, in order to provide some protection for the trademark rights of domain names, Congress enacted the **Uniform Domain Name Dispute Resolution Policy (UDRP)** and the **Anticybersquatting Consumer Protection Act (ACPA)**. **Cyberpiracy** is defined as the registration of a domain name containing a known name with the intention of selling it to the owner of the trademarked name or to a third party for financial gain. In this fashion, the cyberpirate is "squatting" on the name. Prior to the ACPA, the trademark holder could only enforce his or her right to the name if the domain name was identical to the trademarked one. This act affords greater protection for the mark holder.

The Internet Corporation created the UDRP for Assigned Names and Numbers in order to force challenges of infringement to be settled by mandatory arbitration. To initiate proceedings, the challenger to the domain name must prove the following:

1. The domain name is identical or confusingly similar to the marked name
2. The challenger has the mark to that name
3. The domain name holder has no right to the marked name
4. The domain name was registered in bad faith.

The domain name holder can use the same arguments typically raised in all trademark disputes as a defense; for example, fair use, loss of mark, legitimate use, and so forth.

In order to demonstrate bad faith, the following factors are considered:

1. Circumstances indicating that the registrant only registered the domain name primarily to sell or transfer the name to the mark holder or its competitor for value

2. The domain name was registered to prevent the mark holder from using the mark as a domain name

3. The name was registered primarily to disrupt the mark holder's business

4. The registrant intended to acquire the name to confuse the public so that they would believe they were dealing with the mark holder.

Pursuant to the provisions of the UDRP, if successful, the claimant can have the domain name cancelled or transferred to the mark holder. Appeals of these decisions are restricted, and the arbitration does not preclude the parties from instituting judicial proceedings before or after the arbitration.

The Anticybersquatting Consumer Protection Act, 15 USC § 1125 (d), provides civil remedies to a mark holder if it can prove that the domain name holder

1. Has a bad faith intent to profit from the domain name

2. Registers a name that is protected as a registered trademark.

The complainant must indicate bad faith to initiate proceedings under the ACPA and may do so by demonstrating various factors that point to the domain name holder's intent. The decisions that have resulted from challenges under this act have specified certain factors that are deemed automatically to indicate bad faith. Such factors are

1. Using the domain name in connection with a pornographic site

2. Providing inaccurate or false information in the registration of the domain name

typo-piracy
Deliberately misspelling a famous trademark.

3. Using a deliberate misspelling of a famous trademark, known as **typo-piracy**

4. The name was deliberately designed to confuse users with respect to the identity of the seller of the site's products

5. No Web site is created after the domain name is registered

6. The offer to sell the domain name to the mark holder.

One important aspect of the UDRP that must be considered is that it does not protect the user of a personal name absent that name being included as part of a trademark. In other words, it provides no protection for personality rights or privacy rights for personal name use.

Jurisdiction for commencing proceedings under the UDRP is based on the agreement between the license registrar and the registrant, making the jurisdiction automatic by virtue of the registration contract. Further, to initiate a claim, the trademark must be registered in the United States; no jurisdiction may be predicated on a foreign mark.

Modern technology has created greater challenges for the entertainment law professional because new technology means new methods of disseminating creative products as well as new methods of infringing upon the legal rights of artists and other entertainment professionals. Traditional law does not always translate effectively to cyberspace; thus, on an almost daily basis, old laws are being judicially reinterpreted and new laws arc being enacted to afford rights and protections to entertainment professionals. These problems escalate as technology upgrades and changes.

INTERNATIONAL PROTECTIONS

World Intellectual Property Organization (WIPO)
International organization created to protect copyrights and intellectual property worldwide.

WIPO Copyright Treaty
International treaty designed to protect copyrights worldwide.

WIPO Performance and Phonograms Treaty
International treaty designed to protect rights for performances and phonograms.

Berne Convention
Convention for the protection of literary and artistic works.

In an attempt to provide solutions for conflicts resulting from new technological advancements, the **World Intellectual Property Organization (WIPO)** created the **WIPO Copyright Treaty** and the **WIPO Performance and Phonograms Treaty** in accordance with the **Berne Convention**.

The WIPO treaties attempt to lay down recognizable rules and regulations for the protection of ownership of copyrights and performance and phonogram rights. On the tail of the Berne Convention was the Convention for the Protection of Literary and Artistic Works; combined, these treaties act to secure intellectual rights and protections for artists.

The **Convention on Cybercrime**, held November 23, 2001, is the first international treaty on crimes committed via the Internet and computer networks. One of its focuses is the protection of copyrights. It recognizes the need for cooperation between states and private industry in the war against cybercrime. The treaty mandates that all parties to it shall adopt legislative and other measures, under their respective domestic laws, to criminalize offenses that infringe upon copyrights.

In addition, the treaty sets forth much-needed jurisdictional guidelines, as discussed in the following section of this chapter.

CYBERLAW JURISDICTION

Convention on Cybercrime
First international treaty involving crimes committed via the Internet.

Determination as to which court has jurisdiction over Internet issues is problematic because the information disseminated on the World Wide Web crosses all borders, both domestic and international. To determine the appropriate jurisdiction, several factors are considered:

1. Where the Web site is located
2. The laws of the state where the Internet provider is located
3. The laws of the country where the Internet provider is located.

Civil Cases

Generally, the state in which suit is filed determines where jurisdiction falls on a cyberlaw issue. This determination is subject to the **Due Process Clause** of the **Fourteenth Amendment** of the United States Constitution, which states that no person shall be deprived of the right to due process of the laws. To meet these standards, the court that hears the matter must have both subject matter jurisdiction and personal, or *in personam* jurisdiction, over the parties or property in question. Having subject matter jurisdiction means filing the claim in a court that is authorized to hear such cases. Having *in personam* jurisdiction means having jurisdiction over the persons against whom the action is brought. These determinations are directed by federal or state statutes, depending upon the court in which the suit is filed and the basis of the cause of action.

There are several ways to establish personal jurisdiction under the Due Process Clause. One such way is if the aggrieved person can show that the **Long-Arm Statute**, allowing the long arm of the law to reach outside the state's natural boundaries, applies. It will apply if the aggrieved person can show that the wrong doer purposefully established **minimum contacts** (the least amount of contacts necessary) with the forum state. In order to establish minimum contacts, the court developed a three-prong test. First, the court determines whether there is purposeful availment on the part of the aggressor; i.e., whether the wrongdoer made himself available to the claim. Second, the court determines whether the claim arose out of the wrongdoer's activities. Third, the court looks to see if subjecting the wrongdoer to jurisdiction would offend the traditional notions of fair play and substantial justice.

— *Example* —

The owner/operator of a New York nightclub complained that the owner/operator of a nightclub in Missouri used the same name. The Missouri owner created a Web page that allowed people who logged on to purchase tickets for the club. The New York owner claims this site infringes on his, the owner/operator's trademark of the club's name. A New York court would not have jurisdiction over this matter because it was a Web site in Missouri, set up in Missouri, and the purchasers could only pick up their tickets in Missouri.

Example

A Connecticut corporation discovers that a Massachusetts corporation is using their company's name as a domain name. The Connecticut corporation claims that the Massachusetts corporation infringed on its company's trademark. The Massachusetts corporation advertised on the Internet on sites located in Connecticut. The advertisements were frequently accessed by a large number of people in Connecticut over and over again. Because the advertisements were continuously available, the Massachusetts corporation was subject to Connecticut's Long-Arm Statute.

Criminal Cases

Criminal cases arise from the violation of cyberlaw primarily in instances of alleged child pornography, where the right to free speech is curtailed by the obscenity exception. While applying the Due Process Clause, courts have also had to wrestle with other new complications to determine whether or not something on the Internet was obscene, especially since the complained-of files are, for all intents and purposes, intangible. Also to be determined was the intent of Congress, for the federal obscenity statutes do not expressly prohibit or prevent obscene material crossing state lines through the use of **interstate commerce** (sale of goods from state to state).

interstate commerce
The sale of goods from state to state.

── *Example* ─────────────────────

The operator of a California based pornographic bulletin board claimed that a Tennessee Court had no jurisdiction over them because (1) there was no tangible obscene material and (2) Congress did not specifically regulate the area of law. The court may decide that, in looking at Congress' intent, the pornographic material was obscene.

Cyberlaw Jurisdiction for International Cases

International cases pose even more difficulties than do domestic cases when trying to determine proper jurisdiction. There are no judicial decisions that address which is the best forum for an international cyberlaw conflict. While the determination as to whether a party from outside the United States can be confronted in an American court follows the basic determination of whether there is both subject matter and *in personam* jurisdiction, the Supreme Court ruled that there is a higher jurisdictional threshold for international matters.

The Convention on Cybercrime also sets out guidelines for jurisdiction. It states that parties shall adopt legislative and other measures to establish jurisdiction when the offence is committed

1. In its territory
2. On board a ship flying the flag of that party
3. On board an aircraft registered under the laws of that party
4. By one of its nationals, if the offense is punishable under criminal law where it was committed or if the offense is committed outside the territorial jurisdiction of any state.

Additionally, the treaty calls for international cooperation in regard to reciprocal legislation and domestic laws for the purpose of investigation and collection of evidence.

— *Example* —

A California company brings suit against five Swedish citizens for the posting of false and misleading articles about it on the World Wide Web. The court may hold that where the alleged wrongdoer did not have continuous and systematic contacts with the state the American court has no jurisdiction over the foreigners.

CHAPTER REVIEW

Modern technology has greatly affected the entertainment industry. With the increase of technology, many problems have arisen. Cyberlaw has been enacted to regulate cyberspace technology.

One such area where legislative measures have been passed is in the area of pornographic material distributed to minors, although, to date, no such law has been able to pass constitutional muster. Another area that has received attention is defamation on the Web. Commonly, such defamatory statements are made on bulletin boards. Liability is determined based on the degree of control the provider exercises over the material.

Encryption is the use of a code or codes to secure material transmitted via the Internet. Although originally not viewed as copyright eligible, it is now recognized as an outgrowth of speech and the intellectual process.

Cyberlaw also concerns itself with copyright and trademark. MP3, a digital format for storing music, has been attacked as a means of copyright infringement. Deep-linking permits the use of one Web site to link onto another site without first having to access the second site's homepage. Domain names identify particular Web sites and the use of someone else's trademarked name or the use of a similar one can be an infringement.

There is little regulation when it comes to international protection of artist's rights. Several conventions such as WIPO, the Berne Convention, and the Cybercrime Convention have sought to protect artists through international cooperation.

Many problems occur when determining to which is the proper court to bring a cybercrime. The party must have both subject matter and *in personam* jurisdiction over the controversy and the party. The Long-Arm Statute can establish jurisdiction if minimum contacts with the forum state have been met.

JUDICIAL DECISION

The following case highlights the problems associated with acquiring and protecting domain names.

Virtual Countries, Inc. v. Republic of South Africa
148 FSupp2d 256 (2001)

In this action, plaintiff seeks a declaration, pursuant to 28 USC § 2201, that it has the right to the Internet domain name *southafrica.com*, and an injunction preventing defendants from seeking a declaration of their rights in the name in arbitral or court proceedings worldwide. Currently before the Court is defendants' motion to stay or dismiss the action in its entirety. Because the Court finds that it lacks subject matter jurisdiction to hear the action under the Foreign Sovereign Immunities Act ("FSIA"), 28 USC §§ 1330, 1602–10, the action is dismissed.

I. Factual Background

Plaintiff Virtual Countries, Inc. ("Virtual"), a corporation organized and existing under the laws of the State of Washington with its principal place of business in Seattle, Washington, manages country-specific dot-com Internet domain names (Amended Complaint ("Amend. Compl.") § 6). One of the domain names that Virtual has registered is *southafrica.com*, which it has "owned and maintained" since May 13, 1995 and has used in commerce since October 1996 (*Id* §§ 12, 17, 18). Defendant Republic of South Africa ("Republic") is a foreign state, and defendant South African Tourism Board ("SATOUR") is an agency or instrumentality of Republic with its principal place of business in New York, New York (*Id* §§ 7–8).

The two primary international organizations that set policy concerning domain name registration principles and procedures are the Internet Corporation for Assigned Names and Numbers ("ICANN") and the World Intellectual Property Organization ("WIPO") (Defendants' Memorandum of Law in Support of Defendants' Motion for a Stay or to Dismiss ("Def. Mem.") at 3). ICANN was formed in 1998 by a broad coalition of Internet stakeholders, and is responsible for setting policy for and administering the assignment of domain names, including the so-called generic top-level domains ("gTLDs") .com, .net. and .org (The Internet Corporation for Assigned Names

and Numbers, http://www.icann.org, Declaration of David B. Goldstein dated Apr. 30, 2001 ("Goldstein Decl."), Ex. 1). It is also responsible for resolution of Internet domain name conflicts. ICANN makes decisions through its Board of Directors, who are elected from several supporting organizations, and who are advised by several committees (Def. Mem. at 4; About ICANN, http://www.icann.org/general/abouticann.htm; ICANN: A Structural Overview, Declaration of Lora A. Moffatt, Esq. in Opposition to Defendants' Motion to Stay or Dismiss and in Support of Plaintiff's Motion for Summary Judgment ("Moffatt Decl."), Ex. C). One such committee is the Governmental Advisory Committee ("ICANN-GAC"), the membership of which is limited to national governments, multinational government organizations and treaty organizations, and certain "distinct economies" recognized in international forums (*Id*; ICANN Government Advisory Committee (GAC) Home Page, http://www.noie.gov.au/projects/international/DNS/gac/index.htm, Ex. 2 to Goldstein Decl.). Republic is a member of ICANN-GAC (Def. Mem. at 4). WIPO is a specialized agency of the United Nations which, *inter alia*, administers 21 international treaties concerning intellectual property protection. Its membership, like that of the United Nations, is limited to national governments, and the organization currently has 177 members, including Republic (Def. Mem. at 4 n. 2; "The Recognition of Rights and the Use of Names in the Internet Domain Name System: Interim Report of the Second WIPO Internet Domain Name Process ("Interim Report"), Ex. 7 to Goldstein Decl.). WIPO also plays a significant role in the development of Internet domain name policy, in particular by preparing reports and recommendations based upon submissions of its members and commentary by private sector members of the Internet community (Def. Mem. at 4; Marcelo Halpern & Ajay K. Mehrotra, *From International Treaties To Internet Norms: The Evolution of International Trademark Disputes in the Internet Age*, 21 UPaJ Int'l Econ L 523, 550-52 (2000) (describing WIPO's role in the development of ICANN's domain name policy)).

The current international procedure for domain name dispute resolution occurs through ICANN's Uniform Domain Name Dispute Resolution Policy ("UDRP"), which entered into operation on December 1, 1999 (Interim Report at 1; UDRP, Ex. 3 to Goldstein Decl.). This procedure, which was developed by WIPO through the "First WIPO Internet Domain Name Process" ("WIPO-1"), is limited to the abusive registration of domain names in violation of trademark rights, which most commonly encompasses what many courts have referred to as "cybersquatting" (Interim Report at (v); *Sporty's Farm L.L.C. v. Sportsman's Market, Inc.*, 202 F3d 489, 493 (2d Cir 2000) (discussing the practice of "cybersquatting")). However, WIPO left room for amendments. In the WIPO-1 Final Report, for example, WIPO discussed the issue of "geographical indications," which it stated comprise "a class of intellectual property identifiers other than trade or service marks [that are] also frequently the target of abusive cybersquatting practices," and including geographical terms such as country names (Interim Report §§ 187–91). WIPO recommended that such issue be considered in future discussions (*Id* § 188).

Discussions are now underway in WIPO, as part of a second WIPO investigatory process, the WIPO-2 process, concerning possible amendments to the UDRP. In response to a demand by WIPO Member States that the organization address the issue of geographical names, WIPO-2 "requested comments on whether and by which means geographical indications (in the broad sense) should be protected against their bad faith, abusive, misleading or unfair registration or use as domain names" (*Id* § 189, Executive Summary § 3). Republic submitted a formal Comment in March 2001, in which it stated that WIPO should recommend, *inter alia*, a *per se* exclusion on the registration of country names in the second-level domain, and (ii) the adoption of a policy subjecting entities that register country names in the second-level domain to binding arbitration (Submission by Republic of South Africa in Response to WIPO2 RFC-2, Declaration of Andile Abner Ngcaba dated Apr. 26, 2001 ("Ngcaba Decl."), Ex. 1, at 5). Republic has tabled similar proposals in submissions to ICANN-GAC, the Ministerial Oversight Committee of the African Telecommunications Union, and a task force of the G-8 nations addressing issues related to the so-called "digital

divide" between developed and developing nations (*Id* § 5, Exs. 2–3).

WIPO published the WIPO-2 Interim Report in April 2001 (see Interim Report). In a section entitled "Geographic Designations Beyond Intellectual Property," WIPO discusses certain issues raised by a country's attempt to claim ownership of domain names that employ the country's name (*Id* §§ 236–86). The Report states that WIPO "favor[s] the view that a system of *per se* exclusions would *not* be a desirable means of protecting names of countries …" (*Id* § 279) (emphasis added). WIPO's principal concern is that "such strong form of protection might be perceived to lack international legitimacy, in light of the absence of a universally accepted right of countries to the exclusive use of the terms in question in the context of the [Domain Name System]" (*Id* 1). As an alternative, WIPO suggests two other options for further consideration and comment: (i) maintenance of the status quo, with no protective measures for registration of country names through the UDRP; and (ii) permitting countries, through arbitration, to seek to obtain the transfer or cancellation of the name of a country, region, or municipality which is found to be abusive. The Report does not indicate whether the arbitration proposed in the second option would be binding (*Id* §§ 281, 282). Like WIPO-1, the WIPO-2 process will culminate with the release of a Final Report, expected in August 2001, which will constitute WIPO's recommendations to ICANN concerning domain name registration policy (Timetable, Ex. 6 to Goldstein Decl.). WIPO's conclusions are merely recommendations: ICANN and individual WIPO member states will be free to adopt or disregard the conclusions reached in the Final Report and will not be bound by its recommendations (Plaintiff's Memorandum of Law in Opposition to Defendants' Motion to Stay or Dismiss ("Pl. Mem.") at 5). Although defendants state that ICANN will consider the recommendations in the Final Report "by the end of [2001] or early next year," the record does not reflect that ICANN has set a timetable for taking action (Def. Mem. at 7; Pl. Mem. at 5).

This action arises out of a press release issued by Republic's Department of Communications on October 30, 2000 (the "Press Release"). In the Release, Republic stated its position, also reflected in its submissions to WIPO and ICANN-GAC, that "countries ha[ve] the first right to own their domain names" (Press Release, South African Department of Communications, South Africa Seeks to Secure *www.southafrica.com* (Oct. 30, 2000), Ex. 4 to Ngcaba Decl.). Republic further stated that it intended to file an application with WIPO by November 10, 2000 asserting its rights in the *southafrica.com* domain, which it intended to use as a strategic marketing tool in promoting trade and tourism, and in promoting the image of Republic internationally (*Id* at 1). Republic's then-upcoming submissions to WIPO and ICANN-GAC were also mentioned (*Id* at 2). The Release stated that Republic "could be the first country in the world to make a challenge for the right to own its own domain name in the largest of the high-level domain names—dot.com" (*Id* at 1).

Four days later, on November 3, 2000, Virtual filed the instant action, asserting that "Republic's announced intention to litigate and its assertion of rights have injured [Virtual], placing a cloud over [Virtual] in the equity markets by contesting the ownership of [Virtual's] underlying assets" (Amend. Compl. § 28). Virtual requests (i) a declaration that it has the sole right in the *southafrica.com* domain, to the exclusion of defendants, and (ii) an order enjoining defendants from seeking a declaration of their rights to register the domain name in arbitral or court proceedings worldwide (*Id* at 9). Although Republic's submissions reflect that it still seeks to establish a country's right to second-level domains bearing the country's name, including Republic's own rights in the *southafrica.com* name, Republic has not filed an application with WIPO, and maintains that it does not intend to do so under current UDRP procedures (Ngcaba Decl. § 8). Defendants now move to: (i) stay the proceeding pursuant to FedRCivP 7(b) or the Court's inherent power, or (ii) dismiss the action in its entirety, pursuant to FedRCivP 12(b)(1) ("Rule 12(b)(1)"), for lack of subject matter jurisdiction under the FSIA and the Declaratory Judgment Act, 28 USC § 2201, and/or (iii) dismiss the action as to SATOUR pursuant to FedRCivP 12(b)(6) ("Rule 12(b)(6)").

II. Discussion
A. Defendants are Immune from Suit Under the FSIA
1. Motion to Dismiss Standard

On a Rule 12 motion to dismiss, the Court must accept the factual allegations contained in the complaint as true, and draw all reasonable inferences

in favor of the non-movant; it should not dismiss the complaint "unless it appears beyond doubt that the plaintiff can prove no set of facts in support of his claim which would entitle him to relief" (*Conley v. Gibson*, 355 US 41, 45–46 (1957); see also *Leatherman v. Tarrant County Narcotics Intelligence and Coordination Unit*, 507 US 163, 164 (1993) (noting that factual allegations in complaint must be accepted as true on motion to dismiss); *Press v. Quick & Reilly, Inc.*, 18 F3d 121, 128 (2d Cir 2000) (same)). On a motion to dismiss under Rule 12(b)(1) for lack of subject matter jurisdiction, the court may resolve jurisdictional fact issues by referring to evidence outside of the pleadings, such as affidavits and documentary exhibits (see *Zappia Middle East Constr. Co. Ltd. v. Emirate of Abu Dhabi*, 215 F3d 247, 253 (2d Cir 2000) (citing *Cargill Int'l S.A. v. M/T Pavel Dybenko*, 991 F2d 1012, 1019 (2d Cir 1993)).

2. Commercial Activity Exception to the FSIA

"The Foreign Sovereign Immunities Act 'provides the sole basis for obtaining jurisdiction over a foreign state in the courts of this country'" (*Saudi Arabia v. Nelson*, 507 US 349, 355 (1993) (quoting *Argentine Republic v. Amerada Hess Shipping Corp.*, 488 US 428, 443 (1989)). The term "foreign state" includes an agency or instrumentality of a foreign state; thus, both South Africa and SATOUR qualify as foreign states under the statute (see 28 USC §§ 1603(a), (b); see also *Hansen v. Danish Tourist Board*, No. CV 00-1419, 2001 WL 586001, at *3 (EDNY May 19, 2001); (Amend. Compl. § 8); (cf. Pl. Mem. at 1 n. 1 (asserting that SATOUR "has no identity apart from Republic")); Def. Mem. at 18 n. 11 (stating that SATOUR, as a "duly created instrumentality" of a foreign state, is not necessarily its alter ego)). A foreign state is presumptively immune from the jurisdiction of United States courts under the FSIA, unless a specified exception applies (*Nelson*, 507 US at 355 (citing *Verlinden B.V. v. Central Bank of Nigeria*, 461 US 480, 488–89 (1983)); see also 28 USC § 1604). The most significant of the FSIA's exceptions, and the one at issue in this case, is the so-called "commercial activity" exception, codified in 28 USC § 1605(a)(2) ("Section 1605(a)(2)"), which provides that a foreign state is not immune from suit in any case

in which the action is based upon a commercial activity carried on in the United States by the foreign state; or upon an act performed in the United States in connection with a commercial activity of the foreign state elsewhere; or upon an act outside the territory of the United States in connection with a commercial activity of the foreign state elsewhere and that act causes a direct effect in the United States (Section 1605(a)(2); see *Republic of Argentina v. Weltover*, 504 US 607, 610 (1992)).

In this case, Virtual claims that jurisdiction lies under the third clause of Section 1605(a)(2). Therefore, this Court's analysis is limited to considering whether the lawsuit is (i) "based ... upon an act [of Republic] outside the territory of the United States"; (ii) that was taken "in connection with a commercial activity" of Republic outside this country; and (iii) that "cause[d] a direct effect in the United States" *Weltover*, 504 US at 610). The Supreme Court has stated that the phrase "based upon," as it is used in the FSIA, "is read most naturally to mean those elements of a claim that, if proven, would entitle a plaintiff to relief under his theory of the case" (*Nelson*, 507 US at 357). It is undisputed that this action is based upon an "act" of Republic that occurred outside the United States. Specifically, Virtual states that "[t]his action arises from, and is based upon, [Republic's] public challenge of [Virtual's] ownership of *southafrica.com* and the accompanying threat by [Republic] to commence an arbitration against [Virtual]" (Pl. Mem. at 16). Virtual's requests for a declaratory judgment and injunction flow directly from this conduct, which Virtual acknowledges is the only "legally significant conduct" in support of its application to this Court (*Id* at 19).

The principal disagreement between the parties pertains to whether such acts were taken "in connection with a commercial activity" of Republic, and whether the acts had a "direct effect in the United States." The record reflects that both questions should be resolved in the negative. While the FSIA provides that the commercial character of an activity should be determined by reference to its "nature," rather than the foreign state's underlying "purpose" for so acting, 28 USC § 1603(d), "[t]his definition ... leaves the critical term 'commercial' largely undefined" (*Weltover*, 504 US at 612). In *Weltover*, the Supreme Court set forth the standard pursuant to which the existence of commercial activity should be judged, which standard reflects the "restrictive" theory of foreign sovereign immunity first endorsed by the State Department in

1952 (*Id*, see 26 DeptStateBull 984 (1952) (stating that "the purpose of the restrictive theory of sovereign immunity is to try to accommodate the interest of individuals doing business with foreign governments in having their legal rights determined by the courts, with the interest of foreign governments in being free to perform certain political acts without undergoing the embarrassment or hindrance of defending the propriety of such acts before foreign courts")). Under such theory, a state is immune from the jurisdiction of foreign courts as to its sovereign or public acts (*jure imperii*), but not as to those that are private or commercial in character (*jure gestionis*) (*Nelson*, 507 US at 359–60 (citations omitted)). Put differently, a foreign sovereign's acts are "commercial" within the meaning of the FSIA when the sovereign "acts, not as a regulator of a market, but in the manner of a private player within it" (*Weltover*, 504 US at 614). A sovereign may be considered such a private player if the particular actions it performs are "the type of actions by which a private party engages in '*trade and traffic and commerce*'" (*Id* (emphasis added) (citations omitted); see also Restatement (Third) of the Foreign Relations Law of the United States § 451 (1987) ("Under international law, a state or state instrumentality is immune from the jurisdiction of the courts of another state, except with respect to claims arising out of activities of the kind that may be carried on by private persons")). Further, acts of a sovereign are "in connection with" a commercial activity when there is a substantive connection or a causal link between the acts and the commercial activity (*Hanil Bank v. PT Bank Negara Indonesia (PERSERO)*, 148 F3d 127, 131 (2d Cir 1998)).

Virtual contends that Republic has engaged in commercial activity, because "[t]he continuing battle for a stake in cyberspace is hardly the exclusive domain of sovereigns," as private persons frequently challenge domain name ownership and commence arbitrations (Pl. Mem. at 16). Virtual therefore concludes that the Court should accept subject matter jurisdiction here to forestall "[Republic's] misguided foray into this commercial arena" (*Id*). However, while the Court acknowledges that a sovereign's actions in registering or challenging domain names may in certain cases qualify as "commercial," here Republic has not engaged in any transaction or course of conduct that is commercial in nature (28 USC § 1603(d)).

It merely issued a press release stating that it intended to file an application with WIPO for the right to own the *southafrica.com* domain name, and "take the matter up in international fora" (Press Release at 1–2)). The issuance of the Release, without more, is insufficient to establish the requisite commercial activity, because, even assuming it were a form of "public challenge" as Virtual contends, it does not constitute "trade, traffic, or commerce" within the marketplace (see *Weltover*, 504 US at 614; *Nelson*, 507 US at 360; *Hanil Bank*, 148 F3d at 130 (stating that the state must act "like a private player in the marketplace" in order to be deemed to have engaged in commercial activity); cf. *U.S. Fidelity and Guar. Co. v. Braspero Oil Servs Co.*, 199 F3d 94, 98 (2d Cir 1999) (finding that defendants' commercial construction projects constituted commercial activity, and its issuance of a payment default notice to co-defendants was the act in connection with such activity); *Filetech S.A. v. France Telecom S.A.*, 157 F3d 922, 931 (2d Cir 1998) (finding that defendant's sales of marketing lists amounted to commercial activity)). The record reflects that, since the issuance of the Press Release, Republic has taken no further action with respect to the domain *southafrica.com* beyond its submissions to certain international bodies concerning the role of country names within domain name policy. Further, Republic has affirmatively represented that it will not commence an arbitration in WIPO or other organization under existing UDRP procedures, which suggests that it will wait to see how WIPO and ICANN resolve the proposed changes before deciding on a course of action (Ngcaba Decl. § 8; Def. Rep. at 6). Thus, even assuming that the initiation of an arbitration would constitute "commercial" activity under the FSIA, a filing by Republic does not appear imminent, thus removing the "threat" of such filing, on which the majority, if not the entirety, of this action is based (see Pl. Mem. at 17 (stating that the lawsuit "is based upon [Republic's] conduct in announcing to the world through a press release that it intended to commence an arbitration against [Virtual] challenging [Virtual's] rightful ownership of the *southafrica.com* domain name)).

Moreover, the limited activity in which Republic has engaged in support of its position concerning country domain names, namely, its presentation of position papers to WIPO and ICANN-GAC, arises from its role as policymaker within, and indirectly, regulator of, the market of Internet domain names, rather than its role as a participant in such market. Contrary to Virtual's contention, the mere fact that private parties are allowed to submit comments to WIPO concerning domain name policy is irrelevant (Pl. Mem. at 16-17 n. 18). Republic's activities in WIPO, a UN body, and the advisory committee of ICANN comprising national states, are inherently sovereign (see *Heaney v. Government of Spain*, 445 F2d 501, 503 (2d Cir 1971) (stating that a state's acts concerning diplomatic activity are public acts entitled to immunity)).

Even if Republic's actions were deemed to be "commercial" under the FSIA, they would still be insufficient to trigger the commercial activity exception because they did not cause a "direct effect" in the United States (Section 1605(a)(2)). The Supreme Court considered the meaning of "direct effect" in *Weltover*. There, Argentina had issued bonds as part of a currency stabilization plan, which provided for repayment in United States dollars through one of several markets, namely, New York, London, Zurich, or Frankfurt (see *Weltover*, 504 US at 609). When the bonds matured, Argentina lacked sufficient reserves to pay them, so it unilaterally extended the time for their redemption (see *Id* at 610). Two Panamanian corporations and a Swiss bank refused to accept such rescheduling and demanded full payment of the bonds in New York. When Argentina refused, these bondholders filed suit (*Id*) Having determined that the bondholders had sufficiently established that the lawsuit was based upon an act outside the territory of the United States (presumably Argentina's unilateral extension) and that such act was taken in connection with commercial activity (the issuance of the bonds), *Id* at 611–17, the Court turned to direct effect. The Court stated that "an effect is direct if it follows as an immediate consequence of the defendant's activity," although it need not be substantial or foreseeable (*Id* at 618). Because the bondholders in question had designated their accounts in New York as the place of payment, thus making New York the place of performance for Argentina's contractual obligations, "the rescheduling of those obligations necessarily had a 'direct effect' in the United States: Money that was supposed to have been delivered to a New York bank for deposit was not forthcoming" (*Id* at 619).

In the instant case, Virtual claims that it has suffered economic loss as a direct result of Republic's issuance of the Press Release. In the Amended Complaint, Virtual states that Republic's "announced intention to litigate and its assertion of rights" have "plac[ed] a cloud over [Virtual] in the equity markets" (Amend. Compl. § 28). In an affidavit submitted in opposition to defendants' motion to dismiss, Virtual's president and CEO, Gregory Paley ("Paley") elaborates on the "cloud," stating that the release had a "devastating and direct effect ... on [Virtual's] short and long term business operations, [which] ... threatens [Virtual's] continued corporate existence" (Paley Decl. § 10). In particular, Paley states that Virtual has had difficulty "compet[ing] with other ventures for a share of what is now a limited pool of available capital," and that the controversy surrounding the Release has negatively impacted Virtual's cashflow and company morale (Id § 11). He also states that one of several companies that has approached Virtual with an interest in a joint business relationship pulled out of preliminary discussions concerning an alliance related to *southafrica.com* because it "feared that a partnership with us could result in reprisals from the South African government" (Id § 13). Paley concludes that Virtual "urgently requires a ruling from this Court" that Republic "has no basis to publicly challenge" Virtual's ownership of the *southafrica.com* domain name (Id § 16).

The Court finds that Paley's allegations are insufficient to establish the requisite direct effect under Section 1605(a)(2). Virtual's allegation of a loss of competitiveness from the Press Release that has jeopardized the company's entire corporate existence is entirely conclusory; Paley states only that certain unspecified United States investors who initially expressed an interest in investing, later decided not to invest (Paley Decl. § 12). To the extent that Virtual has encountered problems raising money from investors, such problems would more plausibly be the result of the "limited pool of available capital" for dot-com concerns, rather than Republic's Press Release. Moreover, Virtual's statements as to the purported negative impact on its cashflow caused by the Press Release are conclusory and vague, and the alleged harm to company morale, as an outgrowth of the alleged reduction in competitiveness and cashflow problems, is clearly not an immediate consequence of Republic's actions. Finally, Virtual does not provide any details concerning the potential partner that pulled out of negotiations for fear of reprisals from Republic, the type of partnership that was envisaged, or the injury that Virtual allegedly suffered as a result.

Thus, Virtual has not established, under the standard set forth in *Weltover*, that Republic's actions had a "direct effect" in the United States. Moreover, Virtual's allegations fail to satisfy its burden for an independent reason, namely, that an undefined financial loss such as that which is alleged, without more, is not sufficient to trigger the commercial activity exception (*Antares Aircraft, L.P. v. Fed. Republic of Nigeria*, 999 F2d 33, 34–35 (2d Cir 1993) ("[T]he fact that an American individual or firm suffers some financial loss as a result of a tort cannot, standing alone, suffice to trigger the [commercial activity] exception.")). The Second Circuit held in *Antares* that jurisdiction under the FSIA does not lie where, as here, all "legally significant acts" occur outside the United States (*Id* at 36–37; *Filetech*, 157 F3d at 931; (Pl. Mem. at 19 (stating that Republic's "public challenge" of Virtual's ownership in the Press Release was the "legally significant conduct" in this case))). While the court's holding in *Antares* related to a tort cause of action, and in certain cases such holding may not apply to a contract action, the "legally significant acts" test is equally applicable to Virtual's allegations here, which are more akin to tort (e.g. defamation) than to contract (*cf. Hanil Bank*, 148 F3d at 133 (stating that the test was "not directly applicable to the contract at issue," but nevertheless finding that "the most legally significant act—the breach of contract—occurred in the United States")); *Antares*, 999 F2d at 36 (discussing *Weltover* and stating that the legally significant act in that case was the breach that occurred in New York); *Martin v. Republic of South Africa*, 836 F2d 91 (2d Cir 1987) (finding that financial injury of person injured abroad is not a "direct effect" in United States); *Zernicek v. Brown & Root, Inc.*, 826 F2d 415, 418 (5th Cir 1987) (stating that "consequential damages [from personal injury tort abroad] are insufficient to constitute a 'direct effect in the United States' for purposes of abrogating sovereign immunity")).

Accordingly, the Court finds that it lacks subject matter jurisdiction to hear this action, against either Republic or SATOUR, under the FSIA.

C. Dismissal of SATOUR

Republic moves separately to dismiss SATOUR from this action pursuant to Rule 12(b)(6) for failure to state a claim. Because SATOUR is an agency or instrumentality of Republic, the Court lacks subject matter jurisdiction under the FSIA to hear the action against SATOUR (see *supra*). Moreover, even if SATOUR were not an agency or instrumentality of Republic, Virtual has not stated a claim against SATOUR because SATOUR is not alleged to have performed any act apart from its actions as an agency of Republic, let alone an act resulting in injury to Virtual (see *Leeds v. Meltz*, 85 F3d 51, 53 (2d Cir 1996) (stating that "bald assertions and conclusions of law" do not suffice to defeat a motion to dismiss under Rule 12(b)(6))). Accordingly, the action must also be dismissed as to SATOUR under Rule 12(b)(6).

III. Conclusion

For the foregoing reasons, defendants' motion to dismiss is granted. The mere fact that Virtual operates in the volatile electronic commerce industry and is seeking to raise capital under sensitive economic conditions is not grounds for assuming jurisdiction over a foreign sovereign which has performed no commercial act with respect to the subject matter of this dispute. Accordingly, the action is dismissed. The Clerk of the Court is directed to close the file in this action.

SO ORDERED.

KEY TERMS

Anticybersquatting Consumer
  Protection Act (ACPA)

Berne Convention

bulletin-board site

Child Online Protection Act
  (COPA)

Communications Decency Act
  (CDA)

Convention on Cybercrime

cyberlaw

cyberpiracy

cyberspace

deep-linking

Digital Millennium Copyright Act
  (DMCA)

domain name

Due Process Clause

encryption

filtering software

Fourteenth Amendment

framing

Internet Corporation for Assigned
  Names and Numbers

interstate commerce

Long-Arm Statute

minimum contacts

MP3

Network Solutions, Inc.

overbreadth

Telecommunications Act of 1996

typo-piracy

Uniform Domain Name Dispute
  Resolution Policy (UDRP)

vague

Verisign

WIPO Copyright Treaty

WIPO Performance and
Phonograms Treaty

EXERCISES

1. Using the Internet, locate statutes and treaties that have been enacted since the publication of this text that address the problem of the entertainment industry and cyberspace.

2. Determine which countries are party to the recent Convention on Cybercrime Treaty.

3. What is your opinion of the effectiveness of the current protections that are afforded to artists with respect to addressing copyright infringement on the Internet? How would you like to see this problem resolved?

4. Find a chat group that discusses Internet freedom. Log the chatters' opinions over several days.

5. What do you believe is the most effective forum to resolve cyberspace legal conflicts: the state, the federal government, or an international tribunal? Discuss.

6. Read and brief *Universal City Studios, Inc. v. Shawn C. Remerdes*, 82 FSupp2d 211, a case dealing with copyright protection in the face of the new technology.

7. Go to the Web and download the WIPO Performances and Phonograms Treaty. Discuss its provisions.

8. Go to the Web and download the Convention on Cybercrime. What is your opinion of its ability to achieve its stated goals?

9. Using the Internet, obtain a sample of an encryption contract and analyze its provisions.

10. Discuss how modern technology has increased or diminished your enjoyment of your favorite entertainment medium.

EXHIBIT

Exhibit 10-1 shows the World Intellectual Property Organization's copyright treaty.

WIPO **CRNR/DC/94**

ORIGINAL: English

DATE: December 23, 1996

WORLD INTELLECTUAL PROPERTY ORGANIZATION

GENEVA

DIPLOMATIC CONFERENCE
ON
CERTAIN COPYRIGHT AND NEIGHBORING RIGHTS QUESTIONS

Geneva, December 2 to 20, 1996

WIPO COPYRIGHT TREATY

adopted by the Diplomatic Conference on December 20, 1996

The agreed statements of the Diplomatic Conference (that adopted the Treaty) concerning certain provisions of the WCT are reproduced in the original text of the Treaty as footnotes under the provisions concerned. These footnotes do not appear in the present text, but are replaced by bracketed references to the corresponding agreed statements.

Contents

Preamble

Article 1: Relation to the Berne Convention

Article 2: Scope of Copyright Protection

Article 3: Application of Articles 2 to 6 of the Berne Convention

Article 4: Computer Programs

Article 5: Compilations of Data (Databases)

Article 6: Right of Distribution

EXHIBIT 10-1 WIPO Copyright Treaty

Article 7: Right of Rental

Article 8: Right of Communication to the Public

Article 9: Duration of the Protection of Photographic Works

Article 10: Limitations and Exceptions

Article 11: Obligations concerning Technological Measures

Article 12: Obligations concerning Rights Management Information

Article 13: Application in Time

Article 14: Provisions on Enforcement of Rights

Article 15: Assembly

Article 16: International Bureau

Article 17: Eligibility for Becoming Party to the Treaty

Article 18: Rights and Obligations under the Treaty

Article 19: Signature of the Treaty

Article 20: Entry into Force of the Treaty

Article 21: Effective Date of Becoming Party to the Treaty

Article 22: No Reservations to the Treaty

Article 23: Denunciation of the Treaty

Article 24: Languages of the Treaty

Article 25: Depositary

EXHIBIT 10-1 WIPO Copyright Treaty (*continued*)

Preamble

The Contracting Parties,

Desiring to develop and maintain the protection of the rights of authors in their literary and artistic works in a manner as effective and uniform as possible,

Recognizing the need to introduce new international rules and clarify the interpretation of certain existing rules in order to provide adequate solutions to the questions raised by new economic, social, cultural and technological developments,

Recognizing the profound impact of the development and convergence of information and communication technologies on the creation and use of literary and artistic works,

Emphasizing the outstanding significance of copyright protection as an incentive for literary and artistic creation,

Recognizing the need to maintain a balance between the rights of authors and the larger public interest, particularly education, research and access to information, as reflected in the Berne Convention,

Have agreed as follows:

Article 1

Relation to the Berne Convention

(1) This Treaty is a special agreement within the meaning of Article 20 of the Berne Convention for the Protection of Literary and Artistic Works, as regards Contracting Parties that are countries of the Union established by that Convention. This Treaty shall not have any connection with treaties other than the Berne Convention, nor shall it prejudice any rights and obligations under any other treaties.

(2) Nothing in this Treaty shall derogate from existing obligations that Contracting Parties have to each other under the Berne Convention for the Protection of Literary and Artistic Works.

(3) Hereinafter, "Berne Convention" shall refer to the Paris Act of July 24, 1971 of the Berne Convention for the Protection of Literary and Artistic Works.

(4) Contracting Parties shall comply with Articles 1 to 21 and the Appendix of the Berne Convention. [See the agreed statement concerning Article 1(4)]

EXHIBIT 10-1 WIPO Copyright Treaty (*continued*)

Article 2

Scope of Copyright Protection

Copyright protection extends to expressions and not to ideas, procedures, methods of operation or mathematical concepts as such.

Article 3

Application of Articles 2 to 6 of the Berne Convention

Contracting Parties shall apply *mutatis mutandis* the provisions of Articles 2 to 6 of the Berne Convention in respect of the protection provided for in this Treaty. [See the agreed statement concerning Article 3]

Article 4

Computer Programs

Computer programs are protected as literary works within the meaning of Article 2 of the Berne Convention. Such protection applies to computer programs, whatever may be the mode or form of their expression. [See the agreed statement concerning Article 4]

Article 5

Compilations of Data (Databases)

Compilations of data or other material, in any form, which by reason of the selection or arrangement of their contents constitute intellectual creations, are protected as such. This protection does not extend to the data or the material itself and is without prejudice to any copyright subsisting in the data or material contained in the compilation. [See the agreed statement concerning Article 5]

Article 6

Right of Distribution

(1) Authors of literary and artistic works shall enjoy the exclusive right of authorizing the making available to the public of the original and copies of their works through sale or other transfer of ownership.

(2) Nothing in this Treaty shall affect the freedom of Contracting Parties to determine the conditions, if any, under which the exhaustion of the right in paragraph (1) applies after the first sale or other transfer of

EXHIBIT 10-1 WIPO Copyright Treaty (*continued*)

ownership of the original or a copy of the work with the authorization of the author. [See the agreed statement concerning Articles 6 and 7]

Article 7

Right of Rental

(1) Authors of

(i) computer programs;

(ii) cinematographic works; and

(iii) works embodied in phonograms, as determined in the national law of Contracting Parties,

shall enjoy the exclusive right of authorizing commercial rental to the public of the originals or copies of their works.

(2) Paragraph (1) shall not apply

(i) in the case of computer programs, where the program itself is not the essential object of the rental; and

(ii) in the case of cinematographic works, unless such commercial rental has led to widespread copying of such works materially impairing the exclusive right of reproduction.

(3) Notwithstanding the provisions of paragraph (1), a Contracting Party that, on April 15, 1994, had and continues to have in force a system of equitable remuneration of authors for the rental of copies of their works embodied in phonograms may maintain that system provided that the commercial rental of works embodied in phonograms is not giving rise to the material impairment of the exclusive right of reproduction of authors. [See the agreed statement concerning Articles 6 and 7, and the agreed statement concerning Article 7]

Article 8

Right of Communication to the Public

Without prejudice to the provisions of Articles 11(1)(ii), 11*bis*(1)(i) and (ii), 11*ter*(1)(ii), 14(1)(ii) and 14*bis*(1) of the Berne Convention, authors of literary and artistic works shall enjoy the exclusive right of authorizing any communication to the public of their works, by wire or wireless means, including the making available to the public of their works in such a way that members of the public may access these works from a place and at a time individually chosen by them. [See the agreed statement concerning Article 8]

EXHIBIT 10-1 WIPO Copyright Treaty (*continued*)

Article 9

Duration of the Protection of Photographic Works

In respect of photographic works, the Contracting Parties shall not apply the provisions of Article 7(4) of the Berne Convention.

Article 10

Limitations and Exceptions

(1) Contracting Parties may, in their national legislation, provide for limitations of or exceptions to the rights granted to authors of literary and artistic works under this Treaty in certain special cases that do not conflict with a normal exploitation of the work and do not unreasonably prejudice the legitimate interests of the author.

(2) Contracting Parties shall, when applying the Berne Convention, confine any limitations of or exceptions to rights provided for therein to certain special cases that do not conflict with a normal exploitation of the work and do not unreasonably prejudice the legitimate interests of the author. [See the agreed statement concerning Article 10]

Article 11

Obligations concerning Technological Measures

Contracting Parties shall provide adequate legal protection and effective legal remedies against the circumvention of effective technological measures that are used by authors in connection with the exercise of their rights under this Treaty or the Berne Convention and that restrict acts, in respect of their works, which are not authorized by the authors concerned or permitted by law.

Article 12

Obligations concerning Rights Management Information

(1) Contracting Parties shall provide adequate and effective legal remedies against any person knowingly performing any of the following acts knowing, or with respect to civil remedies having reasonable grounds to know, that it will induce, enable, facilitate or conceal an infringement of any right covered by this Treaty or the Berne Convention:

(i) to remove or alter any electronic rights management information without authority;

EXHIBIT 10-1 WIPO Copyright Treaty (*continued*)

(ii) to distribute, import for distribution, broadcast or communicate to the public, without authority, works or copies of works knowing that electronic rights management information has been removed or altered without authority.

(2) As used in this Article, "rights management information" means information which identifies the work, the author of the work, the owner of any right in the work, or information about the terms and conditions of use of the work, and any numbers or codes that represent such information, when any of these items of information is attached to a copy of a work or appears in connection with the communication of a work to the public. [See the agreed statement concerning Article 12]

Article 13

Application in Time

Contracting Parties shall apply the provisions of Article 18 of the Berne Convention to all protection provided for in this Treaty.

Article 14

Provisions on Enforcement of Rights

(1) Contracting Parties undertake to adopt, in accordance with their legal systems, the measures necessary to ensure the application of this Treaty.

(2) Contracting Parties shall ensure that enforcement procedures are available under their law so as to permit effective action against any act of infringement of rights covered by this Treaty, including expeditious remedies to prevent infringements and remedies which constitute a deterrent to further infringements.

Article 15

Assembly

(1)(a) The Contracting Parties shall have an Assembly.

(b) Each Contracting Party shall be represented by one delegate who may be assisted by alternate delegates, advisors and experts.

(c) The expenses of each delegation shall be borne by the Contracting Party that has appointed the delegation. The Assembly may ask the World Intellectual Property Organization (hereinafter referred to as "WIPO") to grant financial assistance to facilitate the participation of delegations of Contracting Parties that

EXHIBIT 10-1 WIPO Copyright Treaty (*continued*)

are regarded as developing countries in conformity with the established practice of the General Assembly of the United Nations or that are countries in transition to a market economy.

(2)(a) The Assembly shall deal with matters concerning the maintenance and development of this Treaty and the application and operation of this Treaty.

(b) The Assembly shall perform the function allocated to it under Article 17(2) in respect of the admission of certain intergovernmental organizations to become party to this Treaty.

(c) The Assembly shall decide the convocation of any diplomatic conference for the revision of this Treaty and give the necessary instructions to the Director General of WIPO for the preparation of such diplomatic conference.

(3)(a) Each Contracting Party that is a State shall have one vote and shall vote only in its own name.

(b) Any Contracting Party that is an intergovernmental organization may participate in the vote, in place of its Member States, with a number of votes equal to the number of its Member States which are party to this Treaty. No such intergovernmental organization shall participate in the vote if any one of its Member States exercises its right to vote and *vice versa*.

(4) The Assembly shall meet in ordinary session once every two years upon convocation by the Director General of WIPO.

(5) The Assembly shall establish its own rules of procedure, including the convocation of extraordinary sessions, the requirements of a quorum and, subject to the provisions of this Treaty, the required majority for various kinds of decisions.

Article 16

International Bureau

The International Bureau of WIPO shall perform the administrative tasks concerning the Treaty.

Article 17

Eligibility for Becoming Party to the Treaty

(1) Any Member State of WIPO may become party to this Treaty.

(2) The Assembly may decide to admit any intergovernmental organization to become party to this Treaty which declares that it is competent in respect of, and has its own legislation binding on all its Member States

EXHIBIT 10-1 WIPO Copyright Treaty (*continued*)

on, matters covered by this Treaty and that it has been duly authorized, in accordance with its internal procedures, to become party to this Treaty.

(3) The European Community, having made the declaration referred to in the preceding paragraph in the Diplomatic Conference that has adopted this Treaty, may become party to this Treaty.

Article 18

Rights and Obligations under the Treaty

Subject to any specific provisions to the contrary in this Treaty, each Contracting Party shall enjoy all of the rights and assume all of the obligations under this Treaty.

Article 19

Signature of the Treaty

This Treaty shall be open for signature until December 31, 1997, by any Member State of WIPO and by the European Community.

Article 20

Entry into Force of the Treaty

This Treaty shall enter into force three months after 30 instruments of ratification or accession by States have been deposited with the Director General of WIPO.

Article 21

Effective Date of Becoming Party to the Treaty

This Treaty shall bind

(i) the 30 States referred to in Article 20, from the date on which this Treaty has entered into force;

(ii) each other State from the expiration of three months from the date on which the State has deposited its instrument with the Director General of WIPO;

(iii) the European Community, from the expiration of three months after the deposit of its instrument of ratification or accession if such instrument has been deposited after the entry into force of this Treaty

EXHIBIT 10-1 WIPO Copyright Treaty (*continued*)

according to Article 20, or, three months after the entry into force of this Treaty if such instrument has been deposited before the entry into force of this Treaty;

(iv) any other intergovernmental organization that is admitted to become party to this Treaty, from the expiration of three months after the deposit of its instrument of accession.

Article 22

No Reservations to the Treaty

No reservation to this Treaty shall be admitted.

Article 23

Denunciation of the Treaty

This Treaty may be denounced by any Contracting Party by notification addressed to the Director General of WIPO. Any denunciation shall take effect one year from the date on which the Director General of WIPO received the notification.

Article 24

Languages of the Treaty

(1) This Treaty is signed in a single original in English, Arabic, Chinese, French, Russian and Spanish languages, the versions in all these languages being equally authentic.

(2) An official text in any language other than those referred to in paragraph (1) shall be established by the Director General of WIPO on the request of an interested party, after consultation with all the interested parties. For the purposes of this paragraph, "interested party" means any Member State of WIPO whose official language, or one of whose official languages, is involved and the European Community, and any other intergovernmental organization that may become party to this Treaty, if one of its official languages is involved.

Article 25

Depositary

The Director General of WIPO is the depositary of this Treaty.

EXHIBIT 10-1 WIPO Copyright Treaty (*continued*)

GLOSSARY

A

absolute (strict) liability Being held legally responsible for injuries regardless of degree of care.

acceptance Manifestation of assent to an offer.

accountant A licensed professional who maintains and creates financial books and records.

Actors' Equity The actors' and stage managers' union that negotiates and administers national and regional agreements with theatrical employers.

actual damages An award of money for an amount actually lost.

adaptation An alteration of an original work to create a new copyrightable work.

adapted from Label generally indicating the original author also wrote the subsidiary work.

administrative law judge Person who presides at administrative hearings.

advance (1) Money given to an artist as initial consideration to produce a record. (2) Upfront payment given to an author before the work is sold, in anticipation of eventual royalties.

agent (1) One permitted to enter into contracts binding all partners in a partnership. (2) One who acts on behalf of another. (3) Someone expressly authorized to act on another's behalf.

amateur performance A performance where there are no professionals or paid actors.

amateur sports Sports in which the participants do not receive compensation for participation.

American Federation of Musicians (AFM) 100,000-member union uniting musicians across the United States and Canada.

American Federation of Television and Radio Artists (AFTRA) National labor union for the entertainment industry.

American Society of Composers, Authors, and Performers (ASCAP) Organization that protects the rights of composers, performers and writers.

Americans with Disabilities Act (ADA) Federal statute providing for equal access for persons with mental or physical impairments.

Anticybersquatting Consumer Protection Act (ACPA) Federal law designed to prevent cyberpiracy.

antitrust laws Statutes designed to prohibit unfair trade or the lessening of competition.

arbitrator An individual who oversees a nonjudicial method of resolving disputes.

articles of organization Document filed to establish a limited liability company.

assignment Transfer of contractual rights.

assumption of the risk Person voluntarily engaging in hazardous acts is assumed to know of the hazard involved.

B

based upon Label indicating that the work is not an original idea.

bequeathed Personal property left to someone in a will.

Berne Convention Convention for the protection of literary and artistic works.

Bill of Rights The first ten amendments to the Constitution of the United States.

blacklisting Placing a performer on a list to ensure that he or she will not be hired.

board of directors Managers of a corporation.

boilerplate Standard clause.

bonus based on budget Method of compensating a writer by granting him a payment above the exercise price for a script based on a percentage of the film's operating budget.

bonus based on credit Method of compensating a writer by granting him a payment above the exercise price for a script based on his eventual credit for the film.

booking agent Person who only negotiates live appearances for the musician.

bootlegging Making an unauthorized tape of a theatrical performance.

boycott Unfair labor practice.

breach of contract Failure to fulfill a contractual obligation.

Broadcast Music, Inc (BMI) Performing-rights society.

budget record A record that sells for 30 to 50 percent of the cost of a top-line record.

bulletin-board site A Web site that provides information on general or specific topics.

business judgment rule Fiduciary standard for corporate directors.

business manager A person responsible for the musician's daily business expenses.

business tax Tax imposed by certain municipalities on businesses that rent commercial property.

bylaws Day-to-day rules of a corporation.

C

Cable Act Amendment to the Communication Act that added cable to the FCC's jurisdiction.

Cable Television Consumer Protection and Competition Act Statute currently regulating cable television.

capital gain Increase in the value of an asset between the time it is bought and the time it is sold.

CATV Cable television transmission.

certificate of incorporation Document filed to create a corporation.

certificate of limited partnership Document filed to create a limited partnership.

charging party Person who files a dispute under the NLRA.

Child Online Protection Act (COPA) Federal statute designed to prevent children from accessing obscene material on the Internet; found unconstitutional.

Children's Television Act of 1990 Federal law regulating broadcasts aimed at children.

chromotoid process A method of colorizing a film based on making prints of a black-and-white film in red, green, and blue and then combining those prints.

Clayton Antitrust Act A federal statute prohibiting monopolies.

clearing house A company who specializes in clearing samples for use in derivative works.

co-authors Label indicating that two or more persons share equal credit as authors.

collaboration agreement A contract that defines each party's interest in a work.

collapsible corporation Corporation formed for one purpose that dissolves when that purpose is completed for tax benefits.

collective bargaining agreement Contract resulting from the collective bargaining process.

collective bargaining Labor law concept requiring good faith negotiation of employment contracts.

collective work Work owned by a group.

colorization process Method of colorizing a film by assigning specific colors to a pixel version of the film.

commission (1) Fee paid to an agent. (2) Fee representing a percentage of the consideration of a contract.

common law Law evolving from judicial precedent rather than statute.

Communications Act of 1934 First federal statute that established the regulation of the airways.

Communications Decency Act (CDA) Federal statute designed to prevent obscene material from being transmitted over the Internet; found unconstitutional.

compilation An album that features several artists who contribute a song or songs.

compulsory mechanical license A compulsory grant of the right to a song by the copyright office.

condition Timing element of a contract.

conflict of interest Representing opposing interests.

consent An implied or express permission.

consideration The bargain element of a contract.

constitutional law Law derived from the United States Constitution that is not otherwise set out in a statute or a legislatively created law.

constructive notice Notice not directly given.

contingent fee arrangement The eventual fee paid is determined as a percentage of profits.

contingent payment Method of purchasing a script by allocating profits and losses rather than having a set price.

contract Legally enforceable agreement.

contract of adhesion Agreement in which one side has an unfair bargaining position.

contractual capacity Legal ability to enter into a contract.

contribution Partner's obligation to pay his or her proportionate share of an award granted to a third person injured by the partnership.

Convention on Cybercrime First international treaty involving crimes committed via the Internet.

copyright Right of exclusive use of a writing or a work of art.

corporation Artificial business entity.

counteroffer Cross-offer.

covenant Contractual promise; obligation.

covering Recording of a song by an artist who does not own the song.

creative rights The legal right to make changes to a copyrighted work.

cross ownership Television and newspaper in the same community owned by one person.

cross-collateralization charge Allocating revenues and expenses over all films produced by the same artist.

cyberlaw Legal doctrines that apply to cyberspace.

cyberpiracy Registering a well-known name as a domain name to prevent the trademark holder from using the mark as a domain name.

cyberspace Technology associated with the Internet.

D

damages Financial repayment for monetary loss.

DBA form Form used to operate a business under an assumed name.

deduction Subtraction from gross income.

deep-linking One Web site providing access to another site by bypassing the second site's home page.

defamation Tort involving false statements about a person that are communicated to another person, resulting in ridicule or contempt of the person they were said or written about.

defamation per se Statements so defamatory so as to be determined defamatory on their face.

derivative work A new song created from the original song.

development fee Method of acquiring the services of a director.

Digital Millennium Copyright Act (DMCA) Federal statute designed to extend copyright protection to new technology.

Digital Rights Management (DRM) Computer encryption program.

direct broadcast satellite (DBS) Satellite for individual homeowner's reception.

director Corporate manager.

Directors' Guild of America (DGA) Directors' union.

dissolved Terminated.

dividend Shareholder's return on investment.

domain name Unique name to identify a Web site.

double add-back Doubling all costs over the budget as an expense of the film.

dramatic work The story.

droit d'auteur European right of authorship.

droit moral European moral rights granted to artists to retain control over their works.

droits partimoniaux European property rights given to an artist over his work.

due process Constitutional guarantee of a fair hearing.

Due Process Clause In accordance with established and sanctioned legal principles and procedures and with safeguards for the protection of individual rights.

duopoly Ownership of several broadcast facilities in the same community by one person.

E

employer identification number (EIN) Number assigned by the IRS that serves as a kind of Social Security Number for a business.

encryption Method of encoding material for security.

endorsement Contract in which a person lends his name and reputation to a product for consideration.

enjoined Stopped.

equal protection Constitutional guarantee that all persons are to be treated the same.

equitable remedies Non-monetary awards.

estimated income tax Quarterly tax filing required for a business.

estoppel The theory that one is barred from applying a principle of law in a given situation.

exclusive right The owner is the only person who holds the right.

exclusivity clause A contract provision that limits a party from entering into contracts with others.

exercise price Consideration given to a writer to purchase a screenplay.

experimental contract Contract for low-budget or advertising production not subject to strict Equity guidelines.

express contract A contract that relies on an unambiguous agreement.

express waiver Voluntary and deliberate actions that relinquish a right.

fair use Use for the purpose of criticism, comment, news reporting, parody, scholarship, or research.

F

false attribution Attributing a characteristic to a person in instances in which such characteristic does not apply.

Federal Communications Commission (FCC) Federal agency that regulates television.

Federal Trade Commission Federal agency that regulates trade.

fiduciary Person in a position of trust.

Film California First Statute designed to attract film production in California.

film rights The right to create a screenplay from another medium.

filtering software Computer program that can screen out specifically designated material.

financial core status Method whereby a union member resigns membership but continues to pay fees.

firm records Albums that a record company promises to produce in a recording contract.

First Amendment The amendment to the constitution that protects free speech and freedom of the press.

First Sale Doctrine An owner of an exclusive right exercises control over that right only until the copyrighted work is sold or otherwise given away. Once the copyrighted work has been sold, the owner has the right to do what he wants with it.

fixed Permanently established.

force majeure Act of God.

Form 1040 Federal individual income-tax return.

Fourteenth Amendment Amendment that ensures that all people who are citizens receive basic fairness.

framing Having one Web site appear in a window on another Web site.

franchising Letting a team operate in a given geographic area.

free option Price to obtain the option is not applied to the eventual purchase price.

freedom of speech The right of a citizen to say (or write) exactly what he or she thinks without fear of governmental retribution.

G

general partner Co-owner of a business with unlimited personal liability.

general partnership Association of two or more persons engaged in business as co-owners for profit.

good faith (1) Negotiating with an open mind. (2) Without prior knowledge or malice.

gross income The total amount that an artist earns before deductions for expenses and taxes.

gross profit Revenue before expenses.

H

handicap Impairment under the Rehabilitation Act.

holdback Period during which certain retained rights cannot be exercised.

home satellite dish (TVRO) Small dish used for receiving multiple channels.

hyphenate Union member performing some supervisory role as well.

I

implied contract A contract based on an understanding.

implied waiver A person's actions that cause another to believe that a right has been relinquished.

incorporation by reference Making a separate agreement part of a contract by mentioning it.

indecency Inappropriate sexual content, foul language, and nudity that is not sexual in its orientation.

initial term Term in a contract that lasts from the date the contract is entered into until a specified time after the delivery of the specified number of albums promised.

injunction Court order to stop doing something.

installment sale Purchase in which purchase price is paid over time.

insurance Contract used to indemnify against loss.

Internet Corporation for Assigned Names and Numbers Agency that licenses organizations to assign domain names.

interstate commerce The sale of goods from state to state.

intestate succession Passed along though the blood line of a deceased person by statute.

ISBN International standard book number.

J

joint and several liability Tort liability for partnerships.

joint liability Contract liability for partnerships.

joint work A copyrightable work prepared by two or more people who have the intent to produce a merged or coproduced work.

K

key man insurance Insurance used to protect against loss occasioned by injury or death of a principal.

L

labels Method of allocating credits among contributors to a finished work.

Lanham Act Federal statute prohibiting unfair trade practices.

legal remedies Monetary awards.

libel Written defamation.

license An authorization to use.

licenses When an individual athlete allows his or her name to be used by another, such as on a T-shirt.

likeness An image or picture.

limitation of damages Agreement to have a ceiling on potential damages.

limited liability company (LLC) Company that gives limited liability to its owners but lets them manage the business.

limited partner Investor in a limited partnership.

limited partnership agreement Contract between limited partners.

limited partnership share Evidence of the limited partner's ownership interest.

limited partnership Association of two or more persons engaged in business for profit as co-owners, with one or more general partners and one or more limited partners.

liquidated damages Contract provision that provides a specified dollar award in case of breach.

literary agent Artist's representative who negotiates publishing contracts.

lockout Employer refusing to let union workers into the workplace.

Long-Arm Statute Allows the long arm of the law to reach outside the state's natural boundaries.

low-power television service Exempt category from FCC regulation for facilities with limited broadcasting ranges.

M

manager The person who acts as a liaison between the musician and the record company, booking agent, and business manager.

managers Persons who manage an LLC.

mass market paperback Softbound book that may be substantially edited from its hardbound version to attract a greater audience.

may-carry rules FCC requirement for cable stations to carry long-distance broadcast transmissions.

mechanical license Similar to the compulsory mechanical license, only it is granted by the publisher.

mechanical rights The legal ability to reproduce a work mechanically, such as on a CD.

mediator A third person who helps parties with a dispute reach a mutual resolution.

members Owners of an LLC.

membership shares Evidence of ownership in an LLC.

merchants Persons who regularly trade in a particular good or goods.

mid-line record A record that sells for 15 to 30 percent less than a top-line record.

minimum contacts The least amount of contact necessary to establish jurisdiction.

minor Person between the ages of 14 and 18.

mirror-image rule Acceptance must exactly match the terms of the offer.

mitigation of damages Duty of the injured party to lessen the amount of the damages the wrongdoer must pay.

MMDS Multi-channel MDS.

moral rights Rights to retain a work's integrity granted to artists under European laws.

MP3 Digital program to condense music.

multiple ownership FCC rule dealing with diversity in ownership.

multi-point distribution service (MDS) Method of television transmission using microwaves.

music publisher Entity that secures commercially released recordings of the songs it controls.

music publishing agreement An agreement between the writer of a song and a music publisher that transfers ownership of copyright in exchange for an advance against royalties.

musical work The score and lyrics.

must-carry rules FCC requirement that cable station must carry all local stations.

mutuality of consideration Contract requirement that both sides give and receive something of legal value.

N

name What one calls oneself.

National Labor Relations Act (NLRA) Federal statute governing labor organizations.

National Labor Relations Board (NLRB) Agency that administers the NLRA.

National Music Publishers Association Organization that represents music publishers in negotiating and collecting royalties.

negligence Failure to adhere to a defined standard of care.

negligent hiring Failure to exercise due care in employing an unqualified person who injures a third party.

net profit Revenues less expenses.

Network Solutions, Inc. Organization licensed to assign domain names.

non-exclusive license The right to license a copyright to more than one person.

notice Warning or indication.

O

obscene Material is obscene if the average person, applying contemporary standards to the dominant theme of the material taken as a whole, appeals to prurient interests.

offer Proposal to enter into a valid contract.

offeree Person to whom an offer is made.

offeror Person who makes an offer.

officers Senior managers of a corporation.

open auditions Tryouts at which anyone can audition.

operating agreement Document used to indicate how an LLC is to function.

option (1) Ability to exercise a contract right. (2) Exclusive right to acquire a work for a set period of time. (3) The right to extend the term of a contract for another specified period of time.

option contract Exclusive right to purchase a story in the future.

option/purchase agreement Contract used by producers to acquire screenplays by writers.

oral contract Binding contract not reduced to writing.

overbreadth Constitutional proscription against having statutes overly inclusive.

P

paparazzi Zealous photographers who often freelance.

partnership rights (interests) Basic rights granted to partners engaged in a business enterprise.

performance plateau This clause will allow the musician to terminate the management agreement in the event that the musician's gross income does not equal or surpass a negotiated amount.

permanent publication Something fixed in a tangible format.

petition Legal paper requesting a court hear a claim.

pitch Proposal used to attract a potential producer.

pixel Microdot.

post-term commission Commission or payment that a manager is entitled to after the artist/management agreement has been terminated.

power of attorney clause A contract provision that allows the manager to enter into legal agreements and to act on issues on the musician's behalf.

preemption Granting priority to FCC rules that may conflict with local rules.

premium Consideration to support an insurance contract.

print publication rights Rights that permit the publisher to authorize reproduction of music in various printed formats.

product liability Area of tort law concerned with defectively manufactured goods.

professional sports Athletic endeavors in which participants receive compensation.

progress-to-production clause Contract provision for directors to permit them to seek other work if the studio does not start film production within a stated period of time.

promisee A person to whom a right is owed.

public domain Intellectual property that anyone has the right to use.

public performance rights The legal ability to determine when and how a work will be performed.

public performance A performance that is done outside a domestic setting.

R

reasonable accommodation An employer/business owner's duty to allow for the special needs of the disabled.

record deal The contract between the artist and the record label that promises that the artist will record for the label and the label will produce the record.

recoupment Taking money received in the form of royalties and applying it to the amount advanced or paid to the artist to make the record.

red shirting Keeping a student back so he can develop physically to play sports.

Rehabilitation Act Federal statute used to permit handicapped persons to participate in amateur sports.

remedies Method of legally compensating an injured party.

reproduction Photocopying, transcribing, or recording.

reserve clause Agreement providing for a perpetual option; now obsolete.

resolution Agreement of the board of directors.

respondeat superior Holding an employer liable for the tortious acts of his employee.

restraint of labor Contracts that prohibit persons from working for others.

restricted competition Brand of amateur sports in which participation is limited to select persons.

rider A clause that states what the musician is entitled to backstage.

right of publicity A right of publicity involves the use of aspects of one's own personality for economic gain.

right to privacy An inherent right to be left alone.

royalty Consideration paid to a copyright holder for the license to use the copyrighted work.

royalty base rate The cost of the record that the royalty rate will be based on.

royalty rate The percentage of money the artist is entitled to for each record sold.

royalty statements Statements issued as an accounting of royalties due an artist.

Rozelle Rule Acquiring team must compensate player's previous team.

rule of reason Antitrust concept looking at actual factors to determine whether there is an antitrust violation.

runaway production Films produced abroad designed for American distribution.

S

sampling The use of a piece of a song that is not owned by the user.

satellite master antenna television (SMATV) Satellite transmission for entire buildings or small communities.

Schedule C Federal tax attachment for sole proprietors.

scope A specified range in a contract.

Screen Actors' Guild (SAG) Actors' union.

script Written words performed by the actors.

security Attachable interest used to satisfy a debt.

security clause Contract provision indicating when a studio may hire nonunion members.

service mark Word, symbol, or group of words that distinguish a service.

services Intangible things performed by one person for the benefit of another.

shareholder Stockholder; owner of a corporation.

Sherman Antitrust Act First federal statute mandating free competition.

shopping Sending material to a studio without compensating the writer.

signing bonus A cash incentive for an artist to sign with a particular label.

slander Verbal defamation.

Society of European Stage Authors and Composers (SESAC) Performing-rights society.

sole proprietor Owner of a sole proprietorship.

sole proprietorship Business owned and managed by one person.

spec script Script written in advance of finding a producer.

specific performance Court order to fulfill a contractual obligation.

spectrum space Airways and cable frequencies.

Statute of Frauds Law requiring certain contracts to be in writing to be enforceable.

Statute of Limitations Time period the artist has to sue the label.

statutory damages A financial amount set by statute usually when loss of profit would be difficult to determine.

step agreement Agreement that proceeds after the completion of certain steps.

step outline Proposal written in outline format.

stock performance A theatrical company formed to perform a repertoire of plays, usually at one theater.

strict liability Being held responsible regardless of the degree of care exercised.

strike Employees' refusal to work.

subchapter S corporation Tax election for qualifying corporations to be taxed as a partnership.

subsidiary rights Rights to exploit the work in different media.

successor in interest Person who takes over a contract right and obligation.

suspended payment Equity classification in which a person may still audition for Equity productions without full membership.

synchronization right The legal ability to permit a composition to be used on a soundtrack.

technical book Book designed for a specific and limited market, like a textbook.

T

Telecommunications Act of 1996 Federal statute regulating the telecommunications industry.

temporary withdrawal Equity classification in which a person may still audition for Equity productions without full membership.

tenancy in partnership Form of multiple owner-ship of property for partners.

term The length of a contract.

tie-in Illegal agreements under the antitrust laws.

Title IX Civil rights act dealing with education.

title Right to own and/or possess property.

top-of-the-line record A top-priced record album.

tort Civil wrong.

trade Transferring a player to another team.

trade book Mass market book.

trade paperback Softbound version of a hard-bound book that is published faithfully to the original but in a less-expensive form.

trademark Word, symbol, or group of words that distinguishes a good.

treatment Proposal written as a short synopsis of the intended work.

turnaround provision Right to take a project to a different studio during the progress-to-production period.

typo-piracy Deliberately misspelling a famous trademark.

U

UHF Ultra-high frequency.

unfair labor practice Certain activities deemed illegal under the NLRA.

Uniform Commercial Code (UCC) Law that regulates contracts for the sale of goods valued at over $500 and contracts between merchants.

Uniform Domain Name Dispute Resolution Policy (UDRP) Act that mandates arbitration of domain name disputes.

Uniform Limited Partnership Act (ULPA) Statute that regulates limited partnerships.

Uniform Partnership Act (UPA) Statute that regulates general partnerships.

union shop Business in which all employees must belong to the union.

United States Patent and Trademark Office The office responsible for registering and issuing patents and trademarks.

universal service FCC requirement that a cable operator make its service available to all home-owners in its area.

unrestricted competition Branch of amateur sports open to all amateur athletes.

V

vague Constitutional mandate that statutes be precise in their wording.

vanity press Private publication of a work that has no readily ascertainable market.

Verisign Took over from Network Solutions, Inc. in 2001.

vests Having a legally enforceable right.

VHF Very-high frequency.

vicarious liability Being held legally responsible for injuries to third persons caused by one's employee.

Visual Artists Rights Act of 1990 Federal statute designed to extend certain rights of control over their works to authors.

W

waiver Relinquishment of a contract right.

warranties Guarantees.

WIPO Copyright Treaty International treaty designed to protect copyrights worldwide.

WIPO Performance and Phonograms Treaty International treaty designed to protect rights for performances and phonograms.

work for hire A contract employee who creates a product but has no ownership right in what is produced.

workers' compensation insurance Insurance to cover employees injured on the job.

World Intellectual Property Organization (WIPO) International organization created to protect copyrights and intellectual property worldwide.

Writers' Guild of America (WGA) Writers' union.

Z

zoning Government regulation of the use of geographic areas.

INDEX